European Union and its Neighbours in a Globalized World

Volume 35

The series publishes monographs and edited volumes in the field of European and international law and policy. A special focus is put on the European neighbourhood policy, current problems in European and international law and policy as well as the role of the European Union as a global actor. The series supports the publishing and distribution of research results of cross-border research consortia. Besides renowned scientists the series is also open for publication projects of young academics. The series emphasizes the interplay of the European Union and its neighbouring countries as well as the important role of the European Union as a key player in the international context of law, economics and politics.

Leonardo Pasquali
Editor

EU Values and International Law

How the EU Upholds and Promotes its Values in the Wider World through its International Agreements

Springer

Editor
Leonardo Pasquali
Department of Law
University of Pisa
Pisa, Italy

ISSN 2524-8928 ISSN 2524-8936 (electronic)
European Union and its Neighbours in a Globalized World
ISBN 978-3-032-20520-9 ISBN 978-3-032-20521-6 (eBook)
https://doi.org/10.1007/978-3-032-20521-6

This Springer imprint is published by the registered company Springer Nature Switzerland AG
The registered company address is: Gewerbestrasse 11, 6330 Cham, Switzerland

Acknowledgements

This book concludes the scientific research conducted within the framework of the 2022–2025 Jean Monnet Chair "Reinforcing EU responsible global leadership: promoting human rights and democracy through solidarity for a rules-based multilateral world—ProSoEULaw Abroad" (Project number: 101085367, Call: ERASMUS-JMO-2022-HEI-TCH-RSCH, Topic: ERASMUS-JMO-2022-CHAIR). I would like to thank everyone who took part in the Chair's activities, helping us to achieve such high-quality results.

Co-funded by
the European Union

Funded by the European Union. Views and opinions expressed are, however, those of the author(s) only and do not necessarily reflect those of the European Union or European Education and Culture Executive Agency (EACEA). Neither the European Union nor EACEA can be held responsible for them.

Leonardo Pasquali

Contents

About the Editor and Contributors

About the Editor

Leonardo Pasquali, PhD, is Full Professor of International Law at the University of Pisa, Italy (Department of Law). He has recently become the Director of the Jean Monnet Centre of Excellence "EU fundamental values as a backbone for a fair, rules-based global order: promoting an inclusive and effective multilateral system in the wider world (EU4GlobalOrder)" at the same university. In the past, he coordinated a Jean Monnet Module and a Jean Monnet Chair. He is a member of the Academic Board of the Doctoral Programme in Law of the University of Pisa and an external member of the PPGD (mestrado e doutorado) Programme in Law of the Catholic University of Pernambuco (UNICAP), Brazil. He is the Director of the academic journal "Science and Peace". He is also a member of the Editorial Board of European and Latin American academic journals. He is the coordinator of the Italian Society of International Law Interest Group on "International and Supranational Organisations". In recent years, he has participated in numerous national and international scientific projects. He has authored around 60 publications in English, French, Italian and Spanish in leading peer-reviewed journals and edited collections on various international and EU law topics. He is the editor of the book "Solidarity in International Law: Challenges, Opportunities and the Role of Regional Organisations" and co-editor of the book "Solidarity and protection of individuals in E.U. Law. Addressing new challenges of the Union". He is also the author of three monographs on international and EU law topics. He has been an invited speaker at a large number of conferences and workshops in Italy and abroad, and teaches and has taught international law, EU law, international humanitarian law, international judicial cooperation and the law of international organisations. Leonardo Pasquali is a founding partner of Studio Legale Pasquali.

Contributors

Raquel Cavalcanti Ramos Machado Malenchini Department of Public Law, Federal University of Ceará, Fortaleza, Brazil

Marcelo Labanca Corrêa de Araújo Catholic University of Pernambuco, Recife, Brazil

Elena Crespo Navarro Department of Legal Science, Miguel Hernández University of Elche, Elche, Spain

Matteo Del Chicca Department of Law, University of Pisa, Pisa, Italy

Andrea Landi Department of Law, University of Pisa, Pisa, Italy

Francesca Martines Department of Law, University of Pisa, Pisa, Italy

Francisco Pascual Vives School of Law, University of Alcalá, Alcalá de Henares - Madrid, Spain

Gabriele Rugani Department of Law, University of Pisa, Pisa, Italy

Teresa Russo Department of Legal Sciences (School of Law), University of Salerno, Fisciano, Italy

Miriam Schettini Department of Law, University of Pisa, Pisa, Italy

Samantha Velluti Sussex Law School, School of Law, Politics and Sociology, University of Sussex, Brighton, UK

Upholding and Promoting EU Values in the Wider World: The Role of FTAs

Leonardo Pasquali

Contents

Abstract This opening chapter articulates the main objective of the monograph by presenting its central research focus. It begins by asserting that the European Union's commitment to promoting and safeguarding its foundational values externally is not a matter of political discretion, but a legal obligation enshrined in its

This chapter, as well as the whole book is a part of the ongoing research project "EU Values and International Law: how the EU upholds and promotes its values in the wider world through its international agreements", carried out in the framework of the Jean Monnet Chair "Reinforcing EU responsible global leadership: promoting human rights and democracy through solidarity for a rules-based multilateral world" (ProSoEULaw Abroad) coordinated by the author and funded by the European Commission under Erasmus+, the EU's program to support education, training, youth and sport in Europe.
Views and opinions expressed are however those of the author(s) only and do not necessarily reflect those of the European Union or European Education and Culture Executive Agency (EACEA). Neither the European Union nor EACEA can be held responsible for them.

L. Pasquali (✉)
Department of Law, University of Pisa, Pisa, Italy
e-mail: leonardo.pasquali@unipi.it

L. Pasquali (ed.), *EU Values and International Law*, European Union and its Neighbours in a Globalized World 35,
https://doi.org/10.1007/978-3-032-20521-6_1

constitutional framework. The discussion then turns to the specific instruments through which the EU pursues this mandate, with particular attention to the "Trade for All" strategy and the deployment of free trade agreements (FTAs) as key policy tools. A concise introduction to the nature and functioning of EU FTAs is subsequently provided. The following paragraph is dedicated to the formulation of the research question and a detailed account of the methodological framework adopted. By analyzing "second-generation" FTAs, the research aims to examine their role in influencing partner countries' legal systems, shaping international law, and addressing global challenges. Through a comparative approach, focusing on patterns and trends across multiple FTAs, it seeks to ascertain the EU's success in leveraging trade policy to foster peace, security, and adherence to international norms, while balancing the promotion of values with strategic interests. The chapter ends with a synopsis of the book's overall structure, including a brief overview of the chapters that follow.

1 Upholding and Promoting EU Values in the Wider World as a Legal Obligation: The "Trade for All" Strategy

The fundamental values of the European Union are expressly enshrined in Article 2 of the Treaty on European Union (TEU), a foundational provision of the Union's primary law. Without seeking to establish a hierarchy of these values, they may be listed as articulated in the text of the Article: "*respect for human dignity, freedom, democracy, equality, the rule of law and respect for human rights, including the rights of persons belonging to minorities… in a society in which pluralism, non-discrimination, tolerance, justice, solidarity and equality between women and men prevail*".

The respect for and promotion of these values constitute a cornerstone of the European Union's actions, which underscores the rationale for dedicating an entire chapter—Chap. 4, authored by Elena Crespo Navarro—to their analysis.

Their significance remains as vital today as at the time of the signing of the Treaty of Lisbon. Indeed, their foundational role has been reaffirmed in recent years by the European Council.

In its *Strategic Agenda 2024–2029*, the EU institution explicitly reaffirmed that these values "*remain the cornerstone of our Union*".[1]

[1] European Council, Strategic Agenda 2024–2029 (2024, p. 3). In the Agenda, the European Council identifies three overarching priorities for the period 2024–2029, the first of which is "A free and democratic Europe." In alignment with this Agenda, the President of the European Commission has outlined seven strategic priorities for the Commission's mandate during the same period, one of which is "Protecting our democracy, upholding our values". See https://commission.europa.eu/priorities-2024-2029_en

The European Union, its institutions, and its Member States must uphold and promote these values not only within the Union but also in their external actions throughout the wider international community.[2]

In the recent words of the European Council: "*Our values and the rule of law are our compass, both internally and externally*".[3]

This is not merely a matter of political discretion but a legal obligation, as clearly established in the binding terms of Article 3(5) TEU.[4] According to this provision, the Union is required to uphold and promote its foundational values in the wider

[2] Books and articles specifically concerned with EU values in EU Foreign Relations include: Cremona (2011), Leino (2008), and Sciso et al. (2016).

[3] European Council, Strategic Agenda 2024–2029 (2024, p. 2). In the same document, the Council has also explained the meaning of upholding and promoting EU values both inside and outside the Union: "*Upholding European values within the Union Our values are our strength. We will protect and promote our founding values—respect for human dignity, freedom, democracy, equality, the rule of law and respect for human rights, including the rights of persons belonging to minorities—which remain the cornerstone of our Union. We will promote and safeguard respect for the rule of law, which is the basis of European cooperation, upholding the principles of objectivity, non-discrimination and equal treatment of Member States. We will strengthen our democratic resilience, including by deepening citizen engagement, protecting free and pluralistic media and civil society, tackling foreign interference and countering attempts at destabilisation, including through disinformation and hate speech. We will strengthen democratic discourse and ensure that tech giants take their responsibility for safeguarding democratic dialogue online. We will promote our cultural diversity and heritage*"—"*Living up to our values at global level. The European Union shall continue to be the strongest supporter of the international legal order, steadfastly upholding the United Nations and the principles enshrined in the UN Charter. In particular, the European Union will pursue efforts to promote global peace, justice and stability, as well as democracy, universal human rights and the achievement of the Sustainable Development Goals in all international fora. We will strive for a reformed multilateral system, making it more inclusive and more effective*"; European Council, Strategic Agenda 2024–2029 (2024, p. 3).

[4] "*In its relations with the wider world, the Union shall uphold and promote its values and interests and contribute to the protection of its citizens*". Scholars, though, have not failed to point out that: "*Beyond their theoretical significance, however, the technical analysis of the two provisions is fraught with problematic issues. Articles 3(5) and 21 TEU do not clarify the nature and effect of the normative notions they lay down. Nor do they clarify the impact of these notions on the EU's competence system and, in particular, on the new external action of the Union. How do they relate to the principle of conferral? Do they blur the line between the diverse areas of the EU's external action? Or are they simply guidelines deprived of any normative effect? These questions cannot be easily answered by referring to the mere terms of Articles 3(5) and 21. Quite the contrary, it is difficult to determine a coherent normative framework integrating these two provisions in the complex system of the EU's external action… The analysis starts from a terminological issue. The legal notions formulated by Articles 3(5) and 21 seem to sprout from a common root; the desire to construe an ethical framework able to give guidance to the exercise of the EU's foreign power. However, the terminology used in the Treaty is highly heterogeneous. Article 3(5) talks about "values and interests"; Article 21 uses the term "objectives". Other Treaty provisions refer to the notions as "objectives and principles". This uncertain terminology should warn against any attempt to draw conclusions on their definite legal nature. The effect of these legal notions appears even more indeterminate. It is not clear whether they constitute mere guidelines for the exercise of the EU's external policies and actions or, rather, whether they have a normative effect, in general terms and, in particular, on the system of EU competence attribution*". Cannizzaro (2021, pp. 4–5). Notable papers debating justiciability of articles 2 and 3 TEU include Rossi (2020) as well as the very recent Di Federico and Lanotte (2025, pp. 352–357).

world with the explicit aim of contributing to key objectives of the international community. These include: the promotion of peace and security; the sustainable development of the Earth; solidarity and mutual respect among peoples; free and fair trade; the eradication of poverty; the protection of human rights—particularly the rights of the child; and the observance and development of international law, notably including respect for the principles enshrined in the Charter of the United Nations.

Additional relevant provisions include Article 21 TEU and Article 205 of the Treaty on the Functioning of the European Union (TFEU), which constitute the cornerstone of the Union's external action framework. These articles unequivocally establish that the Union's engagement on the international stage is directed towards upholding and promoting its foundational values beyond its borders.

Broadly speaking, the European Union seeks to fulfill its mandate of promoting its values globally through its international agreements[5] by employing three distinct approaches.

Primarily, the European Union actively promotes its values through the process of enlargement.[6]

According to Article 49 TEU, respect for and the promotion of the values upon which the European Union is founded constitute fundamental prerequisites for any European State seeking accession to the Union. These values are embedded within the accession agreements concluded between the Member States and the applicant countries. Although the explicit inclusion of such a provision in the EU's primary law dates only to the Treaty of Amsterdam in 1997, the promotion of the Union's core values—particularly respect for democracy and the rule of law—has been integral to the enlargement strategy from its inception. This is evident in the historical accession processes of Greece, Spain, and Portugal, where these principles were emphasized to varying extents and through differing mechanisms.[7]

---

[5]As has been appropriately highlighted in the literature "*The relationship between the European Union (EU) and its partners is essentially based on a network of bilateral, regional or multilateral treaties. In recent years, however, there has been a proliferation of European secondary law that contains provisions regulating people, goods or services located outside the EU territory*" Dero-Bugny Motte-Baumvol (2021, p. 41). To understand if and how this extraterritorial EU Legislation can contribute to uphold and promote EU Values in the Wider World would have to remain a task for a (separate) future project.

[6]A detailed, recent study of EU enlargement is Russo (2024). Federico Casolari, in his insightful study on the external projection of EU values in the context of relations with a former Member State, approaches the issue from a different perspective. He concludes that the influence of these values serves as a metric by which the consequences of the loss of EU membership can be assessed. In this sense, EU values function as a unit of measurement for the degree of participation in the process of European integration. See Casolari (2024).

[7]Greece had, in fact, submitted its application for membership prior to the United Kingdom, Ireland, and Denmark. However, the military coup of 1967, which brought the colonels' regime to power, resulted in the suspension of accession negotiations. In the case of Spain, accession negotiations did not commence until 1975, following the death of Francisco Franco and the subsequent establishment of a democratic government. Spain ultimately acceded to the European Communities in 1986. Portugal expressed an early interest in joining as far back as 1947, despite being under the

Over time, there has been a discernible evolution in the manner in which the European Union promotes its values through enlargement. A significant shift occurred with the fourth enlargement, which involved the accession of ten countries—Poland, Slovenia, Slovakia, the Czech Republic, Cyprus, Hungary, Malta, Lithuania, Latvia, and Estonia. In 1993, the European Council meeting in Copenhagen established precise criteria for accession, thereby conditioning membership on a genuine structural transformation of the institutional frameworks of candidate states. Notably, these countries had previously been under communist regimes and, through protracted accession negotiations, underwent substantive processes of democratization. This approach exemplifies how the Union has advanced and consolidated its core values through enlargement. The same methodology was applied in subsequent enlargements, including the fifth (Romania and Bulgaria) and the sixth (Croatia).

Currently, enlargement discussions are ongoing with the Western Balkans—comprising North Macedonia, Serbia, Montenegro, Albania, Bosnia and Herzegovina, and Kosovo—where respect for the EU values enshrined in Article 2 TEU remains a fundamental condition.

Another mechanism by which the European Union seeks to promote its values globally is through the inclusion of Human Rights clauses in its international agreements. Since the 1990s, the EU has incorporated provisions emphasizing respect for human rights and democratic principles in certain agreements. These clauses operate under both negative and positive conditionality. Negative conditionality involves the threat of withdrawing trade benefits if severe human rights violations persist, whereas positive conditionality entails granting additional trade advantages contingent upon the respect for human rights or fostering trade agreements designed to protect these rights.

Of particular relevance to this study is the third modality employed by the EU to promote its values abroad: the negotiation and conclusion of free trade agreements (FTAs) with third countries or regional organizations on a bilateral basis. The notion of leveraging trade policy as a vehicle for exporting EU values and principles is a cornerstone of the 'Trade for All' strategy, adopted by the European Commission in 2014.[8]

The principal legal basis for the European Union's trade policy is Article 207(1) TFEU, particularly its final sentence, which states: "*The common commercial policy shall be conducted in the context of the principles and objectives of the Union's external action*".

Consequently, free trade agreements negotiated and concluded by the European Union with partner countries and regional organizations on a bilateral basis, in line

authoritarian regime of António de Oliveira Salazar at the time. It was not until 1977, after the restoration of democracy, that Portugal formally applied for membership, and it too became a full Member State in 1986. These cases clearly illustrate that the existence of authoritarian regimes constituted a significant barrier to accession, thereby underscoring the foundational importance of democratic governance and respect for fundamental values in the process of European integration.

[8] European Commission (2014). The "Trade for All" communication is discussed by Bonfanti (2016).

with this strategy, represent a 'new generation' of trade agreements. Moreover, the European Commission's 2021 Communication, *Trade Policy Review—An Open, Sustainable and Assertive Trade Policy*, emphasizes that:

> The EU must fully use the strength provided by its openness and the attractiveness of its Single Market. The EU's openness and engagement on the international scene make it a credible supporter of international cooperation, multilateralism and the rules-based order, which in turn are critical to the EU's interests. The EU works with partners to ensure adherence to universal values, notably the promotion and protection of human rights. This includes core labour standards, and social protection in line with the European Pillar of Social Rights, gender equality, and the fight against climate change and biodiversity loss.[9]

While, as previously noted, EU primary law imposes a clear legal obligation on the Union to uphold and promote its values internationally, the Treaties simultaneously present certain constraints that complicate the EU's capacity to fulfill this mandate. Although the European Union, pursuant to Article 47 TEU, possesses legal personality[10] and thereby qualifies as a subject of international law capable of negotiating and concluding international agreements on its own behalf,[11] the scope of this capacity is limited. According to Article 3 TFEU, the Union's competence to act in international relations extends only to specific subject matters that fall within its exclusive competence.

Among these are undoubtedly 'pure' trade agreements, as provided for under Article 207 TFEU.[12] However, the majority of the Union's values fall outside the scope of exclusive competence defined in Article 3 TFEU and instead fall within the shared competence outlined in Article 4 TFEU. This implies that the European Union does not possess exclusive authority to conclude international agreements concerning these matters, as competence is shared with the Member States. Consequently, any trade agreement aimed at upholding and promoting EU values in non-EU countries cannot be concluded by the Union unilaterally; rather, its finaliza-

---

[9] COM(2021) 66 final.

[10] A detailed study of EU legal personality is Thürer and Marro (2012).

[11] See Pisapia (2019, pp. 4–10).

[12] Scholars, though, warn that: "*Al di là tuttavia del riconoscimento formale, da parte della Corte di giustizia, di poteri autonomi esclusivi in capo all'Unione, non si può negare che, da un lato, la tradizionale ritrosia degli Stati ad abbandonare i propri poteri sovrani e, dall'altra, l'enfatizzazione politico-istituzionale di ogni accordo, anche di apparente natura solo commerciale (unitamente alla maggior complessità degli odierni rapporti commerciali non limitati più, come nel passato, prevalentemente alle merci), ha fatto sì che in concreto fosse assai raro il ricorso alla tecnica negoziale prevista per gli accordi puramente comunitari. In effetti, l'utilizzo nella prassi comunitaria di accordi negoziati prima e ratificati poi da organi dell'Unione "rafforzati" dalla presenza (e firma) di rappresentanti degli Stati membri è sorta fondamentalmente per rispondere all'esigenza di evitare casi di attività* ultra vires *da parte dell'Unione con riferimento, in concreto, a singoli accordi non ricadenti pacificamente (o rientranti solo in parte) nella competenza esclusiva della Unione… La giurisprudenza della Corte di giustizia ha poi avuto modo di chiarire che, in tutti i casi di accordi che comportano oneri finanziari a carico degli Stati membri, si debba escludere la natura esclusiva della competenza dell'Unione*". See Piva (2021, pp. 497–500).

tion requires ratification by the Member States in accordance with their respective constitutional procedures. Such agreements are commonly referred to as 'mixed agreements',[13] to which the consent of all Member States is necessary. In other words, the European Union cannot unilaterally uphold and promote its values on the international stage; it requires the cooperation of all Member States, which inevitably entails various practical challenges. Experience has demonstrated that this requirement can pose a significant obstacle to effective EU action, as each Member State must participate in the negotiation process and, crucially, ratify the agreement according to its national constitutional procedures. This ratification process can substantially delay the agreement's entry into force, often to the dissatisfaction of the other parties involved.[14]

The solution commonly adopted to address this issue is the provisional application of certain chapters of the free trade agreement—specifically those relating to purely commercial aspects. This approach enables the immediate implementation of parts of the agreement, thereby addressing urgent political and economic considerations, while respecting the legal requirements governing the conclusion of treaties.[15] However, this provisional application does not resolve the challenge of promptly implementing provisions aimed at upholding and promoting the European Union's fundamental values.

Neither does the more recent solution, involving the adoption of an agreement composed of two parallel legal instruments, fully resolve the issue. Under this approach, one instrument covers only those parts relating to trade and investment that fall within the EU's exclusive competence and can therefore be concluded solely through the EU's ratification process. The other instrument encompasses provisions on matters requiring ratification by all Member States.

Although this structure allows for a partial and quicker application of the agreement's commercial components, it does not fully circumvent the delays inherent in securing unanimous consent from all Member States for the remaining provisions. Consequently, this can lead to a fragmented implementation timeline, potentially

[13] Suggestions for those interested in reading further on EU mixed agreements include Pisapia (2019).

[14] For example, the EU-Canada Comprehensive Economic and Trade Agreement (CETA) faced protracted ratification processes, with several Member States encountering domestic political opposition that postponed its full implementation. Similarly, the EU-Singapore Free Trade Agreement required extensive coordination to address diverse constitutional requirements among Member States. These instances underscore the complexity inherent in the EU's multi-level governance system and highlight the practical constraints on its ability to act swiftly in promoting its values abroad.

[15] See in particular article 25 of the 1969 Vienna Convention on the Law of Treaties and article 218, paragraph 5, of the TFEU, which allows the Council to decide, unanimously and after consulting the European Parliament, to apply an agreement provisionally pending its entry into force. This mechanism respects the constitutional requirements of Member States while enabling the EU to implement parts of an agreement without delay.

weakening the Union's ability to promptly promote its fundamental values abroad and creating uncertainty for third countries awaiting full treaty enforcement.[16]

2 European Union Free Trade Agreements (EU FTAs)

Generally speaking, the European Union can be regarded as one of the principal actors in global trade, given the extensive network of free trade agreements (FTAs) it has concluded. Currently, the Union has 44 FTAs in force, encompassing 76 partner countries. However, these agreements vary considerably in scope and content, prompting scholars to propose various classification schemes.

One of the more straightforward approaches distinguishes between two categories:

- "First-generation" trade agreements, predominantly concluded prior to 2016, which are essentially traditional trade treaties focused primarily on the reduction or elimination of tariff barriers;
- "Second-generation" (or "new-generation") trade agreements, characterized by the inclusion not only of provisions addressing tariff and non-tariff barriers but also clauses that seek to integrate trade policy with the promotion of fundamental values, such as the protection of human rights, democracy, the rule of law, intellectual property rights, inclusive growth, and sustainable development.[17]

[16] This bifurcated approach has been notably employed in agreements such as the EU-Singapore Free Trade Agreement and the EU-Vietnam Free Trade Agreement. In these cases, the trade and investment chapters—falling under the Union's exclusive competence—were provisionally applied following EU ratification, while other parts of the agreements, addressing issues like sustainable development, labor rights, or dispute resolution mechanisms, required ratification by each Member State. This is also the case of the modernised Agreement between the European Union and Chile, negotiated between 2017 and 2022 to modernize the previous EU-Chile Association Agreement (in force since 2003). On 9 December 2022, a political conclusion was reached and, on 13 December 2023, the modernized Agreement was signed. In truth, it is composed of two parallel legal instruments: the Advanced Framework Agreement (AFA), that includes the political and cooperation pillar, and the trade and investment pillar (inclusive of investment protection provisions), subject to ratification by all Member States; and the Interim Trade Agreement (ITA), covering only those parts of the trade and investment pillar of the AFA that are of EU exclusive competence (i.e. not including the investment protection provisions), adopted through the EU only ratification process. While the ITA entered into force on February 1st, 2025, following the completion of Chile's ratification process, the AFA will enter into force only if and when all EU Member States have completed their respective ratification processes. In that case, the ITA would cease to exist and would be replaced by the AFA.

[17] Notable books dealing with new generation trade agreements include: Adinolfi (2021), Fernández Rozas (2019), Maillo (2021), Ruotolo (2016), and Vincent (2021).

These free trade agreements embody the so-called "deep trade" approach, aiming to intensify economic integration among a select group of partners by progressively harmonizing their respective legal and regulatory frameworks.[18]

Included within this category are the Deep and Comprehensive Free Trade Agreements (DCFTAs), which aim to grant associated non-EU countries—such as Moldova, Georgia, and Ukraine—access to the "four freedoms" of the Single Market: the free movement of goods, workers, capital, and services. It is important to note, however, that the free movement of workers remains under the jurisdiction of individual EU Member States. Another relevant instrument is the Economic Partnership Agreements (EPAs), which are trade and development agreements negotiated between the EU and African, Caribbean, and Pacific (ACP) countries. Generally, these agreements provide for immediate and full access to EU markets for ACP partners, while the latter progressively open their markets to EU imports over transitional periods typically ranging from 15 to 25 years.

Second-generation FTAs are therefore of particular interest for the present study. The research will focus on their detailed analysis to assess whether, and to what extent, they effectively uphold and promote the European Union's fundamental values in its external relations.

At present, the European Union has concluded or is in the process of concluding second-generation free trade agreements (FTAs) with several partners. These include: South Korea (signed on 6 October 2010 and entered into force on 13 December 2015); Colombia/Peru/Ecuador (signed on 26 June 2012 and entered into force in 2013); Central American Association (signed on 29 June 2012 and entered into force in 2013); Canada (CETA) (signed on 30 October 2016 and entered into force in 2017); Japan (entered into force on 1 February 2019); Singapore (signed on 19 October 2018 and entered into force on 21 November 2019); Vietnam (signed on 30 June 2019 and entered into force on 31 July 2020); United Kingdom (signed on 30 December 2020 and entered into force on 1 May 2021); New Zealand (signed on 9 July 2023 and entered into force on 1 May 2024); Kenya (signed on 18 December 2023 and entered into force on 1 July 2024); Chile (in 2022 a political agreement was reached to modernize the previous 2002 Association Agreement and it entered into force on 1 February 2025). Regarding other partners, negotiations have been concluded but the agreements have not yet been signed or ratified. This includes: Mercosur (an agreement in principle reached on 28 June 2019, improved on 6 December 2024, on 17 January 2026, the European Union and Mercosur signed the Partnership Agreement and the Interim Trade Agreement); East African Community (the Economic Partnership Agreement, signed in 2014, is not yet applicable); Kyrgyzstan (agreement initialed in 2019), Uzbekistan (agreement initialed in 2022) and West Africa (the Economic Partnership Agreement signed in 2014, entered into provisional application only with Ivory Coast and Ghana in 2016), India (negotiations involve three separate instruments: a Free Trade Agreement, an Investment Protection Agreement, and an Agreement on Geographical Indications; negotiations

[18] See Melo Araujo (2016).

began in 2007, paused in 2013, resumed in 2022 and concluded on 27 January 2026). Additionally, new generation FTAs are under negotiation with: Australia (since 2018); Indonesia (negotiation ongoing since 2016 with this ASEAN Member); the Philippines (negotiations started in 2015, paused in 2017, resumed in 2024); Tajikistan (since 2023); Thailand (negotiations launched in 2013, paused in 2014, relaunched in 2023). Finally, the EU has initiated modernization negotiations for existing agreements with: Mexico (political agreement reached in 2018 to modernize the 1997 agreement); Azerbaijan (negotiations since 2017, currently on hold since 2019); Eastern and Southern Africa (ESA) partners (since 2019); Kazakhstan (since 2023); Morocco (since 2013, negotiations on hold since 2014); Tunisia (since 2015, negotiations on hold since 2019).

These agreements are particularly significant for understanding if and how the European Union upholds and promotes its values globally due to the diverse nature of their partners and the breadth of their reach. The EU's trade agreements encompass a wide spectrum of countries that collectively represent virtually the entire world. Some agreements involve numerous countries and hundreds of millions of citizens, with estimated trade volumes reaching tens of billions of euros, as exemplified by the agreement with Mercosur. Others are bilateral agreements with individual non-EU countries, which vary considerably in size—ranging from smaller States such as Singapore to larger economies like Canada.

The partners themselves vary economically and politically: some are affluent, highly developed countries such as South Korea and Japan, while others are developing nations like Vietnam and Kenya. Furthermore, the degree of shared values between the EU and its partners differs significantly. Some partners align closely with the EU on fundamental principles, such as Canada and New Zealand, whereas others, such as Vietnam, share fewer common values.

From a geographical perspective, these agreements cover all inhabited continents—Europe, the Americas, Asia, Africa, and Oceania—highlighting the global scope of the EU's external trade policy. However, the heterogeneity of the EU's partners also means that these FTAs are far from uniform. In some cases, certain EU values may not be fully accepted by partners, while in others, partners' own values may diverge from those upheld by the EU. This diversity makes these agreements a critical site for analyzing the EU's ability to uphold and promote its values internationally.

It is accurate to state that the European Union has adopted a differentiated, partner-specific approach,[19] aiming to uphold and promote, within each agreement, at least those values that are mutually accepted. This pragmatic strategy seeks to

[19] Melo Araujo compares this EU flexible approach with the US rigid one, pointing out that "*The EU… in this respect, must be distinguished from the US's competitive liberalization 'take it or leave it' policy towards FTA negotiations*" Melo Araujo (2016, p. 229).

avoid the alternative of foregoing agreements altogether, which would effectively preclude the possibility of advancing any of the Union's core values.[20]

For instance, while democracy occupies a central place in all agreements concluded with American States and regional organizations—reflecting a shared Euro-American commitment—this value is notably absent in agreements with other partners, such as Vietnam. Nonetheless, this divergence should not be overstated. Certain values are broadly upheld and promoted across nearly all EU free trade agreements.

Second-generation agreements, for example, commonly include a dedicated chapter on 'Trade and Sustainable Development' (TSD), wherein the parties commit to continually strive to improve their respective environmental and labor standards. This reflects the promotion of two fundamental EU values enshrined in Article 3(5) TEU: sustainable development and the protection of human (particularly workers') rights.

The EU's flexible approach is further demonstrated by its preference, where possible, to conclude trade agreements not with individual States but rather with regional organizations and their Member States. This strategy aligns with the EU's broader objective of contributing to the development and respect of international law, fostering an inclusive and effective multilateral system, and promoting a fair, rules-based global order grounded in EU fundamental values.

The advantages of this approach are evident: a single agreement with a regional organization enables the adoption of uniform rules, which uphold and promote EU values, across multiple countries simultaneously. The broader and more comprehensive the regional organization, the greater the impact. Consequently, a limited number of such agreements with key regional bodies would effectively cover much of the world, facilitating the creation of a relatively uniform set of international norms and positioning the EU as a prominent global norm-setter.

It is therefore hardly surprising that the European Union actively seeks to conclude free trade agreements with regional organizations, and in certain instances, as exemplified by the EU-Mercosur agreement, it has successfully done so. However, the EU-Mercosur agreement remains an exception rather than the norm.

As noted previously, a significant challenge arises from the limited scope of the EU's competence *ratione materiae* under EU law. Although the Union is

[20]Although, in my view, the assessment of this approach is generally positive, scholarly doctrine cautions against the potential risk of a "race to the bottom" resulting from such regulatory convergence. See Theisinger (2021). Another author considers this EU approach "*a preferable option to the approach adopted by the US in the framework of its competitive liberalization strategy*" although "*it does come with certain pitfalls*" and "*the EU's policy is tantamount to throwing everything at the wall and seeing what sticks*" Melo Araujo (2016, p. 230).

empowered to negotiate, sign, and ratify international agreements, this authority is confined to specific subject matters.

The situation is considerably more complex—and often more restrictive—for other regional organizations,[21] whose founding treaties frequently do not confer upon them the authority to conclude international agreements. In such instances, the European Union has demonstrated considerable flexibility, adapting its *modus operandi* to align with the specific competencies granted to each regional organization under its founding treaty.

In some cases, agreements are initially negotiated with a regional or sub-regional organization but are ultimately concluded with the individual Member States of that organization. Notable examples of this practice include the agreements between the European Union and the Member States of CARIFORUM,[22] the Andean Community,[23] and the Southern African Development Community (SADC).[24]

On other occasions, the European Union has sought to negotiate agreements encompassing all members of a regional or sub-regional organization but has ultimately concluded the agreement exclusively with the most willing Member State, while leaving the option open for other members to join subsequently. Illustrative

---

[21] "*La peculiarità della ripartizione di competenze nell'Unione, e in particolare, di quelle concorrenti con gli Stati membri, si riflette sulla natura stessa dell'Unione e sul* treaty making power *che la distingue rispetto a tutte le altre organizzazioni* internazionali"; Pisapia (2019, p. 10).

[22] The EU has a preferential trade agreement with 14 Member States of the Caribbean Forum (a subgroup of the Organisation of African, Caribbean and Pacific States, which comprises 14 Caribbean Community States and the Dominican Republic, called also CARIFORUM) which entered into provisional application in December 2008.

[23] The EU has a comprehensive trade agreement with Colombia and Peru. The agreement has been provisionally applied with Peru since 1 March 2013 and with Colombia since 1 August 2013. On 1 January 2017, Ecuador joined the trade agreement. The agreement gradually opens up markets on both sides and increases the stability and predictability of the trade and investment environment. Bolivia, a member of the Andean Community, can also seek accession to the trade agreement.

[24] The EU signed an Economic Partnership Agreement (EPA) on 10 June 2016 with the SADC EPA Group comprising Botswana, Lesotho, Mozambique, Namibia, South Africa and Eswatini (formerly Swaziland). Angola has an option to join the agreement in future. The agreement became the first regional EPA in Africa to be fully operational after Mozambique started applying the EPA in February 2018. Southern African Development Community EPA countries: Angola, Botswana, Lesotho, Mozambique, Namibia, South Africa, Eswatini. The other six members of the Southern African Development Community region—the Democratic Republic of the Congo, Madagascar, Malawi, Mauritius, Zambia and Zimbabwe—are negotiating Economic Partnership Agreements with the EU as part of other regional groups, namely Central Africa or Eastern and Southern Africa. On 22 June 2021, the EU started negotiations with Angola on a Sustainable Investment Facilitation Agreement.

examples include the EU-Kenya Economic Partnership Agreement (EPA)[25] and the EU-United Arab Emirates (UAE) Free Trade Agreement.[26]

In any case, with the aim of facilitating the adoption of common rules by a broader group of countries, such agreements are typically designed to remain open for accession by other members of the involved regional or sub-regional organizations at a later stage.

This approach reflects a pragmatic strategy aimed at overcoming the political and legal complexities inherent in multilateral negotiations within regional organizations, where consensus among all members may be difficult to achieve due to divergent interests, levels of development, or political will. By securing an

[25] The EU-Kenya EPA was preceded by another EPA: the "bloc-to-bloc" EPA concluded on 16 October 2014 between the European Union and the East African Community (EAC). The latter is a regional (*rectius* sub-regional) international organisation founded in 1999 that includes countries located in the Eastern part of the African continent. At the time of the conclusion of the agreement, besides the Republic of Kenya, the other EAC Member States were the Republic of Burundi, the Republic of Rwanda, the Republic of Uganda and the United Republic of Tanzania; instead, the Republic of South Sudan, the Democratic Republic of Congo and the Federal Republic of Somalia joined later, respectively in 2016, 2022 and 2024. To fully enter into force, the EU-EAC EPA had to be signed and ratified by each party: the EU, the EAC, and their respective Member States, according to their national ratification procedures. However, while all EU MSs, and the EU itself, signed the EU-EAC EPA, only Kenya and Rwanda have done so on the EAC side; moreover, Kenya is the only EAC State to have ratified the agreement. The latter, consequently, did not enter into force. However, Kenya was still interested in concluding an EPA with the EU and searched a solution to break the deadlock. Upon request of such country, therefore, EAC heads of States declared at their 21st ordinary summit in February 2021 that the EAC shall explore a different strategy: no longer a "bloc-to-bloc" agreement, but a "variable geometry" approach. The latter implied the conclusion of a different EPA with the EU, only involving Kenya, but open for other EAC countries to join later. Negotiations were concluded on 24 May 2023 at technical level, and on 19 June 2023 at political level. On 12 December 2023, the Council adopted its Decision on the signature (Council of the European Union, Press Release—The EU and Kenya sign a landmark Economic Partnership Agreement, 19 December 2023). Finally, as anticipated, on 18 December 2023 the Economic Partnership Agreement between the European Union and the Republic of Kenya was signed. It entered into force on 1 July 2024. An entrance into the literature on the EU-Kenya EPA can be found in Rugani (2024).

[26] The relations between the European Union and the Gulf Cooperation Council (GCC, whose members are Bahrain, Kuwait, Oman, Qatar, Saudi Arabia and the United Arab Emirates) are based on a Cooperation Agreement from 1988, which establishes regular dialogues on cooperation between the EU and GCC on trade and investment issues, macro-economic matters, climate change, energy, the environment, and research. The EU and GCC launched negotiations for a Free Trade Agreement (FTA) in 1990. The FTA was meant to provide for the progressive and reciprocal liberalisation of trade in goods and services. However, negotiations were suspended in 2008 as they faced several challenges. On 10 April 2025, European Commission President Ursula von der Leyen and Sheikh Mohamed bin Zayed Al Nahyan, president of the United Arab Emirates, agreed to launch negotiations on a free trade agreement (FTA). The FTA negotiations with the UAE—which were formally launched on 28 May 2025—focus on liberalizing trade in goods and services, and investment, while deepening cooperation in strategic sectors such as renewable energy, green hydrogen and critical raw materials. The first negotiation round took place on 24 June 2025, and covered all areas of the future FTA.

agreement with the most motivated partner first, the EU can initiate trade relations and promote its values without being indefinitely stalled by less willing members.

The primary advantage of this approach lies in its flexibility and capacity to deliver tangible results within reasonable timeframes. It allows the EU to foster deeper economic integration and normative alignment incrementally, with the possibility of gradual accession by other members. This 'variable geometry' approach can thus maintain momentum in trade policy and value promotion.

However, this strategy also entails certain drawbacks. The exclusion of some members at the outset may fragment regional integration efforts and create asymmetries within the organization, potentially undermining collective bargaining power and coherence. Furthermore, the staggered accession process may delay the uniform application and enforcement of EU values and standards across the entire region, limiting the overall impact of the agreements on promoting democratic principles, human rights, and sustainable development.

3 Research Question and Methodology

This research seeks to examine whether, and to what extent, European Union free trade agreements (FTAs)—particularly the so-called "new generation" FTAs—function as instruments through which the EU effectively upholds and promotes its foundational values on the global stage, as articulated in Articles 2 and 3(5) TEU.

From a theoretical point of view, the core idea is that the legal obligations enshrined in Articles 2 and 3(5) TEU confer upon the European Union a specific role in the international scenario as a value-based normative power. This role is a consequence of the specific features of its legal order: the Union's legal identity as a community founded upon common values, combined with its duty to uphold and promote those values in its external relations, provides the interpretive framework for assessing the extent and nature of the Union's role as a normative power in contemporary international legal order. More specifically, this volume examines the value-oriented clauses incorporated into the EU's new-generation free trade agreements (FTAs), on the premise that these instruments constitute the most effective means by which the Union can play the above-mentioned role as a normative power. This effectiveness is largely attributable to the interest of third countries in trading with the European Union and gaining access to its highly attractive internal market. The investigation will nevertheless demonstrate that the Union's success in performing this function is uneven, as it is contingent upon several factors, including the specific values implicated in each case and the capacity and political willingness of EU's different partners to adhere to those values. Accordingly, the argument advanced is that the European Union can indeed operate as a normative power in the international sphere, albeit in a variable manner.

Therefore, the inquiry is structured around two interrelated dimensions. The first concerns the extent to which the EU, through individual FTAs, has succeeded in advancing its normative agenda by inducing third countries to incorporate and implement EU values within their domestic legal systems. The second addresses the cumulative effect of EU FTAs: whether, taken together, they have contributed to shaping the broader landscape of international law in a manner that reflects and reinforces the EU's fundamental normative commitments.

In essence, the research aims to assess the substantive contribution of EU FTAs to the transformation of both international legal norms and the internal legal orders of partner countries, with a view to determining the extent to which these agreements foster an international legal and political order aligned with EU values.

A further line of inquiry concerns the depth and consistency of the EU's normative influence. Specifically, it explores the degree to which EU FTAs have impacted partner States' internal legal systems and the extent to which they have led to the incorporation of EU values. Additionally, the research investigates whether the values promoted through these agreements vary from one FTA to another, and if so, seeks to identify the underlying causes of such divergences. Finally, it examines whether the EU consistently promotes its entire set of fundamental values across all FTAs, or whether it tends to prioritize certain values over others, both in terms of emphasis and effectiveness.

A useful starting point for understanding how the European Union is able to "convince" third States or other regional organizations to conclude free trade agreements (FTAs) that incorporate EU fundamental values is to consider the EU's considerable market size. As one of the three largest global economies—alongside the United States and China—[27] the EU offers an exceptionally attractive market for international trade partners.[28] The prospect of gaining preferential access to such a market provides strong incentives for third countries to enter into FTAs with the EU, even when such agreements entail commitments to normative provisions reflecting EU values. However, this leverage is not uniformly distributed. According to the gravity model of international trade, the EU's bargaining power is likely to be more limited in negotiations with geographically distant partners, where proximity and trade intensity are lower.[29]

[27] International Monetary Fund World Economic outlook 2024/2025, which estimates the Gross Domestic Product (GDP) based on Purchasing Power Parity (PPP) to be 14.1% with a GDP of 29.18 tn int. dollars (PPP; current prices, estimate 2025), compared to China 19.7% and the United States 14.75% of the global GDP.

[28] Theisinger (2021, p. 20), explains that: "*The EU's market size makes it an important trading partner to many countries, which are anticipated to have an incentive of unilaterally adjusting their regulation to lower trade costs for their exporting companies*". Some scholars, however, argue that when the "carrot" employed is access to the European Union's lucrative market—and the corresponding "stick" is the withdrawal of such access—this dynamic tends to prioritize the promotion of EU economic interests over the advancement of its core values: "*The EU's power is derived from the strength and size of its internal market, the rules of which are designed to further the EU's interests abroad whilst the enhancement of the EU's competitiveness becomes an increasingly prominent justification and goal of its external action*". See Melo Araujo (2016), p. 45. I do not concur with this theory and contend that it can be effectively refuted through a straightforward analysis of the provisions contained in the EU FTAs.

[29] See Theisinger (2021, p. 36).

Another important question that arises is whether, assuming the European Union has indeed succeeded in upholding and promoting its values globally through its free trade agreements, such action could be interpreted as an imposition of its normative model on third countries. In this light, one might ask whether the Union's external trade policy risks being perceived as a vehicle for normative conditionality aimed at extending its regulatory and ideological influence beyond its borders.[30] Alternatively, could this normative projection instead be understood as part of the Union's broader commitment to the maintenance of international peace and stability, grounded in a general principle of solidarity, as an unprejudiced reading and interpretation of the Treaties might suggest?

In order to address the questions outlined above, the authors of this volume undertake a targeted and comparative analysis of EU free trade agreements, with particular attention to the so-called "new generation" FTAs that have either been concluded or for which an agreement in principle has been reached. This analysis aims to highlight the innovative features of these agreements and to examine the mechanisms through which the European Union seeks to promote its fundamental values within them. A central question guiding this inquiry is whether, and to what extent, the EU is deliberately linking the promotion of its values to its external trade policy, leveraging its prominent position in global trade to this end.

Within this theoretical framework, the principal challenge is to assess whether the underlying scientific hypothesis—that the European Union upholds and promotes its values in the wider world through its international agreements— is corroborated by actual legislative choices as well as by current practice. To that end, the authors first analyze the relevant treaty provisions, and subsequently turn to their practical implementations in internal law and practice.

This volume is not a work of international relations or political science, nor does it seek to provide a comprehensive account of the various measures the European Union adopts in order to fulfill its obligation—enshrined in Article 3(5) TEU—to uphold and promote its values in its external relations. Rather, this is a legal study, and as such, its primary focus lies in the normative analysis of the provisions contained within EU free trade agreements.

The methodological approach adopted in this book does not involve a case-by-case examination of each FTA to assess whether, and to what extent, that individual agreement promotes EU values. Instead, the research is guided by a different analytical framework: it seeks to determine whether specific EU values are upheld and promoted across the spectrum of FTAs—particularly in the so-called "new

[30] This perspective is exemplified by Damro (2012, p. 695), who contends that: "*The externalization of internal regulatory measures can take place if, for example, the EU attempts to include standards in bilateral and multilateral trade agreements (i.e., positive conditionality). Even if the EU employs the tools of positive conditionality with the intent of persuading changes in behaviour, the third parties in question may feel they have been coerced into changing their behaviour because they have no alternative: they must agree to undesirable terms in trade agreements because they need access to the large European single market; and they must abide by the EU's relevant internal regulatory measures or they will be subject to sanctioning under the associated implementing legislation*".

generation" agreements—and, if so, to what extent. Emphasis is placed on the most legally and politically significant agreements.

Accordingly, this book constitutes an exploratory and comparative legal study of the extent to which the EU promotes its fundamental values through its free trade agreements. The comparative dimension is essential, as the analysis is not confined to a single agreement but encompasses multiple FTAs in order to identify patterns, divergences, and overarching trends in the EU's legal approach to value promotion through trade.

Among the numerous values enshrined in Articles 2 and 3(5) TEU, this volume focuses selectively on a limited number.

Naturally, the values selected for analysis in this volume do not constitute a random sample.

A substantial body of scholarship supports the view that the central and enduring aim of the European Union since its inception has been the preservation of peace. While the economic dimension of integration has always occupied a prominent position—and has undoubtedly shaped both the evolution and attractiveness of the Union—it has traditionally served as a means to this higher end. This interpretation, which the present author shares, underscores the foundational role of peace in the European integration project.

In the current geopolitical context, the value of peace has assumed even greater prominence. Article 2 TEU affirms that the Union is founded on a set of clearly defined values, including respect for human dignity, freedom, democracy, equality, the rule of law, and human rights. The promotion and safeguarding of these values are not only essential for ensuring peace within the Union itself, but also constitute key objectives of its external action. As such, the EU's commitment to upholding these values through its international instruments—including free trade agreements—may be seen as part of a broader strategy aimed at fostering peace and stability globally.

Democracy and the rule of law form the bedrock of Western political and legal culture. Without them, the effective protection and promotion of the other values enshrined in Articles 2 and 3(5) TEU would be unattainable. These two principles constitute the necessary precondition for the functioning of a value-based legal order, both within the European Union and in its external action.

Other values addressed in this volume reflect evolving priorities and contemporary challenges within the European Union. Sustainable development and data protection, for example, respond to modern societal needs and policy imperatives in a globalized and digitized world. Security—unfortunately—has returned to the forefront of European political discourse in recent times, alongside a renewed emphasis on the observance of international law and respect for the principles of the United Nations Charter, particularly in light of recent geopolitical developments.

Finally, the protection of the rights of persons belonging to minorities remains a matter of paramount importance in the European context. Throughout the continent's history, the violation—or even the perceived violation—of minority rights has often been a source of political tension and conflict. In a region where many States are home to diverse ethnic and cultural groups, the safeguarding of these rights continues to play a crucial role in ensuring peace, stability, and democratic legitimacy.

A careful reader may note that, under Article 3(5) TEU, the European Union is not only required to uphold and promote its values in its external action, but also to advance its interests. On this basis, one might contend that the present analysis is incomplete insofar as it focuses exclusively on the EU's core values, without addressing the extent to which the Union pursues and promotes its interests in its external relations.

This critique might seem particularly pertinent in light of an observable trend in contemporary international relations, whereby the primacy of national interest frequently overrides fundamental values, such as democracy, the protection of human rights, the rule of law, and anti-corruption measures. A number of States—in particular certain major powers—[31] routinely conclude international agreements, namely with developing countries, that contain no substantive provisions relating to these core values.

By contrast, the European Union systematically incorporates value-based conditionality clauses into its international trade and cooperation agreements. While this reflects the EU's self-conception as a normative power and its commitment to foundational principles enshrined in the TEU, it may also diminish the Union's attractiveness as a negotiating partner. This is especially the case when compared to States such as China or Russia, whose agreement-making practices often eschew such conditionalities, prioritising strategic and economic objectives over values promotion.

Although this observation is entirely legitimate, there are sound reasons for the decision to focus this volume specifically on how, and to what extent, the European Union upholds and promotes its values—rather than its interests—in the context of its free trade agreements (FTAs).

The first reason is of a strictly scientific nature. In international relations, States in general—and major powers in particular—typically act in pursuit of their national interests, often adopting approaches that may be characterised as "Bismarckian" or "Machiavellian." As such, an inquiry into how the EU promotes its interests in its external action would offer relatively limited added value to existing scholarly discourse. By contrast, an examination of the extent to which the EU upholds and promotes its values in its FTAs engages a less travelled field of inquiry.

This question is especially pertinent from a legal perspective. As previously noted, the promotion of its values in the wider world is not a matter of political discretion for the EU, but a binding legal obligation.

The second reason is somewhat more complex. To appreciate it fully, one must first reflect on the actual relationship between the promotion of interests and the promotion of values in the EU's external action.

A prevailing view in the literature, as previously noted, is that these two dimensions are either juxtaposed or, at the very least, that the pursuit of values tends to

[31] Not all of them, though: for instance the US in their FTAs often uphold and promote some values.

hinder the effective advancement of interests. However, in my view, such a dichotomous framing is not necessarily accurate, and it is insufficient for scholars to merely restate this tension without deeper analysis.

There are instances in which the effective promotion of fundamental values—such as the rule of law, human rights, or good governance—can in fact serve the EU's long-term strategic and economic interests. Thus, rather than being mutually exclusive, values and interests may, in certain contexts, be mutually reinforcing.

To clarify this point, it may be useful to illustrate it with a concrete example.

Consider a scenario in which a third country—perhaps a developing State—ratifies additional multilateral instruments and raises its environmental and/or labor standards as a result of implementing the sustainability provisions contained in a new-generation free trade agreement (FTA) concluded with the European Union. In such a case, the EU has simultaneously upheld and promoted both its values and its interests.

On the one hand, the values promoted are those of sustainable development and the protection of fundamental rights, specifically workers' rights. On the other hand, a key economic interest is also served: namely, the prevention of market distortions resulting from the importation of goods whose low prices stem from inadequate domestic environmental or labor standards. This concern becomes even more acute in situations where a FTA might incentivize the economically weaker partner to engage in a "race to the bottom"—deliberately lowering labor or environmental protections in order to reduce production costs, increase exports, and maximize profits.[32]

Thus, in such circumstances, the promotion of values and the pursuit of interests are not only compatible but may in fact be mutually reinforcing. This underscores the importance of moving beyond the simplistic binary opposition between "values" and "interests" in the EU's external trade policy.

The second dimension of the research question concerns the extent to which the provisions contained in the EU's bilateral trade agreements reflect the parties' intentions regarding the Union's role in shaping norms within the international

[32] Certain authors, such as Melo Araujo, appear to criticize this approach: "*The EU, through its EU DCFTAs, seeks to increase compliance with international social and environmental standards, and in doing so arguably removes one of the very few areas where developing countries retain a competitive advantage*" Melo Araujo (2016), p. 229. Although he indirectly supports my thesis—that the successful promotion of fundamental values can, at times, advance broader interests—I do not concur with the view that the behavior of the European Union warrants criticism because it "*removes one of the very few areas where developing countries retain a competitive advantage*". What course of action should the European Union pursue? Should it contravene its own foundational legal principles by cooperating in the lowering of environmental and social standards solely to preserve one of the limited areas in which developing countries maintain a competitive advantage? I submit that it should not. The reality is not that: "*behind the EU's commendable drive to promote non- trade values lies a certain degree of self- interest*" Melo Araujo (2016, p. 229), but rather that the (legally binding) promotion of fundamental values can, at times, have the incidental effect of advancing EU interests. This outcome aligns with the legal obligations set forth in Article 2 of the Treaty on European Union (TEU) and reflects a consistent practice of States in the conduct of their international relations.

trade—and more broadly, international legal—order. In other words, this inquiry seeks to determine whether, and to what extent, the EU uses its Free Trade Agreements (FTAs) as instruments to contribute to the development of, and adherence to, international law, in pursuit of an inclusive and effective multilateral system and a fair, rules-based global order grounded in EU fundamental values.

It is important to underscore that, pursuant to Article 3(5) of the Treaty on European Union (TEU), "*the strict observance and the development of international law*" is not merely a policy preference but a fundamental value that the Union is legally obliged to uphold and promote in its external relations. Accordingly, examining whether and how EU FTAs support the international legal order—by incorporating, reinforcing, or even innovating legal norms—constitutes a key aspect of assessing the Union's normative impact beyond its borders.[33]

A comprehensive answer to this latter question, however, necessarily exceeds the scope of the present study and must remain a task for future research. A full assessment of the EU's contribution to the development of international law through its bilateral trade agreements would require a separate, in-depth analysis—both legal and empirical—that goes beyond the objectives of this volume.

This book will provide multiple opportunities to examine the European Union's evolving approach to achieving these objectives through the negotiation and conclusion of free trade agreements. As previously indicated, these agreements reflect a dual-purpose strategy: alongside traditional commercial provisions aimed at trade liberalization, the EU systematically incorporates commitments designed to promote adherence to non-trade values. In this way, the EU seeks to utilize its economic leverage as a leading global trading actor to project and institutionalize its core values beyond its borders.

This development represents a significant shift in the EU's trade policy paradigm.

Notably, the EU's bilateral and regional trade agreements are increasingly positioned as alternatives to the multilateral trading system under the World Trade Organization (WTO), which has remained effectively paralyzed in recent years. One of the key points of contention in the current multilateral negotiations is the proposed expansion of WTO commitments to encompass non-trade-related concerns. The inclusion of such disciplines, particularly in areas like environmental protection, has historically faced resistance from certain WTO members. Nevertheless, it bears emphasizing that the EU has been among the most vocal

---

[33] Barthesaghi et al. (2019, p. 455) argue that: "*cabe destacar el giro que ha mostrado la política comercial de la UE en los últimos años, priorizando los acuerdos comerciales con nuevos socios… y recuperando el liderazgo en cuanto a la definición de las normas comerciales internacionales*". Theisinger (2021, p. 20) points out that: "*Global regulatory competition is becoming increasingly relevant as global value chains (GVCs) and tradable services are of growing importance in international trade. The European Union has proven to be an influential regulator by its market size, regulatory capacities, and past successes in regulatory diffusion… The expectation of the EU's ambitions of influencing global rules and norms in light of its standards comes from the EU's strategy papers, as well as from negotiation successes in adjacent countries*". Other publications on the subject include Damro (2012) and Melo Araujo (2016).

proponents of integrating these issues into the multilateral framework, notably during the Uruguay Round and the subsequent Doha Development Agenda negotiations.

Another important factor to consider is that the failure to incorporate regulatory disciplines into the framework of international trade law under the auspices of the World Trade Organization has prompted a strategic reorientation of the European Union's trade policy. In response, the EU has increasingly pursued its "deep trade agenda" through bilateral and regional avenues, most notably under the "Global Europe" strategy adopted by the European Commission in 2006.[34] This shift marks a significant departure from the EU's prior commitment to multilateralism. The strategy promotes a new generation of Deep and Comprehensive Free Trade Agreements (DCFTAs), through which the EU seeks to advance regulatory cooperation and integration in areas that extend beyond the scope of existing WTO commitments.

A constructive point of departure for assessing how the European Union's free trade agreements (FTAs) may enhance its capacity to act as a global norm-setter lies in a measured evaluation of the continued adequacy of the World Trade Organization's (WTO's) legal framework in addressing contemporary economic realities. There is a growing consensus among scholars that the WTO's normative architecture may no longer sufficiently reflect the complexities of the current global trading system. This is unsurprising, given that the core set of rules was conceived in the 1980s—a markedly different economic context. Since that time, the structure and dynamics of the global economy have evolved significantly and continue to do so at an accelerated pace.

The international community at large, and WTO Member States in particular, are increasingly called upon to advance the development of the multilateral trading system by formulating new legal rules capable of addressing the most pressing global challenges. The failure of the first substantive negotiation round launched in 2001 under the Doha Development Agenda has not facilitated progress in this regard, despite the partial success represented by the adoption of the WTO's Bali Package.[35] Several implications arising from this stagnation, when viewed in conjunction with the profound transformations in the global economy, merit careful consideration. Notably, these include the recent backlash against globalization within high-income countries (and its political consequences), as well as the exacerbation of global economic inequality, persistent unemployment, and escalating environmental risks.

Another critical factor contributing to the current crisis of the WTO is, without doubt, the profound breakdown of its once highly regarded and widely acclaimed[36]

---

[34] European Commission (2006).

[35] References on this topic include Del Vecchio and Di Comite (2014, pp. 387–417).

[36] "*With 146 decisions delivered since 1995, the Appellate Body of the World Trade Organization (WTO) stands as one of the world's most prolific and accomplished international courts*". Miranda and Sánchez Miranda (2023, p. 435).

dispute settlement mechanism.[37] It is well established that the crisis of the WTO's dispute settlement mechanism was precipitated by the United States, which, since May 2016—and notwithstanding the succession of four different administrations under three presidents from both major political parties—has persistently blocked the appointment of new members to the Appellate Body. This obstruction has been justified by the United States on the basis of both procedural and substantive criticisms concerning the functioning and jurisprudence of the Appellate Body.[38]

As a result, since December 11, 2019, the Appellate Body has been unable to attain the minimum quorum of three members required to hear appeals of panel reports.[39] In the absence of a functioning Appellate Body, any party may effectively suspend the adoption of a panel report by filing an appeal, thereby placing the dispute in a legal limbo. This procedural deadlock significantly undermines the complainant's ability to obtain a final resolution through the WTO dispute settlement mechanism, as the Dispute Settlement Body (DSB) is precluded from adopting panel findings that are subject to appeal in the absence of an Appellate Body ruling.

Furthermore, the broader context of international trade governance has deteriorated in recent months, attributable in large part to the unilateral and protectionist tariff measures pursued by the current administration of the United States. These developments pose serious challenges to the stability and credibility of the multilateral trading system.

Within this context, the European Union's free trade agreements (FTAs) may serve as instruments to support the implementation and progressive development of the principles enshrined in the General Agreement on Tariffs and Trade (GATT) and the World Trade Organization (WTO) framework. In doing so, they may help to address and partially remedy the institutional and substantive deficiencies that have emerged as a result of the ongoing crisis in the multilateral trading system.

Notably, EU FTAs incorporate several distinctive features, particularly in relation to: structured policy dialogue and a balanced approach across a broad range of subject matters; the conceptualization of trade as a means to advance societal objectives and promote sustainable development; the inclusion of provisions addressing emerging issues such as e-commerce, transparency, a redefined approach to barriers affecting trade in services and investment and the establishment of dispute settlement mechanisms that diverge in significant ways from the WTO model.

---

[37] Papers in English about the crisis of WTO dispute settlement mechanism and possible solutions include: Baroncini (2020), Miranda and Sánchez Miranda (2023), Petersmann (2019), and Sykes (2024).

[38] Petersmann (2019, p. 503) argues that in doing so the United States—as well as other WTO members—"*have been violating their legal duties and democratic mandates given by national parliaments to maintain the WTO Appellate Body (AB) as legally prescribed in Article 17 of the WTO Dispute Understanding (DSU)*".

[39] The sole Chinese judge, Zhao Hong remained in office, but in March 2020 the U.S. administration asserted that she was not a valid member of the Appellate Body, being a paid affiliate of the People's Republic of China. See Baroncini (2020), p. 2.

Several potential avenues through which the European Union's free trade agreements (FTAs) may exert influence on the World Trade Organization (WTO) legal framework warrant careful consideration. One such possibility is the emulation of the EU's normative model by third countries, either unilaterally or through the negotiation of autonomous agreements incorporating similar provisions. This form of legal transplantation may occur when certain regulatory approaches are perceived as particularly effective, legitimate, or economically advantageous.

A second dimension of potential impact concerns the direct or indirect effect that specific provisions of EU FTAs may have beyond the contracting parties. This may manifest in two distinct ways. First, certain obligations—such as those relating to transparency or the regulation (or prohibition) of public subsidies—may produce *de facto* benefits for third countries, even in the absence of formal participation in the agreements. Second, some provisions may confer *de jure* rights on third countries, particularly through the operation of the Most-Favoured-Nation (MFN) clause contained in Article 4 of the Agreement on Trade-Related Aspects of Intellectual Property Rights (TRIPS).[40] In this context, commitments undertaken within EU FTAs, especially in the field of intellectual property, may become automatically extended to other WTO Members by virtue of the MFN principle.

Finally, the proliferation of "second-generation" trade agreements concluded by the European Union with third countries and regional organizations is progressively constructing a complex and far-reaching network—or "spider's web"—of agreements that incorporate provisions addressing non-trade values. These include, *inter alia*, commitments to the protection of the environment, the promotion of human rights, adherence to democratic principles, and the rule of law. Through these agreements, partner countries assume additional obligations with respect to these core values.

The success of this model is evidenced by the growing number of comprehensive trade agreements the EU has concluded with partners across the globe. Moreover, these agreements are evolving in both breadth and depth, with non-trade values occupying an increasingly prominent place. Notable examples of this development include the EU's recent agreements with Chile, Kenya, and New Zealand.

An additional and significant consideration concerns the potential impact of these agreements on the development of international law. The two primary sources of international law[41] are customary international law and international treaties,[42] the key distinction between them lying in their scope of application: while treaties are binding only upon those States that have ratified or acceded to them, customary international law is generally binding upon the international community as a whole.

[40] The peculiarity of this clause in the TRIPS Agreement, when compared to analogous provisions in the GATT and GATS frameworks, lies in the absence of an exception akin to Article XXIV of GATT or Article V of GATS. These latter provisions permit derogations from the relevant obligations in the context of agreements on economic integration—an exception that TRIPS does not provide.

[41] Books specifically concerned with the sources on International Law include Koskenniemi (2000).

[42] An entrance into the literature on the law of treaties can be found in De Oliveira Mazzuoli (2016).

In this regard, the increasing incorporation of non-trade norms into EU FTAs may, over time, contribute to the crystallization of relevant customary rules, particularly where such provisions are consistently included in treaty practice and reflect a broader normative consensus among States.

That said, the influence of EU FTAs on the development of international law might, at first glance, appear limited, insofar as they are treaty instruments binding only upon the contracting parties. However, such a conclusion is insufficient from a scholarly perspective and warrants deeper examination, particularly with regard to the formation of customary international law.

Traditionally, under the theory of custom as a form of tacit agreement, it was widely held that the express or implied consent of all States was required for a customary rule to emerge. This understanding, however, has evolved in response to significant changes in the composition and character of the international community.[43] The disintegration of colonial empires following the First and Second World Wars resulted in a huge increase in the number of sovereign States—from approximately 40 in the early twentieth century to nearly 200 today. Consequently, the international community is not only significantly larger, but also far more diverse in political, economic, and ideological terms.

Until the early twentieth century, the establishment of general rules of international law was facilitated by a relatively homogeneous group of States, largely rooted in European traditions and guided by shared historical, cultural, and religious values—primarily those of Western, Christian origin.[44] This Eurocentric legal order, while foundational for classical international law, no longer reflects the needs, values, or perspectives of the newly independent States that emerged during the decolonization process, nor of socialist or other ideologically distinct regimes. As a result, the previously prevailing uniformity has given way to a deeply pluralistic and fragmented international order.

In this context, achieving broad consensus on the content of general rules has become increasingly complex. This has made the emergence of universally accepted customary rules more difficult, particularly in areas involving value-laden issues such as environmental protection, human rights, and sustainable development.

As a consequence, the classical theory of custom as tacit agreement is no longer tenable if one aims to construct a general and inclusive international legal system.[45]

---

[43] Simma (2009) reflecting on this development, emphasizes that the formation of customary law today must account for this increased diversity and no longer presumes the kind of normative homogeneity once taken for granted.

[44] See Cassese (2001, p. 27).

[45] Cannizzaro (2023, p. 112) though warns that: "*Le concezioni consensualiste peraltro, non sono mai state abbandonate e, anzi, riemergono periodicamente nella dottrina e nella prassi internazionale. Il motivo del perdurante successo di tali dottrine è duplice. Da un punto di vista politico, esse incontrano il favore degli Stati, i quali costantemente cercano di sottrarsi all'osservanza di regole internazionali che si sono formate indipendentemente dal loro consenso. In una prospettiva teorica, inoltre, l'idea che la consuetudine internazionale tragga fondamento dal consenso degli Stati può risultare attraente per superare le varie difficoltà logiche prospettate da questa singolare fonte di diritto*".

Contemporary doctrine recognizes that customary international law may emerge even in the absence of the express consent or participation of all States. Rather, a customary rule may crystallize when it is supported by a sufficiently representative group of States—both quantitatively and qualitatively—that reflects a broad spectrum of economic systems, political alignments, and ideological perspectives.

In this modern view, States may be bound by a customary norm even if they have remained passive—failing to express either explicit support or opposition.

In other words, the development of customary international law does not require unanimous or universal assent; it is sufficient that there exists a general and consistent pattern of State practice, accompanied by *opinio juris*, and the non-objection of other States, particularly those with a special interest in the matter, and acquiescence by other States.

Today, many scholars also maintain that, in general, a State is not entitled to exempt itself from a customary rule by invoking its consistent opposition—under the so-called "persistent objector" doctrine—once that rule has crystallized into a generally applicable norm of international law.[46]

Although, as a general rule, custom does not arise from a deliberate lawmaking process,[47] it may, in certain instances, be derived from treaty provisions. This occurs when non-party States come to accept that specific provisions of a treaty are capable of giving rise to customary international law. Whether such provisions generate custom depends on various factors, including the nature of the treaty, the number and representativeness of the participating States, and the broader context of international practice.

Treaty provisions may contribute to the formation of customary international law provided that both State parties and non-parties exhibit consistent and general practice (*usus* or *diuturnitas*), accompanied by a belief that such practice is legally required (*opinio juris sive necessitatis*). This phenomenon is commonly referred to either as the generative effect—where the treaty provision initiates the formation of a customary rule—or the crystallizing effect—where the provision consolidates or confirms an emerging customary norm.

---

[46] "*One of the consequences of the theory of custom as 'tacit agreement' was that any time a State could prove that it had tacitly or expressly opposed a customary rule, such rule could not be regarded as binding on it. This view… reflected the real state of affairs existing before the Second World War, when there were few States (mostly European) and their consent was necessary for a general rule to emerge. Whether or not that view rightly reflected the reality of the time, it can no longer be regarded as tenable today*". Cassese (2001, p. 123). Although a substantial portion of the scholarly literature concurs with the current inapplicability of the persistent objector doctrine (while noting that such inapplicability is subject to certain limits and conditions), there are still scholars who continue to uphold its validity (among them the Special Rapporteur Wood in his Third Report on Customary International Law). Suggestions for those interested in reading further on the persistent objector doctrine include Charney (1985), D'Amato (2014), and Green (2016). For a nuanced and comprehensive analysis of the various scholarly interpretations and judicial positions on the doctrine of the persistent objector, the classic (although not very recent) reference is Mendelson (1998).

[47] Kelsen (1966, p. 307) defines custom as: "*unconscious and unintentional lawmaking*".

There are compelling grounds to argue that provisions contained in EU FTAs may serve as generators of customary international law.

As noted in the preceding paragraph, the European Union has concluded such agreements with a substantial number of countries—nearly half of the international community. Moreover, these agreements have been entered into with States that are diverse in terms of economic systems, political orientations, and ideological frameworks, and they span all geographical regions.

While it is true that EU FTAs are not uniform in every respect, it is equally true that many of them contain substantially similar provisions.

Accordingly, for these reasons, such provisions are strong theoretical candidates to exert either a generative or crystallizing effect on customary international law—provided, of course, that other States, whether parties or non-parties to the agreements, exhibit the requisite consistent practice and adhere to the necessary belief in the legal character of such practice (*opinio juris*).

This issue will arise repeatedly throughout the present work, and we shall have multiple opportunities to elaborate upon it. Nonetheless, it is our contention that this conceptual framework serves as a unifying thread for the analysis presented in the following chapters, and is essential for understanding the European Union's contribution to the development of a multilateral, rules-based international order.

4 Plan of the Book

Here is a road-map to the book. As previously mentioned, this study investigates how the European Union upholds and promotes its foundational values in the wider world through its international free trade agreements (FTAs). Accordingly, the initial chapters of the book are dedicated to a thorough examination of the values underpinning the European Union. The subsequent chapters focus individually on how specific, particularly significant values are promoted and protected through the EU's external trade policy, with a specific emphasis on the content and implementation of its FTAs.

The volume begins with an introductory chapter, which outlines the purpose and scope of the book. It begins by demonstrating that, for the European Union, the promotion and protection of its values on the international stage is not merely a matter of political discretion but constitutes a legal obligation under the Treaties. The chapter then highlights the key instruments through which the EU seeks to fulfill this obligation—most notably, the "Trade for All" strategy and the network of bilateral and regional free trade agreements it has concluded.

In this introductory chapter I discuss the aim of the book by detailing its topic. An overview of the structure and functioning of EU FTAs follows, providing essential background for the analyses contained in later chapters. The chapter proceeds by defining the central research question and elaborating on the methodology adopted throughout the study. It concludes with a summary of the book's structure and a brief introduction to the contents of the individual chapters.

This introductory chapter is followed by a series of three chapters focusing on European—and more broadly, Western—values. Each of these chapters is authored by a scholar with specific expertise in the subject matter under discussion. This section is intended to reconstruct the historical and philosophical foundations of shared European values, both from a historical perspective and through comparative legal analysis.

Chapter 2 searches for the roots of European common legal values going back to the Middle Ages. The legal historian Andrea Landi thinks that, despite the coexistence of multiple legal systems, the aspiration for legal unity has been a constant value in the European experience since the medieval centuries. He concludes that contemporary efforts to harmonize law within the European Union are ultimately in line with this long-standing pattern and that current EU values have been built up over the centuries thanks to a sort of "long wave", beginning in the Middle Ages and extending to the present day.

Chapter 3, by Marcelo Labanca, is a comparative study aimed at finding out the degree of convergence (or divergence) between the founding values of the European Union, enshrined in Article 2 of the TEU, and the legal principles of Latin American legal experiences. In particular, the research intends to show whether and to what extent there is a progressive construction of a common core of values between the European Union and Latin America, based on dignity, freedom, equality, democracy, the rule of law and the protection of minorities, in order to find out if there is a transconstitutional legal heritage based on pluralism and the global affirmation of civilizational standards of justice, democracy and human dignity.

Identifying the presence of values common to European States that can also be found in the legal systems of Latin American countries may suggest that there is a shared foundation that minimizes the importance of borders in defining a civilizing legal culture. This common ground ends up encompassing people subjected to similar patterns of formative values, even considering the many differences between the legal systems and cultures of Europe and Latin America.

Labanca's methodological approach is particularly noteworthy, as rather than presuming a unidirectional export of European values, he seeks to explore whether the pluralism inherent in Latin American constitutional experiences may affirm similar values through distinct formulations and institutional commitments.

The last chapter of this part, Chap. 4, is a dynamic analysis of EU founding values. Hence, after mentioning which are the legal basis of EU founding values and explaining how upholding and promoting these values, inside the EU but also in the wider world, is a hallmark of EU action, Elena Crespo Navarro points out how in current times these values are threatened both internally (due to the behavior of some Member States) and from the outside. In order to try to give an answer to the fundamental question about the capability of the EU to face these challenges, she wonders if the EU today has sufficient and adequate instruments to ensure the protection of its values and carries out an exhaustive analysis of the different tools currently available to the EU to promote and protect its values, pointing out how there are instruments not only to react to actual violations but also to act on promotion, awareness-raising and prevention and paying special attention to those linked to the EU Budget.

Following this general introduction to the topic, the central part of the book—comprising Chaps. 5–12—is dedicated to examining whether, and to what extent, the European Union's fundamental values are effectively upheld and promoted in the wider world through its free trade agreements.

This section consists of eight chapters, each authored by a scholar with specific expertise in the respective subject matter. Every chapter focuses on a particular value that holds a central place in the EU's legal and normative framework. The values addressed include: democracy and the rule of law; peace and security; sustainable development; data protection; human rights and the rights of persons belonging to minorities; dispute settlement and access to justice; observance of international law; and respect for the principles enshrined in the Charter of the United Nations.

In the first chapter of this section, Chap. 5, Raquel Cavalcanti Ramos Machado's theory is that an international commitment to promoting and defending democracy, the rule of law, and the respect for human rights is necessary to ensure the continued viability of democratic regimes in societies that uphold them today, in the light of the transnational nature of current democratic challenges and the ongoing crisis affecting the Western model of freedom and human rights. In this scenario, the EU's role in strengthening democracy through concrete actions and legal commitments, and in particular in its FTAs, remains a key contribution to global governance and the protection of fundamental values, in spite of criticisms regarding the selective application of this principle, concerns over the North-South imposition of political models and worries about the so-called "democratic ambiguity" (which arises when democracy is promoted externally but is not sufficiently upheld internally).

A final consideration is that while the inclusion of democratic principles in international law and trade agreements does not guarantee their practical implementation or realization, it remains significant. Such inclusion acknowledges that no single State can fully advance democracy on its own, particularly given the complexities of transnational relations. Enforcing democratic clauses requires oversight, but more importantly, it begins with recognizing their normative value and the collective effort needed to uphold them.

The aim of Chap. 6, by Matteo Del Chicca, is first of all to investigate whether and how certain international agreements between the European Union and third parties uphold and promote the EU's core values of peace and security. Many of these agreements contain similar provisions—such as specific "security exceptions" and "denial of benefits" clauses—which can also be seen as tools to support and advance peace and security. In addition, some agreements include targeted provisions specifically aimed at achieving these goals. A second issue to be considered is the role played by European Union military and civilian missions and operations in reinforcing and promoting the Union's values related to peace and security.

This volume is not an article on current affairs, limited in relevance to a specific moment in time. Rather, it constitutes a broad and systematic study aimed at understanding the place of European Union free trade agreements—particularly the so-called "new generation" FTAs—within the framework of international law. More specifically, it seeks to assess whether, and to what extent, the European Union has succeeded in upholding and promoting its core values in third countries through the conclusion and implementation of these agreements.

This clarification is made for the benefit of the reader who might otherwise expect the book to contain dedicated chapters on each and every value enshrined in the EU Treaties. That is not the objective of the present work. The selection of values analyzed in the central chapters is intended to be illustrative rather than exhaustive, focusing on those values which, by their nature or by the way they are incorporated into trade policy, offer the most meaningful insight into the EU's promotion of its values in the wider world.

That's why we have chosen to devote a large chapter, authored by two scholars, Francesca Martines and Samantha Velluti to a single, particularly significant, value. This choice is by no means arbitrary. In our view, it represents the most compelling example of how the European Union actively upholds and promotes its values in the wider world through its free trade agreements.

The theme addressed in Chap. 7 is sustainable development, a topic that is not only among the most pressing issues of our time, but one that is expected to remain central to the global agenda for many years, if not decades, to come. The rationale for allocating a large chapter, with two different authors to this subject lies in its dual dimension: one section of the chapter, by Francesca Martines, addresses the environmental aspects of sustainable development, while another, by Samantha Velluti, focuses on its labor dimension. This division allows for a more nuanced and in-depth analysis of the ways in which sustainable development is embedded and operationalized in the EU's external trade policy.

After a short introduction contained in Sect. 1 of the chapter, Sect. 2 focuses on the complex relationship between trade, environmental protection and sustainability within the framework of the European Union's free trade agreements (FTAs). After tracing the development of the intricate interaction between international trade regulations and environmental concerns -highlighting both the benefits and drawbacks, challenges, and opportunities- the chapter focuses on the incorporation of sustainable development into EU trade policy. The contribution further delves into the structure of the chapters on sustainable development, with an emphasis on environmental issues in the so-called new generation FTAs. It specifically highlights provisions addressing deforestation as a case study, exploring how the EU's approach to deforestation, through initiatives such as FLEGT and the more recent EUDR, is reflected in the clauses of the latest second generation agreements.

Martines concludes by emphasizing the importance of the provisions in free trade agreements to prevent a "race to the bottom," which could result in a significant decline in domestic environmental standards. This is especially crucial given that the EU's consumption and production patterns may unintentionally cause negative environmental impacts both within its borders and beyond.

Section 3 explores the role of labor provisions in promoting sustainable development within second-generation EU FTAs.

Following the failure of including a "social" clause within the WTO legal framework, the European Union has been increasingly relying on bilateral and regional trade agreements to strengthen the social dimension of its external trade relations.

Many of these agreements feature a dedicated chapter on labor, often labeled as the 'Trade and Sustainable Development' (TDS) chapter, or more simply as 'Labor' or 'Trade and Labor'. These chapters typically include labor-related clauses, where the parties commit to continually improving labor standards and incorporate non-regression clauses to prevent a "race to the bottom" that could undermine domestic labor protections. Furthermore, these provisions reaffirm the parties' existing international labor commitments and aim to incentivize them to adhere to key International Labour Organization (ILO) Conventions. The chapter critically assesses whether these labor provisions effectively enhance labor standards within domestic legal frameworks. It focuses on two case studies: the EU's trade agreements with the United Kingdom (UK) and Japan. After providing an overview of EU social conditionality in trade agreements, the analysis compares the labor provisions found in the 2019 EU-Japan Economic Partnership Agreement (EPA) and the 2020 EU-UK Trade and Cooperation Agreement (TCA). On a broader level, the chapter seeks to shed light on how sustainable development is addressed and incorporated into modern EU FTAs, serving as an example of how the European Union contributes to the development of international law and sets norms for global trade. The author concludes that the findings present a mixed and, at times, disappointing view of the EU's approach to trade sustainability, overall indicating that the EU has not yet fully fulfilled its own TEU obligations as outlined in Article 3(5) TEU and Article 21 TEU.

Chapter 8, by Gabriele Rugani, examines how the European Union seeks to promote fundamental rights to privacy and data protection—enshrined in Articles 7 and 8 of the Charter of Nice—beyond its borders through international agreements. After describing briefly the difference between the two rights and their content, the chapter highlights the inclusion of provisions in various EU free trade agreements aimed at enhancing third countries' protections for these rights. The focus then shifts to a more robust mechanism introduced by the European Commission in 2018: the "Horizontal Provisions for Cross-Border Data Flows and for Personal Data Protection." These are designed to replace outdated clauses in future trade agreements. Rugani explores ongoing negotiations where the EU is pushing to incorporate these Horizontal Provisions, as well as finalized agreements where such clauses have already been implemented, including those with New Zealand, Chile, and the United Kingdom. The chapter ends with some reflections on the effectiveness of the Horizontal Provisions in promoting and extending the fundamental rights to privacy and personal data protection on a global scale. The author concludes that the EU seeks to promote fundamental rights to privacy and data protection globally through a range of instruments—primarily unilateral in nature—that have already yielded significant results. The inclusion of privacy and data protection clauses in international agreements with third countries forms an integral part of this broader strategy, especially with the introduction of the Horizontal Provisions, which represent a clear advancement over the earlier, more outdated formulations.

However, while these provisions contribute to the European Union's overarching objective, they are neither the most central nor the most effective tool in this effort. This is due, in part, to the fact that counterpart countries may not always accept the proposed clauses without modifications, and also because the primary focus of these provisions often lies elsewhere.

In Chap. 9, Miriam Schettini examines the European Union's global human rights promotion, noting its complexity and occasional controversy. Critics argue that the EU imposes a Eurocentric model rooted in the 1948 Universal Declaration of Human Rights, while others question its actual commitment beyond declaratory statements. Schettini outlines the integration of human rights into the EU's common commercial policy and its free trade agreements (FTAs), emphasizing that such rights go beyond the traditional "essential elements" clause and appear in new-generation provisions. She raises concerns about the effectiveness of enforcement mechanisms, particularly regarding minority rights. The EU–New Zealand FTA is highlighted as a model for future agreements, notably for its engagement with the Māori and protections for their cultural identity. The chapter concludes that EU FTAs contribute to international human rights law by incorporating non-trade concerns, promoting EU values through negotiation rather than imposition. While most human rights clauses remain in non-binding sustainable development chapters, some newer agreements signal a shift by embedding these provisions within binding trade sections. However, enforcement remains a critical weakness in most FTAs.

The analysis of how certain new international agreements concluded by the European Union with third countries may contribute to the progressive institutionalization of Investor-State Dispute Settlement (ISDS) mechanisms in international investment law is particularly compelling from a dual perspective. First, it sheds light on how the EU seeks to uphold and promote its fundamental values—such as free and fair trade—not merely by incorporating them into treaty provisions, but by ensuring their effective implementation. This is achieved through the establishment of arbitral tribunals and the adoption of procedural mechanisms aimed at fostering consistency, coherence, predictability, and legal correctness in decision-making. Second, the very act of resolving disputes through binding decisions rendered by judicial or quasi-judicial bodies constitutes, in itself, a manifestation of the EU's commitment to the rule of law—a core value enshrined in Article 2 TEU.

Relatedly, the theme discussed in Chap. 10 also intends to assess the extent to which the provisions of these EU bilateral trade agreements indicate the parties' intentions in relation to the EU's role in setting norms in a specific branch of international law, namely international investment law. In order to prove this, Francisco Pascual Vives first of all analyses some of the new international agreements concluded by the EU with third States (specifically the ones with Canada, Chile, Singapore, and Vietnam). A second factor he further considers is the practice of the EU within UNCITRAL Working Group III, with the objective of comparing if the proposals that the EU has made in this multilateral forum keep in tune or not with the conventional practice of the EU with third States. In particular, the author examines the procedural mechanisms put forward by the EU to enhance the consistency, coherence, predictability, and accuracy of arbitral decisions. This includes proposals for establishing an appellate body and a permanent mechanism for resolving investment disputes, as well as measures aimed at preventing frivolous claims and minimizing the disruptive impact of parallel proceedings.

In order to understand if and to what extent FTAs concluded by the EU with third Parties (and in particular second generation agreements) uphold and promote the respect for the principles of the UN Charter and the observance of international law Chap. 11, also authored by Matteo Del Chicca, begins with a brief introduction and then examines, paragraph by paragraph, how specific provisions within these agreements enable the EU to support and advance individual principles of the UN Charter. The author begins by observing that, in many respects, the international agreements concluded by the EU with third parties inherently require strict adherence to international law and may also contribute to its evolution (for instance, their adoption procedures, interpretation, and legal effects are all governed by the rules of international law). He also points out that in the preambles of many new generation international trade agreements concluded by the EU with third Parties the agreement Parties explicitly reaffirm their commitment to the UN Charter. Subsequently, he investigates how specific articles of FTAs allow the EU to sustain and foster the following UN Charter principles: the settlement of international disputes by peaceful means; domestic jurisdiction; friendly relations among nations; international cooperation as a means to solve international problems, before discussing the observance of international law at large. He ultimately concludes that the new generation of international trade agreements concluded by the European Union with third countries contains numerous provisions that may also be interpreted as instruments through which the EU seeks to uphold and promote respect for certain principles and objectives of the United Nations Charter, as well as adherence to international law.

The last chapter, Chap. 12, authored by Teresa Russo, focuses on the promotion of EU values in a specific category of States—those aspiring to EU membership. For candidate countries, the formal acceptance and effective implementation of fundamental EU values carry particular significance, often requiring legislative changes and influencing every stage of the accession process. This heightened importance is rooted in law: while Article 3(5) TEU imposes a duty on the EU to promote its values externally, Article 49 TEU extends this obligation to candidate countries. According to the Court of Justice of the European Union, the principle of mutual trust—derived from Articles 2 and 49 TEU—prohibits Member States from regressing in their protection of EU values, particularly the rule of law. Unlike in EU trade agreements, where obligations are unilateral, the enlargement process involves reciprocal commitments.

Russo also emphasizes the challenges of aligning with EU principles, which affect both candidate and Member States. Although such alignment should be continuous throughout the integration process, the EU's limited capacity to enforce these standards internally undermines its credibility and weakens the legitimacy and effectiveness of its policies. In particular, the rule of law—an essential accession criterion—must remain non-negotiable. Any inconsistency in its application risks destabilizing the Union's democratic foundations and eroding candidate countries' trust in the transformative process.

References

Adinolfi G (2021) Gli accordi preferenziali di nuova generazione dell'Unione europea. Giappichelli, Torino
Baroncini E (2020) Saving the right to appeal at the WTO: The EU and the multi-party interim appeal arbitration arrangement. Federalismi 22:1–33
Barthesaghi I, De Maria Calvelo N, Melgar Alassio N, Pereira MA (2019) La nueva generación de acuerdos de la Unión Europea y sus implicancias en el sistema internacional. In: Tremolada Alvarez E (ed) Gobernanza, cooperación internacional y valores democráticos comunes. Universidad Externado de Colombia, Bogotá, pp 445–478
Bonfanti A (2016) Diritti umani e politiche dell'Unione europea in materia commerciale e di investimenti stranieri: la comunicazione 'Commercio per tutti', tra regionalismo e multilateralismo economico. Dir umani dir intern (1):233–239
Cannizzaro E (2021) The value of the EU international values. In: Th DW, Eckes C, Van Elsuwege P, Kassoti E, Ott A, Wessel RA (eds) The evolving nature of EU external relations law. Asser Press, The Hague, pp 3–18
Cannizzaro E (2023) Diritto internazionale. Giappichelli, Torino
Casolari F (2024) La proiezione esterna dei valori dell'Unione europea nelle relazioni con un ex Paese membro. Quaderni AISDUE 5(2):1–19
Cassese A (2001) International Law. Oxford University Press, Oxford
Charney J (1985) The persistent objector rule and the development of customary law. Br Yearb Int Law 56:1–24
Cremona M (2011) Values in EU foreign policy. In: Cremona M, Evans M, Koutrakos P (eds) Beyond the established legal orders: Policy interconnections between the EU and the rest of the world. Hart Publishing, Oxford
D'Amato A (2014) Groundwork for international law. Am J Int Law 108(4):650–679
Damro C (2012) Market power Europe. J Eur Public Policy 19(5):682–699
De Oliveira Mazzuoli V (2016) The law of treaties. Editora Forense, Rio de Janeiro
Del Vecchio M, Di Comite V (2014) Da Doha a Bali il futuro dell'OMC tra nuove speranze e antiche questioni. Comunità Internaz:387–417
Dero-Bugny D, Motte-Baumvol J (2021) Shaping EU external relations beyond treaty-making: The scope of extraterritorial EU legislation and its enforcement challenges. In: Th DW, Eckes C, Van Elsuwege P, Kassoti E, Ott A, Wessel RA (eds) The evolving nature of EU external relations law. Asser Press, The Hague, pp 41–59
Di Federico G, Lanotte M (2025) Le conclusioni dell'AG Ćapeta in Commissione c. Ungheria e l'uso a sé stante dell'art. 2 TUE. Eurojus 2025:347–359
European Commission (2006) Communication from the Commission to the Council, the European Parliament, the European Economic and Social Committee and the Committee of the Regions—Global Europe— Competing in the world—A contribution to the EU's Growth and Jobs Strategy, COM/2006/0567 final
European Commission (2014) Trade for all. Towards a more responsible trade and investment policy. Luxembourg Publication Office of the European Union. https://op.europa.eu/en/publication-detail/-/publication/d90eda7c-7299-11e5-9317-01aa75ed71a1
European Commission COM(2021) 66 final Communication from the Commission to the European Parliament, the Council, the European Economic and Social Committee and the Committee of the Regions. Trade Policy Review—An Open, Sustainable and Assertive Trade Policy. https://eur-lex.europa.eu/legal-content/EN/TXT/?uri=celex:52021DC0066
European Council (2024) Strategic agenda 2024–2029. https://www.consilium.europa.eu/en/european-council/strategic-agenda-2024-2029/
Fernández Rozas JC (2019) Permanencia y expansión del bilateralismo: Los acuerdos comerciales de "Nueva Generación" entre la Unión Europea y terceros países. Ley Unión Eur 68:1–59
Green J (2016) The Persistent Objector Rule in International Law. Oxford University Press, Oxford
Kelsen H (1966) Principles of international law. Holt, Rinehart and Winston, New York

Koskenniemi M (2000) Sources of international law. Routledge, London
Leino P (2008) The journey towards all that is good and beautiful: human rights and "common values" as guiding principles of EU foreign relations law. In: Cremona M, De Witte B (eds) EU foreign relations law: constitutional fundamentals. Hart Publishing, Oxford, pp 259–290
Maillo J (2021) Acuerdos comerciales UE de "Nueva Generación": origen, rasgos y valoración. CEU, Madrid
Melo Araujo BA (2016) The EU's deep trade agenda. Oxford University Press, Oxford
Mendelson M (1998) The formation of customary international law. RDC 272: 155–410
Miranda J, Sánchez Miranda M (2023) Chronicle of a crisis foretold: how the WTO Appellate Body drove itself into a corner. J Int Econ Law 26:435–461
Petersmann EU (2019) How should WTO members react to their WTO crises? World Trade Rev 18:503–525
Pisapia A (2019) Gli accordi misti nel quadro delle relazioni esterne dell'Unione europea. Giappichelli, Torino
Piva P (2021) La politica commerciale comune. In: Strozzi G, Mastroianni R (eds) Diritto dell'Unione europea – Parte speciale. Giappichelli, Torino, pp 473–522
Rossi LS (2020) Il valore giuridico dei valori. L'Articolo 2 TUE: relazioni con altre disposizioni del diritto primario dell'UE e rimedi giurisdizionali. Federalismi 19:4–26
Rugani G (2024) The economic partnership agreement between the European Union and the Republic of Kenya: an example of "variable geometry" approach. Quaderni AISDUE (2):1–9
Ruotolo GM (2016) Gli accordi commerciali di ultima generazione dell'Unione europea e i loro rapporti col sistema multilaterale degli scambi. Stud Int Eur (3):329–354
Russo T (2024) Allargamento e *Membership* dell'Unione europea. Editoriale Scientifica, Napoli
Sciso E, Baratta R, Morviducci C (eds) (2016) I valori dell'Unione europea e l'azione esterna. Giappichelli, Torino
Simma B (2009) Universality of international law from the perspective of a practitioner. EJIL 20(2):265–297
Sykes AO (2024) The utility of appellate review at the WTO and its optimal structure. J Int Econ Law 3:424–440
Theisinger M (2021) New approaches in the promotion of EU standards. In: Th DW, Eckes C, Van Elsuwege P, Kassoti E, Ott A, Wessel RA (eds) The evolving nature of EU external relations law. Asser Press, The Hague, pp 19–40
Thürer D, Marro P-Y (2012) The union's legal personality: ideas and questions lying behind the concepts. In: Blanke HJ, Mangiameli S (eds) The European Union after Lisbon: Constitutional basis, economic order and external action. Springer, Heidelberg, pp 47–70
Vincent P (2021) Les nouveaux accords commerciaux conclus par l'Union Européenne. Cah Sci Polit ULg:54–76. https://doi.org/10.25518/1784-6390.999

Further Readings

Bartels L (2005) Human rights conditionality in the EU's international agreements. Oxford University Press, Oxford
Cannizzaro E (2002) The scope of the EU foreign power. Is the EC competent to conclude agreements with third states including human rights clauses? In: Cannizzaro E (ed) The European Union as an actor in international relations. Kluwer Law International, The Hague, London, New York, pp 297–319
Cellerino C (2015) Soggettività internazionale e azione esterna dell'Unione. Fondamento, limiti e funzioni. Aracne, Roma
Circolo A (2022) La condizionalità politica nella dimensione esterna e interna dell'azione dell'Unione europea. DUE:1–57

Cremona M (2004) The Union as a global actor: roles, models and identity. Common Mark Law Rev 41:553–573
D'Agnone G (2016) La condizionalità economica nell'azione esterna dell'Unione europea. DUE (4):653–682
Douma WT, Eckes C, Van Elsuwege P, Kassoti E, Ott A, Wessel RA (2021) The evolving nature of EU external relations law. Asser Press, The Hague
Fernández Esteban ML (1995) Constitutional values and principles in the community legal order. Maastricht J Eur Comp Law 2:129–144
Ghazaryan N (2015) A new generation of human rights clauses? The case of association agreements in the eastern neighbourhood. ELR 40(3):391–410
Lawrence JC (2021) The EU in the mirror of NPE: normative power Europe in the EU's new generation trade and investment agreements. In: Nagy CI (ed) World trade and local public interest. Springer, Cham, pp 33–50
Pasquali L (2020) Il contributo dell'accordo UE-Mercosur alla governance internazionale dell'ambiente. Nomos 40:179–200
Pasquali L (2021) The EU-Mercosur Agreement as a source of development of specific global norms and standards. In: Garcia Segura C, Ibañez J, Pareja P (eds) Actores regionales y normas globales: la Unión europea y los BRICS como actores normativos. Tirant lo blanch, Valencia, pp 131–142
Pasquali L (2024a) La contribución del acuerdo Unión Europea-México a la gobernanza medioambiental internacional. In: Petrucci A, Gómez Alcalá R (eds) Uniformación, internacionalización y regionalismo en el Derecho. Tirant humanidades, Mexico City, pp 199–249
Pasquali L (2024b) La protección de las inversiones en el tratado comercial entre la Unión Europea y México. In: Petrucci A, Gómez Alcalá R (eds) Uniformación, internacionalización y regionalismo en el Derecho. Tirant humanidades, Mexico City, pp 383–438
Woolcock S (2014) EU policy on preferential trade agreements in the 2000s: a reorientation towards commercial aims. ELJ 20(6):718–732

The Aspiration for Legal Unity as a Constant Value of Europe: Broad Outlines of an Idea

Andrea Landi

Contents

Time present and time past
Are both perhaps present in time future,
And time future contained in time past.
If all time is eternally present
All time is unredeemable.

Eliot T S (2003), Four Quartets, I—Burnt Norton. In: Eliot T S (cur Sanesi R) Opere 1939–1962, Bompiani, Milano, p 336.

Abstract The Chapter aims to illustrate, from a historical-legal perspective, how the aspiration for legal unity has been a constant value in the European experience since the medieval centuries, despite the coexistence of multiple legal systems. It also examines how contemporary efforts to harmonize law within the European Union are ultimately in line with this long-standing pattern.

A. Landi (✉)
Department of Law, University of Pisa, Pisa, Italy
e-mail: andrea.landi@unipi.it

L. Pasquali (ed.), *EU Values and International Law*, European Union and its Neighbours in a Globalized World 35,
https://doi.org/10.1007/978-3-032-20521-6_2

1 Preliminary Clarifications

The term 'Europe', even to the untrained eye of the uninitiated, presents a marked polysemy: while on the one hand it refers to the European continent, which is clearly delineated by geographical evidence, on the other hand it has also gradually taken on a meaning that identifies it with the supranational structure represented by the European Union. And while it is perfectly clear that there is no overlap between these two meanings, it is equally evident that they are meant to meet, especially if one looks, from a historical perspective, at the underlying values that characterize the entire continent and are an integral part of Western culture.

Thus, from the humble point of view of the legal historian, it seemed to us that a sort of long wave could be identified, beginning in the Middle Ages and extending to the present day. This wave represents a pervasive aspiration for a legal unity that is precisely an expression of those values that have been built up over the centuries.[1]

2 Unum sit ius, cum unum sit Imperium

The discourse that we are about to make cannot but start from the centuries of exasperated early medieval particularism, namely the centuries in which, as we know, the great migrations of Germanic peoples had led to the affirmation of the principle of the personality of law. Following the reassembly of political unity with Charlemagne, the problem of legal unity for the reconstituted empire arises in an urgent manner. And it is precisely in this context that the heartfelt voice of Bishop Agobard of Lyon (769–840), summarised in the expression "*Unum sit ius, cum unum sit Imperium*", should be placed in order to proceed, as has been said, to overcome multiplicity in unity ("*superamento della molteplicità nell'unità*").[2]

With Agobard, we can see how the foundation of legal unity rests on the existence of a single empire and thus appears as a logical consequence of the achievement of political unity. Indeed, such a political unity requires the harmful multiplicity of civil laws to be removed.

This idea, far from being realized in the early Middle Ages,[3] reappears with greater intensity in the late Middle Ages, during a period characterized by the plurality of legal systems. This was a consequence of the new institutions that had

---

[1] This Chapter is based on the discussions held during a round table at the *Facultate de Direito* of the *Universidade Federal do Ceará* in Fortaleza on 6 March 2002. The event, organised by the Jean Monnet Chair "ProSoEuLaw Abroad" of the University of Pisa (Project 101085367), focused on *A promoção de valores comuns entre a União Europeia e o Brasil*. The present Chapter revisits these themes, adding essential bibliographical references.

[2] Calasso (1965, p. 216).

[3] Agobard himself, in his exhortation, would have wished that the Emperor Ludwig the Pious had adopted the personal law of the sovereign as his only law, i.e. the *lex Francorum*; Calasso (1970, p. 46).

joined the universal authorities of the Pope and the Emperor in the production of legal norms. Such idea is clearly articulated in a little work, full of symbolic meanings, written around the middle of the twelfth century, the *Questiones de iuris subtilitatibus*.[4] However, it is present, we might argue, as the cultural substratum of the majority of the jurists of the period.[5]

The plurality of disparate and often conflicting normative facts was, indeed, brought back to unity by a renewed *scientia iuris*, formed through the study of the rediscovered texts of the Justinian Compilation, which came to create the system of Roman-Canon Law (*ius commune*) that was the normative backbone of European legal experience.[6]

Here we see how the idea of a single European legal system, extending from one side of the continent to the other, has been concretely realized: certainly not in the sense of an indiscriminate identity of normative content, but rather as an identity of legal system, based on the dialectic between Roman-Canon Law (*ius commune*) and the laws of particular institutions (*iura propria*).[7]

We can say that *ius commune* was a system of normative clauses created by non-legislative means and characterised by territorially indeterminate applicability. Its content was variable, and it was intended to be applied in the absence of specific norms belonging to the *iura propria* of individual territories.[8]

A system, therefore, that was able to prevail without any imposition from the authorities of the time, because it was scientifically elaborated in the universities: although it was based on the foundations of an ancient law—namely, Roman Law—this system was kept up to date thanks to the interpretation of legal science, which did not limit itself to the mere exegesis of Justinian's texts, but develop a real "nomopoietic" activity.[9]

Thus, thanks to the jurists, *ius commune* could truly be the law of the whole medieval Europe.

---

[4] The *querelle* over the origin, dating and attribution of this small work is summarised in Cortese (2000, pp. 278–281).

[5] Campitelli (2001) refers to «*una percezione diffusa e concretamente vissuta*», p. 20.

[6] Santarelli (1991, pp. 121–131) and Bellomo (1994, pp. 163–215).

[7] In this regard, it was well emphasized that «*la scienza giuridica continuò a sostenere l'universalità dell'Impero come principio d'ordine universale, ma riconobbe che gli ordinamenti particolari viventi nella sua orbita, pur restandovi subordinati* de iure, *potevano esercitare nella propria giurisdizione gli stessi poteri che esercitava l'imperatore su tutta la terra. Di qui il corollario che il diritto di ciascun ordinamento particolare* (ius proprium) *valesse, entro i confini di questo, quanto il diritto comune* in universo»; Calasso (1987, p 159).

[8] Santarelli (2010, p. 917): "*il* ius commune *fu un sistema di clausole normative, di produzione non-legislativa e di vigore territorialmente indeterminato, variabile nei suoi contenuti e destinato ad essere applicato in mancanza di norme appartenenti agli* iura propria *dei singoli territori*".

[9] Caprioli (1993, pp. 13–25) and Grossi (2006, pp. 162–175).

3 Modern Age

It is well known how the many political and legal formations of the late Middle Ages had significantly limited the role of the Empire in the society of the time, reducing it in most parts of the continent to a mere symbol, almost devoid of effective powers.[10] Thus, on the threshold of the Modern Age, Europe had to face the birth or the consolidation of national and regional States. As far as we are concerned here, such new entities profoundly affected both the particular legal systems and the validity of Roman-Canon Law, which, although it had the two universal authorities—the Pope and the Emperor—as institutional referents, was maintained in force in the individual States thanks to the consent of the prince.

In particular, it is no longer the *ratio imperii* that justifies the application of Roman Law, but the tacit or explicit will of the prince who wants it as a subsidiary law in his domain.[11]

Notwithstanding this, the value of the *ius commune* system as European law remains unaffected. Indeed, on the birth, in almost all these states, of the so-called Superior Courts—supreme State courts that exercised third-degree jurisdiction in place of the prince—has given rise to the European jurisprudential customs. These customs are the result of the same scientific *habitus*—derived from Roman-Canon Law—that is characteristic of the judges who were part of these collegiate courts[12] and which formed the basis of their *decisions.*[13]

Thus, Roman-Canon Law further consolidates its character as a supranational and objectively universal law, an expression of what has been called a true *transnational* spirit.[14]

---

[10] An exhaustive summary of these Institutions and their activities can be found in Bellomo (1991, pp. 213–269).

[11] As the most important figure in Italian practical jurisprudence of the seventeenth century—Cardinal Giovan Battista De Luca—will point out, the necessary observance of Roman laws did not originate from a provision of the ancient legislator of the Roman Empire, but «*dalla podestà diversa di ogni Principe, il quale le ha volute ricevere, e si contenta che s'osservino nel suo Principato, con le moderazioni che gli piacciono*»; De Luca (1673, p. 69, n. 20); and also again: «*l'autorità delle leggi civili, nasce più dal consenso, e dall'uso de' popoli, che dalla precisa, et obbligatoria podestà dell'antico Imperio Romano*»; De Luca (1673, p. 96 n. 9).

[12] For a general overview: Cavanna (1982, pp. 155–171) and Ascheri (2007, pp. 129–153).

[13] These *decisiones* did not coincide with the sentences, but represented a sort of factual and legal prerequisite on the basis of which the sentence was issued. They performed a dual function: one within the trial as its motivation and the other outside the trial, as an indicator of the legal theories followed by the collegiate courts; theories which were very relevant, with their *auctoritas*, for the formation of the so called *communis opinio doctorum*. On this topic, see Santarelli (1997, pp. 72–73) and the proceedings Sbriccoli and Bettoni (1993).

[14] Gorla (1981, pp. 543–617, 602–603); who specifies that "*i tribunali supremi e i gruppi forensi di ciascun Stato italiano dell'epoca erano animati, per usare un'espressione di David, da uno spirito 'transnational' (ove 'nation' è lo Stato)*"; a characteristic which, in our opinion, can also be extended to courts outside the peninsula. Of the famous French comparatist, we refer to David (1967).

4 Contemporary Age

The process of codification will definitively undermine this supranational dimension of law. The triumph of the so-called *legal absolutism*, in the aftermath of the French Revolution, whose primary corollary was the identification of the law with the legislation,[15] indeed lead to the overcoming of internal legal particularism within individual States. In France, for example, the *loi 30 Ventôse an XII* (law of March 21st, 1804), abolished all particular legal regimes with the entry into force of the Civil Code.[16] However, this shift also resulted in a new form of particularism, this time concerning the *ius commune*, which was superseded by distinct national legal systems contained in codes.

We may therefore argue that since the nineteenth century onwards, Europe experienced a shift away from the *ius commune*, a sort of "seamless tunic",[17] which had served as the unifying legal factor for the entire continent from the late Middle Ages to the entire Modern Age, towards a more diverse and often conflicting national laws.

Therefore, the process of European integration, which built on the ruins of the Second World War and led to the creation of the European Union, could not fail to consider this legal particularism. Thus, from the very first Community experiences, the principle was established that the law of the Communities had to affect, in an ever more intense manner, the legal systems of the individual Member States.

It should be noted, however, that this effort to standardise the law in force, first in the Communities and then in the Union, was and is carried out in a way that is diametrically opposed to the historical experience of *ius commune*. In this case, Roman-Canon Law was the general law which was derogated by particular regulations. By the contrary, today, in the Union, EU law permeates the laws of the individual States, which are therefore obliged to comply with it to a greater or lesser extent.[18]

Even if it is not possible to refer, tout court, as is sometimes done, to "a new modern *ius commune*",[19] precisely because of the above-mentioned diversity of functioning, nevertheless it is worth noting an important consonance between contemporary European Union law and the Roman-Canon *ius commune*, at least in its mature phase: it lies, in our opinion, in the fundamental role of jurisprudence.

In fact, just as in the historical experience of the *ius commune* of the Modern Age, the Superior Courts contributed to strengthen what was said to be the

---

[15] Essential information in Grossi (1994, pp. 3–15).

[16] Here is the text of its famous art. 7: «*A compter du jour où ces lois sont exécutoires, les lois romaines, les ordonnances, les coutumes générales ou locales, les statuts, les réglemens, cessent d'avoir force de loi générale ou particulière dans les matières qui sont l'objet desdites lois composant le présent Code*».

[17] The suggestive parallel with the seamless tunic of Christ is thanks to Calasso (1966, p. 69).

[18] *Pedem non inferimus* into the delicate issue of the primacy of European law over national regulations, the cross and delight of international law scholars and constitutionalists; for a quick summary: Arena (2018, pp. 317–340).

[19] So instead Herzog (2024, p. 285).

supranational vision of law. As a consequence, today the process of 'Europeanisation' of the various national laws is led by jurisprudence, first of all of the European Court of Justice and then of the national courts, which have firmly adhered to the idea of promoting the process of integration between the Member States, seeing legal unity as the backbone for the entire European edifice.[20]

5 Judges and Jurists

In this process towards legal unity, we should not overlook the role of the jurists, who are reclaiming functions that they lost with codification and post-revolutionary *legislative monism.*[21] Thus, they are no longer mere exegetes of legal texts, but builders of the new legal system, since they are responsible for reducing the plurality of normative facts—European and national, legislative and jurisprudential, written and unwritten—in ways that are once again similar to those used by jurists of *ius commune*. And this is not with the aim of re-proposing that historical experience that has now definitively disappeared, but to go in search of a new system that is capable of responding effectively to the demand for justice and peace that is also present in our globalized society.[22]

It is precisely for this reason that a distinguished scholar of Western legal history and culture has emphasised that, now more than ever, lawyers must fully embody the virtues that have always defined their role: justice and prudence, together with freedom and imagination.[23]

In this context, a law that is as uniform as possible can certainly prevent disputes from arising in the first place,[24] but ultimately it can really help to build a better society.

And we believe that Europe understood this truth early on: "Time future contained in time past", indeed.

---

[20] Herzog (2024, pp. 288–290).

[21] It is a terminology of Paolo Grossi; on the subject, among many contributions of such Florentine historian, see those collected in Grossi (2021).

[22] Grossi (2009, pp. 17–46).

[23] Del Arenal Fenochio (2016, p. 229): "*nuestros tiempos exigen desplegar, una vez más, con toda fuerza e intensidad, las virtudes que siempre han caraterizado al jurista: la justicia y la prudencia, así como la libertad y la imaginación*".

[24] From this perspective, the various projects aimed at unifying sectors of private law—developed by jurists at the initiative of European institutions—must be taken into account. The most significant of these is the *Draft Common Frame of Reference of the European Private Law* (Dcfr); about these projects, however classifiable as *soft law*, and their results: Petrucci (2018, pp. 45–54).

References

Arena A (2018) Sul carattere 'assoluto' del primato del diritto dell'Unione europea. Studi sull'integrazione europea 13:317–340

Ascheri M (2007) Introduzione storica al diritto moderno e contemporaneo. Giappichelli, Torino

Bellomo M (1991) Società e Istituzioni dal medioevo agli inizi dell'età moderna. Il Cigno Galileo Galilei Edizioni di Arte e Scienza, Roma

Bellomo M (1994) L'Europa del diritto comune. Il Cigno Galileo Galilei Edizioni di Arte e Scienza, Roma

Calasso F (1965) Gli ordinamenti giuridici del rinascimento medievale. Giuffrè, Milano

Calasso F (1966) v. Equità – Premessa storica. In: Enciclopedia del Diritto, vol 15. Giuffrè, Milano, pp 65–69

Calasso F (1970) Il concetto di «diritto comune». In: Calasso F Introduzione al diritto comune. Giuffrè, Milano, pp 31–76

Calasso F (1987) Il diritto comune. In: Calasso F L'unità giuridica dell'Europa. Rubbettino, Soveria Mannelli, pp 155–163

Campitelli A (2001) Europeenses. Presupposti storici e genesi del diritto comune. Cacucci editore, Bari

Caprioli S (1993) v. Interpretazione nel diritto medievale e moderno. In: Digesto IV (ed) Discipline privatistiche – sez. civile, vol 10. Utet, Torino, pp 13–25

Cavanna A (1982) Storia del diritto moderno in Europa. Le fonti. Giuffrè, Milano

Cortese E (2000) Le grandi linee della storia giuridica medievale. Il Cigno Galileo Galilei Edizioni di Arte e Scienza, Roma

David R (1967) I grandi sistemi giuridici contemporanei. Cedam, Padova

De Luca GB (1673) Il Dottor volgare. Stamperia di Giuseppe Corvo, Roma

Del Arenal Fenochio J (2016) El Derecho en Occidente. El Colegio de México, México D.F.

Gorla G (1981) I Tribunali supremi degli Stati italiani preunitari quali fattori della unificazione del diritto nello Stato e della sua uniformazione fra Stati. In: Gorla G Diritto comparato e diritto comune europeo. Giuffrè, Milano, pp 543–617

Grossi P (1994) Legal absolutism and private law in the XIX century. In: Pizzorusso A (ed) Italian studies in law, vol 2. Martinus Nijhoff Publishers, Dordrecht, Boston, London, pp 3–15

Grossi P (2006) L'ordine giuridico medievale. Laterza, Roma-Bari

Grossi P (2009) Il diritto civile tra le rigidità di ieri e le mobilità di oggi. In: Lobuono M (ed) Scienza giuridica privatistica e fonti del diritto, Proceedings of Meeting Bari 4 novembre 2007. Cacucci, Bari, pp 17–46

Grossi P (2021) Il diritto civile in Italia tra moderno e postmoderno. Dal monismo legalistico al pluralismo giuridico. Giuffrè, Milano

Herzog T (2024) Breve storia del diritto in Europa. Dal diritto romano al diritto europeo. Il Mulino, Bologna

Petrucci A (2018) Fondamenti romanistici del diritto europeo. La disciplina generale del contratto, Giappichelli, Torino

Santarelli U (1991) L'esperienza giuridica basso-medievale. Giappichelli, Torino

Santarelli U (1997) Auctor iuris homo. Introduzione allo studio dell'esperienza giuridica basso-medioevale. Giappichelli, Torino

Santarelli U (2010) Il Ius commune, frutto maturo dell'esperienza giuridica medievale. In: Santarelli U, Ubi societas ibi ius. Scritti di storia del diritto, vol 2. Giappichelli, Torino, pp 909–917

Sbriccoli M, Bettoni A (eds) (1993) Grandi Tribunali e Rote nell'Italia di Antico Regime. Giuffrè, Milano

Common Fundamental Values in the EU and Latin America: A Dialogue Through the Inter-American System

Marcelo Labanca Corrêa de Araújo

Contents

Abstract This chapter analyses the convergence between the founding values of the European Union, as set out in Article 2 of the Treaty on European Union (TEU), and the normative structure of the inter-American system for the protection of human rights. It examines whether values such as human dignity, freedom, democracy, equality, the rule of law, and respect for human rights (including minority rights) are present and operative in Latin American legal frameworks. Based on the jurisprudence of the Inter-American Court of Human Rights and the normative force of the American Convention on Human Rights, it is argued that these values are not only mirrored but reinterpreted in light of the specificities of the region and the historical experience of Latin America. The study demonstrates that the region has developed a multilevel protection system that affirms common constitutional

M. Labanca Corrêa de Araújo (✉)
Catholic University of Pernambuco, Recife, Brazil
e-mail: marcelo.labanca@unicap.br

L. Pasquali (ed.), *EU Values and International Law*, European Union and its Neighbours in a Globalized World 35,
https://doi.org/10.1007/978-3-032-20521-6_3

values not through legal transplantation, but through dialogic processes of mutual reinforcement and normative circulation. In conclusion, it is argued that the convergence between the European and Inter-American systems reveals the formation of a transconstitutional legal heritage based on pluralism and the global affirmation of civilisational standards of justice, democracy and human dignity.

1 Introduction

This paper analyses whether the fundamental common values of the European Union are also present in Latin American legal experiences. Identifying the presence of values common to European states that can also be found in the legal systems of Latin American countries may suggest that there is a shared foundation that minimises the importance of borders in defining a civilising legal culture. This common ground ends up encompassing people subjected to similar patterns of formative values, even considering the many differences between the legal systems and cultures of Europe and Latin America.

As a benchmark, this paper uses Article 2 of the Treaty on European Union (TEU),[1] which proclaims a set of founding values that form the normative backbone of the European Union: human dignity, freedom, democracy, equality, the rule of law and respect for human rights (with particular emphasis on the rights of minorities). These values are not merely decorative clauses. On the contrary, they are substantive criteria for membership of the European Union itself. In other words, the presence of these values generates internal cohesion and institutional legitimacy.[2]

It is important to clarify, also from a methodological point of view, that this chapter takes as its reference these fundamental values defined in Article 2 of the Treaty on European Union (TEU). It is possible to adopt a restrictive view, considering only these elements as fundamental values per se. On the other hand, principles such as solidarity, justice, pluralism and tolerance, although mentioned in Article 2 of the TEU as structuring characteristics of European society, also deserve to be considered fundamental values.

However, in this paper, the methodological approach will work with the restricted concept of values listed in the first part of Article 2 TEU from a Latin American perspective, using the regional human rights protection system (norms of the American Convention and decisions of the Inter-American Court of Human Rights). This choice was made so that it would be possible to observe the presence of the European Union's values in Latin America's normative architecture from the point of view of multi-level protection through international arrangements. This study

[1] Charter of Fundamental Rights of the European Union. https://eur-lex.europa.eu/resource.html?uri=cellar:9e8d52e1-2c70-11e6-b497-01aa75ed71a1.0019.01/DOC_2&format=PDF. Accessed 15 April 2025.

[2] von Bogdandy (2024).

will therefore analyse whether the EU's fundamental values are also present in the Inter-American legal system of international law.

The values of Article 2 TEU constitute a privileged point of observation for thinking about the normative conditions of democratic legitimacy in Latin American multi-level contexts. The aim is therefore to assess the degree of convergence or divergence between European constitutional ideals and the common legal space of the selected Latin American states. But it is important to emphasise that, rather than assuming a unidirectional export of European values, the aim is to verify the pluralism of Latin American constitutional experiences that can affirm similar values through different formulations and institutional commitments.

This approach avoids both the trap of Eurocentrism and the illusion of strict equivalence, while at the same time offering an insight into the transconstitutional circulation of central normative concepts linked to civilising standards, such as the rule of law and democracy.

2 The Fundamental Values of the European Union

European Union values work as axiological clauses structuring the European legal order and as criteria for the constitutional legitimacy of member states, serving as parameters for the actions of European institutions, even in contexts of democratic risk. The normative force of these principles, especially after the episodes of institutional regression in countries such as Hungary and Poland, projects Article 2 as a true centre of gravity of contemporary European constitutionalism. However, one cannot fail to recognise that its degree of imprecision allows for a great deal of room for interpretation, making the implementation of Community law in the various member states asymmetrical. As a result, there are more or less democratic[3] countries that are members of the European Union, even though the word 'democracy' is listed in the aforementioned Article 2 as a fundamental value applicable to all.

While it is true that these fundamental values are aimed at EU member states, it is also true that these values are amplified beyond the European Union. It is therefore necessary to identify whether these values are truly universal or whether they are exclusive to European constitutional discourse.Considering that the aim of this paper is to identify whether these values resonate in other constitutional traditions in Latin America, outside of the European Union, it should be noted that this movement does not occur through a direct legal obligation, but rather through the European Union's ability to influence constitutional discourses and institutional practices in other regions around the world. In this context, it is important to investigate the extent to which these values, as expressions of a minimum normative core

[3] European Commission (2024) Special Eurobarometer 104—Charter of Fundamental Rights of the European Union. https://europa.eu/eurobarometer/surveys/detail/2966. Accessed 20 April 2025.

for constitutional democracies, find resonance in Latin American institutional arrangements.

Article 2 TEU mentions a set of fundamental values on which the contemporary European project is built: human dignity, freedom, democracy, equality, the rule of law and respect for human rights, including the rights of minorities. It is a normative reference that gives democratic legitimacy to the member states and guides the European Union's institutional action.

On the subject of 'human dignity', the preamble states that 'the Union is founded on the indivisible and universal values of human dignity'.[4] It is a reference that precedes the citation of other values, corresponding to an axiological foundation that is truly central to the European legal order. The observation about the precedence of the dignity provision is important insofar as, in a normative text, when an institute or norm is inserted at the beginning of its text, this also implies that the other articles of the normative diploma must be interpreted in the light of the initial norms. In other words, as well as having a normative function, the dignity provision also has an interpretative function, since all the other normative provisions will be interpreted in the light of dignity. Perhaps this is why the EU Charter of Fundamental Rights itself included dignity as the first value to be disciplined in Title 1, stating that 'Human dignity is inviolable. It must be respected and protected'.[5]

Freedom, as a fundamental value of the European Union, takes on various dimensions, be they legal, political or economic. There are several provisions in the Charter of Fundamental Rights, from Article 6, which recognise the right of human beings to freedom of expression, assembly, association and movement, even freedom of the arts and science.

The value of democracy is a fundamental element of the European Union's political and legal legitimisation. It is explicitly mentioned in the preamble and in various other provisions of the Treaty on European Union, which even includes provisions on democratic principles in its Title II, providing for the adoption of representative democracy (Article 10). Furthermore, European democracy is the subject of constant institutional surveillance, especially in view of the authoritarian threats that have emerged in recent years in countries such as Hungary and Poland. In this context, mechanisms such as the one provided for in Article 7 TEU represent essential legal instruments for guaranteeing respect for the democratic principle and curbing institutional setbacks that threaten the democratic integrity of the Union.

Article 2 TEU also categorises equality as a value of the European Union, with express provision for respect for the rights of minorities. Equality has a central position in the political structure of the Union, implying a broad commitment to non-discrimination and fair treatment. In addition to its explicit formulation in the Charter of Fundamental Rights (Article 20), clearly stating that 'everyone is equal before the law', there is also equality based on non-discrimination and affirmative action against various forms of discrimination based on gender, race, ethnic origin,

---

[4] EU Charter of Fundamental Rights, Preamble.

[5] EU Charter of Fundamental Rights, Title I: Dignity.

religion, disability, age or sexual orientation. Hence the special treatment of the elderly, children, in short, special groups that can be treated within the limits of the unequal need for protection. Fair treatment thus becomes a legal obligation both internally and in the European Union's external relations.

Finally, the principle of the rule of law is also listed as a European Union value in the aforementioned Article 2. The rule of law is the structuring principle that imposes limits on the exercise of public power and on rulers on duty, subjecting them to the rule of law, the predictability of state actions and judicial control against abuses by the authorities. The legal expression of the rule of law is enshrined in various provisions of the Charter of Fundamental Rights, such as the need for an impartial court, the presumption of innocence and rights of defence (arts. 47 et seq.), i.e. the fundamental right to effective judicial protection.

The recent crisis involving judicial independence in member states such as Hungary and Poland has highlighted the critical relevance of the rule of law to the institutional integrity of the European Union, mobilising significant legal and political responses from European institutions.[6]

Finally, the centrality attributed to fundamental values is also evident in the constant institutional action, particularly in the vigilance exercised by the European Commission and the jurisdictional decisions handed down by the Court of Justice of the European Union, thus ensuring their effective and coherent application throughout the European area.

3 The Multilevel Protection of the Same EU Fundamental Values in Latin America

The identification of fundamental values such as dignity, democracy, equality and the rule of law in Latin American constitutions may, at first glance, suggest a normative convergence with the founding principles of the European Union. However, as Marcelo Neves warns, adopting legal concepts from dominant centres as if they were universally valid categories (without considering local legal traditions and peripheral social contexts) runs the risk of deepening what he calls self-peripheralisation. This is 'a mindset present in academic and scientific work developed in these very peripheries' that 'reinforces the hierarchy among knowledge creation spaces and produces a self-peripheralisation'.[7]

This warning is especially relevant when analysing the transconstitutional circulation of values.[8] The mere inclusion of expressions similar to those in Article 2 of

[6] European Parliament (2018) Rule of law in Hungary: Parliament calls on the EU to act. https://www.europarl.europa.eu/news/en/press-room/20180906IPR12104/rule-of-law-in-hungary-parliament-calls-on-the-eu-to-act. Accessed 18 May 2025.

[7] Neves (2023), p. 208.

[8] According to Neves, in another paper, "a *partir do final do século passado, constitucionalistas de diversas tradições teóricas e de países os mais diferentes, vinculados fortemente ao estudo das*

the Treaty on European Union in Latin American constitutional texts should not be interpreted as evidence of full internalisation or equivalent functionality. As Neves states, "The fascination with legal knowledge and theories generated in these centers, especially Germany, the United States, England, and France, often leads to a kind of cognitive dissonance regarding the legal reality of the country."[9] The uncritical import of normative models can create a mismatch between language and reality, between what is affirmed in the constitution and what is realised in society.

The fact is that this logic of centre and periphery also manifests itself in the field of comparative constitutional theory, where there is a risk of the constitutions of the global South being read only as reflections (and not as sources) of normative innovation. This attitude compromises the possibility of effective dialogue and recognition of the specific density of Latin American constitutional experiences.

As a response to this dynamic, Neves proposes the development of a Trans-Legal Theory, based on transversal rationalities that favour reciprocal learning between different legal orders. In his words, it would be necessary to promote a dialogue between legal theories in order to learn from each other's diverse experiences. involving 'reciprocal learning among diverse experiences'.[10]

This proposal dialogues directly with the aim of this article: to understand the presence of European values in the Latin American legal system not as a reflection of hegemony, but as part of a normatively dense circulation that allows the global South not only to receive, but also to reformulate and radiate constitutional meanings on a transnational level.

Contemporary Latin American constitutionalism is marked by a remarkable normative convergence in terms of the centrality of fundamental rights. Although the historical, political and social contexts vary between the countries in the region, it is possible to identify common traits in the constitutional texts, with the documents incorporating catalogues of rights and linking them to the notion of human dignity, in clear resonance with international standards and the new global constitutionalism.[11]

The centrality of fundamental rights in Latin America's post-democratic transition texts reflects a deliberate effort to break with previous authoritarian experiences, while at the same time seeking to affirm constitutional models based on legitimacy, inclusion and justice. Constitutions such as Brazil's of 1988, Argentina's of 1994 and Mexico's, especially after the 2011 reforms, have placed human rights at the centre of their institutional commitments. This centrality is not limited to declaratory wording: it spills over into the institutional design of states, demanding new standards of control, interpretation and state action in all spheres.

Constituições estatais, passaram a preocupar-se com os novos desafios de um direito constitucional que ultrapassou as fronteiras dos respectivos Estados". That's why the author mentions Tushnet when he talks about the inevitable globalisation of constitutional law. Neves (2014, p. 202).

[9] Neves (2023, p. 209).

[10] Neves (2023).

[11] Mexico's Constitution of 1917 with Amendments through 2015. https://www.constituteproject.org/constitution/Mexico_2015. Accessed 20 April 2025.

One of the factors that most contributed to the density and effectiveness of the constitutional rights discourse in the region was the incorporation of international human rights treaties into domestic legislation. The American Convention on Human Rights, in particular, has come to occupy a central role in this process, influencing not only the jurisprudence of national courts, but also the content of the constitutional texts themselves. The trend towards the expanded reception of international norms reveals a commitment on the part of Latin American constitutions to a post-positivist vision of rights, in which treaties and conventions are given high normative status, in some cases even supra-constitutional status.

The binding of national constitutional orders to human rights treaties has produced a multi-level normative environment in which the content of rights is not only defined internally, but also negotiated at regional and international level. This arrangement contributes to the circulation and internalisation of constitutional values that dialogue directly with the parameters established by Article 2 of the Treaty on European Union, such as dignity, equality, freedom and respect for minorities. Although affiliation with these values does not occur by virtue of a European legal obligation, their presence in multiple normative and institutional layers in Latin America reveals a substantial normative alignment.

In this context, the Inter-American Court of Human Rights has come to play a decisive integrating role, acting as a supranational body for the control and interpretation of fundamental rights recognised in national legal systems. Its decisions have progressively moulded the way states interpret and apply rights, consolidating a logic of blocking setbacks and imposing minimum standards of protection. This action by the Court is not restricted to the federal level, but also directly affects the actions of sub-national authorities, which reinforces the multi-level dimension of protection.

Looking at the recent jurisprudence of the Inter-American Court, one can see a clear concern to ensure that democratic values and fundamental rights are protected regardless of the level of government involved. This is especially important in federations such as Brazil, Mexico and Argentina, where the autonomy of sub-national entities can result in asymmetries in the guarantee of rights. By demanding uniform fulfilment of international commitments, the Court acts as a normative anchor for the transnational protection of fundamental values, as will become evident later.

The existence of a multi-level architecture for the protection of rights in Latin America is therefore a real and relevant fact, even if it is built on different logics to those of the European Union. While the EU operates on the basis of formal institutional integration between sovereign states, Latin America builds its multi-level protection on the basis of international commitments and supranational judicial articulations, above all through the Inter-American System. This is a less hierarchical structure, but with growing normative and symbolic power, especially on issues such as combating discrimination, protecting minorities and guaranteeing due process of law.

The Brazilian Constitution of 1988, for example, not only recognises international treaties as a source of rights, but since EC 45/2004 has also allowed human rights treaties approved in two rounds by three-fifths of the votes in each house of

Congress to have constitutional status. This mechanism brings Brazil closer to the European logic of supranational incorporation of values and reinforces the centrality of rights in its federative pact. Other countries, such as Argentina, explicitly recognise the constitutional hierarchy of international human rights treaties, which shows a regional pattern of normative openness.

The combination of constitutional norms, international norms and supranational jurisprudence thus creates a web of protection for values that transcends borders and institutional levels. In this environment, the values of Article 2 TEU are not only compatible with Latin American systems; in many respects they are reaffirmed in other ways, through political and legal processes specific to the region. The trans-constitutional circulation of these values is facilitated by the open and porous architecture that characterises contemporary Latin American constitutionalism.

Finally, the Latin American experience shows that it is possible to build a robust, multi-level protection of fundamental rights outside the institutional model of the European Union. The region has not only absorbed similar values, but has also developed its own mechanisms to guarantee them, especially through its links to international treaties and the work of the Inter-American Court. This dynamic shows that fundamental values are not the monopoly of a constitutional tradition, but can be shared and promoted in different contexts based on concrete democratic commitments and inclusive normative structures.

4 Fundamental Values of the EU in the Inter-American Regional System for the Protection of Human Rights

The entry into force of the Treaty on European Union, by consolidating Article 2 as the core normative structure, institutionalised a set of values that were already insinuating themselves into the European community ethos and which, in fact, are the civilising values of Western constitutionalism. Their inclusion in the Treaty gains binding force for the member states because it is not just a programmatic clause or a decorative preamble, but a true constitutional identity clause. Human dignity, freedom, democracy, equality, the rule of law and respect for human rights, with special attention to the rights of minorities, no longer appear as rhetorical principles, but as criteria for the validity of political, administrative and judicial practices, and increasingly as parameters for the Union's external action.

This axiological core is echoed in other regional human rights protection systems, such as the Inter-American system. The inter-American system, structured around the American Convention on Human Rights, dialogues on several fronts with European values. But not by mere textual coincidence, but by virtue of a broader process of circulation and consolidation of universal constitutional principles.

This legal globalisation of fundamental values and, above all, to test the hypothesis that there is a transnational legal heritage in the making. The globalisation of human rights, as Jerome J. Shestack points out,[12] should be understood not just as the normative diffusion of universal principles, but as a multifaceted phenomenon that encompasses institutional, judicial and political processes on a global scale. By recognising that human rights have an intrinsically international nature, the author emphasises that their global recognition (to the point of reaching the status of jus cogens norms) demands more than formal consensus: it requires concrete implementation mechanisms, the participation of multiple actors and real influence in the calculation of international relations. The idea of 'universality' expressed in the Universal Declaration of Human Rights thus translates an expectation of civilisational convergence that transcends state borders.

In addition to setting global standards, the globalisation of human rights implies the consolidation of an international system capable of prosecuting violations and generating transnational jurisprudence. The progress of this process is not merely legal, but involves a reconfiguration of the practices and institutions that shape the place of human rights in the contemporary international order and, in this sense, the Convention and the Inter-American Court of Human Rights are very important instruments.

4.1 The American Convention on Human Rights Aligned with European Community Law

Dignity, as an inaugural value in Article 2 TEU, is also centrally affirmed in the inter-American system and is present in a number of provisions:[13]

> Art. 5, 2: No one shall be subjected to torture or to cruel, inhuman, or degrading punishment or treatment. All persons deprived of their liberty shall be treated with respect for the inherent dignity of the human person.
>
> Art. 11, 1: 1: Everyone has the right to have his honor respected and his dignity recognized

Although it does not appear repeatedly, its presence is unequivocal in the Convention, which recognises the foundation of human rights. What's more, the case law of the Inter-American Court has reiterated that dignity operates as a transversal category, guiding the interpretation and application of the entire catalogue of rights. The similarity of functions attributed to dignity in the two systems is indicative of a shared value, albeit differently operationalised.

The same can be said of freedom, which is projected in the Convention as a founding principle of democratic life and which is broken down into specific guarantees such as personal freedom and the right not to be enslaved (Art. 7), freedom of conscience and religion (Art. 12), freedom of thought and expression (Art. 13),

[12] Shestack (1988, pp. 201–234).

[13] OAS—Organization of American States (1969) American Convention on Human Rights. https://www.cidh.oas.org/basicos/english/basic3.american%20convention.htm. Accessed 13 April 2025.

freedom of assembly (Art. 15), freedom of association (Art. 16) and freedom of movement (Art. 22). The protection of freedom in the Convention is not limited to a negative concept; it imposes positive obligations on the State and presupposes the creation of institutional environments that allow pluralism, typical of democratic societies, to flourish. This material density of freedom refers directly to the European model of modern constitutionalism and reinforces the convergence between that system and the inter-American system.

Democracy appears explicitly in the Convention on six occasions. The preamble refers to democratic institutions. Subsequently, the word democracy appears four times as 'democratic society'. In Articles 15 and 16, democratic society is understood as a prerequisite for the exercise of freedom of association, assembly and movement. In Article 32, democratic society is understood as a prerequisite for the peaceful and harmonious coexistence of different rights within a single society.

Equality also appears explicitly in the Convention. In fact, the American Convention on Human Rights enshrines the principle of equality as one of the fundamental pillars of the inter-American system for the protection of human rights. This principle is explicitly affirmed in Article 24, which establishes: "All persons are equal before the law. Consequently, they are entitled, without discrimination, to equal protection of the law".[14] Furthermore, Article 8 also expressly provides for equality in relation to judicial guarantees. Article 17 refers to the need to preserve equality between spouses in a family, and Article 23 applies the principle of equality in the area of political rights, so that citizens may enjoy equal conditions of access to public office.

Although the expression 'rule of law' does not appear literally in the American Convention on Human Rights, its normative presence is unequivocal when one observes the articulation between Articles 8 and 25 of the Convention. Article 8 enshrines fundamental judicial guarantees, requiring judges to act competently, independently, and impartially, all as previously established by law. These can be said to be essential features of a legal system committed to legality and the limitation of power. Article 25 establishes the right of every person to an effective judicial remedy against acts that may violate fundamental rights, including when such acts are committed by state agents in the exercise of their functions. Thus, it can be said that these two provisions, taken together, reveal an effective commitment by the inter-American system to an institutional structure based on the primacy of law, state accountability and judicial protection of rights. Ultimately, this is the enshrinement of the rule of law as an essential condition for the development of democracy and human rights.

The value of protecting human rights, expressly mentioned in Article 2 TEU, is, of course, the raison d'être of the American Convention. Although the Convention does not contain a specific provision aimed at protecting minorities, its general anti-discrimination clause (Article 1.1) and the evolving case law of the Court allow for the recognition of protective measures for vulnerable groups. Inter-American case law has shown itself to be sensitive to particularities of identity and collective

[14] Ibid.

identity, granting these populations not only protection against discrimination, but also cultural recognition and institutional autonomy.

The fact that there are fundamental values expressed in Article 2 of the Treaty on European Union (dignity, freedom, democracy, equality, the rule of law and respect for human rights and minorities) and that these values coincide with the normative foundations enshrined in the American Convention on Human Rights cannot be interpreted as a mere coincidence. Nor can it be interpreted as a simple unilateral acceptance of the Latin American system by the European system. The presence of points of convergence between the two systems reveals, in fact, a convergence that is structured around a broader movement of transnational constitutionalism,[15] in which different legal traditions, despite their specificities, share a common ethical and legal core.

It is important to highlight that this convergence cannot be explained by the direct transplantation of European institutional models to Latin American systems (which would, incidentally, be a reductionist and Eurocentric interpretation), but rather by the gradual consolidation of values that have emerged as universal legal responses to the traumas of authoritarianism, structural inequality and the denial of human dignity. Both the American Convention and the founding treaties of the European Union were conceived in a historical context of democratic reconstruction and the affirmation of the individual as the centre of gravity of legal orders. In this process, values such as dignity and freedom ceased to be the exclusive heritage of national traditions and became part of a universalising constitutional logic.

The convergence between the European and Inter-American systems must therefore be understood in light of the phenomenon of the transconstitutional circulation of normative principles. This circulation does not occur by osmosis, but through a dynamic process of dialogue between legal orders, mutual learning, and the incorporation of transregional experiences that ultimately reinforce contemporary civilisational standards.[16] Human dignity, for example, operates as a cross-cutting category in both the jurisprudence of the European Court and the Inter-American Court, playing an integrative role in the interpretation of the catalogue of rights and imposing substantive limits on state power. It is in this context that it can be said that the similarity between the values of Article 2 TEU and the foundations of the American Convention stems not from imitation or coincidence, but from a common horizon of affirmation of human rights, democracy and constitutional justice as the structural pillars of an international legal order marked by interdependence and the aspiration to multilevel protection of human beings. This convergence of values, with distinct historical roots and specific institutional expressions, points to the existence of converging bases for a pluralist constitutionalism in which systems dialogue and reinforce each other without losing their identity.

Preserving identity is important because the idea of convergence, in this sense, cannot be confused with homogenisation. It is a process of bringing together systems that preserve their normative autonomy but share values. Human dignity in

[15] Neves (2013).

[16] Peters (2007, pp. 251–308).

Latin America, for example, acquires collective density and is linked to demands for social justice and identity recognition, the fight against poverty and the preservation of the environment, such as the Amazon rainforest, which is located in more than one Latin American country.

It is in this area that a comparison between Article 2 TEU and the American Convention on Human Rights reveals a joint interpretation that allows us to glimpse a common constitutional heritage in the making which, while plural in its expressions, is also cohesive in its aim of protecting individuals against arbitrariness and the degradation of the human condition. In this context, Latin American constitutionalism does not position itself as an epistemic periphery, but as a normative partner in addressing the great civilisational challenges of our time.

It should be emphasised that the American Convention on Human Rights not only reflects European values, but also reinterprets them in the light of Latin American history. In doing so, it contributes decisively to the strengthening of a global legal culture committed to dignity, equality, and freedom. Recognising this process is not merely an exercise in comparative law, but also a gesture affirming the centrality of the global South in the development of contemporary constitutionalism.

To reinforce this homogenisation process, the highest body of the inter-American system, the Inter-American Court, plays a strong role. As the judicial body of the regional human rights protection system, it is worth noting that the Court has distinguished itself by its substantive interpretation of these provisions, requiring States not only to demonstrate formal neutrality, but also to take affirmative action to combat historical and structural inequalities and strengthen democracy in Latin America. This is evident, for example, in the enhanced protection afforded to indigenous peoples, women, LGBTI+ persons, persons with disabilities, and minority groups.

Next, we will look at the important role played by the Court in Latin America in dealing with the values set out in Article 2 of the TEU.

4.2 The Role of the Inter-American Court of Human Rights in Building a Common Legal Space of Values

The Inter-American Court of Human Rights, located in Costa Rica, has played a decisive role in the formation of a common legal space in Latin America, structured on values that echo those enshrined in Article 2 TEU (human dignity, freedom, democracy, equality and the rule of law). Inter-American case law, by interpreting the American Convention in a dynamic and evolving manner,[17] has fostered a transnational legal culture that goes beyond national peculiarities and recognises the

[17] Magalhães (2020, p. 587). According to the author, "*a convenção americana, imbuída de seu ideal integracionista e de uma visão naturalista de Direitos Humanos, deve ser interpretada como um acordo internacional que serve à finalidade de criar padrões de direitos decorrentes de inúmeras fontes, internacionais, regionais ou nacionais para melhor proteger as pessoas*".

existence of an axiological heritage shared by the various member countries of the inter-American system. This process of legal integration is evidenced not only by the ratification of the American Convention by the countries, but also by their acceptance of the jurisdiction of the Inter-American Court. This integration is also achieved through the adoption of legislative and administrative measures by national and subnational governments to align their internal rules with inter-American standards. In other words, this movement towards regulatory alignment with inter-American parameters is not limited to the actions of central governments, but also extends to subnational entities. A notable example is the state of Pernambuco (Brazil), which, in response to a decision by the Inter-American Court of Human Rights, acted in coordination with the federal government to prohibit the practice of humiliating searches in the prison system, thereby demonstrating the process of concrete reception of international obligations at the domestic level.[18]

It is not possible to build a common legal space simply by repeating clauses or formally converging constitutional texts. It is built through concrete decisions that generate normative, symbolic, and pedagogical effects. The Inter-American Court, in exercising its jurisdictional function, not only interprets the American Convention, but also produces normative and transformative effects in the domestic law of States.[19] These effects are truly enhanced by the requirement for legislative, administrative and judicial measures to enforce decisions, including legislative reforms, changes to domestic case law and the implementation of reparatory public policies.

The Inter-American Court has established minimum standards for the protection of rights, which have become, in effect, vectors of internal transformation in national legal systems. Examples include the cases of Atala Riffo y Niñas v. Chile[20] (non-discrimination on the basis of sexual orientation) and Gelman v. Uruguay[21] (accountability of state agents granted amnesty) reveal how the Court's jurisprudence leads to the internalisation of normative parameters that bind States and guide domestic constitutional interpretation. The formation of this legal space is also evident in the

---

[18] Federal Government of Brazil (2023). Standing tall, Minister highlights shared responsibility to tackle issues in the Brazilian prison system. Ministry of Human Rights and Citizenship, October. Available at: https://www.gov.br/mdh/pt-br/assuntos/noticias/2023/outubro/em-pe-ministro-destaca-responsabilidade-compartilhada-para-enfrentar-problemas-do-sistema-prisional-brasileiro (accessed 12 May 2025).

[19] States play a dual role as creators and recipients of international law with regard to the normative internalisation and active participation of state entities, including subnational entities, in shaping their domestic legal frameworks in accordance with international human rights treaties. On this point, see Chapter 1. "*Relación entre el Derecho Internacional y el Derecho interno: la internacionalización del Derecho interno y la nacionalización del Derecho Internacional*". Instituto Interamericano de Derechos Humanos (2015, p. 18).

[20] Inter-American Court of Human Rights (2012) Case of Atala Riffo and Daughters v. Chile. Judgment of February 24, 2012 (Merits, Reparations and Costs). https://www.corteidh.or.cr/docs/casos/articulos/seriec_239_ing.pdf. Accessed 11 May 2025.

[21] Inter-American Court of Human Rights (2011) Case of Gelman v. Uruguay. Judgment of February 24, 2011 (Merits and Reparations). https://www.corteidh.or.cr/docs/casos/articulos/seriec_221_ing.pdf. Accessed 11 May 2025.

growing reference made by Latin American constitutional and supreme courts to inter-American jurisprudence. The dialogue between courts, although asymmetrical, highlights the authority of the Inter-American Court, which not only adjudicates contentious cases but also influences the formation of national jurisprudence, even outside direct litigation. This phenomenon is characteristic of the transconstitutional circulation of principles, as discussed by authors such as Marcelo Neves, and denotes an integrative dimension of international human rights law.

The consolidation of this Latin American legal space, therefore, does not mean the standardisation of institutional models, but rather the establishment of a common space of rights based on shared values. This common space allows national experiences to maintain their identity, but under the rule of a common minimum standard, operated through the binding and pedagogical force of the decisions of the Inter-American Court. It is in this sense that the Court's work is similar to what is known in the European Union as multilevel constitutionalism: a system that articulates multiple normative centres around fundamental values.[22]

In order for this system of values to be promoted internationally through the Court, it was necessary to overcome sovereignty as a barrier to the protection of rights. The traditional doctrine of sovereignty, marked by the impermeability of legal borders and the absolute primacy of the State in defining its own duties, has in fact been progressively overcome within the inter-American system.[23] The Inter-American Court of Human Rights, in its jurisdictional role, has categorically and repeatedly affirmed that sovereignty through the primacy of domestic law cannot be a shield for the violation of fundamental rights based on civilisational values protected by international norms.

> esta Corte ha establecido que "[s]egún el derecho internacional las obligaciones que éste impone deben ser cumplidas de buena fe y no puede invocarse para su incumplimiento el derecho interno"[24]

Following the European-inspired logic of limiting state power through law, the inter-American system is moving towards the construction of sovereignty conditioned by international commitments on human rights. In the case of Barrios Altos v. Peru[25] (2001), for example, the Court declared the inadmissibility of amnesty laws that prevented the investigation and punishment of serious human rights violations, affirming that domestic norms cannot prevail over international obligations assumed by States. This decision consolidated the idea that there are supranational legal limits to domestic legislative power, especially when it affects the dignity of

[22] Piovesan (2008, pp. 61–62).

[23] Nikken (1987).

[24] Inter-American Court of Human Rights (2006) Caso Almonacid Arellano y otros vs. Chile, excepciones preliminares, fondo, reparaciones y costas. Judgment of September 26, 2006. Series C No. 154, para. 124. Available at: https://www.corteidh.or.cr/docs/casos/articulos/seriec_154_esp.pdf (accessed 10 May 2025).

[25] Inter-American Court of Human Rights (2001) Case of Barrios Altos v. Peru (Chumbipuma Aguirre et al. v. Peru), Judgment of March 14, 2001 (Merits). Series C No. 75, para. 41. Available at: https://www.corteidh.or.cr/docs/casos/articulos/seriec_75_ing.pdf (accessed 02 May 2025).

victims and compromises the duty of memory, justice, and reparation. As a result, the Court's case law has reaffirmed that the obligation of States to guarantee the rights enshrined in the American Convention also requires the review of sovereign acts, such as judicial rulings and administrative decisions. This possibility of international review is often seen as a partial renunciation of sovereignty in favour of a collective protection pact, in which States mutually submit themselves to supranational control to prevent abuses of power.

This new paradigm shifts the axis of sovereignty from a concept of vertical authority to a conception of horizontal responsibility among the States that make up the regional human rights protection system. In fact, it is a federalism of values at the international level, in which sovereignty is exercised within the limits of the commitments undertaken and in light of a common constitutional morality. Just as Article 2 TEU signals a fundamental normative basis for membership of the Union, fidelity to the American Convention and the jurisprudence of the Court becomes a criterion for the democratic and legal legitimacy of Latin American States.

The work of the Inter-American Court has increasingly favoured the opening up of national constitutions to international human rights standards. This process takes place through a normative dialogue in which constitutional texts and inter-American jurisprudence intertwine, forming a plural model of rights interpretation. This dialogue is not without tensions, but it reveals a fruitful possibility for complementarity between different legal orders, under the common denominator of fundamental rights.

The conventionality review debated by the Court in the case of Almonacid Arellano v. Chile (2006)[26] it is the main mechanism that institutionalises this dialogue. This is a requirement imposed on judges and national authorities to verify the conformity of state norms and acts with the standards of the Convention and the jurisprudence of the Court. This model creates an interface between domestic constitutionalism and the regional system, requiring States to take an active rather than merely reactive stance in incorporating human rights.

In addition to its binding function, the Court's case law serves as an interpretative reference for national courts. In Brazil, for example, the Federal Supreme Court has already relied on inter-American jurisprudence on issues such as the presumption of innocence, freedom of expression and the right to memory, as in the emblematic judgment of ADPF 153, which dealt with the Amnesty Law (even though it was declared valid by the Brazilian Court).[27]

This normative transition between national courts and the Inter-American Court represents more than a vertical overlap of legal orders. It reveals a complex legal

[26] Inter-American Court of Human Rights (2006) *Case of Almonacid Arellano et al. v. Chile, Preliminary Objections, Merits, Reparations and Costs*. Judgment of September 26, 2006. Series C No. 154, para. 124. Available at: https://www.corteidh.or.cr/docs/casos/articulos/seriec_154_ing.pdf (accessed 25 April 2025).

[27] Supremo Tribunal Federal (2010) *Arguição de Descumprimento de Preceito Fundamental (ADPF) No. 153, Rel. Min. Eros Grau, judgment of April 29, 2010*. Diário da Justiça Eletrônico, Brasília, DF, 14 May 2010.

relationship in which different normative levels influence each other. It is a model of legal pluralism guided by the search for more appropriate responses to human dignity, based on a dialogical logic. This characteristic brings the inter-American system closer to experiences such as European multilevel constitutionalism, in which different sources of normative authority legitimise each other in the construction of a common law.

The case law of the Inter-American Court of Human Rights reveals a substantive correspondence with the fundamental values enshrined in Article 2 of the Treaty on European Union. Human dignity, for example, appears as a structuring axis in the decision in the case of Gomes Lund v. Brazil,[28] in which the Court emphasised the need for reparations for victims of the Brazilian military dictatorship and State accountability for serious human rights violations committed during the authoritarian regime.

Freedom and democracy also play a central role in inter-American doctrine, with emphasis on the case of Kimel v. Argentina,[29] in which the Court affirmed the protection of freedom of expression as a pillar of a democratic society, especially in the context of criticism of state agents and the exercise of critical journalism. Also, on this point, there is the case of the film The Last Temptation of Christ, where the Court reaffirmed the need to respect artistic freedom of expression, ordering the Chilean State to amend its domestic legislation to eliminate prior censorship and allow the film to be shown. In compliance with the ruling, it is worth noting that Chile approved reforms, replacing the censorship system with an age rating system, allowing the film to be shown to adults, over the age of 18.[30]

With regard to equality and non-discrimination, values also enshrined in Article 2 TEU, it is worth recalling the decision in the case of Atala Riffo y Niñas v. Chile,[31] a true landmark. The Court recognised that sexual orientation cannot be used as a criterion for restricting parental rights, affirming, in a pioneering manner, the principle of substantive equality based on gender identity and sexual orientation. This is in line with the idea of protection of minorities present in Article 2 TEU.

The rule of law, in turn, is reaffirmed in decisions that consolidate due process and effective judicial protection, especially in judgments involving the independence of the judiciary, such as in the case of the Constitutional Court v. El Salvador,

---

[28] Inter-American Court of Human Rights (2010) Case of Gomes Lund et al. ("Guerrilha do Araguaia") v. Brazil. Judgment of November 24, 2010 (Merits, Reparations and Costs). https://www.corteidh.or.cr/docs/casos/articulos/seriec_219_ing.pdf. Accessed 10 May 2025.

[29] Inter-American Court of Human Rights (2008) Case of Kimel v. Argentina. Judgment of May 2, 2008 (Merits, Reparations and Costs). https://www.corteidh.or.cr/docs/casos/articulos/seriec_177_ing.pdf. Accessed 09 May 2025.

[30] Inter-American Court of Human Rights (2001) Case of Olmedo Bustos et al. ("The Last Temptation of Christ") v. Chile. Judgment of February 5, 2001 (Merits, Reparations and Costs). https://www.corteidh.or.cr/docs/casos/articulos/seriec_73_ing.pdf. Accessed 10 May 2025.

[31] Inter-American Court of Human Rights (2012) Case of Atala Riffo and Daughters v. Chile. Judgment of February 24, 2012 (Merits, Reparations and Costs). https://www.corteidh.or.cr/docs/casos/articulos/seriec_239_ing.pdf. Accessed 10 May 2025.

which reinforces the requirement of impartiality and institutional autonomy of national courts.[32]

The protection of human rights and minorities also finds strong support in the inter-American system. The Court has paid special attention to vulnerable groups, as demonstrated in the case of Comunidad Indígena Yakye Axa v. Paraguay, in which the Court recognised vulnerability as a relevant interpretative criterion for the protection of the territorial and cultural rights of indigenous peoples.[33]

Finally, it should be noted that conventionality control is essential as a mechanism for the circulation of these values and the internal transformation of national legal orders. The duty of States to ensure compatibility between internal norms and inter-American standards reflects a model of multilevel constitutionalism, strongly inspired by the logic of normative dialogue typical of the European experience.

5 Conclusion

The evaluative convergence between the European Union legal system and the Inter-American system is evident when we observe the judicial activity of the Inter-American Court of Human Rights as an instance of projection and consolidation of the values enshrined in Article 2 of the Treaty on European Union. Although this is not a formal reception or textual incorporation, what we see is a substantial manifestation of the same values, reinterpreted and applied in the Latin American context.

The analysis undertaken throughout this paper allows us to affirm that there is an effective normative convergence between the founding values of the European Union, enshrined in Article 2 of the TEU, and the legal principles that structure the inter-American human rights system, which radiates into the national legal systems of the countries participating in that system. More than a mere coincidence of terminology, there is a convergence that reveals the progressive construction of a common core of values between the European Union and Latin America, based on dignity, freedom, equality, democracy, the rule of law and the protection of minorities.

This is the consolidation of a genuine space of intersection, where different constitutional traditions engage in dialogue, learn from each other and influence each other. In this context, the Inter-American Court emerges as one of the main agents for the consolidation and dissemination of these values. Its jurisprudence contributes not only to the strengthening of individual guarantees, but also to the

---

[32] Inter-American Court of Human Rights (2023) Case of the Constitutional Court v. El Salvador. Judgment of October 9, 2023 (Merits, Reparations and Costs). https://www.corteidh.or.cr/docs/casos/articulos/seriec_477_ing.pdf. Accessed 23 May 2025.

[33] Inter-American Court of Human Rights (2005) Case of the Yakye Axa Indigenous Community v. Paraguay. Judgment of June 17, 2005 (Merits, Reparations and Costs). https://www.corteidh.or.cr/docs/casos/articulos/seriec_125_ing.pdf. Accessed 23 May 2025.

consolidation of a regional democratic culture capable of confronting the authoritarian threats and structural inequalities that still deeply mark the Latin American continent.

A comparative reading of the European and Inter-American systems, far from being merely an academic exercise, is a powerful tool for the practical strengthening of democracy and human rights, which are common values. This allows for the identification of good practices, the development of innovative institutional solutions, and the recognition of a legal heritage that revolves around a space of intersection and sharing, essential for the legitimacy of multilevel protection arrangements.

Thus, ultimately, recognising and promoting this convergence of values represents an important step towards building a truly pluralistic constitutionalism, in which Europe and Latin America do not occupy hierarchical positions, but rather engage in dialogue on an equal footing, contributing jointly to the affirmation of a more just and democratic international legal order.

References

Instituto Interamericano de Derechos Humanos (2015) Manual auto-formativo para la aplicación del control de convencionalidad dirigido a operadores de justicia. IIDH, San José, Costa Rica

Magalhães BB (2020) A interpretação evolutiva da Convenção Americana sobre Direitos Humanos: uma revisão documental do período 1988–2018. Rev Direito Int 17(3):578–598

Neves M (2013) Transconstitutionalism (Kevin Mundy, trans). Hart Publishing, Oxford

Neves M (2014) (Não) Solucionando Problemas Constitucionais: Transconstitucionalismo Além de Colisões. Lua Nova 93:201–232. https://doi.org/10.1590/S0102-64452014000300008

Neves M (2023) Self-peripheralization of legal theory: The Brazilian case. Rechtstheorie 54:203–235. https://doi.org/10.3790/rth.2025.395597

Nikken P (1987) La protección internacional de los derechos humanos: su desarrollo progresivo. Instituto Interamericano de Derechos Humanos, Civitas, Madrid

Peters A (2007) The globalization of state constitutions. In: Nijman JE, Nollkaemper A (eds) New perspectives on the divide between national and international law. Oxford University Press, Oxford, pp 251–308. https://doi.org/10.1093/acprof:oso/9780199231942.003.0011

Piovesan F (2008) ¿Hacia un constitucionalismo interamericano? In: Fix-Fierro H (ed) Derechos sociales y doctrina constitucional: el caso de la Corte Interamericana de Derechos Humanos. UNAM – Instituto de Investigaciones Jurídicas, Mexico City, pp 599–622

Shestack JJ (1988) The philosophic foundations of human rights. Hum Rights Q 20(2):201–234

von Bogdandy A (2024) The European renaissance of republicanism: On the future of EU law in light of Article 2 TEU. Max Planck Institute for Comparative Public Law & International Law (MPIL), Research Paper No. 2024-02

EU Founding Values

Elena Crespo Navarro

Contents

Chapter held within the framework of Grant "Hacia un nuevo marco jurídico para las inversiones socialmente responsables y sostenibles: Respuestas desde el Derecho Internacional y de la Unión Europea" (PID 2023-149020NB-100) funded by MCIN/AEI 10.13039/501100011033 and by ERDF/EU, and of *Jean Monnet Chair Strengthening the European Union by reinforcing its values (ReinforcEU)*, Project 101085550, funded by the European Union. Views and opinions expressed are however those of the author only and do not necessarily reflect those of the European Union or the European Education and Culture Executive Agency (EACEA). Neither the European Union nor EACEA can be held responsible for them.

E. C. Navarro (✉)
Department of Legal Science, Miguel Hernández University of Elche, Elche, Spain
e-mail: ecrespo@umh.es

L. Pasquali (ed.), *EU Values and International Law*, European Union and its Neighbours in a Globalized World 35,
https://doi.org/10.1007/978-3-032-20521-6_4

Abstract The EU is founded on certain values such as respect for human rights, democracy and the rule of law. The respect and protection of these values, both internally and in its external actions, constitute its hallmark. However, in recent years, these values have been threatened from within and from outside. The serious and repeated violations of the principles of the rule of law in some Member States such as Poland, Hungary and, more recently, Slovakia, as well as the difficult situation in the international landscape, pose significant challenges that the EU must face with firmness and determination. Is it prepared to do so? Does it have adequate mechanisms to deal with violations of its founding values? This chapter analyses the different tools available to the EU for this purpose.

1 Introduction

The EU is founded on the values of respect for human dignity, freedom, democracy, equality, the rule of law and respect for human rights, including the rights of persons belonging to minorities. This was established by its Member States in one of the initial provisions of the Treaty on the European Union (TEU), its Article 2, which we will return to later. The EU's concern for the respect and guarantee of these values, both internally and in its relations with third countries and other international organisations, is its hallmark.[1]

It is true that when the European Communities were created in the 1950s by the Treaties of Paris and Rome, no reference was made to the protection of fundamental rights, democracy or the rule of law. This was logical, considering that the objectives of the European integration process that was beginning were primarily economic in nature. At the time, it did not seem to be a concern, as rights and freedoms were expressly protected at the constitutional level by the domestic laws of all Member States. However, in practice, it soon became clear that the application of the Treaties and secondary law by Member States and institutions could affect some of these fundamental rights and freedoms. This legal vacuum had to be filled to ensure that both the development and application of the founding Treaties and the rules of secondary law were respectful of such rights and freedoms, given the primacy of Community law over national laws.

The Court of Justice was the first to fill this legal vacuum. Through a comprehensive judicial protection effort, it progressively shaped an important body of case law based on the consideration of fundamental rights as common general principles, the respect of which it was therefore required to ensure. At that time, not only did the constitutions of all the Member States establish a high level of protection, but all of

[1] "They define the very identity of the European Union as a common legal order", Judgments of the Court of 16 February 2022, Case C-156/21, *Hungary v European Parliament and Council of the European Union*, ECLI:EU:C:2022:97, paragraph 127 and Case C-157/21, *Poland v Parliament and Council*, ECLI:EU:C:2022:98, paragraph 145.

them had also ratified the Convention for the Protection of Human Rights and Fundamental Freedoms (hereafter ECHR).[2] For this reason, the Court understood that, when guaranteeing these rights and freedoms as general principles of EU Law, it should take as a reference the constitutional traditions common to the Member States and the ECHR itself.[3]

But the Court of Justice was not alone on this path. The other institutions and the Member States themselves also expressed their commitment to the protection of fundamental rights early on, not only *ad intra* but also *ad extra*,[4] even in the absence of specific provisions in the founding Treaties.

However, it would not be until 1986, with the Single European Act,[5] that concern for human rights and democracy was included for the first time in a text of primary law, although it did not go beyond a couple of references in paragraphs 3 and 5 of the Preamble.

With the Treaty of Maastricht,[6] the EU's commitment to respecting human rights and fundamental freedoms is now expressly recognised in the articles, as general principles of EU law, in line with the case law of the Court of Justice. In addition, these principles, along with the development and consolidation of democracy and the rule of law, become objectives of the Common Foreign and Security Policy and the Common Policy on Development Cooperation.

The Treaty of Amsterdam[7] states for the first time that the EU "is founded on" the principles of liberty, democracy, respect for human rights and fundamental freedoms, and the rule of law, the observance of which becomes a requirement for accession. This condition for EU membership was included at a time when geopolitical changes in Europe were leading a significant number of Central and Eastern European countries to apply to join the club, resulting in a a new, more complex and

[2] Opened for signature in Rome on 4 November 1950 and came into force on 3 September 1953.

[3] Judgments of the Court of 17 December 1970, Case 11/70, *Internationale Handelsgesellschaft mbH v. Einfuhr-und Vorratsstelle für Getreideund Futtermittel*, ECLI:EU:C:1970:114, paraparaphs 3–4; and Case 25/70, *Einfuhr-und Vorratsstelle für Getreideund Futtermittel c. Köster and Berodt & Co.* ECLI:EU:C:1970:115; Judgment of the Court of 14 May 1974, Case 4/73, *J. Nold, Kohlen- und Baustoffgroßhandlung v.. Commission*, ECLI:EU:C:1974:51, paragraphs 13 and 14. Previously, Judgment of the Court of 12 November 1969, Case 29/69, *Erich Stauder v. Stadt Ulm–Sozialamt*, ECLI:EU:C:1969:57.

[4] Examples for action *ad intra*, included the Joint Declaration of the Commission, the Council and the European Parliament (EP) on respect for fundamental rights, 5.4.1977, *JO* C 103, 27.4.1977, pp. 1–2; and the Declaration on democracy of the Copenhagen European Council of 7–8 April 1978. With regard to *ad extra* action, already, in the 1970s, the granting of certain trade preferences to developing countries was linked to respect for certain internationally accepted standards on working conditions; the adoption by Member States in 1977 of a code of conduct for European companies with subsidiaries in South Africa, despite its voluntary nature. Also the numerous direct approaches and statements expressing concern and condemnation by member states within the Council, as well as by the Commission and the EP, in relation to particularly serious situations of human rights violations during the military dictatorships in Chile and Argentina.

[5] *OJ L 169, 29.6.1987.*

[6] *OJ* C 191, 29.7.1992.

[7] *OJ C 340, 10.11.1997.*

far less homogenous reality, which made it necessary to consider the possibility that these principles could be jeopardised or infringed from within.[8] This led to the decision to introduce a binding control mechanism into the TEU, with a sanctioning nature, for the case of serious and persistent violation of such principles by Member States (current Article 7.2 of the TEU, which we will discuss later).

This control was completed with the Treaty of Niza[9] with a preventive mechanism applicable in the event of a case of clear risk of serious breach (current Article 7.1 TEU). In addition, economic, financial and technical cooperation with third countries has also been linked since Nice to the general objective of developing and consolidating democracy and the rule of law and respect for human rights and fundamental freedoms.Recently, in the Strategic agenda 2024–2029,[10] the European Council affirmed:

> Our values and the rule of law are our compass, both internally and externally. They are the foundation for a stronger, more prosperous and more democratic Union for our citizens.

In 2024 the European Council set three priorities for the next years: a free and democratic Europe, a strong and secure Europe, and a prosperous and competitive Europe. The first of these priorities involves a commitment to protect the EU's values *ad extra* and *ad intra*. In this case, promoting and safeguarding respect for the rule of law, and upholding the principles of objectivity, non-discrimination and equal treatment of Member States; strengthen the democratic resilience, including by deepening citizen engagement, protecting free and pluralistic media and civil society, tackling foreign interference and countering attempts at destabilisation, including through disinformation and hate speech; strengthen democratic discourse and ensuring that tech giants take their responsibility for safeguarding democratic dialogue online and promoting our cultural diversity and heritage. Based on that Strategic agenda and the discussions on it with the political groups of the European Parliament (EP), the President of the Commission set out seven priorities for the 2024–2029 period. These include to protect the democracy and EU values. Furthermore, at its meeting in June 2024, the European Council also set out the roadmap for future work on internal reforms, inviting the Commission to present,

---

[8] Fonseca Morillo (2024), p. 27.

[9] *OJ* C 80 de 10.3.2001. The failure of the Treaties to deal with a situation of clear risk of breach of values became evident when such a situation arose in Austria. After the general elections held in that State in October 1999, a coalition was formed that included the far-right party led by J. Haider, known for his xenophobic, racist and anti-Semitic discourse, which led the Member States to resort to the traditional mechanisms of International Law and suspend bilateral contacts with that State. In addition, the 'Report of the Three Wise Men' was commissioned: M. Athisaari, J. Frowein and M. Oreja Aguirre, on the Austrian Government's commitment to common European values'. Available in Spanish at *Revista de Derecho Comunitario Europeo*, n°. 8 (2000), pp. 775—814. The precedent set by this situation led the Member States to supplement Article 7 TEU with a preventive mechanism. See on this topic Ripoll Carulla (2018), pp. 780–785; Cervell Hortal (2022), pp. 41–42; and Fonseca Morillo (2024), p. 29.

[10] Annex to the European Council Conclusions of 27 June 2024, EUCO 15/24.

in the spring of 2025, in-depth reviews on four specific areas for reform, including values, with reference to the instruments and processes necessary to protect the rule of law.[11]

In short, there is no doubt about the EU's concern for the respect, guarantee and protection of its values. A concern that, unfortunately, is on the rise, given not only the internal circumstances, but also the turbulent international landscape. However, it is not a new concern. It is the EU's hallmark. Practically since its origins, its external action has been inspired, with its strengths and weaknesses, by the promotion and defence of such values and the EU has been developing mechanisms to guarantee their protection, also *ad intra*.

But does the EU today have sufficient and adequate instruments to ensure the protection of its values?

The aim of this work is to provide a general overview of the different tools currently available to the EU to promote and protect its values internally. As we will see, these tools have emerged as responses to challenges posed by situations that have occurred in recent years and are focused both on promotion, awareness-raising, and prevention, as well as on reacting to actual violations.

After a brief presentation of the legal bases derived from the founding treaties, we analyse the different instruments contained in the EU's 'toll box', starting with the preventive ones and continuing with the reactive ones, paying special attention to those linked to the EU Budget, and concluding with a brief final reflection to close the study.

2 The Legal Basis

2.1 The Lisbon Treaty: The Current Regulation

In the Preamble to the TEU Member States affirm to be inspired from the cultural, religious and humanist inheritance of Europe, from which have developed the universal values of the inviolable and inalienable rights of the human person, freedom, democracy, equality and the rule of law, and they confirm their attachment to the principles of liberty, democracy and respect for human rights and fundamental freedoms and of the rule of law. The protection of human rights, the rule of law and democracy have acquired enormous relevance since the Lisbon Treaty, as the EU itself is founded on these common values, which means that they should guide all its actions, both internally and externally.Article 2 TEU provides that:

> The Union is founded on the values of respect for human dignity, freedom, democracy, equality, the rule of law and respect for human rights, including the rights of persons belonging to minorities. These values are common to the Member States in a society in which pluralism, non-discrimination, tolerance, justice, solidarity and equality between women and men prevail.

---

[11] Point VII of the Conclusions EUCO 15/24. In June 2025, the Council must present a follow-up report on the internal reforms that reflects these four lines of work.

With regard to internal action, the objectives of the EU, set out in Article 3 TEU, expressly include to promote peace, its values and the well-being of its peoples" (3.1), to combat social exclusion and discrimination, and to promote social justice and protection, equality between women and men, solidarity between generations and protection of the rights of the child (3.3).

More specifically, the commitment to the protection of human rights is included in Article 6 TEU, which incorporates the jurisprudence established by the Court of Justice of the EU (CJEU) when it provides that fundamental rights, as guaranteed by the ECHR and as they result from the constitutional traditions common to the Member States, shall constitute general principles of the Union's law (6.3). Furthermore, this article establishes that the EU recognises the rights, freedoms and principles set out in the Charter of Fundamental Rights of the EU (6.1), and states that the EU shall accede to the ECHR, although it clarifies that such accession shall not affect the EU's competences as defined in the Treaties.

Regarding democracy, Title II (Articles 9–12) of the TEU incorporates certain provisions on democratic principles. On one side, the principle of the equality of its citizens. Furthermore, the requirement that the functioning of the EU will be founded on representative democracy, direct representation of citizens through the EP, and the right to every citizen to participate in the democratic life of the EU. Likewise, the requirement that decisions be taken as openly and as closely as possible to the citizen; and the importance of political parties at european level to contribute to forming european political awareness and to expressing the will of citizens of the EU. The obligation of the institutions to give citizens and representative associations the opportunity to make known and publicly exchange their views in all areas of EU action; the recognition of an open, transparent and regular dialogue between institutions and representative associations and civil society, and the recognition of European Citizens' Initiative.

With respect to all these commitments, it should be remembered that pursuant to the principle of sincere cooperation (Article 4.3 TEU) the EU and the Member States shall, in full mutual respect, assist each other in carrying out tasks which flow from the Treaties. In addition, the Member States shall take any appropriate measure, general or particular, to ensure fulfilment of the obligations arising out of the Treaties or resulting from the acts of the institutions of the EU. They shall facilitate the achievement of the Union's tasks and refrain from any measure which could jeopardise the attainment of the Union's objectives.

For its part, Article 19.1 TEU states in its first paragraph that it is the responsibility of the CJEU to ensure that in the interpretation and application of the Treaties the law is observed. And the second paragraph of the same article requires Member States to provide in their legal systems remedies sufficient to ensure effective legal protection in the fields covered by Union Law.

To guarantee the effective and uniform application of Union Law in all Member States, the Treaties provides national judges with a mechanism for judicial cooperation, the preliminary ruling (Article 267 Treaty on the Functioning of the European Union (TFEU). And to monitor the fulfilment by Member States of their obligations derived from EU Law, the Treaty provides infringement procedure (Articles

258–260 TFEU), which can be brought by any Member State or the European Commission (which is responsible, as the promoter of the general interest in accordance with the mission assigned to it by Article 17 TEU, to oversee the application of Union law under the control of the CJEU). Both mechanisms are important instruments for dealing with specific problematic situations for the rule of law in the Member States when such situations in turn involve violations of EU law.

We will not focus on the EU's external action in this work, but it is worth noting that the EU's commitment to its values also permeates its external action, as reflected in its objectives in Article 3.5 TEU and more specifically in Article 21 TEU and Article 205 TFEU. More specifically in EU policy in the field of development cooperation (Article 208.1 TFEU), economic, financial and technical cooperation (Article 212.1 TFEU), and the Union's operations in the field of humanitarian aid (Article 214.1 TFEU).

However, respect for EU values is an obligation for Member States, not only when they apply EU law, but also in the exercise of their own non-delegated competences, which they must exercise in a way that does not jeopardise the objectives of the EU and by respecting EU law, as the CJEU has repeatedly affirmed in its case law.

In that sense, respect for EU values is, furthermore, a condition for joining the EU and to achieve the Membership Status according to Article 49 TEU. The admission is conditioned to the EU values respect and the commitment to promoting them. To evaluate the membership application, the conditions of eligibility agreed upon by the European Council in 21–22 June 1993, known as the Copenhagen criteria, are taken into account. Among them, they are political criteria, stability of institutions guaranteeing democracy, the rule of law, human rights and respect for and protection of minorities.

2.2 *The Charter of Fundamental Rights of the European Union*

With specific reference to the protection of fundamental rights, although the case law helped fill the gap left by the original founding Treaties on these matter, there was a lack of a specific and defined catalogue of binding rights. To formally address this situation, two possible options were considered: EU accession to the ECHR and the adoption of its own normative text. Both options, that have been debated over the years, are currently included, as we have seen, in Article 6 TEU. The first has not yet been implemented, whereas the second materialised with the adoption of the Charter of Fundamental Rights of the EU.

The Charter was solemnly proclaimed in Nice on December 7, 2000. However, it was not incorporated at that time into the Treaty of Nice, which meant it remained as a political text, without binding legal value. This issue was postponed until the Intergovernmental Conference that approved the Treaty of Lisbon, during which the text of the Charter was revised and adapted to be solemnly proclaimed for a second time in Strasbourg on December 12, 2007 and incorporated into the TEU, whose Article 6.1 granting it binding legal force by giving it the same legal value as the Treaties.

The Charter codifies and reaffirms existing law, bringing together in a single text the fundamental rights derived from various normative instruments (ECHR, the Social Charters adopted by the EU and by the Council of Europe), the constitutional traditions and international obligations common to the Member States, and the case-law of the CJEU and of the European Court of Human Rights. It is about strengthening the protection of fundamental rights in the light of changes in society, social progress and scientific and technological developments (paragraph. 4 of the Preamble). In order to making those rights more visible and clair, improving legal security within the EU, the Charter is a simple text that includes a Preamble and 54 articles distributed in 7 Titles[12] and is limited to determining the essential elements of the rights and freedoms it contains.

However, this regulatory instrument does not extend the field of application of EU Law beyond the powers of the EU or establish any new power or task for the UE, or modify powers and tasks as defined in the Treaties, as its Article 51.2 expressly clarifies. The provisions of the Charter are addressed to the institutions, bodies, offices and agencies of the EU, with due regard for the principle of subsidiarity, and to the Member States, but only when they are implementing Union law (art. 51.1). This obligation applies not only to the central authorities of the State but also to regional or local bodies and, where applicable, to public bodies.

3 The Rule of Law

3.1 The Concept of the Rule of Law

In the absence of a definition in EU Law, the European Commission, in different Communications, has been outlining the concept of rule of law, in the light of the case law of the CJEU and the European Court of Human Rights, as well as the reports of the Committee on Venice of the Council of Europe.[13] As the Commission emphasises, the rule of law is conceived as an organisational model for regulating the exercise of public powers ensuring their actions are within the limits set by law, in accordance with the values of democracy and fundamental rights and under the

[12] Dignity, Freedoms, Equality, Solidarity, Citizens' rights and Justicie, and a Title VII on General provisions. See about the Charter, Mangas Martín and González Alonso (2008).

[13] See, Judgment of the Court of 23 April 1986, Case C-294/83, *Parti écologiste "Les Verts" v. European Parliament,* ECLI:EU:C:1986:166, Report on the Rule of law, adopted by the Venice Commission at its 86th plenary session (Venice, 25–26 March 2011), CDL-AD (2011)003rev; and the Rule of law Checklist, adopted by the Venice Commission at its 106th Plenary Session (Venice, 11–12 March 2016), CDL-AD (2016)007-spa.

control of independent and impartial jurisdictional bodies.[14] A model that is essential to guarantee the trust of citizens and companies in the institutions, as it directly affects their lives, being a necessary condition for equal treatment before the law, for the defence of individual rights, to avoid abuses of power by public authorities and, where appropriate, to demand accountability.[15]

Rule of law, democracy and protection of human rights are inherently interrelated concepts. The rule of law requires an enabling ecosystem based on respect for judicial independence (to guarantee fundamental rights and freedoms), effective anti-corruption policies, a transparent and high-quality public administration, free and pluralistic media, and a free and active civil society.[16]

The specific content of the principles and rules established in each Member State to guarantee the rule of law does not have to be identical; it may vary depending on the peculiarities of each constitutional system. However, there are certain basic principles, whose substantive and not merely formal or procedural nature has been confirmed by the CJEU, that can be considered general principles of law derived from the common constitutional traditions of the Member States. These are the principle of legality (a transparent, responsible, democratic and pluralist legislative process subject to accountability), the principle of legal certainty (clear and predictable rules that cannot be modified retroactively), the principle of prohibition of arbitrariness of public authorities, and in particular the executive branch (any intervention by public authorities in individuals' private sphere must be legally grounded, justified in accordance with the law, and there must be adequate means of protection against arbitrary or disproportionate interventions); the principle of the separation of powers and equality before the law,[17] and the principle of effective judicial protection (which implies the right of access to an independent and impartial judge, in accordance with Article 47 second paragraph of the EU Charter of Fundamental Rights).

Regarding this last principle, the CJEU in its Judgment of 27 February 2018 in case *Associação Sindical dos Juízes Portugueses*[18] interpreted for the first time Article 19.1, second paragraph, of the TEU in relation to Article 2 TEU, understanding that it requires Member States to guarantee the independence of their national judges and courts. The CJEU recalled that effective judicial protection is a general principle of EU law derived from the constitutional traditions common to the Member States, which has been enshrined in Articles 6 and 13 of the ECHR and that

[14] Communication from the Commission to the EP and the Conucil, *A new EU Framework to strengthen the Rule of law*, COM (2014)158 final, 11.3.2014, pp. 3–4.

[15] *Ibid*, p. 1; and Communication from the Commission to the EP, the European Council and the Council, *Further strengthening the Rule of law within the Union: State of play and possible next steps*, COM (2019) 163 final, 3.4.2019, p. 1; and COM (2020) 580 final, pp. 1–2.

[16] Communication from the Commission to the EP, the Council, the European Economic and Social Committee and the Committee of Regions, *2020 Rule of law Report: The rule of law situation in the European Union*, COM (2020) 580 final, 30-9-2020, p. 4.

[17] See Annex I COM (2014)158 final, pp. 1–2 and the CJEU case law cited in that document.

[18] Case C-64/16, ECLI:EU:C:2018:117, paragraphs 29–43.

it is expressly recognised in Article 47 of the Charter. The CJEU stated that the very existence of effective judicial review is inherent in the rule of law and it conclude that every Member State must ensure that its judicial bodies, which form part of the national system of legal remedies in the fields covered by EU law, meet the requirements of effective judicial protection, which implies an obligation to preserve their independence (inherent to the role of judging).

The CJEU acknowledged that the *ratione materiae* application of this provision refers to the areas covered by EU Law, regardless of the situation in which Member States apply it. However, it recalled that mutual trust between Member States (and between their respective courts and tribunals) is based on the fundamental premise that they all share a set of common values on which the EU is founded, such as the rule of law in a society characterised, among other things, by justice. The EU is a Union based on the rule of law, where litigants can legally challenge the legality of any national decision or act by which EU law is applied to them. Article 19.1, second paragraph of the TEU, attributes this judicial control not only to the CJEU but also to national courts which, as ordinary judges of EU Law, perform, in collaboration with the CJEU, the function of guaranteeing compliance with the Law in the interpretation and application of the Treaties. This requires Member States to establish the necessary channels of appeal to ensure effective judicial protection for litigants in areas covered by EU Law, which necessarily implies guaranteeing their independence.[19] The notion of independence, implies, among other things, as clari-

[19] *Ibid*, paragraph 44. Subsequently, the CJEU has had the opportunity to complete and reinforce this reasoning that links the rule of law as an EU value with the obligation of Member states to guarantee judicial independence in order to ensure effective judicial protection in the application of EU Law. In particular, in the series of rulings issued regarding the repeated breaches of the rule of law, especially in Poland and Hungary, either within the framework of the infringement proceedings initiated by the Commission since then, or through the preliminary rulings issued by the national courts themselves. In regard to Poland, in the Judgment of the Court of 24 June 2019, the CJEU declared for the first time the violation of Article 19.1 s paragraph in respect of the measure to reduce the retirement age of Supreme Court judges and the decision to grant the President of the Republic the discretionary power to extend the function of such judges once the new retirement age has been reached., Case C-619/18, *European Commission v. Republic of Poland*, ECLI:EU:C:2019:531, paragraph 124. C-192/18. It is not possible in this study to analyse this jurisprudence, but it can be seen in this regard, among others, Campos Sánchez-Bordona, M. (2020); Cortés Martín, J.M. (2020), pp. 487–494; Cervell Hortal, M.J. (2022), pp. 82–104; Urbaneja Cillán, J. (2023), pp. 208–254 and Fonseca Morillo, F. (2024), pp. 58–68. Among the most recent cases, several requests for prejudicial rulings can be mentioned, such as Case C-792/22, Judgment of the Court of 26 September of 2024, about the disciplinary proceedings against a judge of an ordinary court in the event of failure to comply with a decision of a constitutional court that is contrary to EU law, ECLI:EU:C:2024:788; the one raised by two courts (Polish and Lithuanian) about the modalities of judges' remuneration, resolved by Judgment of the Court of 25 February 2025, Joined Cases C-146/23 and C-374/23, ECLI:EU:C:2025:109; or that referring to the principle of the irremovability of judges and judicial independence, in relation to the decision of the College of a Regional Court of Poland to withdraw cases from a judge without observing objective criteria, and without justifying such a decision, Judgment of 6 March 2025, Joined Cases C-647/21 and C-648/21, ECLI:EU:C:2025:143. In relation to Poland, in Case C-448/23, *Commission v Poland* (*Ultra vires* review of the Court's case-law-Primacy of EU law), the CJEU (Grand Chamber) declared that in light of the Polish Constitutional Court's interpretation of the Poland

fied by the CJEU, that the judicial bodies exercise their functions with full autonomy, without being subject to any hierarchical or subordinating ties with third parties and without receiving orders or instructions of any kind, whatever their origin, in such a way that it is protected from external interferences or pressures that could jeopardise the independence of its members when judging or that could influence their decisions.Based on a concept that focuses on the essential elements of the principle, the Regulation 2020/2092 *on a general regime of conditionality for the protection of the Union budget*[20] defines, for the first time, "the rule of law", for the purposes of the Regulation. Article 2 a) Regulation 2020/2092, disposes that the rule of law:

> Refers to the Union value enshrined in Article 2 TEU and it includes the principles of legality implying a transparent, accountable, democratic and pluralistic law-making process; legal certainty; prohibition of arbitrariness of the executive powers; effective judicial protection, including access to justice, by independent and impartial courts, also as regards fundamental rights; separation of powers; and non-discrimination and equality before the law. The rule of law shall be understood having regard to the other Union values and principles enshrined in Article 2 TEU.

3.2 Rule of Law and Functioning of the EU

Respect for the rule of law is fundamental for the proper functioning of the EU as an organisation based on solidarity, cohesion and mutual trust.[21] Such trust is a prerequisite for the effective and uniform application of EU law in each Member State in accordance with the principles of primacy and direct effect. The rule of law plays a key role in achieving the EU's objective of consolidating an Area of Freedom, Security and Justice, as this requires close cooperation based on mutual trust and recognition. It is also essential to ensure the proper functioning of the internal market, as well as to safeguard the EU's financial interests and the soundness of public

Constitution, Poland had failed to fulfil its obligations under Article 19.1 second paragraph and under the principles of autonomy, primacy, effectiveness and unfiform application of EU Law, as well as the principle of the binding nature of the case law of the CJEU. The CJEU also declared that Polish Constitutional Court did not meet the requirements of an independent and impartial tribunal previously established by law, due to irregularities in the appointment procedures of three of its members and of its president, Judgment of 18 December 2025, ECLI:EU:C:2025:975. Case C-769/22 (Commission v. Hungary), initiated by the Commission against Hungary for violation of Article 2 TEU is still pending. On 5 June 2025, the Advocate General delivered her Opinion proposing that the CJUE declare Hungary's failure to comply with Article 2 TEU, Case C-769/22 (*OJ* C 54 del 13.2.2023, p. 16), Opinion of the Advocate General of 5 June 2025, EU:ECLI:2025:C:408.

[20] Regulation 2020/2092 of the EP and of the Council of 16 December 2020 *on a general regime of conditionality for the protection of the Union budget*, *OJ* L 433 I, 22.12.2020.

[21] See, among others, Opinion of the Court of 18 December 2014, Case opinion 2/13 (Adhesion EU to the ECHR), EU:C:2014:2454, paragraphs 166–168; Case C-64/16, aforementioned, paragraph 30; Judgment of 20 April 2021, *Repubblika v Il-Prim Ministru*, C-896/19, EU:C:2021:311, paragraph 62; and C-156/21, aforementioned, paragraph 125.

finances, which demand effective judicial systems and adequate anti-corruption frameworks.[22] As the Commission graphically highlighted, if the rule of law is not properly protected in all Member States, the Union's foundation stone of solidarity, cohesion, and the trust necessary for mutual recognition of national decisions and the functioning of the internal market as a whole, is damaged.[23]

Warning signs include the failure of public authorities and elected majorities to respect established laws and procedures; attempts by political authorities to undermine judicial independence and the binding force of judicial rulings; the weakening of constitutional courts; excessive recourse to the adoption of regulations by the executive; repeated public attacks between branches of the state; widespread deficiencies in public administration (creating fertile ground for arbitrariness in decision-making) coupled with high levels of corruption; or attempts to limit pluralism by weakening or exerting pressure on civil society and independent media generalised inefficiencies in the public administration.[24]

EU action to protect the rule of law is based on the following premises.[25] First, both the EU itself and its Member States have a legitimate interest in the proper functioning of the rule of law at the national level. However, the primary responsibility lies with each State within its own domestic order, therefore, the first recourse consists of national protection mechanisms. In any case, the duty of the EU and its Member States to assist each other, in accordance with the principle of sincere cooperation, implies a duty for EU institutions to provide assistance to the Member States in this regard. The EU must therefore provide support, prevention and control.

Of course, in the case of specific breaches of the rule of law principles that also constitute violations of EU law, especially if such breaches could undermine sound financial management and negatively affect the EU budget, the Union must act. The EU has mechanisms for this purpose in the Treaty, such as the infringement procedure (arts. 258–260 TFEU) or even the preliminary ruling of art. 267 TFEU. This is a channel of action that has been used on numerous occasions in recent years, especially in the cases of Poland and Hungary. The Commission has also been requesting provisional measures in some of the infringement proceedings it has initiated against these states. In this way, it sought to achieve the suspension until the CJEU's decision, of the measures that were undermining the principles of the rule of law as they occurred over time. Provisional measures, whose non-compliance led in some cases to the imposition of economic sanctions on the State.[26] Obviously, financial

---

[22] COM (2020) 580 final, p. 2.

[23] COM (2019) 163 final, p. 2.

[24] *Ibid*, pp. 8–9.

[25] COM (2014) 158 final, pp. 6–7; and Communication from the Commission to the EP, the European Council, the Council, the European Economic and Social Committee and the Committee of the Regions, *Strengthening the rule of law within the Union. A blueprint for action*, COM (2019) 343 final, 17.7.2019, pp. 3–4 and 13.

[26] On 5 February 2025, the General Court confirmed Poland's obligation to pay a total amount of nearly 320,200.00 euros in respect of a penalty payment imposed by the CJEU for non-compliance with the provisional measures adopted in Case C-204/21, *European Commission v. Republic of*

sanctions are also applied when the state's non-compliance continues even after it has been declared by a CJEU ruling.[27]

However, when national mechanisms cease to function or to be effective and national authorities adopt or tolerate measures that severely and negatively affect these mechanisms, the situation may lead to a systemic threat to the rule of law and, therefore, to the proper functioning of the EU. In that case, the EU has a major interest and must intervene and react to protect the rule of law as a common value of the EU,[28] even if the violations do not constitute breaches of Union law.

In short, the EU's action in relation to guaranteeing the rule of law rests on three pillars: promotion, prevention (to act at an early stage, aiming to avoid the risk of escalation) and reaction (which can be specific to concrete situations of violations that imply in turn a breach of EU Law or that may jeopardize the proper functioning of the EU Budget, or, more general, when a sufficiently significant problem has

Poland, Judgment of 5 June 2023, ECLI:EU:C:2023:442 (on the disciplinary chamber of the Polish Supreme Court). In April 2021, the Commission initiated infringement proceedings and, in parallel, requested interim measures (asking Poland to suspend the application of the contested legislation and to communicate the measures adopted), which were granted by order of the Vice-President of the CJEU of 14 July 2021 (ECLI:EU:C:2021:593). Poland requested the revocation of this order, a request that was rejected by a new order of the Vice-President on 6 October (ECLI:EU:C:2021:834). In view of the inadequacy of the measures adopted by Poland, the CJEU, by order of 27 October 2021 (ECLI:EU:C:2021:878), accepted a new request for interim measures presented by the Commission and ordered Poland to pay a daily penalty of 1,000,000 euros from the date of notification of the order until the obligations were fulfilled or, failing that, until judgment was delivered. Given Poland's failure to pay the daily penalty payments, the Commission recovered their amounts periodically by means of offsetting against various claims held by that Member State with regard to the EU. Poland brought an action before the General Court of the EU seeking the annulment, in total, of six set-off decisions. The sums thus recovered amount to approximately 320,200,000 euros. On the other hand, on 15 June 2022, that State informed the Commission of the adoption of the new Law. Following this change in circumstances, the CJEU, by order of 21 April 2023, (ECLI:EU:C:2023:334), decided to halve the daily penalty payment (500,000 euros). In its Judgments of 5 February in the Joined cases T-830/22 y T-156/23, *Republic of Poland v. European Commission*, ECLI:EU:T:2025:131, the General Court dismissed the actions brought by Poland against the Commission's decisions to collect the amounts due by offsetting. Finally, by Judgment of 5 June 2023, *Commission v Poland (Indépendance et vie privée des juges)*, ECLI:EU:C:2023:442, the CJEU declared Poland's non-compliance with EU Law. About the calculation method for financial sanctions, Communication from the Commission, *Modification of the calculation method for financial sanctions proposed by the Commission in infringement proceedings before the Court of Justice of the European Union*, C/2025/1481, *OJ* 5.3.2025.

[27] For e. g. by means of Judgment of 13 June 2024, Case C-123/22, *European Commission v. Hungary*, ECLI:EU:C:2024:493, the CJEU ruled on the application filed by the Commission for non compliance of the judgment of 17 December 2020, *Commission* v *Hungary* (Reception of applicants for international protection), C-808/18, EU:C:2020:1029), the CJEU confirming Hungary's non-compliance and imposing on that State the obligation to pay a lump sum of 200 million euros and a penalty payment of 1 million euros per day of delay (900.000 euros for the infringement of the rules on procedures for granting international protection and 100.000 euros for the failure to observe the rules on returning illegally staying third-country nationals).

[28] COM (2014) 158 final, p. 6–7; and COM (2019) 343 final, p. 13.

been detected that pose a clear and serious risk or represents a systemic threat).[29] The following sections are dedicated to outlining the different promotion/prevention and reaction mechanisms that currently exist in the EU tool box.

4 Mechanisms of Protection Through Prevention and Promotion

In this section we analyse some mechanisms more specifically aimed at protecting fundamental rights and freedoms and others designed to protect the rule of law. In both cases, through promotion, prevention and awareness-raising.

4.1 The Charter Reports

As a preventive mechanism in relation to the application of the Charter of Fundamental Rights of the EU, the European Commission has been regularly monitoring its application since 2010 by publishing periodic annual reports.[30]

In 2020 the Commission approved a new *Strategy to strengthen the application of the Charter of Fundamental Rights in the EU*,[31] that proposes specific actions to strengthen the application of the Charter, in particular in the Member States. The actions set out in this strategy focus on prevention, promotion, implementation and enforcement. To this end, it focuses on four strands: ensuring the effective application of the Charter by the Member States, empowering civil society organisations, rights defenders and justice practitioners; fostering the use of the Charter as a compass for EU institutions; and strengthening people's awareness of their rights under the Charter. The Strategy falls into the Commission's comprehensive approach to promoting and protecting the fundamental values on which the EU is founded, complementing the European democracy action plan and the plan to strengthen rule of law.[32]

According to said Strategy, from 2021, the Commission presents a new model of annual report on the application of the Charter, which look more closely at its application in the Member States and provide further insight to the Commission for the

[29] COM (2019) 163 final, p. 10.

[30] Communication from the Commission *Strategy for the effective implementation of the Charter of Fundamental Rights by the European Union*, COM (2010) 573 final, 19.10.2010.

[31] Communication from the Commission to the EP, the Council, the European Economic and Social Committee, and the Committee of the Regions, *Strategy to strengthen the application of the Charter of Fundamental Rights in the EU*, COM (2020) 711 final, 2.12.2020.

[32] Communication from the Commission to the EP, the Council, the European Economic and Social Committee, and the Committee of the Regions, *On the European democracy action plan*, COM (2020) 790 final, 3.12.2020; COM (2019) 163 final; and COM (2020) 343 final.

assessment of compliance of national legislation with EU law. It adopts a thematic approach, focusing on areas of strategic relevance governed by EU law. In 2021, the Charter report focused on fundamental rights in the digital age, in 2022 on the role of civil society organisations and rights defenders, in 2023 on effective legal protection and access to justice, and the 2024 Charter report focuses on EU funding directed towards promoting, protecting and enforcing fundamental rights across the EU.[33]

4.2 European Union Agency for Fundamental Rights

On the 1st of March 2007 the EU Agency for Fundamental Rights (FRA) began operating, taking on the functions of the former European Monitoring Centre on Racism and Xenophobia.[34] Its objective is to provide help and advice to the institutions, bodies and organisations of the EU, as well as to the Member States when they apply EU law. It seeks to promote full respect for fundamental rights by all parties when they adopt measures or establish lines of action in their respective spheres of competence.

The FRA's general scope of action corresponds to that of the EU's competences as defined in the Treaties, and its areas of work are: access to justice; victims of crime; the information society; Roma integration; rights of the child; anti-discrimination; immigration and integration of migrants; and racism, xenophobia and intolerance. However, the specific sectors of activity on which it is focusing its attention are set out in the FRA's programming document, which provides detailed information on the projects and activities that the FRA will carry out, indicating human resources and budget allocation. The single programming document 2025–2027 is within the framework of the FRA's strategy for 2023–2028, that consists of three strategic priorities (support the upholding of fundamental rights standards in the development of new EU laws and policies; contribute to ensuring respect, protection, and fulfilment of fundamental rights in the fields covered by existing EU laws and policies; and cross-cutting actions to support the realisation of the EU's fundamental rights goals and vision). Each of these priorities corresponds to a series of strategic objectives. By detailing the specific contributions of each unit and their associated projects, the Annual Work Plan 2025 provides a comprehensive

[33] See Annual Reports on the application of the EU Charter of Fundamental Rights (2021–2024): *Protecting Fundamental Rights in the Digital Age*, COM (2021) 819 final; *A thriving civic space for upholding fundamental rights in the EU*, COM (2022) 716 final, 6.12.2022; *Effective legal protection and access to justice*, COM (2023) 786 final, 4.12.2023; and *Funding to promote, protect and enforce fundamental rights*, COM (2024) 456 final, 10.10.2024. See also Council Conclusions of 7 March 2025 *on the application of the EU Charter of Fundamental Rights: funding to promote, protect and enforce fundamental rights*, Doc. 6878/25.

[34] Council Regulation 168/2007 of 15 February 2007 *establishing a European Union Agency for Fundamental Rights*, *OJ* L 53, 22.2.2007, later replaced by Council Regulation 2022/555 of 5 April 2022, *OJ* L 108, 7.4.2022.

overview of how the FRA aims to address thematic challenges effectively. The Units are: a) Equality, Roma and social rights; c) Justice, digital and Migration; c) Institutional cooperation and networks; d) Communication and events.

To achieve its objectives, the FRA is entrusted with the functions of collect and analyse law and data: provide independent, evidence-based advice on rights; identify trends by collecting and analysing comparable data; help better law making and implementation; support rights-compliant policy responses, and strengthen cooperation and ties between fundamental rights actors.

The FRA, whose headquarters are in Vienna, carries out its functions independently and in the public interest. Its budget for the year 2025 foresees an estimated income of 26,639,755 euros.[35] It works in close coordination with the EU institutions, bodies and agencies competent in these matters, and with the Member States. It also collaborates with international organisations such as the Council of Europe and the OSCE, as well as with civil society, for which a specific network was created, the Fundamental Rights Platform, open to the different sectors of civil society (NGOs, trade unions, business or professional organisations, universities…).

Every year the Agency prepares and publishes two reports: the Agency's Consolidated Annual Activity Report, and the Agency's Annual Fundamental Rights Report. The latter provides an annual review of key developments in the field, identifying both achievements and remaining areas of concern. It is accompanied by FRA's opinions on these developments, including a synopsis of the evidence supporting these opinions. The report also identifies trends and relevant promising practices. The report's overall findings are used by the EP in its report about fundamental rights in the EU, and by the Council.

4.3 Annual Rule of Law Cycle

This mechanism also falls within the framework of preventive action, in which the EU's objective is to foster cooperation and offer support to reinforce the rule of law at the national level. In order to be in a position to identify possible risks and be able to act effectively against them, the EU must have regular knowledge of the situation in each Member State, which requires monitoring on its part. To this end, the Commission, in response to requests from the EP,[36] proposed a Rule of Law Review Cycle in 2019. The aim is to facilitate the early detection of potential risks and, through dialogue, cooperation and practical support, to help improve the

[35] *Statement of revenue and expenditure for the 2025 financial year, OJ* C/2025/841, 28.2.2025.

[36] EP Resolution of 25 October 2016 with recommendations to the Commission on the establishment of an EU mechanism on democracy, the rule of law and fundamental rights (2015/2254(INL)); and EP Resolution of 14 November 2018 on the need for a comprehensive EU mechanism for the protection of democracy, the rule of law and fundamental rights (2018/2886(RSP)).

preparedness and resilience of national systems and institutions to deal with possible situations of tension.[37]

To this end, and also with a view to raising awareness, the Commission has been publishing the Annual Rule of Law Report since 2020. This report is made public and examines developments in all Member States in four key areas: the justice system, the framework for the fight against corruption, media pluralism and freedom, and other institutional issues related to checks and balances. Each pillar is subdivided into different detailed sub-themes and is accompanied by sections for individual countries.

The aim is to make an annual assessment of the situation of the rule of law in each Member State and in the EU as a whole. The report therefore includes a more general section on the situation in the EU and specific chapters for individual countries, in which the Commission makes a qualitative assessment of the situation, highlighting positive aspects and problems detected, as well as good practices, and shows the evolution, possible progress or setbacks since the previous report. In the words of the Commission: "the country chapters do not purport to give an exhaustive description of all relevant elements of the rule of law situation in Member States but to present significant developments". Nevertheless, the European Court of Auditors, in its 02/2024 review of the Commission's reports, regretted the lack of presentation of trends in the evolution of the rule of law over the years, despite repeated requests from the EP that the report identify with sufficient clarity positive and negative trends, as well as cross-cutting trends, including possible systemic vulnerabilities at EU.[38]

So far, the Commission has published four reports. Specific recommendations to Member States have been included since 2022 and, from the 2023 report there is also an evaluation of the implementation of recommendations.[39] The 2024 report adds an analysis of the situation in certain candidate countries (Albania, North Macedonia, Montenegro and Serbia) as a way to support the reforms these countries are implementing to advance in the areas of democracy and the rule of law.

As it is a preventive and awareness-raising mechanism that is conceived as a regular process of dialogue, the methodology used[40] is based on the collaboration of

---

[37] COM (2019) 343 final, p. 16; and COM (2019) 163 final, p. 12.

[38] COM (2024) 800 final/2, p. 11; and COM (2020) 580 final, p. 5; and 02/2024 Review of the European Court of Auditors, *The Commission's rule of law reporting*, points 55 y 82. Said institution clarifies that document is not an audit, it is a review that only provides a descriptive and informative analysis, but do not formulate recommendations, and instead may identify potential challenges and opportunities or issues for further scrutiny (Point 5).

[39] The 2024 Rule of law report refers to a positive evolution in the fulfilment of the recommendations, indicating that in 2023 almost 65% of the set of specific recommendations made in the 2023 report had been followed and that in 2024 compliance reached 68%, COM (2024) 800 final/2, 24.7.2024, p. 3. In its 02/2024 Review, already cited, the European Court of Auditors details that, in 2023, 11% of the recommendations had been fully implemented, 55% had been partially implemented and no progress had been made on 34% of them (point VIII of the summary).

[40] The Commission adopted a document detailing this methodology, *European Rule of Law mechanism: Methodology for the preparation of the Annual Rule of Law Report*, latest version available in: https://commission.europa.eu/document/e80a08e9-a5cd-4100-833d-f87548004226_en.

the Member States. To this end, a 'Network of National Contact Points' was created as a permanent channel of communication, in which the aforementioned third countries also currently participate.[41]

The participation of the Member States and other stakeholders takes place in several stages. Initially, through their written contributions. The Commission sends the Member States standardised questionnaires that follow the four pillars of the Report, divided into more detailed sub-themes, and launches a public consultation with stakeholders. After the initial analysis of these contributions, the Commission prepares a series of follow-up questions, which it uses to structure its virtual visits to the country. During these visits, the Commission holds meetings with national authorities and other stakeholders.[42] In the final phase, before the publication of the Report, States are once again given the opportunity to provide updated information.[43]

The Commission's assessment is based on compliance with Union Law, but also with the relevant standards approved by the Council of Europe and the case law of the European Court of Human Rights. The European Court of Auditors has pointed out the absence of specific indicators to measure compliance with each of the issues to be analysed in the four pillars.[44]

The dialogue continues after the publication of the Report, both with the Member States and within the EU institutions. Specifically, during the Commission's national dialogues in the Member States, in the EP's debate and resolution on each edition of the Report and within the framework of the Council's annual dialogue on the rule of law.[45]

Furthermore, the EU toolbox includes other instruments that reinforce and complement this prevention and awareness-raising work, for which the Commission Report serves as reference point, such as the Justice Scoreboard and the European Semester.

[41] COM (2024) 800 final/2, p. 9.

[42] COM (2020) 580 final, pp. 4–5; and Review 02/2024 of the European Court of Auditors, points 41, 43–46.

[43] With regard to the information provided by the Member States at this last stage, the European Court of Auditors makes it clear that, in general, the Commission takes account only of the Member States' comments relating to factual accuracy, and rejects most of those which change its assessment, unless they are justified by additional evidence. In any case, the Commission does not explain directly to the Member States the possible changes introduced by the specific comments, but the changes are already reflected in the final report that it publishes. Furthermore, the draft recommendations are not included in this final consultation with the Member States, so that they can comment on the draft country chapters, but do not have the opportunity to accept or reject the recommendations in advance, Reviews 02/2024, points 63 y 72.

[44] Review 02/2024 of the European Court of Auditors, point 50.

[45] The annual dialogue of the Council about the rule of law began as a result of some Council Conclusions of 16 December 2014, Doc. 17,014/14. From 2020, the dialogue is divided into horizontal debates, covering the general evolution of the rule of law in the EU, and country-specific debates, focusing in detail on the situation in each Member State. Both debates are based on the Commission's annual reports about the rule of law, See Presidency Conclusions of 12 December 2023, *Evaluation of the annual Rule of law*, Doc. 16,547/23.

The Justice Scoreboard, launched in 2013,[46] is a comparative information tool aimed at helping the EU and Member States improve the effectiveness of national judicial systems based on three main elements: efficiency, quality and independence. To assess efficiency, aspects such as the length of judicial proceedings and the resolution rate (i.e., the number of cases resolved compared to the number of incoming cases and of pending cases) are taken into consideration. Regarding quality, data on accessibility (access to free legal assistance, court fees), human resources, digitisation, training, budget and salaries of judges and prosecutors are analysed. With regard to independence, the perception of judicial independence in society (for example, based on Eurobarometer surveys), safeguards related to structural independence, and the functioning of public prosecutor's offices are considered.

The information included in the Justice Scoreboard contributes to the monitoring carried out through other mechanisms, as it serves as one of the sources that provide input for the Commission's Rule of Law Report, the country-specific assessment within the framework of the European Semester and the monitoring and evaluation of the implementation of the national Recovery and Resilience plans which we will discuss later.

The European Semester is not in itself a mechanism for protecting the rule of law. It is an annual process of coordination of the economic, social, employment, structural and budgetary policies of the Member States which has its legal basis in Articles 121, 126 and 148 TFEU. It provides a country-specific analysis and allows for the formulation of structural reform recommendations. Within the framework of this analysis, relevant aspects related to the protection of the rule of law are addressed, such as the fight against corruption, the effectiveness of judicial systems and the reform of public administration.[47]

5 Reaction Mechanisms

5.1 EU Framework to Strengthen the Rule of Law

Faced with the situation in Poland and the difficulties of applying art. 7 TEU, the Commission launched in 2014 a new EU Framework to strengthen the rule of law,[48] applying prior to art. 7 TEU. The objective was preventively confronting systemic threats through political dialogue. It is intended to be activated in situations where the authorities of a Member State are taking measures or are tolerating situations which are likely to systematically and adversely affect the integrity, stability or the

[46] Communication from the Commission to the EP, the Council, the European Central Bank, the European Economic and social Committee and the Committee of the Regions, *The EU Justice Scoreboard. A tool to promote effective justice and growth*, COM (2013), 160 final, 27.3.2013.

[47] COM (2019) 163 final p. 5.

[48] COM (2014) 158 final. See Mangas Martín, A. (2018), pp. 2-5.

proper functioning of the institutions and the safeguard mechanisms established at national level to secure the rule of law.

How does it work? The process, which is reminiscent of the pre-litigation phase before the Commission in the infringement procedure, is composed of three stages: a Commission assessment, a Commission recommendation and a follow-up to the recommendation. The EP and the Council will be kept regularly and closely informed of progress made in each of the stages.

In the face of a systemic threat of violation of EU values, the first stage opens in which the Commission carry out a preliminary assessment. If the Commission considers that there is indeed a situation of systemic threat to the rule of law, it initiate a dialogue with the Member State concerned, by sending a "rule of law opinion" and substantiating its concerns, giving the Member State concerned the possibility to respond. The launching of the Commission assessment and the sending of its opinion will be made public by the Commission, but the content of the exchanges with the Member State concerned remains confidential.

If a satisfactory solution is not reached in the first phase, the Commission will issue a "rule of law recommendation". In that recommendation, the Commission will clearly indicate the reasons for its concerns and indicate a time limit to resolve the situation and to informs of the steps taken to that effect. Where appropriate, it may include specific indications on ways and measures. The sending of its recommendation and its main content will be made public.

In a third stage, the Commission will monitor the follow-up given by the Member State concerned to the recommendation. If there is no satisfactory follow-up, the Commission will assess the possibility of activating one of the mechanisms set out in art. 7 TEU.

In practice, the Framework did not allow to remedy the detected deficiences. It was implemented with respect to Poland without improving nor avoiding the situation (only postponing the activation of Article 7.1 TEU). Between January 2016 and December 2017, the Commission issued one opinion and four recommendations,[49] which were successively ignored by the Polish government.

According to the Commission, the dialogue developed in the Framework helped to identify the problems and frame the discussion. In any case, on December 2017, the Commission triggered the procedure set out in art. 7.1. It did so after the EP had adopted three Resolutions on the situation of the rule of law and democracy in Poland,[50] in which it stated that the situation in that State represented a clear risk of

---

[49] Opinion of 1 June 2016; and Commission Recommendation regarding the rule of law in Poland 2016/1374, of 27 July 2016 (*OJ* L 217, 12-8-2016, p. 53); 2017/146 of 21 December 2016 (*OJ* L 22, 27.1.2017, p. 65); 2017/1520 of 26 July 2017; and 2018/103. of 20 December 2017 (*OJ* L 17, 23.1.2018).

[50] EP Resolutions of 13 April 2016 on the situation in Poland [(2015/3031(RSP)]; of 14 September 2016 on the recent developments in Poland and their impact on fundamental rights as laid down in the Charter of Fundamental Rights EU [2016/2774(RSP)]; and of 15 November 2017 on the situation of the rule of law and democracy in Poland, [2017/2931 (RSP)].

serious violation of EU values. It is true that the EP itself did not propose the activation of this article, although it had the legitimacy to do so.

5.2 *Preventive and Sanctioning Mechanisms Under Article 7 TEU*

As the CJEU has pointed out, compliance with the EU values cannot be reduced to an obligation which a candidate State must meet in order to accede to the EU and which it may disregard after its accession.[51] For this reason, the TEU incorporates in its art. 7 an instrument to address serious breaches to the EU values by Member States. It is an exceptional tool that the EU can use to address the most serious rule of law failings in a Member State, whose purpose is not to resolve individual violations, but to address a general situation. Therefore, the risk or breach of values must concern a systemic problem. The very high thresholds for activating this mechanism make it a last resort mechanism. Its scope is not confined to areas covered by EU law, but empowers the EU to intervene with the purpose of protecting the rule of law also in areas where Member States act autonomously.

When can it be activated? The article includes two mechanisms. A preventive mechanism, applicable in case of clear risk of a serious breach of the EU's values (7.1) and a sanctioning in case of serious and persistent breach (7.2).

The preventive procedure allows the Council to determine the existence of a clear risk of a serious breach of the EU's values and to follow up on such risks. This procedure can be activated on a reasoned proposal by one third of the Member States, by the EP or by the Commission. Then, the State in question must be given the opportunity to give its explanations and, subsequently, as long as the EP gives its consent, the Council (by a majority of 4/5 of Members States excluding EU country concerned) may adopt a Decision to determine that there is a clear risk of a serious breach for the EU's values, and can issue recommendations to the State in question in this regard. The Council shall carry out a regular verification of the grounds.

Through the sanctioning mechanism the European Council may first determine the existence of a serious and persistent breach; and the Council may then determine the action to be taken in terms of suspension of the rights of a Member State under the Treaties. The mechanism can be activated by one third of the Member States or by the Commission (not by the EP in this case). After the observations submitted by the Member State concerned, and with the consent of the EP (2/3 majority of the votes representing the majority of its members) the European Council determines the existence of a serious and persistent breach (by unanimity excluding EU country concerned). In such a case, the Council may adopt measures in this regard, such as

[51] C-156/21, aforementioned, paragraph 126 and C-157/21, paragraph 144.

suspending their membership rights, including voting rights.[52] In doing so, the Council shall take into account the possible consequences of such suspension on the rights and obligations of natural and legal persons. In any case, the obligations assumed under the Treaty continue to be binding on that State. Thereafter, the Council, acting by a qualified majority, may decide to amend or revoke measures adopted in response to changes in the situation that led to their imposition.

So far, the preventive mechanism has been triggered twice: first by the Commission in respect of Poland in 20 December 2017, and then by the EP in respect of Hungary in 12 September 2018.[53] Seven formal hearings have taken place so far as regards Hungary, without however taking a decision to take either procedure to the next stage. As regards Poland, six hearings took place before the withdrawal of the Commission's proposal and the decision to close the art. 7 procedure on 29 May 2024. Following a series of positive developments in Poland, the Commission concluded that the conditions for maintaining the procedure no longer existed. The Polish authorities adopted an action Plan that was presented at the General Affairs Council of 20 February 2024.[54]

Nevertheless, the mechanism of Article 7 raises several issues that seriously hinder its practical application, as has been demonstrated in the two situations in which it has been activated to date. On the one hand, it grants significant discretion, both in determining the risk and for the determination of the existence of the violation. The activation requirements are very strict, especially the requirement of unanimity for establishing the existence of a serious and persistent breach. In the event of clear risk, only recommendations can be made, the content of which, moreover, is not specified. The Council *may*, but is not obliged, to issue such recommendations to the Member State. Nor specific deadlines are provided (the preventive procedure regarding Hungary was initiated in 2018 and remains open since then). It is up to the Council to decide whether to impose sanctions if a serious and persistent breach is found (it is not required to adopt them). Judicial control by the CJEU over the legality of Council/European Council acts under this procedure is limited to procedural compliance (Article 269 TFEU), and does not include monitoring compliance with recommendations or, where applicable, sanctions by the concerned State.

[52] The vote requires a qualified majority (72% of Member States, excluding the Member State concerned, and 65% of the EU's population of the Member States participating in the vote. EU country concerned does not participate in the vote), art. 354 TFEU and art. 238 TFEU.

[53] Proposal for a Council Decision, COM (2017) 835 final, 20-12-2017; and EP Resolution of 12 September 2018 (2017/2131(INL)), approved by 448 votes to 197.

[54] COM (2024) 800 final/2, p. 7. See Poland Action Plan for restoring the rule of law of 21th February 2024 on https://www.gov.pl/web/justice/polish-minister-of-justice-presents-action-plan-for-restoring-the-rule-of-law.

6 Values and the EU Budget

6.1 Positive Measures: Financing

An important line of action developed by the EU to promote and protect its values is funding aimed at strengthening the role of organised civil society or improving democratic structures.

Among the existing programmes, one example is specific support aimed at awareness-raising on fundamental rights and capacity-building through the *Citizens, Equality, Rights and Values programme*. An EU funding programme that specifically seeks to protect and promote the rights and values enshrined in the Treaties and in the Charter, to sustain open, rights-based, democratic, equal and inclusive societies based on the rule of law.[55] The programme, which is run through grants, funds activities encouraging democratic, civic and social participation, and the diversity of the European society. The budget of this Program for the 2021–2027 period amounts to more than 1,5 billion euros, and funds a broad range of actors in both Member States and third countries. It includes a specific chapter on EU values, with its budget of 668 million euros, whose projects, during the first year of implementation, funded supported more than 800 grassroot civil society organisations.[56]

Another noteworthy initiative is the *Justice programme*[57] that, with a total budget of 296.8 million euros for 2021–2027, funds the training of justice practitioners, supports judicial cooperation in civil and criminal matters and effective access to justice for citizens and businesses.

Other programmes also contribute in one way or another to the promotion of EU values. For instance, the *Digital Europe Programme* plays a role in creating safe and secure online environments and combating disinformation, while the *Creative Europe Programme* fosters media freedom, artistic freedom, cultural diversity, pluralism, and gender equality.[58]

---

[55] Regulation 2021/692 of the EP and of the Council establishing the Citizens, Equality, Rights and Values Programme, *OJ* L 156, 5-5-2021.

[56] COM (2024) 456 final, p. 6.

[57] Regulation 2021/693 of the EP of the Council of 28 April 2021 establishing the Justice Programme and repealing Regulation 1382/2013, *OJ* L 156, 5.5.2021.

[58] See COM (2024), 456 final, and Council Conclusions of 7th March 2025 on the application of the Charter of Fundamental Rights: funding to promote, protect and enforce fundamental rights.

6.2 The Horizontal Enabling Condition on the Charter

The horizontal enabling condition is a measure under Regulation 2021/1060 *laying down common provisions on the European Funds*,[59] which aims to ensure compliance with the Charter of Fundamental Rights in the context of EU funding.

The Article 9 of the Regulation establishes a series of horizontal principles applicable to the implementation of the funds. Among them, it stipulates that Member States and the Commission shall ensure respect for fundamental rights and compliance with the Charter in the implementation of the funds (Article 9.1). Also that equality between men and women, gender mainstreaming and the integration of a gender perspective are taken into account and promoted throughout the preparation, implementation, monitoring, reporting and evaluation of programmes (Article 9.2). Furthermore, Member States and the Commission must take appropriate steps to prevent any discrimination based on gender, racial or ethnic origin, religion or belief, disability, age or sexual orientation during the preparation, implementation, monitoring, reporting and evaluation of programmes. In particular, accessibility for persons with disabilities shall be taken into account throughout the preparation and implementation of programmes (Article 9.3).

The Regulation introduces enabling conditions for the specific objectives applicable to funds, that must be fulfilled by each Member State to ensure the effective and efficient implementation of these funds throughout the programming period (Article 15 C). The horizontal enabling conditions, applicable to all specific objectives, and the criteria necessary for the assessment of their fulfilment are included in the Annex III. One of these conditions is the effective application and implementation of the Charter of Fundamental Rights, setting as a fulfilment criteria, the existence of effective mechanisms in place to ensure compliance with the Charter. These mechanisms should include: 1) arrangements to ensure compliance of the programmes supported by the Funds and their implementation with the relevant provisions of the Charter; 2) reporting arrangements to the monitoring committee regarding cases of non-compliance of operations supported by the Funds with the Charter and complaints regarding the Charter submitted in accordance with the arrangements made pursuant to Article 69.7.[60]

[59] Regulation 2021/1060 of the EP and of the Council of 24 June 2021 laying down common provisions on the European Regional Development Fund, the European Social Fund Plus, the Cohesion Fund, the Just Transition Fund and the European Maritime, Fisheries and Aquaculture Fund and financial rules for those and for the Asylum, Migration and Integration Fund, the Internal Security Fund and the Instrument for Financial Support for Border Management and Visa Policy, *OJ* L 231, 30/06/2021.

[60] The Article 69.7 Regulation states: "Member States shall make arrangements to ensure the effective examination of complaints concerning the Funds. The scope, rules and procedures concerning those arrangements shall be the responsibility of Member States in accordance with their institutional and legal framework. This is without prejudice to the general possibility to address complaints to the Commission by citizens and stakeholders. Member States shall, upon request by the Commission, examine complaints submitted to the Commission falling within the scope of their programmes and shall inform the Commission of the results of these examinations. For the pur-

The Member State shall assess whether the enabling conditions linked to the selected specific objective are fulfilled when preparing a programme (Article 15 paragraphs 4 and 5 of the Regulation). They identify in each programme (or in the programme amendment) the fulfilled and non-fulfilled enabling conditions and shall provide a justification where it considers that an enabling condition has been fulfilled. If an enabling condition is not fulfilled at the time of approval of the programme (or the amendment), the Member State shall inform the Commission as soon as it considers that the enabling condition has been fulfilled with a justification. The Commission must evaluate it and inform the Member State in question. The expenditure linked to the specific objectives will not be reimbursed until the Member State provides sufficient guarantees that effective mechanisms are in place (Articles 15.4 y 5). The blocking of funds does not prevent programmes from being implemented or pre-financing from being received. However, reimbursements will only be made for technical assistance (which represents around 3% of the total fund allocation under the Regulation) or for operations that contribute to the fulfilment of the favourable condition.

In practice, the vast majority of Member States have been complying with the horizontal favouring condition of the Charter. Hungary is currently the only non-compliant State.

Poland indicated that it did not comply with the horizontal condition of the Charter when submitting its programme to the Commission for approval. The Commission initially confirmed this non-compliance, blocking a total amount of 74.1 billion euros in reimbursement for cohesion fund expenditure. Therefore, the funds for Poland were not initially disbursed. However, Poland submitted on January 2024 an official request to consider the horizontal enabling condition on the Charter as fulfilled, including a revised self-assessment and a justification. The Commission later confirmed that the condition had been met, allowing Poland to request the release of the total of 76.5 billion euros corresponding to the 2021–2027 cohesion funds.[61]

With regard to Hungary, the Commission decided on 22th December 2022 that this country did not comply with the horizontal enabling condition on the Charter due to several issues of concern, including judicial independence. This resulted in the blocking of the majority of the total of 21.900 million euros of allocated funds.[62] On 13 December 2023,[63] following a new assessment and various exchanges with

poses of this Article, complaints cover any dispute between potential and selected beneficiaries with regard to the proposed or selected operation and any disputes with third parties on the implementation of the programme or operations thereunder, irrespective of the qualification of means of legal redress established under national law".

[61] See COM (2024), 456 final, note 145. Special Report 03/2024, of the European Court of Auditors, Annex IV.

[62] Commission reply of 27 September 2024 to the Petition 0072/2024 by J. H. (German) calling for the return of funds released to Hungary, CM\1311261EN.docx.

[63] Decision C (2023) 9014 of 13 December 2023 on the approval and signature of the Commission assessment, in accordance with Article 15(4) of Regulation 2021/1060, of the fulfilment of the

the Hungarian government, the Commission decided that Hungary had taken the necessary measures to be considered compliant with the horizontal enabling condition on the Charter, although only in relation to judicial independence. This implied the possibility of being able to start requesting funds for a part of the funding, up to 10,200 million euros charged to the funds of the Regulation. However, the Commission understood that Hungary does not yet fulfil the horizontal enabling condition under several programmes, as serious concerns related to several fundamental rights remain. In particular, regarding the inviolability of human dignity, and the rights to private and family life, to freedom of expression and information, to non-discrimination, as well as academic freedom and the right to asylum.[64] The EP regretted the Commission's decision as it considered that Hungary still did not meet the level of judicial independence required by the Charter. The EP also expressed its disappointment for not having been adequately informed during the procedure and announced that it would appeal the decision for annulment. On 25 March 2024, the EP brought an action before the Court seeking the annulment of the Commission's decision, allegin infringement of applicable law, manifests errors of assessment. infringement of its duty to state reasons (required by Article 296 TFEU) and misure of powers.[65]

6.3 *The General Regime of Conditionality for the Protection of the Union Budget*

The General Regime of conditionality emerged as a reaction to serious situations of systemic breaches of the rule of law that have arisen in practice in certain Member States, where existing mechanisms have not produced positive results. The objective is to protect the financial interests of the EU and the sound financial management of its budget in such situations. It is therefore based on the consideration that,

horizontal enabling condition '3. Effective application and implementation of the Charter of Fundamental Rights' with regard to the deficiencies in judicial independence in Hungary.

[64] COM (2024) 456 final, p. 24, note 146; and Communication from the Commission to the EP and the Council, on the application of Regulation 2020/2092 of the EP and of the Council of 16 December 2020 on a general regime of conditionality for the protection of the EU Budget, COM (2024) 17 final, document modified by COM (2024) 17 final/2, de 23.2.2024. p. 12.

[65] Case C-225/24, *Parliament v Commission*, *OJ* C 2025/3063, 13.5.2024 (pending). With the exception of the misure of powers, the allegations of the EP were accepted by Advocate General Capeta in her Opinion presented on 12 February 2026, in which she proposes that the CJEU annul the Commission's Decision, ECLI:EU:C:2026:88. See EP Resolution of 18 January 2024 on the situation in Hungary and frozen EU funds (2024/2512(RSP)), paragraphs 5 and 11; European Commission press release of 13 December 2023, *Questions and Answers on Hungary: Rule of law and EU funding*; and Communication from the Commission to the EP and the Council on the application of Regulation 2020/2092 of the EP and of the Council of 16 December 2020 on a general regime of conditionality for the protection of the Union Budget, COM (2024) 17 final 2, 23.2.2024, p. 12.

in the implementation of the EU budget, respect for the rule of law is an essential precondition for compliance with the principles of sound financial management enshrined in Article 317 TFEU (Recital 7 of the Regulation).

This regime was established, with legal basis in article 322.1 a) TFUE, by Regulation 2020/2092.[66] Initially, Poland and Hungary tried to avoid it, by blocking (given the requirement for unanimity) the approval of the Multiannual Financial Framework 2021–2027 to which the Recovery Instrument (Next Generation EU) was linked.[67] However, at the European Council meeting on December 10–11, 2020,[68] an agreement was reached in exchange for certain commitments regarding the way the Regulation would be applied. The Member States agreed to ensure that the Regulation fully respects Article 4.2 TEU (national identity of Member States) as well as the principles of attribution, subsidiarity and proportionality (Article 5 TEU) and of objectivity, non-discrimination and equal treatment of Member States in the adoption of measures. They also agreed on the requirement of a direct link between the infringement and the consequences for the budget or the financial interests of the EU, as well as on maintaining constant dialogue with affected State throughout the procedure. It was also agreed that the Commission would draw up, in close consultation with the Member States, guidelines on how the Regulation should be applied and on the method for carrying out the evaluation required therein. The agreement also included the Commission's commitment not to finalise such guidelines or propose measures under the Regulation until there was a ruling from the CJEU, in the event that any State filed an action for annulment, in order to incorporate the consequences of the judgement.

On 16 December 2020, the Regulation was approved with Poland and Hungary voting against it. On 11 March 2021, they submitted actions for annulment before the CJEU, which would be dismissed by the Court on Judgments of February 16, 2022.[69] The Commission then published its Guidelines on the application of the Regulation.[70]

The Regulation provides for the possibility of adopting appropriate measures when breaches of the principles of the rule of law in a Member State affect or seriously risk affecting the sound financial management of the EU budget or the protection of the financial interests of the Union in a sufficiently direct way (Article 4.1).

Therefore, in order for measures to be adopted, there must be a sufficiently direct link between the violation and the financial interests of the EU. For this reason, such a violation must refer to one of the aspects listed in Article 4.2 of the Regulation, namely: the proper functioning of the authorities implementing the EU budget, in

[66] Regulation 2020/2092 of the EP and of the Council of 16 December 2020 on a general regime of conditionality for the protection of the Union budget, *OJ* L *433 I, 22.12.2020.*

[67] Conclusions adopted on the European Council special meeting on 17–21 July 2020, Doc. EUCO 10/20, 21.7.2020.

[68] Conclusions adopted on the European Council meeting on 10–11 December 2020, Doc. EUCO 20/22, 11.7.2020. See De Gregorio Merino (2022), pp. 14–17.

[69] Case C-156/21; and Case C-157/21, aforementioned.

[70] C (2022) 1382 final, 2.3.2022.

particular in the context of public procurement or grant procedures; the proper functioning of the authorities carrying out financial control, monitoring and audit, with effective and transparent financial management and accountability systems; the proper functioning of investigation and public prosecution services in relation to the investigation and prosecution of fraud, including tax fraud, corruption or other breaches of EU law relating to the implementation of the EU budget or to the protection of its financial interests; the effective judicial review by independent courts; the imposition of effective and dissuasive penalties; the prevention and sanctioning of fraud and corruption; the recovery of funds unduly paid; the effective and timely cooperation with OLAF, and with de European Public Prosecutor's Office.

They may be considered indicative of breaches: endangering the independence of the judiciary; failing to prevent, correct or sanction arbitrary or unlawful decisions by public authorities, including by law-enforcement authorities, withholding financial and human resources affecting their proper functioning or failing to ensure the absence of conflicts of interest; limiting the availability and effectiveness of legal remedies, including through restrictive procedural rules and lack of implementation of judgments, or limiting the effective investigation, prosecution or sanctioning of breaches of law (Article 3 Regulation).

The measures to be taken in these cases refer, among others, to suspension of payments or suspensión/reduction of the implementation of the legal commitments; interruption of payment deadlines, reduction of pre-financing; prohibition on entering into new legal commitments; prohibition on entering into new agreements on loans, early repayment of loans guaranteed by the EU Budget (Article 5).

Certain precautions are foreseen to protect the legitimate interests of the final recipients or beneficiaries, because the imposition of measures do not affect the obligations of government entities to make the corresponding payments and, in the case of execution of funds under shared management, they must regularly report to the Commission on their compliance. In order to ensure compliance with this obligation, the Commission must inform and receive information from beneficiaries and final recipients and provide them with Internet -based tools to report non-compliance. To this end, the Commission provides a specific complaint form on its website.[71]

In accordance with the commitments made at the European Council in December 2020, the procedure is of a subsidiary nature, as it will be initiated by the Commission, unless it considers that other procedures allow for more effective protection of the budget (Article 6.1). It must also be applied in accordance with the principle of proportionality, in light of the actual or potential impact of the breaches of the principles of the rule of law on the sound financial management of the Union budget or the financial interests of the EU. The nature, duration, gravity and scope of the breaches of the principles of the rule of law shall be duly taken into account, and the

[71] https://commission.europa.eu/strategy-and-policy/eu-budget/protection-eu-budget/rule-law-conditionality-regulation_es. By 12 January 2002, almost 300 complaints had been received, but only a few were submitted using the standard form provided by the Commission. None were considered by the Commission to be supported by sufficient data to enable it to corroborate evidence and initiate proceedings, COM (2024) 17 final/2, p. 4.

measures shall, insofar as possible, target the Union actions affected by the breaches (Article 5.3).

When and how can the procedure be initiated? At the initiative of the Commission, if after a thorough, qualitative, objective, impartial, and fair assessment,[72] it finds reasonable grounds for infringement. A dialogue is then opened with the Member State concerned, to which the Commission will send a written notification outlining the objective elements and specific reasons on which its findings are based. The Commission will inform the EP and the Council of this notification without delay. This dialogue with the State is maintained throughout the entire procedure, for which deadlines are set at all stages.[73]

When the State receives the Commission's notification, it must provide the required information, and may submit its observations, and propose the adoption of corrective measures. The Commission will then evaluate the information and observations provided by the State as well as the adequacy of the proposed corrective measures.

If the Commission finally concludes that the conditions are met and that the corrective measures proposed by the Member State do not provide an adequate response, it will submit a proposal for an implementing decision to the Council to adopt specific measures, outlining the reasons and evidence on which it is based. However, it will once again give the Member State the opportunity to submit its observations, in particular on the proportionality of the proposed measures. The Council has 1 month (which can be extended to a maximum of two in exceptional cases) to decide (by a qualified majority) whether to adopt the decision and it may amend the Commission's proposal. The Commission shall immediately inform the EP of any proposed measures (Article 8).

The Member State concerned may, at any time, adopt corrective measures and notify them in a writing notification to the Commission, including supporting evidence. In any case, the Commission should carry out regular monitoring and a new evaluation if the Member State adopts new corrective measures. If the situation has been sufficiently remedied, the Council, acting on a proposal from the Commission, should lift the measures or adjust them if the situation has only been remedied in part (Article 7 and recitals 24 and 25).

In accordance with the agreement reached at the European Council of December 2020, the Regulation clarifies that the entire procedure must be guided by the principles of objectivity, non-discrimination and equal treatment of Member States, and

---

[72] Recital 16 of the Regulation. The Commission should take into account relevant information from available sources from EU institutions and bodies (CJEU, Court of Auditors, OLAF, European Public Prosecutor's Office...), and from relevant international organisations, such as the Council of Europe bodies like the Council of Europe Group of States against Corruption (GRECO) and the Venice Commission.

[73] In its report on the application of the Regulation, the Commission affirms that the procedure is relatively quick from the moment a written notification is sent, as it can be completed within a time-limited of between 5 and 9 months. However, the Commission stresses that these deadlines allow little flexibility and are particularly challenging at certain stages, COM (2024) 17 final/2, p. 17.

be carried out in accordance with an impartial and evidence-based approach. It is worth noting in this regard that if the State concerned considers that serious breaches of these principles have occurred, the Regulation provides for the possibility for this State to request the President of the European Council to refer the matter to the its next meeting. The decision on the adoption of measures would then be suspended until the institution has deliberated on the matter. In any case, this possibility of postponing the application of the Regulation is not included in the Articles, but rather in recital 26.

The Commission was required to report to the EP and the Council by 12 January 2024 on the application of the Regulation and the effectiveness of the measures adopted. It did so by its Report on January 12, 2024.[74]

To date, the Regulation has been applied to two Member States. On 24 November 2021, the Commission sent two administrative letters to request from Poland and Hungary, both of which responded on January 2022.

Following its assessment of Poland, the Commission did not find that all the conditions for the application of the measures were fulfilled, and therefore continued to address issues related to breaches of the rule of law in that State through other instruments.

In contrast, in the case of Hungary, once the CJEU had dismissed the actions for annulment against the Regulation and the Commission's guidelines had been published, on April 27, 2022, the Commission launched the procedure, by sending a written notification to Hungary. The violations concerned public procurement, judicial proceedings, conflicts of interest, the fight against corruption and public interest trusts.

Hungary rejected all the Commission's conclusions and did not propose any corrective measures until July 2022, which, in the Commission's view, did not resolve the problems detected. It therefore notified Hungary of its intention to propose that the Council adopt measures, which it did in September of that same year. The Council adopted the budgetary protection measures in December 2022,[75] but in accordance with Article 6.11, of the Regulation and for reasons of proportionality, amended the Commission's proposal and reduced the percentage of commitments to be suspended from 65% to 55% for the three operational Cohesion programmes concerned, for a total amount of approximately 6.3 billion euros for the period 2021–2027. It also prohibited entering into new legal commitments with Hungarian public interest trusts and entities maintained by them when executing the Union budget under direct and indirect management.[76]

One year later, in accordance with the provisions of Article 7.2 of the Regulation, the Commission reassessed the situation in Hungary based on the available information (since the State had not formally adopted or notified the Commission of any

[74] COM (2024) 17 final/2, already cited.

[75] Council implementing Decision 2022/2506 of 15 December 2022 *on measures for the protection of the EU budget against breaches of the principles of the rule of law in Hungary*, *OJ* L 325, 20.12.2022.

[76] See COM (2024) 17 final 2, pp. 3–5 y 7.

new solution to address the outstanding issues). In its reassessment Decision,[77] the Commission considered that the situation had not been remedied, concluding that the measures adopted by the Council a year earlier should be maintained. The decision was welcomed by the EP.[78]

On December 2, 2024, Hungary officially notified the Commission of specific legislative amendments relating to public interest trusts and the entities that comprise them, requesting the Commission to propose adapt or lift the measure on trusts. Nevertheless, on December 16, 2004, the Commission decided that the legislative amendments were not sufficient to address conflicts of interest in the boards of trustees of public interest trusts. Therefore it decided to maintain the measure and identified the necessary adjustments. The suspension of budgetary commitments was also maintained as Hungary did not notify corrective measures to address the corresponding issues.[79]

In 2024 the European Court of Auditors published a Special Report about the rule of law in the UE[80] auditing the European Commission's implementation of the Conditionality Regulation. The report, which covers the period from the entry into force of the Regulation in January 2021 to December 2023, concluded that the combined application of this instrument, with the horizontal conditionality of the Charter and the specific provisions of the Recovery and Resilience Mechanism, represents an improvement in the rule of law framework, and that, regarding the only case in which it had been implemented (Hungary), the Commission's action complied with the Regulation and adequately complemented the other budgetary mechanisms.

However, the European Court of Auditors identified implementation difficulties in some aspects of the Regulation and it highlighted certain shortcomings in the procedure. It emphasized the lack of clarity and detail in some aspects of the Commission's guidelines to ensure the uniform and effective application of the Regulation across all Member States, and in all situations. On the one hand, the Court of Auditors emphasised the difficulty of determining compliance with the

[77] Commission Decision of 13.12.2023 on the reassessment, on the Commission's initiative, of the fulfilment of the conditions under Article 4 of Regulation (EU, Euratom) 2020/2092 following Council Implementing Decision (EU) 2022/2506 of 15 December 2022 regarding Hungary, C (2023) 8999 final.

[78] With regard to the application of the procedure to Hungary, COM (2024) 17 final/2; and COM (2024) 800 final/2. See EP resolution of 18 January 2024 *on the situation in Hungary and frozen EU funds* (2024/2512(RSP)), P9_TA (2024)0053. point 4.

[79] See press release of 16 December 2024, https://ec.europa.eu/commission/presscorner/detail/en/ip_24_6465.

[80] Special Report 03/2024 of the European Court of Auditors, *The Rule of Law in the EU*, 28.02.2024, This EU institution had already issued an opinion on the Commission's draft regulation, in which it made several recommendations. All of them have been taken into account, except for the one concerning the need for the Commission to assess the potential budgetary impact of a reduction in EU funding on the national budget of the Member State concerned before deciding on the appropriate measures to propose. See Opinion 01/2018 concerning the proposal of 2 May 2018 for a Regulation on the protection of the Union's budget in case of generalised deficiencies as regards the rule of law in the Member States, *OJ* C 291, 17.8.2018, paragraph 10.

requirement of a sufficiently direct link between breaches of the principles of the rule of law and the financial interests of the EU, as the Regulation and the guidelines do not include detailed criteria for evaluating and determining the existence of such a link, nor sufficient guidance on what form of threats to judicial independence can constitute such a sufficiently direct link. On the other hand, it raised the risk that blocking of funds could have a negatively impact on the achievement of the EU's political objectives, such as social and territorial cohesion, and the professional and personal development of people, with potential short-term negative consequences for EU citizens if national authorities did not have the financial or legal capacity to implement the programmes.

It also found a lack of clear criteria on whether or not to apply the Regulation. It noted that the Commission did not comprehensively document the reason why it decided not to use it to protect the EU's financial interests, for example, in the case of Poland.[81] Also the lack of sufficient information about the reasons why the Commission decides to move from one phase of the procedure to another. In the opinion of the European Court of Auditors, the assessment of the potential impact of breaches of the principles of the rule of law and the need for new measures is not systematically documented, and no evidence was found that the Commission applies a systematic risk analysis according to predefined criteria to support its decisions.

The Court of Auditors is also concerned about the effectiveness of the measures adopted, given their limited impact on the rule of law.[82] In particular, it stresses that formal compliance with corrective measures by a Member State does not necessarily result in a effective and lasting improvements and that, in any case, there is a risk that the State could reverse the remedial measures once the budgetary measures are lifted, especially given that it may be easier to decide to unblock funds than to block them. The Court of Auditors suggests that the application of the Regulation should not be reduced to a mere exercise of routine verification, which does not represent a real change on the ground leading ton effective and sustained improvement. It therefore suggests that decisions should be based on considerations that go beyond mere technical analysis, that any proposal to lift budgetary measures should be based on

[81] In its report on the application of the Regulation, the Commission states that this 'complementarity test' will be refined based on the practical experience gained in applying the Conditionality Regulation. The Commission dedicates Section 3 of the report to explaining complementarity with other instruments, focusing on clarifying that in the case of Hungary, the procedure under the conditionality regulation was carried out in parallel with other procedures and after the Commission considered that no other procedure provided for in EU law would allow it to protect the EU budget from the breaches found, COM (2024) 17 final/2, pp. 9–13.

[82] As regards Hungary, the Court of Auditors emphasises that the direct budgetary impact in the short term is much more limited than the figures would suggest. On the one hand, because the measures adopted do not affect advances and, on the other, because most of the amounts only refer to future payments. Furthermore, they do not eliminate the risks, because their scope of application is partial with respect to the three cohesion programmes with the highest risk of violations of the principles of the rule of law in relation to public procurement, which represents only 55% of the commitments. Regarding the Commission's assessment of the effectiveness of the measures adopted for Hungary see, COM (2024) 17 final/2, pp. 15–18.

solid evidence, that long-term monitoring of remedial measures be carried out to prevent them from being diminished or revoked at a later stage, and that annual reports on their effectiveness be provided, monitoring their real impact.

6.4 The Mechanism of Recovery and Resilience

Although the Regulation 2021/241 *on the Recovery and Resilience*[83] is not specifically aimed at addressing breaches of the principles of the rule of law in Member States, it does include tools that can be used to protect the EU's financial interests against such violations.

In accordance with the Regulation, States must submit their national recovery and resilience plans, which must be consistent with the specific challenges and priorities of each country as determined under the framework of the European Semester and with the information included in the national reform programmes proposed within that framework (Article 17.3 Regulation). Such specific recommendations may lead to the introduction in national plans of milestones and targets for reforms or investments aimed at addressing rule of law challenges, some of which may be linked to measures concerning fundamental rights. National plans should include an explanation of how they will contribute to effectively addressing all or a significant subset of the milestones and targets (Article 18.4 b).

On this basis, the Commission assesses the plans submitted by the Member States before presenting its proposal for an implementing decision to the Council determining the amount allocated to each Member State (Article 19.2 and Annex V Regulation). In addition, Member States are required to report twice a year, in the context of the European Semester, on the progress made implementing their recovery and resilience plans (Article 27).

It should be noted that the Mechanism, which is directly managed by the Member States, is performance-based, which means that the Commission disburses funds to Member States only when they have satisfactorily met the agreed targets and milestones.[84] In its assessment, the Commission must evaluate whether Member States have an effective and efficient internal control system to protect the EU's financial interests, with adequate provisions to prevent, detect and correct fraud, corruption and conflicts of interest when using the Mechanism's funds. If the Commission's assessment is negative, it shall suspend all or part of the financial contribution or

[83] Regulation 2021/241 of the EP and of the Council of 12 February 2021 *establishing the Recovery and Resilience Facility*, *OJ* L 57, 18.2.2021, p. 17.

[84] Once the corresponding agreed milestones and objectives have been achieved, the Member State must submit a duly justified request to the Commission for the disbursement of the financial contribution/loan, and may do so twice a year (Article 24.2). Once the request has been received, the Commission has 2 months to assess whether the milestones and objectives set out in the Council implementing decision have been satisfactorily achieved. Only if the evaluation is positive will it authorise the disbursement of the funds.

loans, and this suspension is lifted only when the Member State concerned has taken the necessary measures to ensure satisfactory fulfilment of the milestones and targets. If the Member State concerned does not take the necessary measures, it is also possible to terminate the agreements related to the financial assistance, which include the commitment to make a financial contribution (Article 23). Pre-financing already provided may also be reduced and recovered if the Member State has not implemented its plan satisfactorily or in the event of serious irregularities (Article 24).

On December 8, 2023, the Council approved Poland's revised recovery and resilience plan,[85] which covered reforms and investments worth 59.8 billion euros (34.5 billion euros in loans and 25.3 billion euros in grants). The plan included two milestones related to judicial independence. On 15 December 2023, Poland submitted to the Commission its first payment request for the disbursement of 6.3 billion euros (2.7 billion in grants and 3.6 billion in loans net of pre-financing). On 29 February 2024, the Commission completed its preliminary assessment, concluding that the State had satisfactorily met the two milestones by reforming the disciplinary regime for judges and using a computer tool that supports auditing and control systems, guaranteeing the necessary safeguards against fraud. This decision, once confirmed by the Council, allows the disbursement of these 6.3 billion euros and the rest will released as the Commission considers that it is satisfactorily meeting the milestones and targets outlined in its plan.[86]

Hungary's Recovery and Resilience Plan was initially approved by the Council on 15 December 2022. Subsequently, Hungary submitted its revised plan on 31 August 2023, which was approved by the Council's implementing Decision of 5 December 2023[87] for a total amount of just over 10.4 billion euros (just over 6.5 billion euros in financial contributions and 3.9 billion euros in loans). Hungary included 27 super-milestones, some directly related to the rule of law and others related to the protection of fundamental rights, which the Commission has not fully considered as met. As a result, no payments have been disbursed to Hungary to date.[88]

---

[85] The Council decision of 17 June 2022, by which the Plan was initially approved was subsequently revised after Poland submitted its amended Plan on 31 August 2023. Three associations and a foundation representing European judges requested the General Court to annul the Council decision because they considered that the milestones set out in the plan were incompatible with EU law (They argued that those milestones are in fact defined too flexibly, allowing Poland not to comply with the case-law of the CJEU regarding the rule of law). The Court dismissed those actions as inadmissible on understanding that the applicant organisations were not entitled to bring proceedings either in their own name or on behalf of the judges whose interests they defended, Order of the General Court of 4 June 2024, Joined Cases T-530/22 to T-533/22, ECLI:EU:T:2024:363.

[86] See European Commission press release, *Poland's efforts to restore rule of law pave the way for accessing up to €137 billion in EU funds; and Questions and answers on rule of law and EU funds for Poland*, 29.02.2024. https://ec.europa.eu/commission/presscorner/detail/en/qanda_24_1223.

[87] Doc. 15,964/23.

[88] See press release, *Commission considers that Hungary has not sufficiently addressed breaches of the principles of the rule of law and therefore maintains measures to protect the Union Budget*, 16.12.2024. https://ec.europa.eu/commission/presscorner/detail/en/ip_24_6465.

7 Brief Concluding Reflection

The rule of law, democracy, and respect for fundamental rights—particularly human dignity, freedom, and equality—represent, as EU founding values, the foundation of a construction that began in the 1950s with the aim of ending conflicts between European States and seeking peace through integration. Over the years, this construction has evolved into what is today the European Union—a international organization of regional integration composed of 27 European States, much more heterogeneous than it was at its origins, combining economic and political objectives, and in which, in recent times, the weight of intergovernmentalism has perhaps been felt excessively.

The EU currently faces serious challenges, some of which originate from external factors, stemming from the turbulent international geopolitical reality, and can only be addressed through unity. However, achieving that unity is not easy when the functioning of the Union is threatened from within. The challenges to the EU's values posed by systemic threats to the rule of law in certain Member States—such as the case of Poland, the ongoing situation in Hungary, and the emerging issue in Slovakia—seriously compromise the functioning of the EU and the principles of mutual trust, sincere cooperation, and solidarity on which it rests. In this context, respecting, promoting, and protecting such values must remain, now more than ever, a priority for the Union. They are its hallmark, as confirmed by the Treaty, which provides the necessary legal foundations for this purpose.

In this effort, it is worth highlighting the key role played, once again, by the CJEU, which has risen to the occasion by using the tools at its disposal to address breaches of the rule of law principles. It has responded to numerous requests for a preliminary ruling, declared infringements, adopted interim measures, and imposed financial penalties when requested by the Commission. Its joint interpretation of Articles 2 and 19.1 TEU has made it possible to tackle the challenges to the rule of law through the guarantee of judicial independence. The Commission's reaction has been slower, but especially following the CJEU's case law, it has gradually, timidly, assumed its role as the guardian of the Treaties, as assigned by Article 17 TEU, by initiating infringement proceedings to respond to breaches of values by some Member States.

However, beyond infringement procedure and preliminary rulings, applicable when the violation of values entails a breach of EU law, the EU has developed, as we have seen, a set of tools to promote and protect its values.

Such mechanisms have been created as problems have arisen, and not always successfully, as in the case of the EU Framework to strengthen the rule of law. This is a slow procedure, with several phases, reminiscent of the pre-litigation phase of the infringement procedure. This tool turned out to be a failure. It was unable to tackle the problem effectively, merely postponing for several years the activation of the mechanism under Article 7.1 TEU. It was essentially a political mechanism, as also the Article 7 TEU mechanism is, which is considered the primary reaction tool. Its shortcomings have become clearly evident in the cases of Poland and Hungary, as we have pointed out. The Article 7 TEU mechanism could be an appropriate tool, but it would require sufficient political will. Moreover, a review would be needed to make it truly operational, something that does not seem feasible in the short term.

Currently, the most effective mechanisms may be the reaction mechanisms linked to the EU Budget, such as the horizontal enabling condition on the Charter, the general regime of conditionality, and (indirectly) the Recovery and Resilience Mechanism. However, even the application of these mechanisms is influenced by political considerations. A significant factor in this regard is the requirement for unanimity in decision-making on particularly relevant issues, which allows the State concerned to use the veto power to block decision-making. In any case, the threat of economic sanctions plays a deterrent role.

Preventive and awareness-raising mechanisms through the evaluation of State behavior are also noteworthy. This evaluation is based on dialogue and cooperation, as seen in the reports on the application of the Charter, the Annual Rule of Law Report, or indirectly, through the European Semester or the Justice Scoreboard. These mechanisms help shed light on the main challenges to values at the national level, facilitating early response. The recommendations made and their follow-up can motivate improvements in the situation, while also serving as an exchange of best practices. On the other hand, their public nature can have an impact on national and European public opinion, thus exerting pressure on governments. This effect would certainly be enhanced if the EU made a greater effort to prevent growing disaffection engagement of citizens. Offering and making information easily accessible in all official languages would be a step worth considering in that direction.

Also the promotional measures through specific funding programs aimed at different sectors of society, or the FRA's support to States and institutions in protecting fundamental rights, are tools that can be considered positive.

These are not good times for values. The proliferation of illiberal regimes, populism, and autocracies, along with the open questioning of the rules of peaceful coexistence and the foundations of the system, does not allow for great hopes. In this context, the EU cannot afford to falter. Its own survival is at stake. Upholding, promoting, protecting, and strengthening its values must be a priority task. Values must inspire all its actions, as required by the Treaty. The EU must also be rigorous in ensuring that the requirement to respect values is strictly adhered to as a condition for the accession of new States, as established in Article 49 TEU and agreed upon by the Member States at the 1993 Copenhagen European Council. The EU already knows the consequences of taking this requirement lightly. It cannot afford laxity. As the CJEU has pointed out, compliance with the EU values cannot be reduced to an obligation which a candidate State must meet in order to accede to the EU and which it may disregard after its accession. This requires the ability to react swiftly, clearly and decisively against violations. The EU's survival depends on it.

References

Campos Sánchez-Bordona M (2020) La protección de la independencia judicial en el Derecho de la Unión Europe. Revista de Derecho Comunitario Europeo 65:11–31

Cervell Hortal MJ (2022) Una Unión de valores: ¿realidad o desiderátum? La protección del Estado de Derecho en el seno de la UE. Aranzadi, Pamplona

Cortés Martín JM (2020) Sorteando los inconvenientes del artículo 7 TUE: el advenimiento del control jurisdiccional del Estado de Derecho. Revista de Derecho Comunitario Europeo 66:473–517

De Gregorio MA (2022) El nuevo régimen general de condicionalidad para la protección del presupuesto de la UE. Revista de Derecho Comunitario Europeo 71:11–26

Fonseca Morillo F (2024) El Estado de Derecho en la Unión Europea: de un valor político a su dimensión financiera. Real Academia de Doctores, Barcelona

Mangas Martín A (2018) Polonia en el punto de mira: ¿Solo riesgo de violación grave del Estado de Derecho? Revista General de Derecho Europeo 44:1–12

Mangas Martín A, González Alonso LN (2008) Carta de los derechos fundamentales de la Unión Europea. Comentario artículo por artículo, Fundación BBVA, Madrid

Ripoll Carulla S (2018) Unión Europa y fortalecimiento y defensa del estado de Derecho. Anuario de Derecho Internacional 34

Urbaneja Cillán J (2023) La crisis del Estado de Derecho en los Estados miembros de la Unión Europea. Aranzadi, Pamplona

Democracy and Rule of Law: The Democratic Regime, International Relations, and the Role of the European Union

Raquel Cavalcanti Ramos Machado Malenchini

Contents

Abstract Despite the expansion of democracy and the rule of law since World War II, they remain subject to continuous progress and setbacks. Due to its conceptual complexity and the principle of self-determination, democracy was not immediately recognized as a foundational value in international law. However, its role in safeguarding fundamental rights and reinforcing the rule of law led to its incorporation into international legal instruments. The European Union has become a central actor in promoting and protecting democracy, both through its treaty-based commitments and concrete actions, including internal policies and external relations, particularly in new-generation trade agreements with third countries. Other regional and international frameworks have also acknowledged democracy as a legal and political standard. Given the transnational nature of current democratic challenges and the

R. Cavalcanti Ramos Machado Malenchini (✉)
Department of Public Law, Federal University of Ceará, Fortaleza, Brazil
e-mail: raquelramosmachado@ufc.br

L. Pasquali (ed.), *EU Values and International Law*, European Union and its Neighbours in a Globalized World 35,
https://doi.org/10.1007/978-3-032-20521-6_5

ongoing crisis affecting the Western model of freedom and human rights, international efforts to uphold democratic principles—such as those advanced by the EU, especially in new-generation trade agreements—warrant close analysis. While criticisms persist regarding the selective application of this principle and concerns over the North-South imposition of political models, the EU's role in strengthening democracy remains a key contribution to global governance and the protection of fundamental values.

1 Introduction

After Athens, Western society resumed practical engagement with democracy in the eighteenth century. The French Revolution and the Declaration of the Rights of Man and of the Citizen (1789) emphasized popular participation, aligning democracy with the consolidation of fundamental rights. Political rights, accordingly, are considered first-generation rights. However, unlike fundamental rights, democracy did not achieve universal status. Understanding this disparity is key to assessing its current state and the international commitment to its protection in legal instruments, norms, and state relations.

This study seeks to explore the commitment (or lack thereof) in international and regional legal norms and documents, as well as in international relations and in trade agreements, to the democratic regime and its consequences for the defense of democracy, the rule of law, and the respect for human rights in contemporary society. Considering its global leadership in this context, the European Union's role will be emphasized.

Understanding the international and regional protection of democracy requires an analysis of its waves, challenges, crises, and paradoxes in societies that seek to implement it, along with a review of historical data on democracy in legal instruments and the evolving stance of the international community.

To this end, the study is structured into four main sections. First, it examines the democratic waves, critically assessing the framework proposed by Samuel Huntington while considering the motivations behind states' adoption of democracy within international and regional legal frameworks, as well as in foreign relations. Next, it explores the extent to which political regimes can shape political, institutional, and legal practices in other countries within a globalized context, considering the inherently transnational nature of contemporary relations and the need to position democracy within international and regional legal instruments. The third section analyzes normative and institutional mechanisms for democracy promotion and defense by regional blocs and within international relations, investigating its expansion, contradictions, and limitations through a critical lens. Special attention is given to the role of the European Union, given its explicit recognition of democracy as a foundational value in both its internal governance (among member states) and external relations, and above all, considering the European Union's use of its economic power to include democratic values and the rule of law in trade agreements with countries or regional blocs. It is not possible, in fact, to fully understand the emergence of so-called new-generation agreements without considering the context of democratic waves, transnational relations, and the broader commitment to democracy at the international level. Trade agreements, regardless of their specific purposes, are not isolated events but rather the result of a coherent set of foreign policy efforts.

Finally, the study reflects on the persistent challenges of employing democracy as a criterion in international legal instruments, regional agreements, trade agreements and foreign policy. The underlying hypothesis is that an international commitment to promoting and defending democracy is necessary to ensure the continued viability of democratic regimes in societies that uphold them today, and that the use of trade agreements can be a respectful path to this end, even though it is difficult to monitor the effectiveness of the application of these agreements and rules.

The methodology follows a hypothetico-deductive approach, drawing on data, legal norms, and doctrinal analysis of the subject. The study adopts a dialogical framework, considering opposing perspectives before reaching a final position.

2 Democratic Waves and the International Commitment to Democracy: Challenges

Analyzing the various moments of expansion and regression of democracy, Samuel Huntington uses the analogy of waves to explain the historical cycles of democratic expansion and regression worldwide.[1] Huntington's historical analysis begins with the first democratic wave, marked by the establishment of American democracy, and extends to what he defines as the third wave. Later, other scholars expanded on his framework, proposing the existence of a fourth wave,[2] while contemporary discussions suggest the emergence of a fifth wave—or at least a reaction to the third and fourth counter-waves. This potential fifth wave, or the attempt to prevent a fourth counter-wave, could serve as the basis for a more internationally coordinated expansion of the democratic model and efforts to safeguard democracy.

When identifying these waves, it is essential to make some critical observations regarding democracy as an exemplary government model to be universally enshrined or integrated into foreign policy.

When Western society experienced what can be considered the first democratic wave, the absolutist monarchical model was so deeply entrenched, and civic electoral participation so limited, that it would have been nearly impossible for any universal legal document to define democracy as a form of government. Across Europe, political regimes fluctuated between different models, and only gradually

---

[1] Huntington (1993), *passim*.

[2] McFaul (2002), pp. 213–214.

did suffrage expand. Thus, the principle enshrined in the Declaration of the Rights of Man and of the Citizen—that 'the law is the expression of the general will' (Article 6)—could not yet be equated with a recognized right to democracy. Despite the absence of a consistent theoretical debate on democracy at the international level, Kant, in Perpetual Peace, emphasized the importance of nations adopting a republican form of government as a path to peace.[3] Although he used the term 'republic,' his focus was on individual liberty in political participation—one of the fundamental principles of the democratic regime.

Even after the second democratic wave, when more nations adopted democracy as a model, significant obstacles remained that prevented its universal recognition as a normative standard or a criterion in international relations. Two key challenges stand out: (i) the semantic plurality of the term democracy and (ii) the principle of self-determination.

The multiple meanings of democracy[4] and the resulting difficulty in defining precise criteria for determining whether a country qualifies as democratic highlight its multidimensional nature (maximalist democracy). As Bobbio observes, democracy encompasses both a formal concept, referring to the 'set of rules whose observance is necessary to ensure that political power is effectively distributed among the majority of citizens,' and a substantive concept, linked to the idea of equality.[5] Even within the political dimension (minimalist democracy), there was no universal consensus on the criteria that should be followed.[6] Democracy involves the people's ability to participate in governance, grounded in liberty, equality, legal predictability, and proper deliberation.[7] However, how should equality be measured? Should it be confined to electoral participation and representative decision-making, or should it also take into account access to public services and wealth distribution within a country?

The complexity of this issue required collective efforts to establish standardized parameters. So much so that, following World War II and amid the emergence of numerous international legal entities, UNESCO launched a survey on the parameters of the democratic model.[8]

Furthermore, the recognition of self-determination[9] and the possibility of securing fundamental rights (beyond the political sphere) under alternative governance

---

[3] Kant (1991), pp. 101–102.

[4] Hodges (1965), pp. 9–10.

[5] Bobbio (2018), pp. 53–54.

[6] This point will be addressed again in the following section, given that it is a problem that persists in the adoption of democracy as a criterion in international relations.

[7] As Simone Goyard-Fabre highlights, the foundations of Athenian democracy were constitutionality, citizenship, legality Goyard-Fabre (1998). Polybius invokes freedom and equality as its specific characteristics, although freedom and equality had another meaning at the time, since aspects of public life were more accentuated, freedom had another meaning, and the understanding of equality was more restricted. Polybius (1986).

[8] Unesco (1951), p. 7.

[9] Mustafa (1971), pp. 486–487.

models, including authoritarian regimes[10] complicate the imposition or adoption of democracy at the international level. Moreover, since liberty is one of democracy's foundational principles, enforcing it as a legal requirement poses a paradox; instead, it must be a voluntary choice by the peoples who embrace it. In other words, democracy cannot be imposed—it must be desired. Otherwise, it risks becoming a form of oppression itself. Democratic commitment requires not only institutional and procedural reforms in political life but also a transformation in civic culture.[11]

On the one hand, the Universal Declaration of Human Rights (1948) states in Article 21 that 'everyone has the right to take part in the government of their country, directly or through freely chosen representatives.' On the other hand, this provision does not explicitly recognize a right to democracy.

Even in the post-war period, during the second democratic wave, countries with significant global influence continued to uphold authoritarian regimes—such as Portugal (1926–1974) and Spain (1939–1975) in Europe—while the Cold War further complicated the discourse on democracy. The expansion of the Soviet Union and the tensions between free societies and egalitarian ideals hindered the establishment of democracy as a normative criterion in international relations. Moreover, even after the third democratic wave, authoritarian regimes persisted across various regions, including Latin America, Africa, and Asia. Paradoxically, in some cases, these regimes were supported or tolerated by liberal democracies due to economic interests or fears of communist expansion, as exemplified by the establishment of military dictatorships in Latin America (e.g., Chile,[12] Bolivia,[13] and Brazil[14]) with the acquiescence of the United States.

In any case, it is important to highlight an aspect of the second wave that is related to the possible use of international trade agreements to promote democracy. From the moment notions begin to act with a sense of community, "with pursuit of common interests with those outside one's immediate Community,"[15] there is a democratic concern in the sense developed by John Dewey. Thus, one of the seeds of the European Union, the European Coal and Steel Community, a common market for the commercialization of coal and steel products, aimed not only to achieve economic balance between nations, but to allow them to develop trade with respect for values that mattered to state organizations that respected the free will of citizens and their fundamental rights, in an environment of peace. In other words, economic development compatible with democracy.[16] During this period, the focus was on promoting economic recovery after the Second World War, but concern with the

[10] Lehfeld (2024).

[11] Fox and Roth (2001), pp. 351–352.

[12] Girard (2015), pp. 2–3.

[13] Field Jr. (2014), pp. 160–162.

[14] Pereira (2018), pp. 8–9.

[15] Ryder (2008).

[16] Petzina et al. (1981), pp. 465–466.

balance between economic agreements, a healthy political environment and a prosperous society can already be seen, albeit in an embryonic form.[17]

The third democratic wave is marked by the democratization of countries such as Spain and Portugal in the late 1970s, already influenced by European Union integration efforts. The fourth wave is often associated with the democratization of the Global South, particularly African nations, following the end of apartheid. These waves play a crucial role in the discussion of democracy as a criterion in international relations, as they illustrate how the persistence of undemocratic regimes can set a negative global precedent. Furthermore, at this moment in history it is possible to see more clearly how economic, commercial and political integration agreements begin to use gradually democracy and the rule of law as one of their elements. The Lomé convention (in which the European Community established a trade agreement with countries in Africa, the Caribbean and the Pacific—ACP) can be used as an example. Despite its more economic character, since the Lomé I Convention (1975–1980) there has been a concern between international agreements that provide socioeconomic development and political stability. Gradually, these concerns increased until the Cotonou agreement (2000–2023) when the commitment to cooperation for the promotion and maintenance of democracy was expressly referred. Indeed, the European Union's generations of trade agreements reflect growing engagement with democratic values. If in the first-generation agreements economic values prevailed, in the new generation agreements political commitments are highlighted more clearly, with occasional express references to democracy and specific chapters for commitments to sustainable development and the participation of civil society.

A movement worth considering—given its relevance to the growing prominence of the democratic principle in treaties, agreements, charters, and international declarations—is the advancement of participatory democracy in environmental protection, as discussed in the following sections. While democracy was not initially recognized as a universal model due to its semantic variability and the principle of self-determination, it gained traction as environmental rights became more firmly established, not just in international treaties, but in trade agreements.

3 Democratic and Anti-Democratic Contagion, Cross-Border Relations, and the Importance of Its Defense in the International Context

Geographical and technological isolation, along with the prevalence of regimes with limited political rights until the early twentieth century, contributed to the lack of international debate on protecting democracy. The rise of authoritarian regimes, culminating in World War II, highlighted the global risks of such governance.

[17] Ryder (2008).

During World War II, in discussions on U.S. aid to the Allies, Jean Monnet referred to the "democratic arsenal,"[18] a term later echoed in Roosevelt's speech announcing military support for Britain.[19] Meanwhile, the link between totalitarian regimes, war, and human rights violations became evident.

Ironically, many totalitarian regimes initially enjoyed popular legitimacy, though electoral processes were often manipulated through populist strategies. Hitler, for instance, held two referendums: one on Germany's withdrawal from the League of Nations' Disarmament Conference and another consolidating presidential powers after Hindenburg's death. Despite overwhelming approval, these referendums lacked essential procedural safeguards, underscoring concerns about the integrity of electoral processes and the formal aspects of democracy.[20]

In the post-war period, with the emergence of international legal entities and the proclamation of universal rights, democracy became an unavoidable issue.

Due to the semantic complexity of defining democracy and the global diversity of political regimes, debates on democracy in universal international declarations and agreements remained limited. A clearer international stance emerged with the EU's expansion, regional democratic charters, and increased cross-border social and political interactions, leading to a demand not only for international legal norms but also for trade agreements.

Since the 1970s, transnational social relations have grown more complex. In environmental matters, localized damage can have global repercussions, necessitating harmonized policies. Recognizing a shared responsibility for environmental protection, the global community embraced participatory democracy for environmental decision-making, as exemplified by the Rio Declaration on Environment and Development (1992) and the Aarhus Convention (1998), to which the EU is a signatory.

In today's "risk society,"[21] where collective responsibility is expanded, political engagement is vital. Here, democracy is valued not only for liberty but also for solidarity, requiring participation in both government elections and ongoing political decisions. This solidarity, which unites individuals within a nation, is expected to extend internationally.

In a globalized world, a country's political models and practices inevitably influence its neighbours, as political decision-making methods often transcend borders—a phenomenon reflected in Huntington's concept of democratic waves. Moreover, authoritarian regimes tend to employ violence and disregard rights, and both democratic and anti-democratic movements can spread contagiously. As Held

[18] Monnet (1978), p. 160.

[19] Roosevelt (1941), p. 640.

[20] As Arnold Zurcher further observes, the forms of participation envisaged during the Nazi government proved to be authoritarian, by attributing the capacity for initiative only to the executive power, removing it from the people, and by admitting that the Constitution and the law were reformed by demonstrations determined by a simple majority and no longer by an absolute majority, as during the Weimer Republic. Zurcher (1935), pp. 94–95.

[21] Beck (1992), pp. 19–21.

observes, "democracy within the nation-state requires democracy within an interwoven network of international forces and relationships."[22]

The proliferation of the internet has significantly increased the complexity of political and social relations. Key events—such as the Cambridge Analytica scandal, the Arab Spring,[23] and widespread disinformation campaigns—illustrate the transnational impact of digital information. Due to their openness, democratic societies are particularly vulnerable to external attacks when protective mechanisms are lacking, and territorial sovereignty may be undermined in the absence of legal frameworks regulating cross-border digital information flows.

It is very important to understand the development of environmental democracy—a form of participatory democracy—and its transnational nature, to also grasp the efforts made to promote it through international trade agreements, such as the new-generation agreements signed by the European Union, which emphasize sustainable development with contractual provisions reinforcing civil society participation. As Pasquali observes regarding the EU-Mexico bilateral agreement, a model of latest-generation agreements, there is a "growing trend by the European Union to use its trade agreements to influence global regulatory standards concerning the environment and sustainable governance."[24]

Purely domestic regulations aimed at protecting internal democratic institutions, ensuring environmental democracy, safeguarding digital freedoms, or promoting citizen participation in governance may prove insufficient in contemporary societies. Given the transnational nature of political threats, a coordinated international effort is necessary. Moreover, it is legitimate to use democracy as a criterion for expanding or restricting international relations, particularly for democratic nations seeking to uphold their political values on the global stage.

4 Legal and Institutional Action in International Relations for the Promotion and Defense of Democracy: The Role of the European Union

A comprehensive analysis of trade agreements in promoting democracy and the rule of law requires understanding their historical evolution alongside treaties and institutional efforts. This is crucial in a global context where democracy's protection is shaped by transnational challenges and regime contagion.

From the second half of the twentieth century onward, and especially in the twenty-first century, democracy has increasingly been recognized as a core value by groups of countries due to its close connection with the rule of law, human rights

---

[22] Held (1991), p. 207.

[23] After the Arab Spring, in 2011, the European Union prepared a study on the topic entitled "A new response to a changing Neighborhood".

[24] Pasquali (2023), pp. 244–245.

development, and often, societal prosperity. In this context, democracy has evolved from being merely a regime adopted by certain nations to a fundamental value, regarded as a pathway to achieving an ideal model of society.

The most emblematic example of this development is the European Union, which not only enshrines democracy as one of its foundational values (Article 2 of the Treaty on European Union) but also, through the Copenhagen Criteria established in 1993, requires candidate and member states to maintain stable institutions that guarantee democracy, the rule of law, human rights, and respect for and protection of minorities. Furthermore, democracy serves as a guiding principle for the European Union's international actions, as stated in Article 21 of the Treaty on European Union. Furthermore, pursuant to art. 3.5. of the Treaty, "in its relations with the wider world, the Union shall uphold and promote its values and interests and contribute to the protection of its citizens. It shall contribute to peace, security, the sustainable development of the Earth, solidarity and mutual respect among peoples, free and fair trade, eradication of poverty and the protection of human rights...".

These criteria initially led to political and institutional restructuring in many nations that joined the bloc, with a key step being the promotion of free and fair elections and the establishment of independent institutions to safeguard citizens' freedom of choice. While these measures face cultural and legal challenges,[25] they represent a concrete commitment to defending European values.

In the early twenty-first century, as democratic crises emerged in some member states, such as Poland and Hungary, the European Union demonstrated the practical significance of these criteria, not only in the context of its enlargement but also in defending democracy and the rule of law within the bloc. The EU withheld financial transfers and imposed sanctions on these countries for violating democratic principles and rule of law standards.[26]

Regarding the assessment of democracy as a criterion in international relations, the European Union has not only implemented measures to support and promote democracy but has also imposed restrictions on countries and entities involved in democratic violations. The European Parliament plays an active role in promoting global democracy through activities such as election observation, mediation, and political dialogue facilitation, working with political parties and parliaments to strengthen democratic institutions.

Additionally, the Council of the European Union conducts meetings, studies, and reports with specific conclusions on strategic actions for democracy promotion in foreign policy. Financial instruments such as the Neighbourhood, Development and International Cooperation Instrument (NDICI) are also available to support democracy-related initiatives in third countries.

---

[25] Malová, Darina and Dolný, Branislav (2008), pp. 71–72.

[26] Case C-156/21 e C-204/21.

As will be exemplified in more detail in the title below, the European Union also makes extensive use of trade agreements, which provide for commitment to democratic values.

Sometimes as a result of such agreements or foreign policy measures with third countries, the European Commission has implemented various restrictive measures, some of which have been reviewed by the General Court of the Court of Justice of the European Union. Certain rulings have being upheld while others were overturned. Nonetheless, it is evident that democracy remains a key criterion in the EU's external relations.

In 2023, for instance, reaffirming its commitment to global democracy, the General Court of the Court of Justice of the European Union upheld restrictions against Venezuela and a group of related individuals due to their disregard for democratic principles.[27] These restrictions included bans on exporting certain goods to Venezuela and the freezing of financial assets belonging to individuals and entities associated with the regime. This decision is significant for several reasons, both procedurally and substantively, particularly in relation to the defense of democracy. By considering Venezuela's democratic decline as grounds for imposing restrictions, the Court recognized the validity of information contained in an Organization of American States (OAS) report, which documented violations of political rights, including restrictions on peaceful protests and the right to vote.

Similarly, in 2024, the General Court confirmed sanctions imposed by the European Council on individuals involved in democratic violations in Belarus.[28] Since 2004, the European Union has enforced restrictive measures against Belarus due to its failure to uphold democratic principles, including the freezing of assets belonging to individuals who support or benefit from Lukashenko's regime. In the case under review, employees of a sanctioned individual had been punished for participating in peaceful strikes and demonstrations following fraudulent elections. The Court determined that these actions constituted repression of civil society and direct support for Lukashenko's regime, further reinforcing the European Union's commitment to defending democracy.

Some of the restrictions imposed by the European Union have significant economic consequences, affecting access to financial resources, contracts, and trade. Given the interconnected nature of global financial markets, these measures effectively strengthen democracy's normative power as a standard in international relations.

Beyond the European Union, other regional organizations have also recognized democracy as a legal standard. The Inter-American Democratic Charter (2001) and the African Charter on Democracy, Elections, and Governance (2007) define democracy not only as a fundamental right but also as a clearly institutional and procedural concept—something not explicitly outlined in the Treaty on European Union. Their greater specificity likely results from their exclusive focus on

[27] T-65/18 RENV.

[28] T-528/22.

democracy. Both reference electoral integrity, voter equality (including gender), anti-corruption measures, institutional stability, separation of powers, and link democracy to human rights. Although these charters include sanctions for non-compliant members, they lack the enforceability of the EU's restrictive measures affecting third countries and private entities.

Beyond binding legal norms, institutional actions and soft law instruments also support democracy. United Nations increasingly recognizes its importance and the need for international efforts to protect it. In 1993, the Vienna Declaration recommended prioritizing national and international measures promoting democracy, development, and human rights, acknowledging their mutually reinforcing relationship. In 2000, the UN's Millennium Declaration pledged to promote democracy, strengthen the rule of law, and recognized participatory democracy as essential to freedom. In 2005, the UN created the United Nations Democracy Fund (UNDEF) to support democratization worldwide. Additionally, in 2007, it proclaimed September 15 as the International Day of Democracy, emphasizing democracy as an ongoing process requiring international commitment—an essential factor in relations among democratic nations. Since 2015, the UN has held a Forum on Human Rights, Democracy, and the Rule of Law (Human Rights Council Resolution 28/14). Additionally, the 2030 Agenda for Sustainable Development emphasizes global democratic efforts in both substantive and formal aspects, particularly Goal 16.7, which calls for inclusive and participatory decision-making at all levels.

The European Union stands out by integrating democracy into international relations, formally enshrining it in its legal framework and enforcing it through mechanisms affecting third countries and private entities. Since 2020, the EU has implemented the European Democracy Action Plan, and in 2024, it launched an initiative to protect democracy (Defence of Democracy package), considering transnational[29] threats and the need for democratic safeguards in international relations.[30]

This increasing use of democracy as a value in regional and international instruments—both as a criterion for international relations and as a guiding principle for assessing the actions of third countries and international legal entities—demonstrates that the democratic principle has become more clearly defined in international relations. It also demonstrates how the evolution of trade agreements, moving from a more economic approach to a more substantial one linked to the promotion of democracy, occurs within a context in which other international efforts are made in the same direction.

Although no country can be forced to adopt democracy, the absence of its universal recognition under international law should not weaken democracy in nations

---

[29] As paragraphs 2 and 39 in Document 32023H2829, the Commission Recommendation (EU) 2023/2829 of 12 December 2023 on inclusive and resilient electoral processes in the Union and enhancing the European nature and efficient conduct of the elections to the European Parliament C/2023/8626.

[30] As in Document 52023PC0637, the Proposal for a Directive of the European Parliament and of the Council establishing harmonised requirements in the internal market on transparency of interest representation carried out on behalf of third countries and amending Directive (EU) 2019/1937

already practicing it. Defending democracy within democratic states remains a legitimate criterion in international relations, warranting global attention, especially when other universally recognized rights—such as environmental protection with stakeholder participation, the right to information, and electoral integrity—are at stake in the digital era and amid AI interference risks. Ultimately, democracy will continue to serve as a foundational principle in international relations when embraced by regional blocs and seen as essential for promoting human rights.

4.1 The European Union's Specific Role in Promoting Democracy and the Rule of Law Through Trade Agreements

As stated in the previous section, among the various actions undertaken by the European Union to promote democracy in international relations, in line with Article 3(5) of the Treaty on European Union, many of its trade agreements—whether concluded with individual countries or regional blocs—establish democracy, the rule of law, or elements intrinsic to democratic governance as fundamental principles. These agreements serve as mechanisms to foster mutual respect among nations and to ensure free and fair trade.

The potential for utilizing trade agreements to promote democracy is particularly evident—as previously stated—in new-generation agreements, where these instruments are employed not solely for economic purposes but also to advance legal values. Moreover, using trade agreements for objectives that go beyond the economic dimension and align them with the European Union's legal values confers upon them even greater democratic legitimacy.[31]

Given the semantic complexity that a mere invocation of the term "democracy" might entail, the concept is often operationalized in trade agreements through specific commitments, such as transparency measures or anti-corruption initiatives. These provisions ultimately contribute to the broader objective of promoting democracy and the rule of law.

At this juncture, two previously discussed themes converge to highlight the significance of the European Union's approach to democracy promotion through trade agreements: the semantic plurality of the term "democracy" and the principle of national sovereignty. Trade agreements, by their very nature, result from negotiations freely undertaken by the contracting parties, thereby respecting national sovereignty rather than undermining it. In fact, they reinforce it, as the signatory states voluntarily commit to implementing democratic values. Regarding the multifaceted nature of democracy, the EU carefully considers the geopolitical and contractual limitations when establishing obligations related to democratic governance. As a result, while some agreements explicitly reference commitments to democracy and

[31] Maillo (2021), p. 5.

fundamental rights, others prioritize obligations concerning governmental transparency and anti-corruption measures.

In certain agreements, civil society engagement is emphasized, particularly through mechanisms that encourage public participation in monitoring compliance with the agreed commitments—an approach aligned with the concept of participatory democracy.

Thus, the strategic value of these agreements lies in creating an economic incentive for adherence to key democratic and rule-of-law principles. The European Union leverages its economic influence to promote legal values that it considers fundamental. Legal texts and agreements are shaped by social and political contexts while also influencing them. The openness introduced by new agreement models allows for a critical assessment of their democratic character. This includes examining whether societal aspirations were considered in negotiations, whether the text reflects democratic commitments, and whether its implementation fosters democratic values. For methodological clarity, this analysis will focus on the approved text, with particular emphasis on civil society participation.

Numerous agreements exemplify this approach:

• The Free Trade Agreement between the European Union and its Member States and the Republic of Korea (2010, updated 2023) contains a dedicated clause requiring the parties to implement transparency measures and adhere to principles of good administrative behavior. Additionally, the agreement mandates that the parties "contribute to the objective of sustainable development" by recognizing that "economic development, social development, and environmental protection are interdependent and mutually reinforcing components of sustainable development." This acknowledgment reinforces democracy in a substantive sense. Furthermore, the agreement underscores the importance of transparency and scientific evidence in decision-making (Article 13.8), which relates to the right to information, and mandates dialogue with civil society (Article 13.13), which relates to the right to civic participation. This forum is held annually and allows opinions and recommendations to be forwarded directly to the parties, promoting a balanced representation among stakeholders.

Before moving on to references to other trade agreements signed by the European Union, it is important to highlight that certain provisions are standardized in new-generation agreements, which include a commitment to sustainable development in its three dimensions (economic, social, and environmental), with a dedicated chapter addressing the subject. This provision, as stated in the previous paragraph, reveals an attempt to implement democracy in its material sense, guaranteeing not only the right to participation but also a good quality of life. They also all refer to the right to civil society participation and the pursuit of decision-making based on scientific evidence. These aspects are more closely related to democracy in its formal sense, with the right to information and participation. What varies from one agreement to another is the degree of depth and commitment with which these issues are addressed. In each agreement, for instance, depending on the period in which it was signed, the commitment to sustainable development differs. The specific obligations related to environmental issues will not be explored here, as the focus is solely on the generic provision of sustainability insofar as it pertains to environmental democracy.

In the Trade Agreement between the European Union and Colombia and Peru (2012), respect for democracy, the rule of law, and fundamental rights is considered a fundamental element. Furthermore, beyond standard provisions related to sustainable development, the agreement recognizes the importance of scientific information (art. 278), dialogue with society (art. 282), and obligations to prevent corruption.

The EU-Central America Association Agreement (2012) explicitly refers to democracy multiple times, linking it to citizen security (Article 21), the promotion of human rights (Article 29), and good governance, requiring joint efforts to "promote transparent, accountable, efficient, stable, and democratic institutions" (Article 30). It also emphasizes anti-corruption measures (Article 38). Furthermore, the agreement considers democracy in its material sense when the parties agree on the importance of reinforcing efforts to reduce poverty (Article 23), protect and promote the rights of indigenous peoples (Article 45), cooperate in favor of vulnerable groups (Article 46), and strengthen policies, programs, and mechanisms to ensure, promote, and expand equal participation and opportunities for men and women (Article 47). The agreement with Central America provides for the establishment of a bi-regional forum for dialogue with civil society (art. 295), where economic, social, and environmental interests are represented in a balanced manner. This forum also meets annually and aims to promote dialogue on how cooperation can contribute to sustainable development. Transparency is ensured by allowing the forum to express views and recommendations on the objectives of the agreement.

The Comprehensive Economic and Trade Agreement (CETA) between the EU and Canada (2016) recognizes "the importance of democracy, human rights, and the rule of law for the development of international trade and economic cooperation." Beyond transparency requirements, multiple provisions emphasize the significance of public consultation and civil society participation, including references to a dedicated forum (Article 22.5), which includes representatives from independent organizations such as employers, trade unions, and environmental groups. The agreement emphasizes balanced representation, and participation can occur through virtual means, increasing accessibility and transparency.

The Free Trade Agreement between the European Union and the Republic of Singapore (2018) does not explicitly mention democracy. However, it includes provisions on anti-corruption measures, good administrative behavior civil society engagement (Chapter 13, Article 13.7).

The Agreement between the European Union and Japan for an Economic Partnership (2018), despite not directly referencing democracy, includes obligations related to sustainability, to decisions based on scientific truths and civil society participation (Article 16.16), ensuring a balanced representation of economic, environmental, and social stakeholders. This dialogue is held regularly, and opinions can be published, promoting transparency.

The Trade and Cooperation Agreement between the European Union and the European Atomic Energy Community and the United Kingdom of Great Britain and

Northern Ireland (2021) expressly mentions democracy in the preamble and in three articles (arts. 524, 525, 763). Furthermore, it refers to obligations to gender equality (art. 399), decisions based on scientific truths and dialogue with civil society with the provision of a specific forum (arts. 12 to 14), with broad representation, including NGOs, trade unions, and employers. Meetings are held at least once a year and can take place virtually, ensuring transparency and accessibility.

The Economic Partnership Agreement between the European Union and the Republic of Kenya (2023) also does not explicitly mention democracy but underscores commitments to substantive equality and the role of civil society in governance. Its emphasis on the egalitarian dimension of democracy is evident when the parties recognize that inclusive trade policies contribute to advancing women's economic empowerment and gender equality.

In the Interim Agreement on trade between the European Union and the Republic of Chile, the democratic principle is expressly referred to. As in the Economic Agreement with Kenya, the egalitarian dimension of democracy is highlighted when parties "agree on the importance of incorporating a gender perspective into the promotion of inclusive economic growth, and on the key role that gender-responsive policies can play in that regard" (art. 27). There is also recognition of the need for decisions based on scientific evidence and dialogue with civil society, including references to a dedicated forum for civil society (Article 33.7). The need for measures to prevent corrupt practices is also mentioned. (art. 21.4).

In the Free Trade Agreement between the European Union and New Zealand (2023) similarly omits direct references to democracy but, like CETA, contains multiple provisions emphasizing the role of civil society in monitoring the agreement's implementation. It also establishes a dedicated civil society forum (Article 24.7). This forum emphasizes the balanced participation of NGOs, businesses, and trade unions, in addition to explicitly including minority groups such as the Māori. Furthermore, the material and egalitarian aspect of democracy is highlighted when the Parties recognize the need to advance gender equality and women's economic empowerment (art. 19.4).

It is particularly noteworthy how certain legal expressions are more or less prominent in different agreements, as already mentioned above when referring to predictions about sustainable development and civil society participation. For instance, in the agreements with Canada and New Zealand, civil society participation is frequently referenced as a procedural requirement for the contracting parties.

Given the scope of trade agreements signed by the European Union, affecting a large geographical area and involving a significant volume of transactions, it can be argued that, although these are agreements between specific parties, they ultimately influence global governance, especially regarding environmental protection[32] and the promotion of environmental democracy.

---

[32] Pasquali (2020), pp. 197–198.

Ultimately, despite these nuanced variations, it is evident that trade agreements with the European Union, regardless of their specific wording, lead to commitments that align with the expected characteristics of a democratic regime, especially considering the concept of environmental democracy. This, in turn, contributes to the broader and collective promotion of democratic governance.

5 Persistent Challenges and the Value of Democracy Beyond Domestic Relations

As discussed in previous chapters, the definition of democracy remains complex.[33] Moreover, its link to self-determination has led some nations to demand more direct public participation in state decision-making—even in foreign policy, raising concerns about the imposition of a Global North model on the Global South.[34] Some scholars argue that standardizing political behavior through international law enables Northern countries to impose their will on the Global South, thereby shaping economic, social, and political expectations in ways that create global governance asymmetries.

Another challenge relates to the promotion of democracy itself with its provisions in international treaties or trade agreements is that the mere provision of democratic clauses can be difficult to implement and can end up leading countries with democratic challenges to disadvantageous situations.

Three questions arise: 1. How to impose demographic criteria in international relations given the multiplicity of meanings of the word democracy? 2. Are regional and international organizations justified in using democracy as a criterion for economic agreements, diplomatic recognition, or political intervention? 3. Do these provisions (whether in international treaties or in trade agreements) have practical effectiveness in promoting democracy?

Rather than dismissing efforts to promote democracy, it is essential to critically evaluate how these commitments are implemented so as not to reinforce existing inequalities.

Given the semantic challenges of defining democracy, a procedural approach is arguably effective means for its international institutionalization. Nonetheless, substantive dimensions remain crucial. Without robust procedures, mere access to material benefits fails to secure genuine public participation or effective control over state power. This view aligns with Amartya Sen's reflections on the intrinsic, instrumental, and constructive values of democracy[35]: (a) Intrinsic value: Fostering

[33] In 2021, for example, the Chinese government, through its State Council, published a white paper entitled "China: Democracy That Works" in which it defends the Chinese political regime model, with just one party, as a democracy that effectively gives more power to its people. The State Council Information Office of the People's Republic of China (2021).

[34] Tonetto et al. (2023), pp. 10–11.

[35] Sen (2000), pp. 10–11.

civic engagement and a sense of belonging; (b) Instrumental value: Ensuring citizens' voices are heard and governments remain accountable; (c) Constructive value: Enabling societies to evolve in response to their unique needs.

These observations demonstrate how a procedural framework for democracy can serve as an inclusive governance model rather than as a rigid imposition of one system over another. Legal certainty in international relations requires a clear definition of democratic criteria. Contributions from legal scholars, international organizations, and regional institutions are vital. For example, Robert Dahl—in both Polyarchy (1971)[36] and On Democracy (1998)[37] —has identified key characteristics of democratic governance, a view corroborated by indices such as V-Dem, the Democracy Index, Freedom House, and International IDEA.

Although the European Union does not explicitly define democracy in its treaties, its institutional practices and legal decisions establish implicit benchmarks. Following the Arab Spring, the EU's "deep democracy" study identified core components—free and fair elections; freedoms of association, expression, and assembly; an independent press; judicial independence; anti-corruption measures; security sector reform; and democratic oversight—that closely align with the Inter-American Democratic Charter (2001) and the African Charter on Democracy, Elections, and Governance (2007). In the current trade agreements signed by the European Union, prevails the concern with the promotion of sustainable development in its three dimensions, in an attempt to use trade agreements to promote democracy in a material and formal sense (considering the sense of participatory environmental democracy).

Trade agreements that include clauses referring to the democratic principle represent a significant pathway for promoting democracy in international relations, as exemplified by the European Union. On the one hand, they respect the autonomy of nations, stemming from a voluntary commitment to measures that all contracting parties freely agree to implement. On the other, they address the semantic multiplicity of "democracy" by specifying concrete measures, such as the commitment to sustainable development (in its three dimensions), the engagement with civil society (which typically advances environmental democracy), the right to objective information (based on scientific data), or the fight against corruption.

6 Concluding Remarks

Although, in respect for the principle of self-determination of peoples and the semantic difficulty of conceptualizing it, the democratic regime is not unanimously acclaimed as a universal value in international norms and international relations, an international commitment to its promotion is essential. This is because democracy

[36] Dahl (1998), pp. 55–58.

[37] Dahl (1971), pp. 13–14.

is the most suitable regime for the protection and promotion of fundamental rights in all their dimensions. As social relations become more complex and transnational, international democratic commitments become increasingly urgent. For regional organizations like the European Union, democracy serves not only as a criterion for diplomatic and economic relations but also as a membership requirement; however, such conditionality must be applied uniformly to avoid reinforcing global asymmetries.

In today's interconnected and polarized world—where disinformation abounds—the promotion of democracy is both a strategic necessity and a means to safeguard domestic governance. This normative push can be described as a "fifth democratic wave" or as a counter-reaction to recent backsliding. The consolidation of democracy in international relations is evident in its explicit inclusion in regional charters (e.g., the EU's Copenhagen Criteria, the Inter-American Democratic Charter, and the African Charter on Democracy), its integration into foreign policy tools like sanctions and diplomatic engagements, and the use of democratic clauses in trade agreements. Trade agreements cannot be considered separately when analyzing the promotion of European values, because they are part of a context of multiple normative and practical, political and economic actions to try to promote democracy.

Furthermore, democratic nations—and particularly those in regional blocs championing democracy—must avoid "democratic ambiguity." This ambiguity arises when states advocate for democratic governance but fail to uphold it domestically (a criticism sometimes directed at the EU),[38] or when democratic standards are applied selectively to justify disparities between developed and developing countries. Effective global promotion of democracy requires coherent legal and institutional measures—a concept referred to as "transdemocracy" by Professor Marcelo Neves[39]—and a clear framework to define a democratic state. In trade agreements, given geopolitical variations, different aspects of democracy can be more or less intensified, but some standards need to be established. The new generation trade agreements arrived in a context where other international efforts are being made by the European Union. Despite the challenges they present, their importance is notable. The relational structure they propose is often innovative and contributes, at least as a proposed model, to better governance.

It is true that the prediction of democracy in norms of International Law and in international trade agreements will not necessarily lead to its implementation, or its realization, but such prediction is relevant insofar as it is a recognition that each nation alone will not be able to promote democracy in all its dimensions, especially in the face of the challenges brought by transnational relations. The implementation of clauses on democracy requires monitoring, but it first involves recognizing their normative importance, and the collaborative effort that it requires.

---

[38] One of the criticisms directed at the European Union, for example, is regarding the power of initiative in the legislative process by the European Commission to the detriment of the European Parliament. Francesca Martines, however, analyzes the topic from another perspective. (Martines, 2017), pp. 155–156.

[39] Neves (2017), pp. 386–388.

Despite the costs, the benefits of democracy—full human emancipation, individual and collective development, and the prevention of authoritarian rule—underscore the imperative to sustain efforts to preserve and advance democratic governance.

References

Beck U (1992) Risk society: towards a new modernity. Sage, London and New York

Bobbio N (2018) Liberalismo e democrazia. Simonelli Editore, Lombardia

Dahl R (1971) Polyarchy: participation and opposition. Yale University Press, New Haven

Dahl RA (1998) On democracy. Yale University Press, New Haven. https://doi.org/10.2307/j.ctv18zhcs4

Field TC Jr (2014) From development to dictatorship: Bolivia and the Alliance for Progress in the Kennedy era. Cornell University Press, Ithaca, NY, and London

Fox GH, Roth BR (2001) Democracy and international law. Rev Int Stud 27(3):327–352. https://doi.org/10.1017/S0260210501003278

Girard G (2015) Disillusionment in action: the origins and outcomes of US solidarity with Chilean refugees. Ezra's Arch 5(1)

Goyard-Fabre S (1998) Qu'est-ce que la démocratie? La généalogie philosophique d'une grande aventure humaine. Armand Colin, Paris

Held D (1991) Democracy, the nation-state and the global system. Econ Soc 20(2):138–172. https://doi.org/10.1080/03085149100000007

Hodges DC (1965) Political democracy: its informal content. Am J Econ Sociol 24(1):9–20

Huntington S (1993) The third wave: democratization in the late 20th century, vol 4. Univ of Oklahoma Press, Oklahoma

Kant I (1991) Perpetual peace: a philosophical sketch. In: Reiss HS (ed) Nisbet HB (trans) Kant: political writings: Cambridge texts in the history of political thought. Cambridge University Press, Cambridge, pp 93–130

Lehfeld LS (2024) A legitimidade de regimes autocráticos com base na autodeterminação dos povos frente aos princípios defendidos pelos direitos humanos. Available via https://www.diritto.it/a-legitimidade-de-regimes-autocraticos-com-base-na-autodeterminacao-dos-povos-frente-aos-principios-defendidos-pelos-direitos-humanos/. Accessed 19 Jan 2025

Maillo J (2021) Acuerdos comerciales UE de "nueva generación": origen, rasgos y valoración. Documento de Trabajo n 110/2021, Serie Unión Europea y Relaciones Internacionales. Real Instituto Universitario de Estudios Europeos, Universidad CEU San Pablo, Madrid

Malová D, Dolný B (2008) The eastern enlargement of the European Union: challenges to democracy? Hum Aff 18(1):67–80. https://doi.org/10.2478/v10023-008-0006-4

Martines F (2017) Institutional balance, democracy and agenda setting in the European Union. https://doi.org/10.1007/978-3-319-53895-2_7

McFaul M (2002) The fourth wave of democracy and dictatorship: noncooperative transitions in the postcommunist world. World Polit 54(2):212–244. https://doi.org/10.1353/wp.2002.0004

Monnet J (1978) Memorie. Collins, London, chap 5, II. Available via https://archive.org/stream/MonnetJeanMemoirs/Monnet%2C%20Jean%20-%20Memoirs_djvu.txt

Mustafa Z (1971) The principle of self-determination in international law. Int Law 5(3):479–487. http://www.jstor.org/stable/40704674. Accessed 24 Jan 2024

Neves M (2017) From transconstitutionalism to transdemocracy. Eur Law J 23:380–394

Pasquali L (2020) Environmental protection in the EU-Mercosur agreement and its legal enforceability. Rev Nomus 40(2):179–200

Pasquali L (2023) La contribución del acuerdo Unión Europea-México a la gobernanza medioambiental internacional. Available via https://www.eld.edu.mx/Pisa/8-

UNIFORMACION-INTERNACIONALIZACION-Y-REGIONALISMO-EN-EL-DERECHO/Capitulos/8-La-contribucion-del-acuerdo-Union-Europea-Mexico-a-la-gobernanza-medioambiental-internacional.pdf. Accessed 21 Feb 2025

Pereira AW (2018) The US role in the 1964 coup in Brazil: a reassessment. In: Special issue: reflections on repression and resistance: the vivid legacies of dictatorship in Brazil, vol 37(1), pp 5–17

Petzina D, Stolper WF, Hudson M (1981) The origin of the European coal and steel community: economic forces and political interests. Z Gesamte Staatswiss J Inst Theor Econ 137(3):450–468. http://www.jstor.org/stable/40750370

Polybius (1986) Selección de historias. Akal, Madrid, VI

Roosevelt FD (1941) Fireside chat on the "great arsenal of democracy." In: Rosenman SI (ed) The public papers and addresses of Franklin D. Roosevelt, 1940. Macmillan, New York, pp 633–644. Also available via https://web.mit.edu/21h.102/www/Primary%20source%20collections/World%20War%20II/FDR,%20Arsenal%20of%20Democracy.html. The speech can also be accessed in audio on YouTube. Miller Center, University of Virginia. MCamericanpresident: A collection of presidential speeches, addresses and photos, all for public consumption. Available via https://www.youtube.com/watch?v=G7BKvlobfBY

Ryder J (2008) Prospects for a thick democracy. AMERICANA E-J Am Stud Hung 4(1). https://www.analecta.hu/index.php/americanaejournal/article/view/45352

Sen A (2000) Democracy as a universal value. Am Educ 10. https://doi.org/10.1353/jod.1999.0055

The State Council Information Office of the People's Republic of China (2021) China: democracy that works. Available via https://english.www.gov.cn/archive/whitepaper/202112/04/content_WS61aae34fc6d0df57f98e6098.html. Accessed 10 Jan 2025

Tonetto AP, Cofferri HA, Tonetto FF (2023) O direito internacional do norte enquanto ferramenta biopolítica de enfraquecimento da democracia representativa no sul global. Inter Rev Dir Int Dir Hum UFRJ 6(1):6–20

UNESCO (1951) Democracy in a world of tensions: a symposium prepared by UNESCO. In: McKeon RP, Rokkan S (eds). UNESCO, Paris. Available via https://unesdoc.unesco.org/ark:/48223/pf0000133513. Accessed 19 Jan 2025

Zurcher AJ (1935) The Hitler referenda. Am Polit Sci Rev 29(1):91–99. Available via https://www.jstor.org/stable/1947171. https://doi.org/10.2307/1947171

Peace and Security

Matteo Del Chicca

Contents

Abstract This chapter examines how some international agreements concluded by European Union with third Parties uphold and promote peace and security European Union values. Such agreements often include certain quite identical provisions—such as a particular "security exception" and some "denials of benefits"—which could be considered also as means to sustain and foster peace and security. Additionally, some of such agreements comprise a few specific contents aimed at

Data in this chapter are updated to February 2025.

M. Del Chicca (✉)
Department of Law, University of Pisa, Pisa, Italy

L. Pasquali (ed.), *EU Values and International Law*, European Union and its Neighbours in a Globalized World 35,
https://doi.org/10.1007/978-3-032-20521-6_6

the same purposes too. Furthermore, this chapter surveys the role played by European Union military and civilian missions and operations in supporting and promoting peace and security European Union values.

1 Introduction

Peace and security are important elements of the Treaty of the European Union. The Preamble of the Treaty of the European Union states that European Union (hereafter: 'EU') is "resolved to implement a common foreign and security policy including the progressive framing of a common defence policy, which might lead to a common defence in accordance with the provisions of Article 42, thereby reinforcing the European identity and its independence in order to promote peace, security and progress in Europe and in the world".[1]

Moreover, it must be reminded that Article 3 of the Treaty of the EU lists all the objectives of the EU and that Paragraph 1 of such Article states that "The Union's aim is to promote peace, its values and the well-being of its peoples"; additionally, Paragraph 5 of Article 3 affirms that EU shall contribute, among other things, to peace and security.

Such objectives are more specifically enforced in the Title V of the Treaty of the EU (hereafter: 'TEU'), related to the "General Provisions on the Union's External Action and Specific Provisions on the Common Foreign and Security Policy": indeed, the first Article of such Title (i.e., Article 21) *inter alia* declares that "The Union shall define and pursue common policies and actions, and shall work for a high degree of cooperation in all fields of international relations, in order to [...] preserve peace, prevent conflicts and strengthen international security, in accordance with the purposes and principles of the United Nations Charter, with the principles of the Helsinki Final Act and with the aims of the Charter of Paris, including those relating to external borders" (Article 21, Paragraph 2, Letter C). As indicated by Article 22, the strategic interests and objectives of the EU on this matter are identified by the European Council[2]: after all this part of TEU is related to the

[1] It must be mentioned that even the Preamble of the Treaty on the Functioning of the European Union refers to peace: "Resolved by thus pooling their resources to preserve and strengthen peace and liberty, and calling upon the other peoples of Europe who share their ideal to join in their efforts".

[2] Article 22 TEU states that "1. On the basis of the principles and objectives set out in Article 21, the European Council shall identify the strategic interests and objectives of the Union. Decisions of the European Council on the strategic interests and objectives of the Union shall relate to the common foreign and security policy and to other areas of the external action of the Union. Such decisions may concern the relations of the Union with a specific country or region or may be thematic in approach. They shall define their duration, and the means to be made available by the Union and the Member States. The European Council shall act unanimously on a recommendation from the Council, adopted by the latter under the arrangements laid down for each area. Decisions

foreign policy of EU, and foreign policy is traditionally considered by States one of their prerogatives. This is one of the main reasons because Member States—through European Council and, as we will see later, the Council[3]—want to be in charge on this crucial topic.[4]

The general provisions of Articles 21 and 22 are implemented by all the specific norms on the common foreign and security policy included in Chap. 2 of Title V of TEU (Articles 23–46). A part of such specific provisions is mainly dedicated to a mutual defence policy between Member States, but there are also some norms which highlight how the EU may uphold and promote peace and security in wider world. On this regard, it should be particularly underlined what stated at Article 42, Paragraph 1, of TEU: "The common security and defence policy shall be an integral part of the common foreign and security policy. It shall provide the Union with an operational capacity drawing on civilian and military assets. *The Union may use them on missions outside the Union for peace-keeping, conflict prevention and strengthening international security* in accordance with the principles of the United Nations Charter. The performance of these tasks shall be undertaken using capabilities provided by the Member States" (italics added). Article 43 of TEU specifies that "The tasks referred to in Article 42(1), in the course of which the Union may use civilian and military means, shall include joint disarmament operations, humanitarian and rescue tasks, military advice and assistance tasks, conflict prevention and peace-keeping tasks, tasks of combat forces in crisis management, including peace-making and post-conflict stabilisation".

Since such EU missions and operations represent means of greatest significance in order to sustain and foster EU peace and security values, they will be examined in this chapter after taking into consideration how some international agreements concluded by EU with third Parties follow such purpose.

2 Peace and Security in International Agreements Concluded by EU with Third Parties

The international agreements concluded with third Parties are essential instruments of the EU to sustain and disseminate its peace and security values.

Such agreements often encompass certain quite identical provisions related to international peace and security: those provisions will be therefore first surveyed in

---

of the European Council shall be implemented in accordance with the procedures provided for in the Treaties. 2. The High Representative of the Union for Foreign Affairs and Security Policy, for the area of common foreign and security policy, and the Commission, for other areas of external action, may submit joint proposals to the Council".

[3] *Infra* par. 3.

[4] For the same reason, EU Parliament has a limited role on this matter: see, for examples, Articles 27, 36, 41 of TEU.

this paragraph, before considering a few specific contents of some agreements concluded by EU with third Parties.

2.1 A "Security Exception"

One of such quite identical provisions is a particular "security exception", which states that nothing in the agreement shall be construed to prevent either Party from taking any action for the purpose of maintaining international peace and security.

Such provision is included in almost all the international agreements concluded by EU with third Parties, even if the wording is sometimes slightly different from one agreement to another. For example, in many agreements such security exception more specifically states that nothing in the agreement shall be construed to prevent a Party "from taking any action *in pursuance of its obligations under the Charter of the United Nations* for the maintenance of international peace and security" (italics added).[5] In other agreements the wording of such security exception is more generic instead, stating that nothing in the agreement shall be construed to prevent any Party "from taking any measures necessary *in pursuance of the obligations it has accepted* for the purpose of maintaining or restoring international peace and security" (italics added).[6]

The different wordings could be dictated by disparate reasons, including the diverse periods of conclusion of such agreements. The more generic wordings of this security exception are, in fact, mainly embedded in the international

[5] In: Free Trade Agreement between the European Union and New Zealand, OJ L 2024/866, 25.3.2024, at Article 25.2, Letter c. An identical—or very similar—provision is included also in many other agreements; see, for example: Agreement between the European Union and Japan for an Economic Partnership, OJ L 330, 27.12.2018, Article 1.5, Paragraph 1, Letter c; Free Trade Agreement Between the European Union and the Socialist Republic of Viet Nam, OJ L 186, 12.6.2020, Article 17.13, Letter c; Trade and Cooperation Agreement between the European Union and the European Atomic Energy Community, of the one part, and the United Kingdom of Great Britain and Northern Ireland, of the other part, OJ L 149, 30.04.2021, Article 415, Letter c; Economic Partnership Agreement between the European Union, of the one Part, and the Republic of Kenya, Member of The East African Community, of the other Part, OJ L 2024/1648, 1.7.2024, Article 129, Paragraph 1, Letter c; Interim Agreement on Trade between the European Union and the Republic of Chile, OJ L 2024/2953, 20.12.2024, Article 32.2, Paragraph 1, Letter c.

[6] In: Trade Agreement between the European Union and its Member States, of the one part, and Colombia and Peru, of the other part, OJ L 354, 21.12.2012, at Article 295, Paragraph 1, Letter c. A provision with selfsame—or almost identical—wording is included also in several other agreements; see, for example: Free Trade Agreement between the European Union and its Member States, of the one part, and the Republic of Korea, of the other part, OJ L 127, 14.5.2011, Article 15.9, Letter c; Agreement establishing an Association between the EU and its Member States, on the one hand, and Central America on the other, OJ L 346, 15.12.2012, Article 357, Paragraph 1, Letter c; Comprehensive Economic and Trade Agreement (CETA) between Canada, of the one part, and the European Union and its Member States, of the other part, OJ L 11, 14.1.2017, Article 28.6, Letter c; Free Trade Agreement between the European Union and the Republic of Singapore, OJ L 294, 14.11.2019, Article 16.11, Letter c.

agreements less recently concluded[7]; the specific reference to the Charter of the United Nations is instead usually inserted in the agreements more recently concluded.[8]

Despite the variants of the wording, this security exception is clearly a provision that EU wished to incorporate in its international agreements with third Parties and it represents an evident EU way of upholding and promoting its peace and security values.

2.2 *The "Denials of Benefits"*

Other typical provisions in support of peace and security—often included in the international agreements signed by EU with third States—are particular "denials of benefits". They are for example inserted in many recent EU agreements, such as the Interim Agreement on Trade between the EU and the Republic of Chile, the Free Trade Agreement between the EU and New Zealand, the Trade and Cooperation Agreement between the EU and the European Atomic Energy Community, of the one part, and the United Kingdom of Great Britain and Northern Ireland, of the other part (hereafter: 'the Trade and Cooperation Agreement between the EU and UK'), the Agreement between the EU and Japan for an Economic Partnership[9] and the Comprehensive Economic and Trade Agreement between Canada and the EU and its Member States.[10]

Such provisions usually state that a Party may deny the benefits of determined Parts of the agreement—typically related to cross-border trade in services and investment—to an investor or service supplier of the other Party or to a covered enterprise if the denying Party adopts or maintains measures related to the maintenance of international peace and security which prohibit transactions with that investor, security supplier or covered enterprise, or would be violated or circumvented if the benefits of that Parts were accorded to that investor, security supplier or covered enterprise, including where the measures prohibit transactions with a natural or juridical person who owns or controls the investor, the security supplier or the covered enterprise.[11]

---

[7] *Ibidem.*

[8] *Supra* footnote 5.

[9] *Ibidem.*

[10] *Supra* footnote 6.

[11] More precisely, Article 10.12 of the Interim Agreement on Trade between the EU and the Republic of Chile states what follows: "A Party may deny to an investor of the other Party or a covered enterprise the benefits of this Chapter if the denying Party adopts or maintains measures related to the maintenance of international peace and security, including the protection of human rights, which: (a) prohibit transactions with that investor or covered enterprise; or (b) would be violated or circumvented if the benefits of this Chapter were accorded to that investor or covered enterprise, including if the measures prohibit transactions with a person who owns or controls

As noted also about the security exception above, even the contents of such denials of benefits sometimes are slightly different from one agreement to another.

For example, in the Trade and Cooperation Agreement between the EU and UK the denials of benefits are related not only to cross-border trade in services and investment, but also to capital movements, payments, transfers and temporary safeguard measures.[12] Such kinds of differences are mainly dictated by the specific context and contents of the trade agreement: the Trade and Cooperation Agreement between the EU and UK now mentioned, for example, was elaborated to regulate trade between EU and UK after the withdrawal of the UK from the EU.

Another difference is that, in the less recent agreements which include such denials of benefits, the provisions specifically refer to a third State: for example, such specification is stated in the Agreement between the EU and Japan for an Economic

---

either of them". Additionally, Article 11.9 of the same agreement states that "A Party may deny a service supplier of the other Party the benefits of this Chapter if the denying Party adopts or maintains measures related to the maintenance of international peace and security, including the protection of human rights, which: (a) prohibit transactions with that service supplier, or with a person who owns or controls that service supplier; or (b) would be violated or circumvented if the benefits of this Chapter were accorded to that service supplier".

Article 10.12 of the Free Trade Agreement between the EU and New Zealand is quite identical to Article 10.12 of the Interim Agreement on Trade between the EU and the Republic of Chile, stating that "A Party may deny the benefits of this Section to an investor of the other Party or to a covered enterprise if the denying Party adopts or maintains measures related to the maintenance of international peace and security, including the protection of human rights, which: (a) prohibit transactions with that investor or covered enterprise; or (b) would be violated or circumvented if the benefits of this Section were accorded to that investor or covered enterprise, including where the measures prohibit transactions with a natural or juridical person who owns or controls the investor or the covered enterprise". Analogously, Article 10.19 of the Free Trade Agreement between the EU and New Zealand is quite identical to Article 11.9 of the Interim Agreement on Trade between the EU and the Republic of Chile, stating that "A Party may deny the benefits of this Section to a service supplier of the other Party if the denying Party adopts or maintains measures related to the maintenance of international peace and security, including the protection of human rights, which: (a) prohibit transactions with that service supplier; or (b) would be violated or circumvented if the benefits of this Section were accorded to that service supplier, including where the measures prohibit transactions with a natural or juridical person who owns or controls that service supplier".

[12] Article 125 of the Trade and Cooperation Agreement between the EU and UK states what follows: "1. A Party may deny the benefits of this Title and Title IV of this Heading to an investor or service supplier of the other Party, or to a covered enterprise, if the denying Party adopts or maintains measures related to the maintenance of international peace and security, including the protection of human rights, which: (a) prohibit transactions with that investor, service supplier or covered enterprise; or (b) would be violated or circumvented if the benefits of this Title and Title IV of this Heading were accorded to that investor, service supplier or covered enterprise, including where the measures prohibit transactions with a natural or legal person which owns or controls any of them. 2. For greater certainty, paragraph 1 is applicable to Title IV of this Heading to the extent that it relates to services or investment with respect to which a Party has denied the benefits of this Title".

Partnership,[13] as well as in the Comprehensive Economic and Trade Agreement between Canada and the EU and its Member States.[14]

Notwithstanding such variations it is evident that the EU wished to embed such denials of benefits in many international agreements with third Parties, because these provisions are also modes to sustain and stimulate its peace and security values.

2.3 Specific Contents Aimed to Uphold and Promote Peace and Security in Some International Agreements Concluded by EU with Third Parties

Some international agreements concluded by EU with third Parties include specific contents aimed to support and foster EU peace and security values.

For example, the Agreement establishing an Association between the EU and its Member States, on the one hand, and Central America on the other (hereafter: 'Association Agreement between EU and Central America') is based on political

[13] Article 8.13 of the Agreement between the EU and Japan for an Economic Partnership states that "A Party may deny the benefits of this Section to an entrepreneur of the other Party that is a juridical person of the other Party and to its covered enterprise if that juridical person is owned or controlled by a natural or juridical person of a third country and the denying Party adopts or maintains measures with respect to the third country that (a) are related to the maintenance of international peace and security, including the protection of human rights; and (b) prohibit transactions with that juridical person or its covered enterprise, or would be violated or circumvented if the benefits of this Section were accorded to them". Article 8.19 of the same agreement states that "A Party may deny the benefits of this Section to a service supplier of the other Party that is a juridical person of the other Party and to services of that service supplier if that juridical person is owned or controlled by a natural or juridical person of a third country and the denying Party adopts or maintains measures with respect to the third country that: (a) are related to the maintenance of international peace and security, including the protection of human rights; and (b) prohibit transactions with the service supplier, or would be violated or circumvented if the benefits of this Section were accorded to the service supplier or to its services".

[14] Article 8.16 of the Comprehensive Economic and Trade Agreement between Canada and the EU and its Member States affirms that "A Party may deny the benefits of this Chapter to an investor of the other Party that is an enterprise of that Party and to investments of that investor if: (a) an investor of a third country owns or controls the enterprise; and (b) the denying Party adopts or maintains a measure with respect to the third country that: (i) relates to the maintenance of international peace and security; and (ii) prohibits transactions with the enterprise or would be violated or circumvented if the benefits of this Chapter were accorded to the enterprise or to its investments". Article 9.8 of the same agreement states that "A Party may deny the benefits of this Chapter to a service supplier of the other Party that is an enterprise of that Party and to services of that service supplier if: (a) a service supplier of a third country owns or controls the enterprise; and (b) the denying Party adopts or maintains a measure with respect to the third country that: (i) relates to maintenance of international peace and security; and (ii) prohibits transactions with the enterprise or would be violated or circumvented if the benefits of this Chapter were accorded to the enterprise".

dialogue, cooperation and trade between Parties,[15] and such political dialogue is aimed to "establish a privileged political partnership based notably on *the respect for and the promotion of* democracy, *peace*, human rights, the rule of law, good governance and sustainable development" (italics added).[16] Analogously, with regard to cooperation, such agreement expressly states that priority shall be *inter alia* given to the following objective: "strengthening peace and security".[17] Furthermore, in the field of cooperation particularly set to "achieve full compliance with all human rights and fundamental freedoms, [...] as well as the building and strengthening of democracy", the Association Agreement between EU and Central America affirms that it could involve also "awareness raising and education in human rights, democracy and *culture of peace*" (italics added).[18] Moreover, Article 32 of such agreement, titled "Conflict Prevention and Resolution", states that "cooperation in this field *shall promote and sustain a comprehensive peace policy*" and that such cooperation "shall strengthen capacities to resolve conflicts and may include, among others, the provision of *support to* [...] *strategies promoting peace*" (italics added).[19]

---

[15] Article 2 of the Association Agreement between EU and Central America *inter alia* states that "The Parties agree that the objectives of this Agreement are to: (a) strengthen and consolidate the relations between the Parties through an association based on three interdependent and fundamental parts: political dialogue, cooperation and trade, based on mutual respect, reciprocity and common interest [....]".

[16] Article 12, Letter a, of the Association Agreement between EU and Central America states what follows: "The Parties agree that the objectives of the political dialogue between the Republics of the CA Party and the EU Party are to: (a) establish a privileged political partnership based notably on the respect for and the promotion of democracy, peace, human rights, the rule of law, good governance and sustainable development".

[17] Article 24, Paragraphs 1, 2 Letter a, of the Association Agreement between EU and Central America states what follows: "1. The general objective of cooperation is to support the implementation of this Agreement in order to reach an effective partnership between the two regions by facilitating resources, mechanisms, tools and procedures. 2. Priority shall be given to the following objectives, which are further developed in Titles I to IX of this Part: (a) strengthening peace and security".

[18] See Article 29, Paragraphs 1, 2 Letter c, *ibidem*.

[19] Article 32 of the Association Agreement between EU and Central America states what follows: "1. The Parties agree that cooperation in this field shall promote and sustain a comprehensive peace policy, including the prevention and resolution of conflicts. This policy shall be based on the principle of commitment and participation of society and shall focus primarily on developing regional, subregional and national capacities. It shall ensure equal political, economic, social and cultural opportunities for all segments of society, reinforce democratic legitimacy, promote social

cohesion and an effective mechanism for peaceful conciliation of the interests of different groups, and encourage an active and organised civil society, in particular making use of existing regional institutions. 2. Cooperation shall strengthen capacities to resolve conflicts and may include, among others, the provision of support to mediation, negotiation and reconciliation processes; to strategies

promoting peace; to efforts to strengthen confidence and security building on the regional level; to efforts developed to help children, women and elderly people and to actions in the fight against anti-personnel mines".

Additionally, in such agreement the Parties "consider that the establishment and effective functioning of the International Criminal Court constitutes an important development for international peace and justice".[20] It could be also pointed out that the Parties of the Association Agreement between EU and Central America "agree to cooperate in fighting the illicit trade and excessive accumulation of small arms and light weapons, including their ammunition" explicitly because such crimes "continue to pose a serious threat to peace and international security".[21]

On this regard, it could be recalled that also the Trade and Cooperation Agreement between the EU and UK comprises similar norms about small arms and light weapons, for the same purposes.[22] In addition, the Parties of such agreement "recognise the importance of domestic control systems for the transfer of conventional arms in line with existing international standards", and "the importance of applying such controls in a responsible manner, as a contribution to international and regional peace, security and stability".[23] Beyond what detailed until now,[24] peace is in general a diffused value in the Trade and Cooperation Agreement between the EU and UK: for example, in its Preamble, where the Parties express their desire "to promote the peaceful use of the waters adjacent to their coasts"[25]; especially in the Article 1, which sets out as purpose of the agreement the establishment of "the basis for a broad relationship between the Parties, within an area of prosperity and good neighbourliness characterised by close and peaceful relations"[26]; and in the cooperation on cyber issues, "aimed at promoting and protecting an open, free, stable, peaceful and secure cyberspace"[27]; and even in the Parties endeavors "to cooperate on current and emerging global issues of common interest such as peace and security".[28]

Lastly, it could be noted that such agreement comprises also some norms about the fulfillment of obligations described as essential elements[29]: in this respect, "the Parties consider that, for a situation to constitute a serious and substantial failure to fulfil any of the obligations described as essential elements in Article 771, its gravity and nature would have to be of an exceptional sort that threatens peace and

[20] In: Article 17, Paragraph 2, *ibidem*.

[21] Article 14, Paragraph 3, of the Association Agreement between EU and Central America states that "The Parties furthermore recognise that the illicit manufacture, transfer and circulation of small arms and light weapons, including their ammunition, and their excessive accumulation and uncontrolled spread continue to pose a serious threat to peace and international security. They therefore agree to cooperate in fighting the illicit trade and excessive accumulation of small arms and light weapons, including their ammunition, and also agree to work jointly to regulate the licit trade of conventional arms".

[22] See Article 766 of the Trade and Cooperation Agreement between the EU and UK.

[23] *Ibidem*, Paragraph 3.

[24] See also *supra* parr. 2.1 and 2.2.

[25] In: Preamble of the Trade and Cooperation Agreement between the EU and UK, 18.

[26] In: Trade and Cooperation Agreement between the EU and UK, Article 1.

[27] *Ibidem*, Article 704.

[28] *Ibidem*, Article 770.

[29] *Ibidem*, Article 772.

security".[30] Similar provisions are included in the Free Trade Agreement between the EU and New Zealand too.[31]

3 EU Missions and Operations as Means to Uphold and Promote Peace and Security Values in Wider World

On the legal bases surveyed above in Paragraph 1, the EU launched a large number of missions and operations abroad over the years, also in order to sustain and foster peace and security in wider world. Such missions and operations could be of different types: military missions, military operations, and civilian missions[32] will be taken into consideration for the purposes of this chapter.

Under Article 31, Paragraph 1, of TEU, the decision to establish such missions or operations "shall be taken by the European Council and the Council acting unanimously" (except where Chap. 2 provides otherwise), and such decision requires unanimity in the Council (even if the same Article 31 envisages also some ways for the Council to decide by qualified majority vote).[33]

---

[30] *Ibidem*, Article 772, Paragraph 4.

[31] See Article 27.4 of the Free Trade Agreement between the EU and New Zealand.

[32] See Bilquin B (2024) EU missions and operations abroad. European Parliament Briefing, European Parliamentary Research Service.

[33] Article 31 TEU states what follows: "1. Decisions under this Chapter shall be taken by the European Council and the Council acting unanimously, except where this Chapter provides otherwise. The adoption of legislative acts shall be excluded. When abstaining in a vote, any member of the Council may qualify its abstention by making a formal declaration under the present subparagraph. In that case, it shall not be obliged to apply the decision, but shall accept that the decision commits the Union. In a spirit of mutual solidarity, the Member State concerned shall refrain from any action likely to conflict with or impede Union action based on that decision and the other Member States shall respect its position. If the members of the Council qualifying their abstention in this way represent at least one third of the Member States comprising at least one third of the population of the Union, the decision shall not be adopted. 2. By derogation from the provisions of paragraph 1, the Council shall act by qualified majority:—when adopting a decision defining a Union action or position on the basis of a decision of the European Council relating to the Union's strategic interests and objectives, as referred to in Article 22(1),—when adopting a decision defining a Union action or position, on a proposal which the High Representative of the Union for Foreign Affairs and Security Policy has presented following a specific request from the European Council, made on its own initiative or that of the High Representative,—when adopting any decision implementing a decision defining a Union action or position,—when appointing a special representative in accordance with Article 33. If a member of the Council declares that, for vital and stated reasons of national policy, it intends to oppose the adoption of a decision to be taken by qualified majority, a vote shall not be taken. The High Representative will, in close consultation with the Member State involved, search for a solution acceptable to it. If he does not succeed, the Council may, acting by a qualified majority, request that the matter be referred to the European Council for a decision by unanimity. 3. The European Council may unanimously adopt a decision stipulating that the Council shall act by a qualified majority in cases other than those referred to in

Furthermore, from an economic point of view, it must be noted that administrative and operating expenditure for implementation of the common foreign and security policy—thus, also for such missions or operations—must be charged to the EU budget (*ex* Article 41, Paragraphs 1 and 2, of TEU), except for operating expenditure "arising from operations having military or defence implications": in such case, "it shall be charged to the Member States".[34] It means that apparently only expenditure for missions and operations with no military or defence implications could be charged to the EU budget. However, EU has continuously found ways to handle the financing of common costs related to EU military missions and operations under the EU's common security and defence policy: the latest is the 'European Peace Facility', created through the Council Decision (CFSP) 2021/509 of 22 March 2021, which is an off-budget tool financed by contributions of EU Member States that allows also to finance the common costs of EU military missions and operations.[35]

3.1 *EU Military Missions*

The EU has launched several military missions over the course of time; there are currently four military missions ongoing: the EU Training Mission in Somalia, the EU Training Mission in Central African Republic, the EU Military Assistance Mission in support of Ukraine, and the EU Military Assistance Mission in Mozambique. As indicated also by the titles of the missions, there are currently two types of EU military missions ongoing: training missions and military assistance missions. Since there is no room in this chapter to properly survey all such missions, only the longer ongoing training mission (i.e., the EU Training Mission in Somalia) and the longer ongoing military assistance mission (i.e., the EU Military Assistance

paragraph 2. 4. Paragraphs 2 and 3 shall not apply to decisions having military or defence implications. 5. For procedural questions, the Council shall act by a majority of its members."

[34] Actually Article 41, Paragraphs 1 and 2, of TEU affirms that "1. Administrative expenditure to which the implementation of this Chapter gives rise for the institutions shall be charged to the Union budget. 2. Operating expenditure to which the implementation of this Chapter gives rise shall also be charged to the Union budget, except for such expenditure arising from operations having military or defence implications and cases where the Council acting unanimously decides otherwise.

In cases where expenditure is not charged to the Union budget, it shall be charged to the Member States in accordance with the gross national product scale, unless the Council acting unanimously decides otherwise. As for expenditure arising from operations having military or defence implications, Member States whose representatives in the Council have made a formal declaration under Article 31(1), second subparagraph, shall not be obliged to contribute to the financing thereof."

[35] It could be reminded that the 'European Peace Facility' in some way replaced the 'Athena' mechanism: about such mechanism see Council Decision (CFSP) 2015/528 of 27 March 2015 establishing a mechanism to administer the financing of the common costs of European Union operations having military or defence implications (Athena) and repealing Decision 2011/871/CFSP.

Mission in support of Ukraine) will be succinctly taken in consideration: the longer lifespan of those missions would allow to better value the EU efforts over the years in upholding peace and security around the world.

3.1.1 The EU Training Mission in Somalia

The EU Training Mission in Somalia (hereafter: 'EUTM Somalia') was originally established by the Council Decision 2010/96/CFSP of 15 February 2010 on a European Union military mission to contribute to the training of Somali security forces and it was launched on 7 April 2010.[36]

Such mission was an essential element of the "comprehensive EU approach to the situation in Somalia",[37] which included also a maritime military operation—the EU Naval Operation 'Atalanta'[38]—and which has subsequently comprised a civilian mission, i.e. the EU Capacity Building Mission in Somalia.[39]

EUTM Somalia was also created in order to implement what adopted by Security Council by its Resolution 1872 (2009): in fact, by such Resolution Security Council determined that the situation in Somalia constituted "a threat to international peace and security in the region"[40] and—acting under Chapter VII of the Charter of the United Nations (hereafter: 'UN')—among other things urged "Member States, regional and international organizations to [...] offer technical assistance for the training and equipping of the Somali security forces".[41]

It should be underlined that Somali Transitional Federal Government—by two letters (dated 18 November 2009 and 23 January 2010 respectively)—"expressed its appreciation for the Union's efforts to coordinate the training of the Somali security

---

[36] See Council Decision 2010/197/CFSP of 31 March 2010 on the launch of a European Union military mission to contribute to the training of Somali security forces (EUTM Somalia), Article 2.

[37] In: Council Decision 2010/96/CFSP of 15 February 2010, Whereas (3). About the situation in Somalia at that time see, for example: Yannis A (1997) State Collapse and Prospects for Political Reconstruction and Democratic Governance in Somalia. African Yearbook of International Law:23–47; Giorgetti C (2010) A Principled Approach to State Failure: International Community Actions in Emergency Situations. Martinus Nijhoff, Leiden/Boston; Jiménez Piernas C (2010) Los Estados fracasados y el derecho internacional: el caso de Somalia. Revista Española De Derecho Internacional:17–59; Kreuter A (2010) Self-Determination, Sovereignty, and the Failure of States: Somaliland and the Case for Justified Secession. Minnesota Journal of International Law:363–397; Pustorino P (2010) Failed States and International Law: The Impact of UN Practice on Somalia in Respect of Fundamental Rules of International Law. German Yearbook of International Law:727–752; Del Chicca M (2020) Recenti tendenze in tema di gestione degli Stati "falliti" da parte dell'ONU: il caso della Somalia. Ordine internazionale e diritti umani:863–890. See also the following Reports of the Secretary-General (on the situation in Somalia when EUTM Somalia was established): S/2009/132, 9 March 2009; S/2009/373, 20 July 2009; S/2010/23, 11 May 2010; S/2010/447, 9 September 2010; S/2010/675, 30 December 2010.

[38] See *infra* par. 3.2.2.

[39] *Infra* par. 3.3.

[40] In: S/RES/1872 (2009), p 2.

[41] *Ibidem*, par. 8.

forces and its efforts towards peace and stability in Somalia, and assured the Union of its commitment to bear its responsibility with regard to the recruitment, training and retention of recruits; it also emphasised its commitment to a broader security sector policy in Somalia".[42] It should be additionally reminded the appreciation expressed in this regard by African Union Deputy Special Representative for Somalia (by letter dated 30 November 2009)[43] and by the Minister of Defence of Uganda (by letter dated 5 January 2010): the latter "welcomed the Union's envisaged mission in support of the Somali security sector and invited the Union to participate in the training of Somali security forces in Uganda for a period of at least 1 year".[44]

These are clear examples of the relevance of EU military missions—like EUTM Somalia—to uphold and promote peace and security EU values around the world.

Since its launch date, the EUTM Somalia mandate has been extended several times, with some changes reflecting the modified circumstances of the situation in Somalia[45]: on 16 December 2024, the Council decided to extend the EUTM Somalia mandate until 28 February 2027.[46]

Such prolonged EU efforts have been appreciated many times by the international community: for example, UN Security Council also recently welcomed "the financial, in-kind and logistical support provided by the European Union and its Member States since the beginning of operations in Somalia in 2007".[47]

3.1.2 The EU Military Assistance Mission in Support of Ukraine

It could be preliminary reminded that European Council, in its conclusions of 24 February 2022, "condemned in the strongest possible terms the Russian Federation's unprovoked and unjustified military aggression against Ukraine" and "reiterated its unwavering support for the independence, sovereignty and territorial integrity of Ukraine within its internationally recognised borders".[48] Additionally, the Minister for Foreign Affairs and the Minister of Defence of Ukraine, by letter dated 30 September 2022, "jointly requested military support to Ukraine from the Union, confirmed that Ukraine's current needs in that regard include basic and collective military training, as well as specialised military training of personnel [...]" in

---

[42] Council Decision 2010/96/CFSP, Whereas (5).

[43] *Ibidem*, Whereas (6).

[44] *Ibidem*, Whereas (9).

[45] See, for example, Council Decision (CFSP) 2015/441 of 16 March 2015, Council Decision (CFSP) 2020/2032 of 10 December 2020, Council Decision (CFSP) 2022/2443 of 12 December 2022.

[46] See Council Decision (CFSP) 2024/3184 of 16 December 2024 amending Decision 2010/96/CFSP on a European Union military mission to contribute to the training of Somali security forces.

[47] In: S/RES/2767 (2024), par. 36.

[48] In: Council Decision (CFSP) 2022/1968 of 17 October 2022 on a European Union Military Assistance Mission in support of Ukraine (EUMAM Ukraine), Whereas (1).

various fields, “and welcomed the establishment for that purpose, as a matter of urgency, of a Union military assistance mission in support of Ukraine”.[49]

The EU Military Assistance Mission in support of Ukraine (hereafter: ‘EUMAM Ukraine’) was therefore established by the Council Decision (CFSP) 2022/1968 of 17 October 2022 and it was launched on 15 November 2022.[50] Conversely to an EU training mission—like the EUTM Somalia (surveyed above)[51]—the EUMAM Ukraine strategic objective is “to contribute to enhancing the military capability of Ukraine’s Armed Forces (UAF) to regenerate and to effectively conduct operations, in order to allow Ukraine to defend its territorial integrity within its internationally recognised borders, effectively exercise its sovereignty and protect the civilians in Ukraine”.[52]

The Council Decision (CFSP) 2022/1968 states also that “international humanitarian law, human rights, protection of civilians including against gender-based violence, as well as the ‘Women, Peace and Security’, ‘Youth, Peace and Security’ and ‘Children and Armed Conflict’ agendas shall be fully integrated in EUMAM Ukraine’s operational planning, training and reporting”.[53] It should be highlighted that this is also a way for the EU to support its peace and security values abroad.

Additionally, EUMAM Ukraine must coordinates its activities with “like-minded international partners, in particular the United States of America (USA), the United Kingdom of Great Britain and Northern Ireland (UK), Canada”,[54] and this is also an opportunity for EU to uphold its peace and security values with third States. Recently, such opportunity could be taken by EU also with a significant international organization—NATO—because Council Decision (CFSP) 2024/2876 of 8 November 2024 added the following paragraph to Article 7 of Decision (CFSP) 2022/1968: “EUMAM Ukraine shall cooperate with NATO, in particular NATO Security Assistance and Training for Ukraine (NSATU), in full respect of the principles of transparency, reciprocity and inclusiveness, as well as the decision-making autonomy and procedures of both organisations”.[55]

Furthermore, it should be reminded that EU has also the possibility to invite third States to participate in EUMAM Ukraine.[56] No third State joined EUMAM Ukraine nowadays, but such possibility opened new ways of dialogue with some third States,

[49] *Ibidem*, Whereas (4).

[50] See Council Decision (CFSP) 2022/2243 of 14 November 2022 launching the European Union Military Assistance Mission in support of Ukraine (EUMAM Ukraine), Article 2.

[51] *Supra* par. 3.1.1.

[52] In: Council Decision (CFSP) 2022/1968, Article 1, Paragraph 2.

[53] *Ibidem*, Article 1, Paragraph 4.

[54] *Ibidem*, Article 7, Paragraph 3.

[55] Council Decision (CFSP) 2024/2876 of 8 November 2024 amending Decision (CFSP) 2022/1968 on a European Union Military Assistance Mission in support of Ukraine (EUMAM Ukraine, Article 1.

[56] Council Decision (CFSP) 2022/1968, Article 8.

so offering additional opportunities to foster peace and security values.[57] EUMAM Ukraine mandate has been at the present time extended until 15 November 2026.[58]

3.2 *EU Military Operations*

The EU has started many military operations in its history. The main difference between EU military operations and EU military missions (surveyed above)[59] is that military operations involve military forces which could possibly rely on the use of force. There are currently four military operations ongoing: the EU military operation in Bosnia and Herzegovina ALTHEA, the EU military operation to contribute to maritime security in the West Indian Ocean and in the Red Sea ATALANTA, the EU military operation in the Mediterranean IRINI, and the EU maritime security operation to safeguard freedom of navigation in relation to the Red Sea crisis ASPIDES. As specified above also for military missions, since there is no room in this chapter to adequately survey all such operations, only the longer ongoing military operations—i.e., the EU military operation in Bosnia and Herzegovina ALTHEA and the EU military operation to contribute to maritime security in the West Indian Ocean and in the Red Sea ATALANTA—will be taken in consideration for the purpose of ponder how EU upholds and promotes its peace and security values in wider world.

3.2.1 The EU Military Operation in Bosnia and Herzegovina

The EU military operation in Bosnia and Herzegovina ALTHEA (hereafter: 'EUFOR ALTHEA') was originally established by Council Joint Action 2004/570/CFSP of 12 July 2004 on the European Union military operation in Bosnia and Herzegovina and it was launched on 2 December 2004.[60] Such military operation has been really appreciated by the international community: it could be reminded, for example, that UN Security Council—determining that the situation in the region continued to constitute a threat to international peace and security, and acting under Chapter VII of the Charter of the UN—by its Resolution 1551 (2004) welcomed "the EU's intention to launch an EU mission to Bosnia and Herzegovina, including a military component, from December 2004".[61] Additionally, by its Resolution 1575 (2004), UN Security Council—once again acting under Chapter VII of the Charter

[57] See, for example, Norway: fourth Dialogue on Security and Defence with the EU takes place in Brussels, EEAS Press, 06.12.2024.

[58] Council Decision (CFSP) 2024/2876, Article 4.

[59] *Supra* par. 3.1.

[60] See Council Decision 2004/803/CFSP of 25 November 2004 on the launching of the European Union military operation in Bosnia and Herzegovina, Article 1.

[61] In: S/RES/1551 (2004), par. 10.

of the UN—authorized "the Member States acting through or in cooperation with the EU to establish for an initial planned period of 12 months a multinational stabilization force (EUFOR) as a legal successor to SFOR under unified command and control, which will fulfil its missions [...] in cooperation with the NATO HQ presence in accordance with the arrangements agreed between NATO and the EU [...]".[62] It must be underlined that such arrangements between NATO and EU recognized "that the EUFOR will have the main peace stabilization role under the military aspects of the Peace Agreement".[63]

The UN Security Council has periodically renewed the above authorization[64] along with its appreciation to EUFOR ALTHEA efforts for peace and security in the region: for example, by its Resolution 2183 (2014), UN Security Council emphasized its appreciation to *inter alia* "the Commander and personnel of the multinational stabilization force (EUFOR ALTHEA)".[65] Furthermore, by such Resolution, UN Security Council also welcomed both "the continued presence of EUFOR ALTHEA, successfully focusing on capacity building and training while also retaining the capability to contribute to the Bosnia and Herzegovina authorities' deterrence capacity if the situation so requires", and "the EU's readiness [...] to continue at this stage an executive military role to support Bosnia and Herzegovina authorities to maintain the safe and secure environment" as well.[66]

Moreover, still by Resolution 2183 (2014), UN Security Council highlighted several times the fundamental role of EUFOR ALTHEA in upholding peace and security in the region.[67] Such role has been emphasized also in the last UN Security Council Resolution related to this topic, when "delegates welcomed the renewal of the authorization of EUFOR-Althea, hailing it as vital in safeguarding peace and security in Bosnia and Herzegovina, as well as in maintaining stability in the region".[68]

As already pointed out in this paragraph, EUFOR ALTHEA cooperates with another international organization, i.e. NATO,[69] and this is an additional opportunity for the EU to uphold its peace and security values.[70] In addition to such cooperation, it should be reminded that third States could give a contribution to EUFOR

[62] In: S/RES/1575 (2004), par. 10.

[63] *Ibidem.*

[64] The mandate of EUFOR ALTHEA has been extended lately for a further period of twelve months by UN Security Council Resolution 2757 (2024), adopted on 1 November 2024, par. 1.

[65] In: S/RES/2183 (2014), 1.

[66] *Ibidem*, 2–3.

[67] *Ibidem*, parr. 7–10, 12–19.

[68] Security Council Renews for One Year Mandate of European Union-led Stabilization Force in Bosnia and Herzegovina, Unanimously Adopting Resolution 2757 (2024), SC/15884, 9774th Meeting (PM), 1 November 2024.

[69] See Articles 13 and 14 of Council Joint Action 2004/570/CFSP, respectively titled "Relations with NATO" and "Release of information to NATO and to third States".

[70] The same opportunity has been mentioned above for EUMAM Ukraine: *supra* par. 3.1.2.

ALTHEA[71]: there are currently some troops contributing third States in EUFOR ALTHEA (like, for example, Chile, Switzerland, and Türkiye)[72] and such third States participation could also show a certain effectiveness of EU efforts in sustaining and promoting its peace and security values in wider world.

3.2.2 The EU Military Operation to Contribute to Maritime Security in the West Indian Ocean and in the Red Sea

The EU military operation to contribute to maritime security in the West Indian Ocean and in the Red Sea ATALANTA (hereafter: 'EUNAVFOR ATALANTA') scored two temporal records: it has been the first naval military operation in EU history, and it has been also the first naval military operation launched in the international community to deter, prevent and repress piracy and armed robbery at sea off the Somali coast.

Before EUNAVFOR ATALANTA was launched, UN Security Council—by its Resolution 1816 (2008), acting under Chapter VII of the Charter of the UN—had determined "that the incidents of piracy and armed robbery against vessels in the territorial waters of Somalia and the high seas off the coast of Somalia exacerbate the situation in Somalia which continues to constitute a threat against international peace and security in the region".[73] For such reason, by the same Resolution, UN Security Council had urged "all States to cooperate with each other [...] and, as appropriate, with the relevant regional organizations in connection with, and share information about, acts of piracy and armed robbery in the territorial waters and on the high seas off the coast of Somalia, and to render assistance to vessels threatened by or under attack by pirates or armed robbers".[74] Again by Resolution 1816 (2008), UN Security Council had also decided that for a period of 6 months States cooperating with the Somali Transitional Federal Government in the fight against piracy and armed robbery at sea off the coast of Somalia were able to enter the territorial waters of Somalia and to use, within such territorial waters, all necessary means for the purpose of repressing acts of piracy and armed robbery at sea.[75]

Afterwards, still before EUNAVFOR ATALANTA was launched, UN Security Council—by its Resolution 1838 (2008)—calling upon "States interested in the security of maritime activities to take part actively in the fight against piracy on the high seas off the coast of Somalia, in particular by deploying naval vessels and military aircraft",[76] and urging "also States and regional organizations [...] to continue

---

[71] See Article 11 (titled "Participation of third States") of Council Joint Action 2004/570/CFSP.

[72] See, for example, Common Security and Defence Policy, EUFOR Operation Althea Mission Factsheet, updated January 2025.

[73] In: S/RES/1816 (2008), 2.

[74] *Ibidem*, par. 3.

[75] *Ibidem*, par. 7.

[76] In: S/RES/1838 (2008), par. 2.

to take action to protect the World Food Programme maritime convoys", expressly commended "the ongoing planning process towards a possible European Union naval operation".[77]

EUNAVFOR ATALANTA was therefore launched on 8 December 2008[78] for the protection both "of vessels of the WFP delivering food aid to displaced persons in Somalia", and "of vulnerable vessels cruising off the Somali coast, and the deterrence, prevention and repression of acts of piracy and armed robbery off the Somali coast"[79] as well.

Since its launch date, EUNAVFOR ATALANTA mandate has been extended many times, and it has been adapted to face in the most appropriate way the changing situation in the Indian Ocean and in the Red Sea[80]: on 16 December 2024, the Council decided to extend the EUNAVFOR ATALANTA mandate until 28 February 2027.[81]

EUNAVFOR ATALANTA has often given a significant boost to EU upholding and promotion of its peace and security values. For example, such EU military operation has been distinctly appreciated right from its beginning by UN Security Council, which immediately welcomed "in particular the decision by the EU on 10 November 2008 to launch [...] a naval operation to protect WFP maritime convoys bringing humanitarian assistance to Somalia and other vulnerable ships, and to repress acts of piracy and armed robbery at sea off the coast of Somalia".[82] UN Security Council has indeed repeatedly praised "the efforts of the European Union Naval Forces (EUNAVFOR) Operation ATALANTA [...] to suppress piracy and to protect ships transiting through the waters off the coast of Somalia"[83] over the course of the years.[84]

Additionally, EUNAVFOR ATALANTA offered the opportunity to EU to conclude agreements with some States near the piracy attacks in the Indian Ocean, so

---

[77] *Ibidem*, 1.

[78] Council Decision 2008/918/CFSP of 8 December 2008 on the launch of a European Union military operation to contribute to the deterrence, prevention and repression of acts of piracy and armed robbery off the Somali coast (Atalanta), Article 2.

[79] Council Joint Action 2008/851/CFSP of 10 November 2008 on a European Union military operation to contribute to the deterrence, prevention and repression of acts of piracy and armed robbery off the Somali coast, Article 1, Paragraph 1.

[80] See, for example, the following Council Decisions amending Joint Action 2008/851/CFSP: Council Decision 2014/827/CFSP of 21 November 2014, Council Decision (CFSP) 2016/2082 of 28 November 2016, Council Decision (CFSP) 2018/1083 of 30 July 2018, Council Decision (CFSP) 2020/2188 of 22 December 2020, Council Decision (CFSP) 2022/2441 of 12 December 2022, Council Decision (CFSP) 2024/3186 of 16 December 2024.

[81] Council Decision (CFSP) 2024/3186, Article 1.

[82] In: S/RES/1846 (2008), par. 6.

[83] In: S/RES/2608 (2021), 2.

[84] See, for example, S/RES/1851 (2008), S/RES/1897 (2009), S/RES/1918 (2010), S/RES/2020 (2011), S/RES/2077 (2012), S/RES/2125 (2013), S/RES/2184 (2014), S/RES/2246 (2015), S/RES/2316 (2016), S/RES/2383 (2017), S/RES/2442 (2018), S/RES/2500 (2019), S/RES/2554 (2020).

that persons detained by EUNAVFOR ATALANTA in connection with piracy and associated property seized by such military operation would be submitted to that States competent authorities for the purpose of investigation and prosecution.[85] On this regard, EU has concluded agreements, for example, with Kenya,[86] Mauritius,[87] Seychelles,[88] and Tanzania,[89] and such agreements could be also seen as EU means to uphold its security value abroad.

From the same point of view, it should be noted that—according to Article 13 of Council Joint Action 2008/851/CFSP—units of EUNAVFOR ATALANTA could be boarded on merchant ships of third States,[90] and this also represents an evident possibility for EU to support and disseminate its peace and security values.

---

[85] Such possibility was established by Article 12 of Council Joint Action 2008/851/CFSP, titled "Transfer of persons arrested and detained with a view to their prosecution", which so states: "1. On the basis of Somalia's acceptance of the exercise of jurisdiction by Member States or by third States, on the one hand, and Article 105 of the United Nations Convention on the Law of the Sea, on the other hand, persons having committed, or suspected of having committed, acts of piracy or armed robbery in Somali territorial waters or on the high seas, who are arrested and detained, with a view to their prosecution, and property used to carry out such acts, shall be transferred:—to the competent authorities of the flag Member State or of the third State participating in the operation, of the vessel which took them captive, or—if this State cannot, or does not wish to, exercise its jurisdiction, to a Member States or any third State which wishes to exercise its jurisdiction over the aforementioned persons and property.

2. No persons referred to in paragraphs 1 and 2 may be transferred to a third State unless the conditions for the transfer have been agreed with that third State in a manner consistent with relevant international law, notably international law on human rights, in order to guarantee in particular that no one shall be subjected to the death penalty, to torture or to any cruel, inhuman or degrading treatment".

[86] See Exchange of Letters between the European Union and the Government of Kenya on the conditions and modalities for the transfer of persons suspected of having committed acts of piracy and detained by the European Union-led naval force (EUNAVFOR), and seized property in the possession of EUNAVFOR, from EUNAVFOR to Kenya and for their treatment after such transfer, Official Journal of the European Union, L 79/49–59, 25.3.2009.

[87] See Agreement between the European Union and the Republic of Mauritius on the conditions of transfer of suspected pirates and associated seized property from the European Union-led naval force to the Republic of Mauritius and on the conditions of suspected pirates after transfer, Official Journal of the European Union, L 254/3–6, 30.9.2011.

[88] See Council Decision 2009/877/CFSP of 23 October 2009 on the signing and provisional application of the Exchange of Letters between the European Union and the Republic of Seychelles on the conditions and modalities for the transfer of suspected pirates and armed robbers from EUNAVFOR to the Republic of Seychelles and for their treatment after such transfer.

[89] See Council Decision 2014/198/CFSP of 10 March 2014 on the signing and conclusion of the Agreement between the European Union and the United Republic of Tanzania on the conditions of transfer of suspected pirates and associated seized property from the European Union-led naval force to the United Republic of Tanzania.

[90] Article 13 of Council Joint Action 2008/851/CFSP, titled "Relations with the flag States of protected vessels", states that "The conditions governing the presence on board merchant ships, particularly those chartered by the WFP, of units belonging to Atalanta, including privileges, immunities and other guarantees relating to the proper conduct of the operation, shall be agreed with the flag States of those vessels".

3.3 EU Civilian Missions

EU has launched numerous civilian missions over the years; there are currently twelve EU civilian missions ongoing: the EU Border Assistance Mission for the Rafah Crossing Point, the EU Police and Rule of Law Mission for the Palestinian Territories, the EU Rule of Law Mission in Kosovo, the EU Monitoring Mission in Georgia, the EU Integrated Border Management Assistance Mission in Libya, the EU Advisory Mission for Civilian Security Sector Reform in Ukraine, the EU Capacity Building Mission in Mali, the EU Capacity Building Mission in Somalia, the EU Advisory Mission in Iraq, the EU Advisory Mission in Central African Republic, the EU Mission in Armenia, and the EU Partnership Mission in Moldova.[91]

As shown by the titles of the missions too, there are several types of EU civilian missions ongoing at present; for the same methodological reasons indicated also for military missions and for military operations,[92] only the two longer ongoing civilian missions will be taken into consideration for the purposes of this chapter: the EU Border Assistance Mission for the Rafah Crossing Point and the EU Police and Rule of Law Mission for the Palestinian Territories.

3.3.1 The EU Border Assistance Mission for the Rafah Crossing Point

It should be preliminary reminded that the EU, as part of the Quartet,[93] was "committed to assisting and facilitating the implementation of the Roadmap, which lays out reciprocal steps by the Israeli Government and the Palestinian Authority in the political, security, economic, humanitarian, and institution-building fields, that will result in the emergence of an independent, democratic, and viable Palestinian state living side by side in peace and security with Israel and its other neighbours".[94] In October 2005 the Palestinian Prime Minister requested the EU's assistance in several areas at the Rafah crossing point.[95] "On 15 November 2005 the Government of Israel and the Palestinian Authority concluded an Agreement on Movement and Access at border crossing points with Gaza, which, *inter alia*, indicated the role of

[91] The EU Border Assistance Mission to Moldova and Ukraine could be added to this list, but it is not technically a Common Security and Defence Policy mission: see also the Memorandum of Understanding between the European Commission, the Government of the Republic of Moldova and the Government of Ukraine of 7 October 2005 on the European Union Border Assistance Mission to the Republic of Moldova and to Ukraine.

[92] *Supra* parr. 3.1 and 3.2.

[93] The Quartet, comprised of the EU, Russia, UN, and United States was established in 2002 to facilitate the Middle-East Peace Process negotiations: on this regard see also UN Security Council Resolution 1397 (2002).

[94] In: Council Joint Action 2005/889/CFSP of 12 December 2005 on establishing a European Union Border Assistance Mission for the Rafah Crossing Point (EUBAM Rafah), Whereas (1).

[95] *Ibidem*, Whereas (7).

the EU as a third party regarding the operation of the relevant crossing points".[96] Some days later "the Palestinian Authority and the Government of Israel invited the EU to establish a European Union Border Assistance Mission for the Rafah Crossing Point".[97]

Following such premises, the EU Border Assistance Mission for the Rafah Crossing Point (hereafter: 'EUBAM Rafah') was initially established by Council Joint Action 2005/889/CFSP: its mandate, sometimes amended to deal with some situation's changes, has been extended periodically[98] (at the moment until 30 June 2025).[99]

EUBAM Rafah for its part contributed to uphold and promote peace and security EU values abroad: the aim of such civilian mission is indeed providing a Third-Party presence at the Rafah Crossing Point in order to build up confidence between the Government of Israel and the Palestinian Authority.[100] Furthermore, EUBAM Rafah has been the first EU Border Management mission, which opened the way to the EU to launch other analogous civilian missions in different scenarios: for example, the EU Integrated Border Management Assistance Mission in Libya, which was established by Council Decision 2013/233/CFSP in order "to support the Libyan authorities to develop capacity for enhancing the security of Libya's land, sea and air borders in the short term and to develop a broader Integrated Border Management strategy in the longer term".[101]

EUBAM Rafah is an important element of the multiple efforts of EU for the question of Palestine and, as reminded above, EU is also part of the Quartet, which has been appreciated by Security Council more than once.[102] In this context, another key element of the EU comprehensive approach to the question of Palestine is the EU Police and Rule of Law Mission for the Palestinian Territories.

---

[96] *Ibidem*, Whereas (8).

[97] *Ibidem*, Whereas (9).

[98] See the following Council Joint Actions: 2006/773/CFSP of 13 November 2006, 2007/359/CFSP of 23 May 2007, 2008/133/CFSP of 18 February 2008, 2008/379/CFSP of 19 May 2008, 2008/862/CFSP of 10 November 2008, 2009/854/CFSP of 20 November 2009. See also the following Council Decisions: 2010/274/CFSP of 12 May 2010, 2011/312/CFSP of 26 May 2011, 2011/857/CFSP of 19 December 2011, 2012/332/CFSP of 25 June 2012, 2013/355/CFSP of 3 July 2013, 2014/430/CFSP of 3 July 2014, 2015/1065 of 2 July 2015, 2016/1107 of 7 July 2016, 2017/1193 of 4 July 2017, 2018/493 of 29 June 2018, 2019/1115 of 28 June 2019, 2020/955 of 30 June 2020, 2021/1065 of 28 June 2021, 2022/107 of 27 June 2022, 2023/1303 of 26 June 2023.

[99] See Council Decision (CFSP) 2024/1806 of 25 June 2024, Article 1, Paragraph 2.

[100] See, for example, Council Joint Action 2005/889/CFSP, Article 2.

[101] In: Council Decision 2013/233/CFSP of 22 May 2013 on the European Union Integrated Border Management Assistance Mission in Libya (EUBAM Libya), Article 2.

[102] See, for example, S/RES/1397 (2002) and S/RES/1850 (2008).

3.3.2 The EU Police and Rule of Law Mission for the Palestinian Territories

The EU Coordinating Office for Palestinian Police Support was formally established by an Exchange of Letters on 20 April 2005 between the Palestinian Prime Minister and the EU Special Representative to the Middle-East Peace Process.[103]

Following on the creation of such EU Coordinating Office, in October 2005—in addition to the Palestinian Prime Minister request to the EU's assistance in many areas at the Rafah crossing point[104]—"the Palestinian Authority invited the EU to launch an European Union Police Mission for the Palestinian Territories".[105]

The EU Police Mission for the Palestinian Territories (hereafter: 'EUPOL COPPS') was therefore established by Council Joint Action 2005/797/CFSP, and its original structure consisted of four elements (Head of Mission/Police Commissioner, Advisory Section, Programme Coordination Section, and Administration Section)[106]: in 2008 a Rule of Law Section was added by Council Joint Action 2008/958/CFSP.[107]

EUPOL COPPS mandate has been amended several times to reflect the changes that have taken place in the Palestinian Territories, and it has been repeatedly extended[108] (today until 30 June 2025).[109]

EUPOL COPPS represents one means for the EU to sustain and foster its peace and security values in wider world. For example, on December 2011 EUPOL COPPS signed an agreement with UN Development Programme and with the Palestinian Authority creating a joint programme—based on rule of law and respect for human rights—aimed at strengthening internal police accountability, national anti-corruption efforts and the oversight role of civil society in democratic governance and preparation for statehood in Palestinian Territories.[110] Additionally, it must be mentioned that Council Joint Action 2005/797/CFSP provided for the

[103] See Council Joint Action 2005/797/CFSP of 14 November 2005 on the European Union Police Mission for the Palestinian Territories, Whereas (3).

[104] *Supra* par. 3.3.1.

[105] In: Council Joint Action 2005/797/CFSP, Whereas (6).

[106] *Ibidem*, Article 5.

[107] See Council Joint Action 2008/958/CFSP of 16 December 2008 amending Joint Action 2005/797/CFSP on the European Police Mission for the Palestinian Territories, Article 1.

[108] *Ibidem*. See also the following Council Decisions: 2009/955/CFSP of 15 December 2009, 2010/747/CFSP of 2 December 2010, 2011/858/CFSP of 19 December 2011, 2012/324/CFSP of 25 June 2012, 2013/354/CFSP of 3 July 2013, 2014/447/CFSP of 9 July 2014, 2015/1064 of 2 July 2015, 2016/1108 of 7 July 2016, 2017/1194 of 4 July 2017, 2018/942 of 29 June 2018, 2019/1114 of 28 June 2019, 2020/902 of 29 June 2020, 2021/1066 of 28 June 2021, 2023/1302 of 26 June 2023.

[109] See Council Decision (CFSP) 2024/1813 of 25 June 2024 amending Decision 2013/354/CFSP on the European Union Police Mission for the Palestinian Territories (EUPOL COPPS), Article 1.

[110] See UNDP Signs Partnership Agreements in Support of Democratic Governance and Rule of Law, UNDP Press Release, 01/12/2011.

possible participation of third States to EUPOL COPPS[111] and that this possibility has been progressively enhanced by some subsequent Council Decisions related to such civilian mission. For example, Council Decision 2009/955/CFSP introduced into EUPOL COPPS "a project cell for identifying and implementing projects" and added to the mission the task to "coordinate, facilitate and provide advice on projects implemented by Member States and third States under their responsibility".[112] Council Decision 2010/747/CFSP then stated that "nationals of third States participating financially in the mission, of host parties and, if required for the operational needs of the mission, of neighbouring countries shall be allowed to tender for contracts".[113] Council Decision 2013/354/CFSP later added that "subject to the Commission's approval, the Head of Mission may conclude technical arrangements with Member States, participating third States, and other international actors regarding the provision of equipment, services and premises to EUPOL COPPS".[114] All such norms related to the participation of third Sates have been subsequently rearranged,[115] but their contents have remained the same, potentially offering EUPOL COPPS the opportunities seen above for EUFOR ALTHEA.[116]

4 Conclusions

The international agreements concluded by the EU with third Parties, examined in this chapter, comprise several provisions which contribute to uphold and promote peace and security EU values in wider world.

For example, a security exception, which prohibits construe anything in such agreements that could prevent either Party from taking any action for the purpose of

---

[111] Article 12 of Council Joint Action 2005/797/CFSP stated what follows: "1. Without prejudice to the decision-making autonomy of the EU and its single institutional framework, acceding States shall be invited and third States may be invited to contribute to EUPOL COPPS provided that they bear the cost of the staff seconded by them, including salaries, medical coverage, allowances, high-risk insurance and travel expenses to and from the mission area, and contribute to the running costs of EUPOL COPPS, as appropriate. 2. Third States making contributions to EUPOL COPPS shall have the same rights and obligations in terms of day-to-day management of the mission as Member States taking part in the mission. 3. The Council hereby authorises the PSC to take the relevant decisions on acceptance of the proposed contributions and to establish a Committee of Contributors.

4. Detailed arrangements regarding the participation of third States shall be subject of an agreement to be concluded in accordance with the procedures laid down in Article 24 of the Treaty. The Secretary-General/High Representative, assisting the Presidency, may negotiate such arrangements on its behalf. Where the EU and a third State have concluded an agreement establishing a framework for the participation of this third State in the EU crisis management operations, the provisions of such an agreement shall apply in the context of EUPOL COPPS".

[112] In: Council Decision 2009/955/CFSP, Article 1.

[113] In: Council Decision 2010/747/CFSP, Article 1.

[114] In: Council Decision 2013/354/CFSP, Article 12, Paragraph 3.

[115] See, for example, Council Decision 2014/447/CFSP and Council Decision 2015/1064.

[116] *Supra* par. 3.2.1.

maintaining international peace and security. It must be underlined that such a security exception has been always incorporated in the international agreements taken into consideration in this chapter.[117]

Other relevant provisions are the denials of benefits—very often inserted in such agreements—which state that a Party may deny the benefits of determined Parts of the agreement—usually concerning cross-border trade in services and investment—to an investor, service supplier or to a covered enterprise of the other Party, when the denying Party adopts or maintains measures related to the maintenance of international peace and security dealing with that investor, security supplier or covered enterprise.[118]

Furthermore, some specific contents—embedded in a few international agreements concluded by EU with third Parties—should be taken into account, because they are aimed to support and foster peace and security EU values. Such aim is widely present in the Association Agreement between EU and Central America, for instance: the privileged political partnership—established by such agreement—is for example expressly based also on the respect for and the promotion of peace. It must be especially recalled that Article 32 of such agreement is entirely dedicated to conflict prevention and resolution, stating that "cooperation in this field shall promote and sustain a comprehensive peace policy" too.[119] Similarly, in the same agreement, one priority objective of the cooperation between Parties is explicitly "strengthening peace and security", and such cooperation involves also fighting the illicit trade and excessive accumulation of small arms, light weapons, and their ammunition, because they "continue to pose a serious threat to peace and international security".[120]

Analogous norms about small arms and light weapons, and for the same reasons, are included also in the Trade and Cooperation Agreement between the EU and UK, in which, by and large, peace looks often like an important value.[121]

Additionally, the EU upholds and promotes its peace and security values also through the several missions and operations launched all around the world over the course of time. Such missions and operations, in fact, are mainly active when and where there is a potential or current threat to international peace and security. They are not only crucial and lasting instruments for EU to sustain and foster peace and security values "on the field"; moreover, they give the opportunity to do that directly with third Parties, also facilitating often an enhanced cooperation with them in this regard. Furthermore, the international community frequently and widely expressed its appreciation for such missions and operations, which so show to be of greatest significance to uphold and promote peace and security EU values.[122]

---

[117] *Supra* par. 2.1.

[118] *Supra* par. 2.2.

[119] *Supra* par. 2.3.

[120] *Ibidem.*

[121] *Ibidem.*

[122] *Supra* par. 3.

However, it could be reminded that international peace and security are regulated by contemporary international law: from some points of view, EU should not therefore properly need to "promote" such values in wider world, because there is hitherto an international legal framework on these matters[123]; in short, such values are already become international rules. EU should anyway always "uphold" international peace and security values, because there is a continuous need to support them.[124]

References

Bilquin, EU (2024) missions and operations abroad, European Parliament Briefing, European Parliamentary Research Service, See url.

Del Chicca M (2020) Recenti tendenze in tema di gestione degli Stati "falliti" da parte dell'ONU: il caso della Somalia. Ordine internazionale e diritti umani 4:863–890

Giorgetti C (2010) A Principled Approach to State Failure: International Community Actions in Emergency Situations. Martinus Nijhoff, Leiden/Boston

Jiménez Piernas C (2010) Los Estados fracasados y el derecho internacional: el caso de Somalia. Revista Española De Derecho Internacional 62:17–59

Kreuter A (2010) Self-Determination, Sovereignty, and the Failure of States: Somaliland and the Case for Justified Secession. Minnesota Journal of International Law 1–28:363–397

Pustorino P (2010) Failed States and International Law: The Impact of UN Practice on Somalia in Respect of Fundamental Rules of International Law. German Yearbook of International Law 53:727–752

Yannis A (1997) State Collapse and Prospects for Political Reconstruction and Democratic Governance in Somalia. African Yearbook of International Law 5:23–47

Further Reading

Abass A (2004) Regional Organisations and the Development of Collective Security. Beyond Chapter VIII of the UN Charter. Hart Publishing, Oxford/Portland

Acconci P (2023) Investimenti stranieri sostenibili. Diritto e *governance* internazionale e dell'Unione europea. Editoriale Scientifica, Napoli

Adinolfi G (ed) (2021) Gli accordi preferenziali di nuova generazione dell'Unione europea. Giappichelli, Torino

Alagappa M (1997) Regional Institutions, the UN and International Security: A Framework for Analysis. Third World Q 18:421–441

---

[123] For example, this is in some way also expressed in the 'Declarations annexed to the final act of the intergovernmental conference which adopted the Treaty of Lisbon'; see 13 'Declaration concerning the common foreign and security policy', which *inter alia* so states: "the European Union and its Member States will remain bound by the provisions of the Charter of the United Nations and, in particular, by the primary responsibility of the Security Council and of its Members for the maintenance of international peace and security".

[124] For example, this could be observed also in the Association Agreement between EU and Central America, where Parties "consider that the establishment and effective functioning of the International Criminal Court constitutes an important development for international peace and justice". See *supra* footnote 20.

Alvarez JE (2017) The Impact of International Organizations on International Law. Brill/Nijhoff, Leiden/Boston
Arangio-Ruiz G (2000) On the Security Council's "Law-Making". Rivista di diritto internazionale 3:609–725
Bailliet CM, Larsen KM (eds) (2015) Promoting Peace Through International Law. Oxford University Press, Oxford
Bargiacchi P (2005) La riforma del Consiglio di Sicurezza delle Nazioni Unite. Giuffrè, Milano
Bianchi A (2009) The International Regulation of the Use of Force: The Politics of Interpretive Method. Leiden Journal of International Law 22:651–676
Biscop S, Fiott D (eds) (2013) The State of Defence in Europe: State of Emergency? Academia Press, Gent
Boisson de Chazournes L (2010) Les relations entre organisations régionales et organisations universelles. Recueil des cours de l'Académie de droit international de La Haye, Tome 347:79–406
Boutros-Ghali B (2000) Le droit international à la recherche de ses valeurs: paix, développement, démocratisation. Recueil des cours de l'Académie de droit international de La Haye, Tome 286:9–38
Bretherton C, Vogler J (2006) The European Union as a Global Actor, 2nd edn. Routledge, New York
Cadin R (2008) I presupposti dell'azione del Consiglio di sicurezza nell'articolo 39 della Carta delle Nazioni Unite. Giuffrè, Milano
Cannizzaro E (ed) (2002) The European Union as an Actor in International Relations. Kluwer Law International, The Hague
Cassese A (ed) (1986) The Current Legal Regulation of the Use of Force. Martinus Nijhoff, Dordrecht/Boston/Lancaster
Cellamare G (2015) Le operazioni di *peacekeeping* delle organizzazioni regionali. Cacucci, Bari
Chamon M, Govaere I (eds) (2020) EU External Relations Post-Lisbon. The Law and Practice Of Facultative Mixity. Brill/Nijhoff, Leiden/Boston
Cimiotta E (2018) L'uso della forza nei rapporti tra Nazioni Unite e organizzazioni regionali e sub-regionali. Jovene, Napoli
Cremona M (ed) (2018) Structural Principles in EU External Relations Law. Hart Publishing, Oxford/Portland
Czuczai J, Naert F (eds) (2017) The EU as a Global Actor—Bridging Legal Theory and Practice. Liber Amicorum in honour of Ricardo Gosalbo Bono. Brill/Nijhoff, Leiden/Boston
Daudet Y. (dir)(1995) Les Nations Unies et la restauration de l'Etat. Pedone, Paris
De Coning C, Peter M (eds) (2019) United Nations Peace Operations in a Changing Global Order. Palgrave Macmillan, Cham
De Pasquale P, Ligustro A. (a cura di)(2024) La gestione delle emergenze nel diritto dell'Unione e nel diritto internazionale. Emergenza energetica, ambientale e bellica, vol. I. Editoriale Scientifica, Napoli
De Waele H, Kuipers J-J (eds) (2013) The European Union's Emerging International Identity. Views from the Global Arena. Brill/Nijhoff, Leiden/Boston
De Wet E (2004) The Chapter VII Powers of the United Nations Security Council. Hart Publishing, Oxford/Portland
Droubi S, d'Aspremont J (eds) (2020) International Organisations, Non-State Actors, and the Formation of Customary International Law. Manchester University Press, Manchester
Fahey E, Mancini I (eds) (2022) Understanding the EU as a Good Global Actor. Edward Elgar, Cheltenham
Findlay T (2002) The Use of Force in UN Peace Operations. Oxford University Press, Oxford
Frederking B, Diehl PF (eds) (2015) The Politics of Global Governance: International Organizations in an Interdependent World, 5th edn. Lynne Rienner Publishers, Boulder
Frulli M (2012) Le operazioni di *peacekeeping* delle Nazioni Unite: continuità di un modello normativo. Editoriale Scientifica, Napoli
Gazzini T, Tsagourias N (eds) (2012) The Use of Force in International Law. Routledge, Ashgate

Hamonic A (2018) Les relations entre l'Union européenne et l'ONU dans le domaine de la gestion des crises. Bruylant, Brussels
Henderson C (2023) The Use of Force and International Law. Cambridge University Press, Cambridge
Hettne B, Söderbaum F (2006) The UN and Regional Organizations in Global Security: Competing or Complementary Logics? Glob Gov 12:227–232
Hoffmeister F (2023) Strategic Autonomy in the European Union's External Relations Law. Common Market Law Review 60:667–700
Hurd I (2008) After Anarchy: Legitimacy and Power in the United Nations Security Council. Princeton University Press, Princeton
Hyde-Price A (2007) European Security in the Twenty-First Century. The Challenge of Multipolarity. Routledge, New York
Ingravallo I (2008) Il Consiglio di sicurezza e l'amministrazione diretta di territori. Editoriale Scientifica, Napoli
James A (1994) Is there a Second Generation of UN Peacekeeping? International Peacekeeping 1:110–113
Kolb R (2018) International Law on the Maintenance of Peace: Jus Contra Bellum. Edward Elgar, Cheltenham
Koops JA, Tercovich G (2016) A European return to United Nations Peacekeeping? Opportunities, Challenges and Ways Ahead. International Peacekeeping 23:597–609
Koops JA, Tardy T, N MQ, Williams PD (eds) (2015) The Oxford Handbook of United Nations Peacekeeping Operations. Oxford University Press, Oxford
Kronenberger V, Wouters J (eds) (2004) The European Union and Conflict Prevention. Policy and Legal Aspects. T.M.C. Asser Press, The Hague
Lattanzi F, Spinedi M. (a cura di)(2004) Le organizzazioni regionali e il mantenimento della pace nella prassi di fine XX secolo. Editoriale Scientifica, Napoli
Ligustro A (2024) Principio pacifista e uso della forza nel diritto internazionale contemporaneo. DPCE Online 63:21–63
Marquardt S, Blockmans S (eds) (2023) The European Union's Contribution to International Peace and Security. Liber Amicorum in Honour of Gert-Jan van Hegelsom. Brill/Nijhoff, Leiden/Boston
Merket H (2016) The EU and the Security-Development Nexus. Bridging the Legal Divide. Brill/ Nijhoff, Leiden/Boston
Muldoon JP (2004) The Architecture of Global Governance. An Introduction to the Study of International Organizations. Routledge, New York
Murphy R (ed) (2012) Post-Conflict Rebuilding and International Law. Routledge, Ashgate
Orakhelashvili A (2011) Collective Security. Oxford University Press, Oxford
Pasquali L (2012) Il contributo delle organizzazioni regionali al mantenimento della pace e della sicurezza internazionale con mezzi non implicanti l'uso della forza. Giappichelli, Torino
Pease K-KS (2019) International Organizations. Perspectives on Global Governance, 6th edn. Routledge, New York
Picone P. (a cura di)(1995) Interventi delle Nazioni Unite e diritto internazionale. CEDAM, Padova
Pietrobon A, Gazzini T (2020) Reconsidering Multilingualism in EU Trade and Investment Agreements in Light of the 'Relocation Case'. European Journal of Legal Studies 12:43–78
Plank F (2022) Evaluating the Africa-EU Partnership on Peace and Security. Interregional Cooperation in Peace Operations. Palgrave Macmillan, Cham
Pohl B (2014) EU Foreign Policy and Crisis Management Operations. Power, Purpose and Domestic Politics. Routledge, London/New York
Rosanò A (2019) At the Frontier: Values and Borders in the EU's External Relations. In: Natoli T, Riccardi A (eds) Borders, Legal Spaces and Territories in Contemporary International Law. Springer, Cham, pp 237–262
Ruotolo GM (2016) Gli accordi commerciali di ultima generazione dell'Unione europea e i loro rapporti col sistema multilaterale degli scambi. Studi sull'integrazione europea 11:329–354

Ruys T (2011) 'Armed Attack' and Article 51 of the UN Charter. Evolutions in Customary Law and Practice. Cambridge University Press, Cambridge

Sarooshi D (2005) International Organizations and their Exercise of Sovereign Powers. Oxford University Press, Oxford

Scalese G (2015) Le fonti della politica estera e di sicurezza comune dell'Unione europea. Editoriale Scientifica, Napoli

Schmidt J (2021) The European Union and the Use of Force. Brill/Nijhoff, Leiden/Boston

Sciso E, Baratta R, Morviducci C. (a cura di)(2016) I valori dell'Unione Europea e l'azione esterna. Giappichelli, Torino

Sezgin FS (2022) The European Union's Role in United Nations Peacekeeping Operations. International Peacekeeping 29:351–383

Società Italiana per l'Organizzazione Internazionale (2021) L'azione dell'ONU per il mantenimento della pace, 75 anni dopo: risultati e prospettive (La Comunità Internazionale—Quaderni, 22). Editoriale Scientifica, Napoli

Tomuschat C (ed) (1995) The United Nations at Age Fifty. A Legal Perspective. Kluwer, The Hague/London/Boston

Verwey DR (2004) The European Community, the European Union and the International Law of Treaties—A Comparative Legal Analysis of the Community and Union's External Treaty-Making Practice. T.M.C. Asser Press, The Hague

Villani U (2001) Les rapports entre l'ONU et les organisations régionales dans le domaine du maintien de la paix. Recueil des cours de l'Académie de droit international de La Haye, Tome 290:225–436

Virzo R, Ingravallo I (2015) Evolutions in the Law of International Organizations. Brill/Nijhoff, Leiden/Boston

Von Bogdandy A, Smrkolj M (2010) European Community and Union Law and International Law. The Max Planck Encyclopedia of Public International Law. Oxford University Press, Oxford

Von Bogdandy A, Häußler S, Hanschmann F, Utz R (2005) State-Building, Nation-Building, and Constitutional Politics in Post-Conflict Situations: Conceptual Clarifications and an Appraisal of Different Approaches. Max Planck Yearbook of United Nations Law 9:579–613

Weller M (ed) (2015) The Oxford Handbook of the Use of Force in International Law. Oxford University Press, Oxford

Winand P, Benvenuti A, Guderzo M (eds) (2015) The External Relations of the European Union. Historical and Contemporary Perspectives, Peter Lang, Brussels

Winther D (2013) Regional Maintenance of Peace and Security under International Law. The Distorted Mirrors. Routledge, London

Sustainable Development in Free Trade Agreements of the European Union

Francesca Martines and Samantha Velluti

Contents

Attribution of the different parts of the Chapter is as follows. Francesca Martines: Section 2; Samantha Velluti: Section 3.

F. Martines (✉)
Department of Law, University of Pisa, Pisa, Italy
e-mail: francesca.martines@unipi.it

S. Velluti (✉)
Sussex Law School, School of Law, Politics and Sociology, University of Sussex, Brighton, UK
e-mail: S.M.Velluti@sussex.ac.uk

L. Pasquali (ed.), *EU Values and International Law*, European Union and its Neighbours in a Globalized World 35,
https://doi.org/10.1007/978-3-032-20521-6_7

Abstract The first part of this chapter analyses the complex interplay between trade, environmental protection and sustainability in the context of the European Union's (EU) free trade agreements (FTAs). After tracing the evolution of the relationship between international trade rules and the environment, highlighting positive and negative aspects, challenges and opportunities, the article focuses on the integration of sustainable development into EU trade policy, referring to the relevant provisions contained in the Lisbon Treaty and to recent European Commission documents on the topic of international cooperation and in particular trade agreements to achieve sustainable development goals. The contribution then analyses the structure of the chapters dedicated to sustainable development and more specifically to the environment in the so-called new generation FTAs, with a particular focus on the provisions on combating deforestation as a case study. The chapter examines how the EU's approach to deforestation, through instruments such as FLEGT and the more recent EUDR, is reflected in the specific clauses included in most recent FTAs. The scope of provisions on deforestation in various agreements is briefly analysed, highlighting an evolution towards a broader approach that integrates conservation and sustainable forest management, going beyond the issue of legality of timber trade. The second part of this contribution seeks to examine the labour dimension of sustainable development in modern EU free trade agreements (FTAs). Many of these agreements contain a specific chapter on labour, namely the 'Trade and Sustainable Development' (TDS) chapter or entitled more simply 'Labour' or 'Trade and Labour'. This chapter includes labour provisions whereby the parties agree to continue to strive to raise their respective standards and non-regression clauses, aimed at preventing a "race to the bottom" that might lead to a significant deterioration of domestic labour standards. Additionally, these provisions include a reaffirmation of the parties' existing international commitments regarding labour standards and/or have the aim of incentivising them to commit to key International Labour Organisation (ILO) Conventions. This contribution seeks to critically evaluate the extent to which these labour provisions are an effective way of improving labour standards in domestic legal systems. To meet its intended aim this section focuses on two EU trade agreements with middle-power countries, namely, the United Kingdom (UK) and Japan. These middle-power states constitute an interesting case-study because they still exert influence in the EU and play a significant role in contemporary international relations and global trade. After an overview of EU social conditionality in trade agreements, the contribution undertakes a country-specific analysis, examining the labour provisions of the 2019 EU-Japan Economic Partnership Agreement (EPA) and the 2020 EU-UK Trade and Cooperation Agreement (TCA). On a broader scale, the aim of this chapter is to contribute to the academic discussion about how sustainable development issues are elaborated and included in modern EU FTAs. Relatedly, it also intends to assess the extent to which the provisions of these EU bilateral trade agreements indicate the parties' intentions in relation to the EU's role in setting norms for the international trade order.

1 Introduction

Sustainable development has become a cornerstone of the European Union's external trade policy, receiving particular emphasis in the Treaty of Lisbon. Recognising the interconnectedness of economic, social and environmental progress, the EU is increasingly using trade agreements—especially the 'new generation' of free trade agreements (FTAs) with Trade and Sustainable Development (TSD) chapters—as key instruments to advance these objectives. These agreements promote environmental and labour standards, often referencing Multilateral Environmental Agreements (MEAs) and International Labour Organization (ILO) conventions, respectively.

Recognizing the limitations of multilateral approaches, the EU has increasingly turned to bilateral and regional trade agreements to embed a stronger social dimension in its external trade. This development underscores the understanding that trade, environmental sustainability, and social well-being are not isolated concerns but rather mutually reinforcing elements of sustainable progress.

The following chapters will contribute to this discussion by evaluating the integration and potential impact of these social and environmental dimensions in Free trade agreements as a problematic way to reinforce and promoting SD as one of the crucial values for the Union, but also for international relations in a rapidly changing world.

2 Sustainable Development and the Environment in Free Trade Agreements of the European Union

2.1 The Complex Interplay Between Trade, Environmental Protection and Sustainability

The intricate interplay between trade and the environment has developed as a subject of ongoing scrutiny and debate in the international arena among legal scholars ,[1] institutional actors[2] and citizens and activists.[3] There is a growing pressure for

[1] The bibliography is extensive. The volume of Delimatsis and Reins (2021) gathers more than 100 entries covering the most relevant issues of the relationship between trade and the environment in international law, WTO and in some states and regional areas. See also Wold and Gaines (2023). According to Van Hasselt (2021) trade law can hinder environmental agreement adoption/implementation, while trade-restrictive environmental policies risk "green protectionism" or "eco-imperialism. See also Gehring and Cordonier (2005). For earlier but seminal work on the environment and trade Brown Weiss et al. (2002); Steinberg (2002); Francioni (1998) p. 162.

[2] In the WTO one can consult the page dedicated to the connection between trade and the environment, https://www.wto.org/english/tratop_e/envir_e/envir_e.htm. For the EU approach see infra paragraph 2.

[3] See, for example, the public rallies against the ratification of the agreement between the EU and Canada (Ceta) and against the ratification of the Transatlantic partnership between the EU and th

integrating environmental issues into trade agreements[4] driven by a confluence of factors, including pressure from civil society, growing awareness of climate change, and the increasing impact of natural disasters and resource scarcity on economies and societies.

In the post-war international order, trade, influenced by historical and political imperatives, was subject to a regime of regulation and liberalization, most notably through the General Agreement on Tariffs and Trade (GATT47) and later GATT94 and other WTO annexed agreements. Trade was often seen as an engine of economic growth regardless of its environmental consequences.[5]

It is well known that GATT includes provisions that allow countries to adopt measures necessary to protect human, animal, or plant life or health and to conserve exhaustible natural resources as a defence for WTO members who have taken measures that are inconsistent with their GATT obligations. However, these measures must not be applied in a manner that constitutes arbitrary or unjustifiable discrimination between countries where the same conditions prevail or a disguised restriction on international trade (Chapeau).[6] In the WTO context of dispute resolution, the

USA (TTIP). A European citizens' initiative was launched in 2017 ("Stop TTIP!") to repeal the negotiating mandate for the Transatlantic Trade and Investment Partnership (TTIP) and not to conclude the Comprehensive Economic and Trade Agreement (CETA). According to the promoters the initiative, which was withdrawn in 2018, aimed at preventing employment, social, environmental, privacy and consumer standards from being lowered. As regards the Agreement with Mercosur, five civil society organisations complained before the EU Ombudsman that by not finalising a Sustainability Impact Assessment before concluding the trade negotiations with Mercosur the Commission breached EU law and in particular article 21 TEU. They argued that "the EU should not conclude trade agreements without knowing whether they have the potential to undermine the principles set out in the EU Treaties concerning the protection of human rights and the promotion of sustainable economic, social and environmental development". The Ombudsman concluded for a case of maladministration of the Commission. See decision in case 1026/2020/MAS. On the mobilization and influence of environmental groups on the expanding scope of trade policies and content of trade agreement, Toenshoff (2024), p. 953 ss. considers the "defensive issue linkage": as international trade law has broadened its reach, it has started to affect environmental policies, as a consequence environmental actors and policymakers link environmental concerns to trade discussions as a defensive measure to protect their policies from being undermined or challenged by trade rules.

[4] The document produced by the OECD Joint Working Party on Trade and Environment, *Greening regional trade agreements (RTAS) on non-tariff measures (NTMs) through technical barriers to trade (TBT), and regulatory co-operation*, investigates how environmental objectives can be further integrated into regional trade agreements. See COM/TAD/ENV/JWPTE(2020)1/FINAL, 25 November 2020,

[5] Brown Weiss (1992), p. 728, maintained that most discussion of trade and environment issues focused on facilitating freer trading relationships, and hence on fitting environmental issues into the framework of trade law.

[6] See, for example, United States—Standards for Reformulated and Conventional Gasoline Appellate Body Report WT/DS2/AB/R) of 1996 found that the contested US rules failed to meet the requirements of the "chapeau" of Article XX. In the United States—Import Prohibition of Certain Shrimp and Shrimp Products, the Appellate Body (WT/DS58/AB/R) concluded that the US measure while qualifying for provisional justification under Article XX(g) did not meet meet the chapeau requirements. At multilateral level cooperation led to the signing of the Agreement on the elimination of subsidies to vessels practicing illegal or illicit fishing.

approach to environmental protection, sustainability and trade has followed a case-by-case approach.

Besides the above-mentioned hypothesis of states measures adopted for preserving endangered species or clean air as an exception to WTO obligations, there are other unilateral measures aimed at protecting the environment, such as the Carbon Border Adjustment Mechanism (CBAM[7]), the European Union Deforestation Regulation (EUDR)[8] or standards or technical regulation, such as ecolabelling or energy efficiency measures, to name but a few, that intersect with trade obligations. The former can in fact be qualified as non-tariff barriers in the WTO.[9] It is, in fact, under this perspective that India has strongly criticised the EU CBAM.[10] One can also mention the issue of intellectual property protection that in case of so called green technologies might require flexible application of the TRIPS provisions to allow more affordable access for developing countries (Kim 2011, Azam (2022). Another crucial topic concerns public financing for supporting environmental transition or sustainable development goals (SDG) (green subsidies[11]) which are not explicitly provided for in the WTO but which shall be in line with the WTO provisions of the Agreement on Subsidies and countervailing measures.[12]

At bilateral levels, mechanisms are in place to avoid that standards or unilateral measures such as those mentioned above are qualified as barriers to trade. Promotion of good regulatory practices and regulatory co-operation among Parties are provided, for example, in CETA's Chapter on Regulatory Co-operation.[13] In fact, the

[7]The mechanism, which is scheduled to enter in force from January 1, 2026 has been conceived to ensure that goods imported in the EU bear a carbon price equivalent to that paid by EU producers under the EU Emissions Trading System (ETS). Importers are required to purchase "CBAM certificates" that correspond to the carbon emissions embedded in the goods they import.

[8]More specifically on the deforestation measures see, infra, paragraph … according to the regulation exports to the European Union must be accompanied by evidence demonstrating that they were not cultivated on land subject to deforestation after December 31, 2020.

[9]On the issue see Durel (2024), p.18 ss. See also WTO, *Joint report explores scope for coordinated approaches on climate action, carbon pricing, and policy spillovers.*

[10]A document was submitted by India, Job/TE/78 "Concerns on Emerging Trends of Using Environmental Measures as Protectionist Non-Tariff Measures". Access to the document is currently restricted, but see the Third World Network WTO: India galvanizes South over North's unilateral environment measures available at https://www.twn.my/title2/wto.info/2023/ti230303.htm. See infra on the issue of the compatibility in the WTO of the Deforestation regulation.

[11]According to Charnovitz (2014), p.1, "'green subsidy' is the allocation of public resources for the purpose of improving sustainability over what would otherwise occur via the market".

[12]Cima Esty (2024) propose a reframing of WTO subsidy rules to assess their permissibility not just on the basis of trade distortions, but also on their alignment with sustainable development goals. The 1994 Marrakesh Agreement includes a reference to sustainable development although only in its Preamble

[13]Bellmann Van der Ven (2020). Article 28.3 of the EU-Canada Comprehensive Economic and Trade Agreement states that environmental measures are covered under Article XX(b) and that the reference to "exhaustible natural resources" in Article XX(g) covers living, as well as non-living, resources. (Client earth) (CETA, USMCA, EU-Japan) also lists the protection of the environment as one of the specific objectives of regulatory co-operation

trade-environment nexus is primarily addressed in bilateral, rather than multilateral, agreements. As the EU's 2006 Communication "Global Europe: Competing in the World" (COM(2006) 567 final) makes clear, bilateral trade agreements are instruments for enhancing, among other things, environmental protection objectives. It is interesting to note that the FTA of the EU with Mercosur (Argentina, Brazil, Paraguay and Uruguay) establishes that: "the measures in Art. XX(b) GATT "include environmental measures, such as measures taken to implement multilateral environmental agreements, which are necessary to protect human, animal or plant life or health" (article 13).

The difficulty to find consent at multilateral but even at plurilateral level has been demonstrated by the case of agreement on the liberalization of environmental goods and services[14] whose negotiations ended as a result of the lack of agreement on the definition of environmental goods.[15]

On the other hand, there are multilateral agreements such as the Convention on International Trade in Endangered Species of Wild Fauna and Flora (CITES) and the Montreal Protocol on Substances that Deplete the Ozone Layer, which regulate international trade of species listed in its Annexes classifies according to the risk of extinction.

In general terms, it is clear that trade still poses significant challenges as it has both positive and negative environmental consequences, hence the difficulty of finding a correct balance between trade liberalization as a driver of development and environmental protection as a crucial element of a sustainable development.

On the positive side of trade liberalization: potentially expansion of access to environmentally friendly products[16] or raw materials used for new technologies; access to sustainable goods and environmentally friendly technology product; creation of incentives for countries to enhance their environmental standards. For instance, reduction of trade barriers for some products such as wind turbines can enhance the dissemination of this environmental-friendly technology. Trade can contribute to environmental protection through facilitating and promoting trade and foreign direct investment in environmental goods and services, or through promoting trade in goods that are the subject of schemes such as fair and ethical trade Article (see EU FTA with South Korea13.6)

---

[14] Article 31(iii) of the 2001 Doha Development Agenda of the WTO. The declaration called for the "reduction, or, as appropriate, elimination of tariff and non-tariff barriers to environmental goods and services." On the *WTO failure in this sense see the study of the European Parliament Research Service, The WTO's negotiating function Towards plurilaterals and new trade challenges*, April 2024, available: https://www.europarl.europa.eu/RegData/etudes/BRIE/2024/760443/EPRS_BRI(2024)760443_EN.pdf

[15] See WTO Reinsch et al. (2021),

[16] Costa Rica, Iceland, New Zealand, and Switzerland signed the Agreement on Climate Change, Trade and Sustainability (ACCTS) that aims to achieve environmental policy objectives through legally binding trade rules. It provides for the liberalisation of tariffs on environmental goods and services, the definition of rues to eliminate fossil fuel subsidies, and the development of high integrity eco-labels. It is not a free trade agreement, as the MFNC applies https://www.iddri.org/en/publications-and-events/billet-de-blog/there-case-eu-join-agreement-climate-change-trade-and

On the negative side: trade can increase greenhouse gas emission,[17] particularly through the use of air, maritime, and road transport. Preferential access to rich markets can encourage the productions that are dangerous for environmental protection.[18] The practice of deforestation for the cultivation of high-demand products (monoculture) might result in direct environmental harm. Illegal trade in protected species is a serious risk. The presence of less stringent environmental policies in developing countries reduces the relative cost of producing environmentally damaging goods, thereby establishing a comparative advantage for these commodities and incentivizing "dirty" Foreign Direct Investment.

The sustainability dimension in trade[19] has made more complicated the relationship between trade and the environment by encompassing social (labor)[20] and economic dimensions. Environment is one of the pillars of sustainable development which refers to the ability to preserve and protect the natural environment over time, ensuring that human activities do not compromise the availability of resources for future generations.[21] This concept is based on the balance between human needs and the planet's capacity to regenerate. It has been increasingly recognized that sustainable trade is fundamental for development[22] but "policy effects on growth have—everything else being equal—initially a negative environmental impact, especially

[17] WTO, Trade and Climate Change, The carbon content of international trade, Information brief no. 4, 2022. The documents highlight that international trade, while generating greenhouse gas (GHG) emissions, can sometimes *reduce* overall emissions. This occurs when the exporting country produces goods or services with lower GHG emissions than the importing country, and this production difference outweighs the emissions from transportation. Furthermore, policy and technological advancements in environmental and energy efficiency can decrease emissions from both production and transport related to trade, with trade itself facilitating the spread of green technologies and improved carbon efficiency. See also the Briefing published in the webpage of the organisation for clean transport and energy, available at https://www.transportenvironment.org/articles/strike-a-balance-trade-agreements-for-resilient-and-responsible-supply-chains

[18] According to legal opinion commissioned by Greenpeace "EU-Mercosur FTA does not comply with EU and international law". The opinion is available in the website of Greenpeace, https://www.greenpeace.de/publikationen/Rechtsanalyse%20Handelsvertrag%20EU-Mercosur%20verst%C3%B6%C3%9Ft%20gegen%20Klimagesetze%20englisch.pdf. See also "FTA's Sustainability Impact Assessment (SIA) commissioned by the EU Commission to the London School of Economics (LSE). It calculates that the FTA would lead to a global increase of methane and nitrous oxide.

[19] CJEU, *Opinion* 02/15, para. 147: The objective of sustainable development henceforth forms an integral part of the common commercial policy.

[20] See the contribution of Samantha Velluti in this volume.

[21] See the definition by the Brundtland Commission in 1987 in its 1987 report "Our Common Future". As reported by the UN in the webpage dedicated to sustainability, available https://www.un.org/en/academic-impact/sustainability.

[22] The Ministerial Declaration of the High-Level Segment of the 2021 Session of the Economic and Social Council and the 2021 High-Level Political Forum on Sustainable Development recognized the importance of sustainable development and initiated negotiations on trade and environment issues. See also Environmental Goods Agreement (EGA) negotiations: Launched in 2014, these negotiations aim to reduce or eliminate tariffs and non-tariff barriers on a wide range of environmental goods.

in developing countries, but unfold positive effects when they have surpassed the pollution peak”.[23]

Thus, the most difficult objective is to achieve a correct balance between trade, development and environmental protection (conceived at large, that is covering different elements such as fight against climate change, maintenance of biological diversity, policies against deforestation etc.).

2.2 *Trade, Environmental Protection and Sustainability in the EU Legal Order, in Recent Documents of the EU Commission*

The integration of sustainable trade into EU trade policy is grounded in the foundational principles of the EU Treaties. Article 3.5 of the TEU defines the general objective of the EU in its relationship with the rest of the world. The EU is committed to the goal of sustainable development and fair and equal trade. Article 21 TEU[24] expands and further elaborates on the general objectives defined in the previously mentioned provision. For the present analysis, the relevant letters in article 21 are those concerning the objective of fostering sustainable economic, social and environmental development of developing countries with the primary aim of eradicating poverty (21.2.d); of encouraging integration of all countries into the world economy by means of the progressive abolition of restrictions on international trade (21.2.e); of helping to develop international measures to preserve and improve the quality of the environment and the sustainable management of global natural resources, in order to ensure sustainable development (21.2.f). These objectives have to be connected to specific goals pursued by the EU through other policies. In particular, article 11 of the Treaty on the Functioning of the European Union (TFEU) mandates that “environmental protection requirements must be integrated into the definition and implementation of the Union’s policies and activities, in particular with a view to promoting sustainable development”. This article provides the legal basis for incorporating environmental considerations into the EU’s Free Trade Agreements (FTAs). Article 191 TFEU indicates the aim of ‘preserving, protecting and improving the quality of the environment and (…) prudent and rational utilisation of natural resources”. Additionally, Article 207 TFEU stipulates that the EU’s common commercial policy “be conducted in the context of the principles and objectives of the Union’s external action”. Moreover, the general principle of consistency requires that the Commission and the Council must ensure that the commercial policy is “compatible with internal Union policies and rules” (Art 207.3 TFEU). There is undirect reference to sustainability in article 208 TFEU, the legal basis of the EU development cooperation policy as it is specified that the latter “shall be conducted

[23] https://coleurope.eu/sites/default/files/research-paper/EDP_5_2024_Peridy.pdf

[24] Van Elsuwege (2010), p. 987; Lonardo (2018), p. 584; Montini (2025), p. 47.

within the framework of the principles and objectives of the Union's external action". Moreover, the same provision refers to the obligation of the EU (and its member states) to comply with the commitment "and take account of the objectives they have approved in the context of the United Nations and other competent international organisations".[25] One of these principles is sustainable development.

The reference to the above-mentioned provisions contained in primary law suggests that the interconnection of policies and objectives complicates the relationship between the areas of intervention and the interconnection between goals such as sustainable development (economic, social, environmental), fair and equal trade, poverty eradication, global economic integration, environmental protection, prudent use of natural resources. The means are to be attained through the progressive abolition of restrictions on international trade, integration of the environmental protection requirements into EU policies (including FTAs), developing international environmental measures, EU development cooperation policy. It is clear that the relationship between goals and means is not always linear. Sustainable development, for example, is at the same time an objective but also an instrument which is functional to contributing to the attainment of the general goal of the eradication of poverty. The EU is required, from a constitutional point of view, to design its policies in a manner that ensures that those objectives are effectively and consistently pursued.

In any case, on the basis on these treaty provisions, the EU has progressively strengthened its commitment to sustainable trade. After the entry into force of the Lisbon treaty, *the Europe 2020 Strategy* adopted in 2010 emphasized the importance of including social and environmental objectives in the economic development. In the *Trade for All: Towards a more responsible trade and investment policy* (2015) the Commission highlighted the importance of integrating sustainable development objectives into trade agreements (point 4.2) recognising trade as a tool to promote sustainable development (point 4.2.2). One of the most significant aspects of the document was the stated intention of aligning EU trade policy with the United Nations' 2030 Agenda for Sustainable Development. The EC recognized that trade could contribute to achieving the Sustainable development goals (SDGs), particularly those related to poverty reduction, social inclusion, and environmental sustainability. The concept of greater transparency in trade negotiations was also mentioned.

The European Commission's 2018[26] non-paper, Feedback and way forward on improving the implementation and enforcement of Trade and Sustainable Development chapters in EU Free Trade Agreements, announced the intention to enhance the effectiveness of TSD chapters. The European Green Deal,[27] launched

---

[25] See the UN's Sustainable Development Goals (SDGs).

[26] European Commission Service *Feedback and way forward on improving the implementation and enforcement of Trade and Sustainable Development chapters in EU Free Trade Agreements.* Non-paper. February 2018, cited in the Commission Communication COM(2021) 654 final.

[27] The European Green Deal. Communication from the Commission to the European Parliament, the European Council, the Council, the European Economic and Social Committee and the Committee of the Regions: COM/2019/640 Final.

by the European Commission further accentuated the inclusion of environmental and social concerns into EU trade policy. The 2021 Trade Policy Review[28] outlined a new direction, representing a necessary adaptation to new realities: changed global context with increased tensions, protectionism, urgency of climate change and green transition with higher environmental and sustainability targets.

The 2022 Communication on The Power of Trade Partnerships[29] revised the EU strategy to include TSD chapters in EU trade policy, indicating six policy priorities: proactive partner cooperation, country-specific approaches, mainstreaming sustainability beyond TSD chapters, enhanced TSD commitment monitoring, reinforced civil society engagement.

Although it is not easy to summarise the complexity of these communications a clear trend can be identified: the EU's trade policy intends to embed environmental concerns in trade policy. Moreover, sustainability clauses are not only included in TSD chapters (Adinolfi 2020). The idea is to integrate these principles across all trade agreement elements. The EU also intends to strengthen enforcement and monitoring mechanisms (Marín Durán 2020). The New 2022 strategy proposes to "further align TSD enforcement with the general state-to-state dispute (SSDS) settlement" and to "extend the possibility to apply trade sanctions in cases of failure to comply with obligations that materially defeats the object and purpose of the Paris Agreement on Climate Change or in serious instances of non-compliance with the ILO fundamental principles and rights at work".

Finally mentions should be made to the Political guidelines of the Commission for the period 2024–2029 (the Commission's pluriannual programme) and the Compass for Competitiveness (as an answer, although limited, to the Draghi report).[30] The first document endorses an integrated approach where trade policy actively supports the European Green Deal and the sustainable competitiveness of the EU. It intends to enhance trade relationships with partner countries alongside infrastructure development (Commission, p. 27). The *Compass* highlights the necessity for European companies not to find themselves in a competitive disadvantage as a consequence of EU to less stringent environmental standards in non-EU countries.

A further interesting initiative announced is the *Clean Trade and Investment Partnerships*.[31] This is aimed at securing "supply of raw materials, clean energy and clean tech from across the world" (p. 8 and p. 27). It is clear that the EU's trade

[28] European Commission, Trade Policy Review—An Open, Sustainable and Assertive Trade Policy. Communication from the Commission to the European Parliament, the Council, the European Economic and Social Committee and the Committee of the Regions: COM/2021/66 Final. Brussels, 18 February 2021.

[29] The Power of Trade Partnerships: Together for Green and Just Economic Growth. Communication from the Commission to the European Parliament, the Council, the European Economic and Social Committee and the Committee of the Regions: COM/2022/409 Final. Brussels, 22 June 2022.

[30] The Draghi Report suggests a strategic approach to decarbonization, where environmental goals are integrated into a broader economic vision.

[31] They intend to implement sustainability commitments through targeted trade and investment rules, regulatory cooperation, sustainable procurement, raw materials management, and support for partner countries' green transitions. European Parliament EPRS, 2015.

interests need to be protected (indeed, this objective is enshrined in article 21, lett. e) (supra).

The inclusion of sustainable development chapters in FTAs and the prospect of strengthening their enforcement seems to indicate that the EU considers trade as a tool functional to the attainment of the sustainability objectives rather than conceiving liberalised trade as an end in itself. In other terms this means that the EU intends, at least in principle, to enhance the positive effect of trade on sustainability. Through this approach, the EU aims to demonstrate its commitment to these values, respond to its citizens' concerns about the environment and climate change, and create a level playing field for EU companies and industries. It also aims to encourage its partners to adopt legislation and practices in line with sustainability goals.

However, it is not clear whether the EU will be able to maintain a coherent approach, particularly, but not only, in the light of recent developments in the international community affecting trade and security relations and the growing challenges related to the EU's environmental objectives.

Even if not produced by the Commission but ordered by it, it is worth shortly mentioning the Letta Report as he refers to standard (not specifically to environmental ones) and agreements. Letta underlines the necessity to involve third countries into the definition of (high) standards and not imposing them through regulation harming their economies; at the same time, he also warnes that trade agreements should not be used as "trojan horse to weaken legislative framework" (Letta, p. 137), thus suggesting a balance between opening of markets and the defence of European values and standards.

2.3 Trade and Sustainable Development Chapters and the Environment in Recent Free Trade Agreements. The Reference to Multilateral Environmental Agreements

EU Free Trade Agreements (FTAs) primarily aim to enhance trade flows by liberalizing markets.[32]

Trade and Sustainable Development (TSD) chapters have been included to address environmental and labor issues since 2009 (FTA with South Korea).[33]

[32] As for FTAs with Mercosur, according to the data reported by the legal opinion for Greenpeace the EU will remove custom duties on 95% of the tariff lines for imports from the Mercosur countries within 10 years after the FTA's entry into force. This accounts for 100% of industrial goods and 82% of agricultural goods. The Mercosur countries must fully liberalise 91% of the tariff lines, including 93% of the agricultural tariff lines and key (industrial) sectors like cars, car parts, machinery, chemicals and pharmaceutical products. The report is available at https://table.media/en/climate/news/legal-opinion-mercosur-treaty-violates-climate-laws/.

[33] Remondino (2022), p. 168; Bronckers and Gruni (2021). For the latter authors standards in FTAs fall into three different groups: obligations based on existing international agreements, obligations related to existing domestic legislation, and more aspirational clauses referring to higher levels of protection.

The structure of environmental provisions within TSD chapters varies across FTAs, often reflecting the timing of the agreement and negotiation outcomes. Agreements concluded after 2018 tend to reflect the EU's 15-point Action Plan for improved TSD, with a strong emphasis on environmental considerations.

Unlike labor provisions, environmental clauses are often non-prescriptive, they encourage rather than require specific actions. This difference illustrates the delicate balance between encouraging the adoption of environmental standards and respecting national sovereignty, that is the right to regulate (see, for example, FTA with Canada, article 24.3; FTA with New Zeeland, article 19.2).[34] Thus the agreements do not aim at harmonization of legislation (with a partial exception in the Association agreement with Ukraine and Moldavia and Georgia[35] which are particular case in the perspective of accession to the EU).

All TSD chapters—which open with an introductory Provisions on Sustainable Development Objectives—recognize the importance of the environment for sustainable development and the potential positive impact of trade in this regard (see FTA with New Zeeland article 19.1.2; FTA with Mercosur article 1 of the TSD chapter). The Mercosur new Annex is worth mentioning as regards sustainable development and trade. Article B.3 specifies: "… the Parties agree to have a cooperative approach to address challenges associated with meeting a Party's sustainability measures affecting trade, taking into account the different levels of development, capacities, priorities and national circumstances and legislations, as well as the specific challenges of landlocked developing countries". Among the aforementioned challenges, the Parties recognize the need to facilitate the implementation of actions to support compliance with the sustainability measures of the other Party affecting trade, in order that exports can benefit fully from the market access opportunities provided for by the Agreement.

FTAs cover a range of environmental topics, including reference to Multilateral Environmental Agreements (MEAs), Trade and climate change, Trade and biodiversity, Sustainable Forest management Sustainable fisheries and aquaculture (see infra for further specifications).

However, the specific inclusion and emphasis of these topics vary significantly between FTAs. For example, South Korea agreement focuses[36] on promoting trade in environmental goods and services, but lacks specific provisions on climate, bio-

[34] For example, in FTA with New Zeeland specified that: trade in forest products harvested in accordance with the law of the country of harvest and from sustainably managed forests.

[35] Those agreements contain the commitment to align the partner's legislation to the EU's environmental Remondino (2022), p. 168. This approach is justified by the objective of the agreement of integrating the economies of those countries into the EU market.

[36] Article 13.6 paragraph 2: "The Parties shall strive to facilitate and promote trade and foreign direct investment in environmental goods and services, including environmental technologies, sustainable renewable energy, energy efficient products and services and eco-labelled goods, including through addressing related non-tariff barriers. The Parties shall strive to facilitate and promote trade in goods that contribute to sustainable development, including goods that are the subject of schemes such as fair and ethical trade and those involving corporate social responsibility and accountability".

diversity, fisheries, and forests. The agreement with Canada includes provisions on MEAs, forest management, and aquaculture but climate change is referred to in the article dedicated to cooperation on environmental issues (24.12) and on trade favouring environmental protection (article 24.19 where trade and investment are conceived as tools to advance environmental goals, particularly in the areas of general environmental protection and the fight against climate change); FTA with Central America, Colombia, Peru,[37] and Georgia contain TSD chapters with different emphasis on environmental protection, including forest management. The agreement with Vietnam in article 13.8, specifically addresses "Sustainable Forest Management and Trade in Forest Products". The FTA with New Zealand contains Article 19.4, "Trade and Gender Equality," and an article addressing "Trade and Fossil Fuel Subsidy Reform" (a proposal also considered with India). While the agreement with Singapore does not contain provisions on biodiversity, it includes an article on Trade in Timber and Timber Products. The proposed FTA with China does not include provisions relating to biodiversity, forests, or aquaculture.[38]

Most FTAs refers to Multilateral Environmental agreements. In FTA with Canada, the article on MEA is broadly formulated: each Party commits to effectively implement in its law and practices, in its whole territory, the multilateral environmental agreements to which it is Party. In case of the FTA with New Zeeland each Party commits to adopt or maintain measures to further the objectives of MEAs to which it is a Party (article 19.5). Similarly, in the Mercosur FTA each Party reaffirms its commitments to promote and effectively implement, multilateral environmental agreements (MEAs), protocols and their amendments to which it is a party. For other MEA Mercosur FTA specifies that Parties will exchange information on their respective progress as regards the ratifications of MEAs.

The Trade and Climate Change sections include (see for example FTA with New Zeeland, article) reference to the United Nations Framework Convention on Climate Change (UNFCCC). In this case each Party undertakes to implement this Convention "including commitments with regard to nationally determined contributions", (self-defined targets and plans for reducing greenhouse gas emissions). Thus, the

---

[37] The text is available at https://publications.europa.eu/resource/cellar/42e02e6c-1698-465e-923c-d2d12f91c728.0017.04/DOC_1.

[38] Agreement containing biodiversity provision: Trade Agreement between the European Union and its Member States, of the one part, and Colombia and Peru; Association Agreement between the European Union and the European Atomic Energy Community and their Member States, of the one part, and Georgia, of the other part (EU-Georgia FTA); Association Agreement between the European Union and the European Atomic Energy Community and their Member States, of the one part, and the Republic of Moldova, of the other part (EU-Moldova FTA); Comprehensive and enhanced Partnership Agreement between the European Union and the European Atomic Energy Community and their Member States, of the one part, and the Republic of Armenia, of the other part; Economic Partnership Agreement between the European Union and Japan; EU-Mexico trade agreement—agreement in principle (EU-Mexico FTA). The texts of the agreements can be downloaded from the EU Commission trade webpage https://policy.trade.ec.europa.eu/eu-trade-relationships-country-and-region/negotiations-and-agreements_en.

Parties are legally bound within their trade agreement to actively work towards their climate goals as defined by the UNFCCC and the Paris Agreement

The most relevant new provisions (reproducing analogous clauses in the Agreement with UK and New Zeeland) in the revised Mercosur agreement is the reformulation of the Climate Change provision which define the obligation for each Party to remain a party, in good faith, of the UNFCCC and its Paris Agreement an essential element of the agreement.[39] Since the Paris Agreement differentiate the commitments of the developing countries parties to the agreement, not providing for sanctions or quantified obligations, the inclusion of this reference is rather symbolic. However, an interesting case is reported by Bronckers and Gruni (2021, p. 29). Brazil, under its Nationally Determined Contribution (NDC) to the Paris Agreement, has stated its intention to achieve zero illegal deforestation in the Brazilian Amazonia and to restore/reforest 12 million hectares of forests by 2035. The inclusion of the obligation to "effectively implement" the Paris Agreement in the EU-Mercosur FTA removes any doubt that Brazil's NDC is a voluntary intention, at least in its relationship with the EU. The FTA, according to the authors, consolidates this commitment.

In general terms, all the above cited agreements engage the Parties to consult and cooperate, as appropriate, on trade-related environmental matters of mutual interest in the context of multilateral environmental agreements (see, for example, the agreement with Canada, article 24.4)

As a further example of mention to MEA, one can consider that chapters on biodiversity refer to the Convention on Biological Diversity (CBD), the Convention on International Trade in Endangered Species of Wild Fauna and Flora (CITES[40]) or to the United Nations Sustainable Development goals. It is to be noted that the legal value of these instruments differs, as the former are binding international law conventions, while the latter is a soft law instrument.

The reference to binding MEAs within FTAs establishes a link between trade and environment, providing a contextual framework for interpreting the agreement. According to Article 31, paragraph 3[41] of the Vienna Convention on the Law

---

[39] On 6 December 2024, the EU and Mercosur reached a political agreement on an improved and additional parts of the EU-Mercosur Partnership Agreement. The new parts include the reference to Paris Agreement as an essential element of the Agreement. This clause refers to the values that are considered of essential relevance and the basis of the partnership. A violation of the essential element clause might lead to the suspension or the termination of the agreement.

[40] The Convention on International Trade in Endangered Species of Wild Fauna and Flora (CITES) is an international conservation instrument for ensuring forest products trade does not threaten the survival of international wildlife species. The central element of CITES trade procedures is verifying the origin and legal sourcing of timber species listed under CITES. In each country, national CITES Management Authorities are responsible for this verification. They evaluate timber exports containing CITES species and, if the consignment meets their requirements, issue Legal Acquisition Findings (LAFs).

[41] McLachlan (2005), p. 279 affirms that "Article 31(3)(c) expresses a more general principle of treaty interpretation, namely that of systemic integration within the international legal system." (p. 280). See also van Gellecum (2012).

of Treaties, treaties should be interpreted with reference to the context, which includes "any relevant rules of international law applicable in the relations between the Parties". Consequently, one could submit that the reference to a MEA requires the Parties to interpret the FTA's provisions related to trade and environment in accordance with the obligations defined in the MEAs.[42] This could also imply that their trade relationship is consistent with and supportive of their climate objectives. In this case the FTA provisions to "effectively implement" the MEA reinforce the obligations undertaken by the Parties with the ratification of the previous agreement.

The above-mentioned view[43] is maintained also by a legal opinion by ClientEarth considering that this process aims to ensure that obligations stemming from MEAs are actively implemented.

The reference to international agreements in the field of labour has been underlined by the EU-South Korea Panel.[44] The latter highlights that FTAs can incorporate and reaffirm existing MEA obligations, making them enforceable under the FTA's mechanisms.[45] The revised TSD chapter of the Agreement with Mercosur invests the Parties with the task of discussing and monitoring the application by the Parties of the commitments made in the Chapter on Sustainable Development of the Agreement, and this will include the verification of how they are implementing the multilateral environmental and social agreements to which they are contracting Parties (the annex, article A.2 par. 12, refers to a longer list of agreements if compared with the 2019 version of the TSD chapter).

It is worth mentioning that in the Green Deal Communication the EU Commission tabled the proposal to include the Paris Agreement in the essential element clause and reaffirmed this in the 2021 review;[46] the same reference is contained in the latest version of the EU's Generalised Scheme of Preferences (GSP). As Adinolfi (2017) highlights, this reflects the EU's efforts to balance economic interests with environmental protection in its trade policy. This suggestion has been implemented in the UK, New Zeeland and Mercosur agreements (see *infra*).

---

[42] The relationship between Meas and trade can be considered the other way round, as MEAs may contain provisions that directly impact trade, for example prohibiting or restricting the export of certain products, such as protected species (CITES), ozone-depleting substances (Montreal Protocol), or hazardous waste (Basel Convention). Brandi (2017).

[43] Partner countries often ratified key MEAs, including the Paris Agreement, the Convention on Biological Diversity (CBD), and CITES, prior to or concurrently with the implementation of FTAs. Therefore, isolating the specific influence of FTAs on MEA implementation proves difficult, as highlighted by the ex-post impact assessment.

[44] See the contribution of Samantha Velluti in this volume.

[45] Panel Report, Panel of Experts proceeding constituted under Article 13.15 of the E.U.-Korea Free Trade Agreement, par. 107 (Jan. 20, 2021).

[46] Trade Policy Review—An Open, Sustainable and Assertive Trade Policy. Communication from the Commission to the European Parliament, the Council, the European Economic and Social Committee and the Committee of the Regions: COM/2021/66 Final. Brussels, 18 February 2021. The EU will propose that the respect of the Paris Agreement be considered an essential element in future trade and investment agreements, point 3.2.2.

In summary, the inclusion of MEAs within FTAs serves to reinforce environmental commitments, provide a contextual framework for interpretation, and acknowledge the interplay between trade and environmental policies. Application is limited, underscoring the importance of viewing MEAs as tools for integration and interpretation.

2.4 The Provisions on the Fight against Deforestation as a Case Study

The present author considers that the focus on sustainable forest management and trade in forest products, a specific part of the TSD chapter, provides an interesting model to illustrate the scope of Sustainable development and its link with EU values and objectives.

2.4.1 The Policy to Counter Deforestation

Sustainable development is central to forestry policy since the 1992 United Nations Conference on Environment and Development (UNCED) (Hickey 2004). Reducing Emissions from Deforestation and Forest Degradation[47] is a framework developed by the United Nations to combat climate change by incentivizing developing countries to protect their forests.

Sustainable forest management, a notion which refers to human intervention necessary to the maintenance of a functioning forest ecosystem, that aims to balance environmental, social, and economic objectives,[48] and the fight against deforestation (that is conversion of forest to other land use independently of whether human-induced or not) is considered essential to achieve the objectives set in the UN 2030 Agenda for Sustainable Development and the Paris Agreement.

In fact, deforestation undermines the three pillars of sustainable development: economic growth, social equity, environmental protection. As regards the former, it affects water and climate regulation, loss of soil fertility and biodiversity compromising long-term development; social equality can be affected as the result of a reduced access to essential resources (water, food) by displacement, loss of traditional knowledge, cultural identity; environment can be damaged as deforestation causes releasing stored carbon, contributing to climate change. Deforestation also leads to the loss of biodiversity, as it leads to the damage of habitats and the extinction of species. It also contributes to soil erosion, which can degrade land and water

[47] https://unfccc.int/topics/land-use/workstreams/redd/what-is-redd.

[48] See the dedicated web page of the EU Commission, https://single-market-economy.ec.europa.eu/sectors/raw-materials/related-industries/forest-based-industries/sustainable-forest-management_en.

quality. While deforestation is a global phenomenon, it is particularly concentrated in certain regions, notably Latin America, and is increasing in Africa, and Asia.[49]

The fundamental elements of sustainable development are also integral part of policies to combat deforestation: it demands a balance between present needs with and long-term ecological, economic, and social necessities related to forests.

As a central aspect of its environmental sustainability policy, the EU is committed to combating deforestation.[50] The forest strategy of the EU clarifies that the EU is responsible for 7–10% of global consumption of crops and livestock products that are associated with deforestation in their countries of origin.[51] One has to consider that the EU does play a role in the deforestation process in third countries as it imports agricultural and timber products from deforested areas.[52]

The Commission has established three pillars to integrate forest protection into comprehensive sustainability policies: protecting existing forests, ensuring sustainable forest management, and creating new forested areas.

The first pillar, protecting existing forests, covers actions such as the EU Forest Law Enforcement, Governance, and Trade (FLEGT) plan and the Deforestation Regulation (EUDR).

The FLEGT action plan was adopted in 2003[53] to combat illegal logging[54] and to promote sustainable forest management at an international level. The objective is to ensure that timber imported into the European Union originate from legal and sustainably managed sources. To ensure the implementation of the plan, in 2005 Regulation 2173[55] was adopted which set up a licensing scheme to ensure that only timber legally produced in accordance with national laws as set out in Voluntary Partnership Agreements, concluded with a variety of countries,[56] is imported into

[49] See the FAO report available at https://www.europarl.europa.eu/RegData/etudes/IDAN/2020/603513/EXPO_IDA(2020)603513_EN.pdf. FAO. 2020. *Global Forest Resources Assessment 2020—Main report*. FAO. https://doi.org/10.4060/ca9825en

[50] The EU is part of the International tropical timber organization (as all its member states). The International Tropical Timber Organization (ITTO) focuses specifically on sustainable management of tropical forests and trade in tropical timber. The ITTO developed criteria and indicators for the sustainable management of natural tropical forests. See https://www.itto.int/direct/topics/topics_pdf_download/topics_id=4872&no=1&disp=inline. The EU is a signatory of the Glasgow Leaders' declaration on Forest and Land Use of 2021. The EU is a contracting Party of the Convention on Biological Diversity, the 2014 New York Declaration on Forests.

[51] Legislative train, https://www.europarl.europa.eu/legislative-train/theme-environment-public-health-and-food-safety-envi/file-eu-driven-global-deforestation.

[52] Fournier and Ozinga (2018), p. 15.

[53] COM/2003/0251 final.

[54] Annual synthesis report on the enforcement of regulation 2173/2005, COM (2018) 448, p. 3.

[55] *OJ L 347, 30.12.2005, p. 1. In 2008 regulation* 1024/2008 was adopted laying down detailed measures for the implementation of the FLEGT Regulation.

[56] For a complete list see the dedicated web page of the Commission, available at https://eur-lex.europa.eu/EN/legal-content/summary/voluntary-partnership-agreements-on-forest-law-enforcement-governance-and-trade.html?fromSummary=12. However, the Commission has recently required the termination of VPA with Camerun and Liberia.

the EU.[57] The policy's external aspects are integrated with its internal regulations. The VPA can become a tool to encourage the partner country to develop and strengthen its legal framework as it requires the former to set up and apply a timber legality assurance system (TLAS) which verifies the legality of timber.[58] Only legally verified timber can enter the EU market as it is covered by the FLEGT licence.

In 2010, the EU adopted regulation 995/2010 (EU Timber Regulation, EUTR) laying down due diligence obligations for operators who sell timber and timber products on the market. The EUDR requires operators to provide information on the origin of their products.

The fight against deforestation system has recently been reinforced by regulation 2023/1115[59] (European Union deforestation regulation, EUDR)[60] which actually repeals the EUTR, providing for new due diligence obligations for importers who are required to prove legality, asses the risk, and mitigate the risk of placing products (such as cocoa, wood, coffee, rubber, palm oil, beef and soy, as well as products made from them, such as furniture, paper, chocolate and tires[61]) for which forests were cleared or degraded after December 31, 2020. The system is also based on the classification of countries according to the risk they pose in terms of deforestation (low, standard, or high risk). An agreement containing provisions on combating deforestation could positively influence the assessment of some of the criteria

---

[57] See, for example, the Voluntary Partnership Agreement between the European Union and the Socialist Republic of Viet Nam on forest law enforcement, governance and trade (10861/2018). *The VPA contains a clause for the involvement of stakeholders (non-governmental organisations, forest associations, enterprises, trade unions, local communities and people living in forest areas) in the implementation of the agreement (article 15) and a social safeguard clause for monitoring the impacts of this Agreement on ethnic minorities and local communities concerned and on their way of life, as well as on households and the timber industry. While taking reasonable steps to mitigate any adverse effects. Vietnam is also importer of illegal timber from Cambodia and Laos (see Report of the Environmental investigating agency, available at* https://eia-international.org/wp-content/uploads/Vietnam-EU-Timber-Briefing-English-version.pdf. *See also* https://ilbolive.unipd.it/it/news/societa/dalla-cambogia-nostre-tavole-lindustria-zucchero. *An example of illegal timber* is when it derives from Cutting down trees in protected areas or natural reserves without the necessary permits or exceeding the allowed logging quotas.

[58] Before a country can start issuing FLEGT licences, the EU and the partner country must certify that the country's legality assurance system is functioning as described in the VPA.

[59] See the proposal of the Commission COM (2021) 776 final. The proposal was a partial answer to the request of the European Parliament's own-initiative legislative resolution 2020/2006(INL) with recommendations to the Commission on an EU legal framework to halt and reverse EU-driven global deforestation (2020/2006(INL)) OJ C 404 which required action by the Commission.

[60] The EUDR framework of reference is the green deal. See also, at the international level, the 2030 United Nations Sustainable Development Goals (SDGs), SDG 15, to protect, restore and promote sustainable use of terrestrial ecosystems, sustainably manage forests, combat desertification, and halt and reverse land degradation and halt biodiversity loss. See also the State of the World's Forests 2018—Forest Pathways to Sustainable Development, FAO (2018).

[61] Cattle, cocoa, coffee, oil palm, rubber, soy, and wood. And products derived from these commodities, such as beef, chocolate, furniture, and tires. As a consequence of Parliament amendments the regulation also covers rubber, charcoal, printed paper products and several palm oil derivatives. (Forest degradation, see Vietnam FTA)

applied to consider a country's risk level.[62] On 29 June 2023 the regulation came into force, and it was to take effect on 30 December 2024. However, a 12-month delay was approved by the legislators as a consequence of concerns on the capacity to fully comply by traders and operators.[63] The regulation will be applicable from December 30, 2025, for large companies and from June 30, 2026, for micro and small companies.

It is to be underlined that while the EUTR approached the issue of deforestation from a perspective of legality, the EUDR extends beyond the compliance approach: what is relevant is not (only) that the commodity has been produced in accordance with national legislation of exporting country[64] to have access to the EU market, but that it has been produced in land that after 2020 has not been subject to a deforestation process (after 2020).

The idea is that the EU shall not contribute to deforestation and this aim is pursued by limiting or prohibiting the entry to its market of products derived from deforestation. This approach intends to encourage importers to find supply chains that respond to the above-mentioned requirements (deforestation free) incentivizing good practices from suppliers. However, this means that producers have to adapt to the information requirements and traceability systems needed to be part of supply chains accessing the EU market.

In the WTO, some WTO members contested the EUDR regulation for its one-size-fits-all approach, the consequences for small farmers in the developing countries, its qualification as technical regulation, the lack of specific information and documentation that producers must provide to European operators, the risk of disruption of trade flows.[65] It is clear that for small farms, especially those located in poor countries, the administrative burden required by the EUDR is very demanding as they have to register their farm and the geolocalisation (van Noordwijk (2025), p. 75).

The second EU pillar of fight against deforestation policy is to support Sustainable Forest Management through cooperation programs with partner countries, promoting certification and traceability of forest products. The EU third pillar is the creation of New Forested Areas.

---

[62] These are: rate of deforestation and forest degradation; rate of expansion of agricultural land for relevant commodities; production trends of relevant commodities and relevant products; land governance (article 29, par. 3 regulation 2023/1115).

[63] (COM(2024)0452—C10-0119/2024—2024/0249(COD))(1)). The Parliament approved amendments introducing, for example, the category of no-risk country, but these were finally not approved by the legislators. See regulation 2024/3234, 9 December 2024.

[64] These concern, inter alia, land use rights, forest regulations but also labour and human rights law.

[65] WTO—Committee on Trade and Environment, European Union Regulation on Deforestation and Forest Degradation-Free Supply Chains: Communication from Argentina, Brazil, Colombia, Ecuador, Guatemala, Honduras, Mexico, Paraguay and Peru of 10 November 2023, WT/CTE/GEN/33.

2.4.2 The Provisions on Deforestation in Trade and Sustainable Development Chapters

Some of the most recent EU FTAs have bene concluded (Mercosur and Vietnam) or are being negotiated with forest rich countries (Indonesia (first to sign a VPA on forest licence system FLAGT) Malaysia (also negotiating VPA).

The EU policy on deforestation explains the inclusion of a specific part dedicated to deforestation in the Chapters of Sustainable Development in the recent FTAs.

It is trivial to note that the conclusion of a free trade agreement that provides for a preferential access for timber (this is the case, for example for Vietnam) and for commodities embedding deforestation encourages trade and thus could encourage deforestation process of certain commodities. However, such a consideration needs to be further specified because the relationship between trade in certain products and land conversion for agricultural use or for raising livestock depends on a series of factors that change from country to country and from commodity and commodity. For example, beef exports from Brazil will not be liberalized as a consequence of the entry into force of Mercosur FTA and this would thus not impact on deforestation.[66] The ex-post impact assessment on the FTA with Colombia and Peru found that the agreement has had substantially no effect on deforestation.[67]

A telling different case, although in the legal context of the General system of preferences (GSP) is provided by Fournier and Ozinga (2018). A deforestation process in Cambodia has been linked to the production of sugar which, among other products, benefited from the EBA scheme for sugar exports of the GSP and was considered to have forced thousands of rural people off their land.

FTAs provisions on Sustainable development follow a similar template, as mentioned above. They include, with some notable exception, such as the FTA with South Korea,[68] provisions on trade and forest. Some relevant differences can be remarked in the older agreements such as the Free trade Agreement signed in 2012 with Columbia and Peru (joined in 2017 by Ecuador). It contains a part dedicate to Trade in forest products[69] (only timber is explicitly mentioned). Although the objective is sustainable management of forest to be attained through domestic legislation and practices, emphasis is on legal trade. The examples of procedures listed in the agreement in fact concerns measures to ensure legal origin of timber through measures like CITES implementation, legal origin verification, promoting recognized

[66] https://www.sciencedirect.com/science/article/pii/S1462901124002090#fn3. Nolte (2021).

[67] Ex post evaluation of the implementation of the Trade Agreement between the EU and its member states and Colombia, Peru and Ecuador. Final Report, Prepared by BKP Economic Advisors. "No effect on deforestation is found in Ecuador and Peru, and a small contribution to deforestation arising from agricultural activity in Colombia (about 0.5 % of total deforestation arising from agricultural activity in the country", p. 16.

[68] TSD chapter with South Korea contains provisions on environmental and climate protection.

[69] There is a difference between trade in timber and trade in forest product as the latter includes products obtained from forest but different from timber (medicinal plants and herbs, resin, gums, etc.)

certification. Some FTAs explicitly connect sustainable management of forest with environmental social and economic objectives.[70] Other agreement such as the Andean FTA seems more specific, referencing to international instruments (as the above-mentioned CITES) and mechanisms (traceability systems, certification).

Another interesting issue is the fact that some EU partners import illegal logging from third countries. The case of India provides an interesting example. The FTA negotiated with India takes into account such a situation and it requires the adoption of "measures to combat illegal logging and related trade, including with respect to third countries". A specific reference is made to "deforestation-free supply chains minimising the risk that products associated with deforestation or forest degradation are being put on the market".

Not all FTAs contain explicit mechanisms to trace and verify the status of commodities other than timber, like cocoa and soy (a relevant difference with EUDR regulation which requires proof that the products are not derived from deforested land).

Recent agreements such as the one with New Zeeland, and the negotiated India agreement (2022), seem to prioritize broader sustainable development aspects, including conservation, alongside deforestation and sustainable management.[71] It is to be noted that in the FTA with India (in a negotiating phase at the time of writing), and in the FTA with New Zeeland there is a shared understanding of the environmental consequences on climate and biodiversity.[72]

Most agreements call on cooperation and exchange of information (India, Mexico article 7) to maximize the effectiveness of their forest-related policies.

Having observed that, a few considerations can be made on some specific aspects of the Forest provisions. The main concepts are *conservation* and *sustainable forest*

[70] See for example: Article X.8 of FTA with India refers to "the importance of the conservation and sustainable management of forests for the environmental functions and economic and social opportunities for present and future generations and the role of trade in pursuing this objective". Analogous provision is contained in New Zeeland FTA. The contribution of conservation and sustainable management of forest for economic social and environmental objectives is recognised in the FTA with Georgia. See also the FTA with Canada (article 24.10).

[71] In the FTA with New Zeeland (identical to that in India FTA) it is stated: "The Parties recognise the importance of the conservation and sustainable management of forests for providing environmental functions and economic and social opportunities for present and future generations, and the role of trade in pursuing this objective".

[72] "Recognising that deforestation is a major driver of global warming and biodiversity loss, the Parties shall exchange knowledge and experience[s] on ways to encourage the consumption and trade in products from deforestation-free supply chains, minimising the risk that products associated with deforestation or forest degradation are being placed on the market" (FTA with India, and FTA with New Zealand).

management[73] (SFM)[74]: this reproduces the first two pillars of the EU approach to combating deforestation. *Sustainable use* is contained (with reference to forest) only in the Mercosur agreement and can be considered a further development if compared to the principle of sustainable *management*. The latter refers to planning, organizing, and controlling resources and requires implementation strategies, while *use* refers[75] to the utilization of forest resources in a way that doesn't deplete them or damage the forest's ability to regenerate.

As for *conservation*, this is related to the issue of preserving the forest ecosystem by, for example, enhancing the biodiversity in forests, creating protected areas, etc.

What is to be underlined is that the fight against deforestation needs to be based on cooperation from third countries. A system of traceability and licences (FLAGT and the EUDT) is crucial for attaining the goals of sustainable development. The EU system has produced important reforms and the involvement of the civil society and local population (receiving a percentage of revenues from timber concessions as a consequence of the VPA).

Most agreements refer to trade of forest products harvested in accordance with sustainable management of forest and with national legislation, which means that logging and extraction activities must comply with the relevant national laws and regulations. Most agreements focus on the promotion of legal timber trade.[76] FTAs do no at usually include provisions requiring the Parties to have mechanisms in place to verify the legality of their timber exports; reference exists to obligations to

[73] Singapore, article 12.7 (recognising the importance of global conservation and sustainable management); Japan, article 16.7 (recognise the importance and the role of trade and investment in ensuring the conservation and sustainable management of forests); Canada article 24.10 (The Parties recognise the importance of the conservation and sustainable management of forests for providing environmental functions and economic and social opportunities for present and future generations, and for market access); Georgia article 233 (The Parties recognise the importance of ensuring the conservation and the sustainable management of forests and of forests' contribution to the Parties' economic, environmental and social objectives.); Mercosur article 8 (The Parties recognise the importance of sustainable forest management and the role of trade in pursuing this objective and of forest restoration for conservation and sustainable use). Vietnam article 13.8 (The Parties recognise the importance of ensuring the conservation and sustainable management of forest resources in contributing to their economic, environmental and social objectives.)

[74] Forest strategy 2030: "The strategy also sets out the policy framework to deliver growing, healthy, diverse and resilient EU forests, which contribute significantly to our biodiversity ambition, secure livelihoods in rural areas and beyond and support a sustainable forest bioeconomy that relies on most sustainable forest management practices. The latter build on a recognised and internationally agreed dynamic sustainable forest management concept that takes into account the multifunctionality, the variety of forests and the three inter-dependent pillars of sustainability". p. 3.

[75] Sustainable use is defined by the Convention on Biological Diversity since 1992 as "the use of components of biological diversity in a way and at a rate that does not lead to the long-term decline of biological diversity, thereby maintaining its potential to meet the needs and aspirations of present and future generations."

[76] See, for example, New Zealand, article 2.a; Mercosur, article 8.2.c); Canada, article 24.10.2.b).

"implement measures to combat illegal logging" which of course can also cover measures of traceability, but the primary way this is achieved is through VPA.[77]

Legality, as mentioned above, does not automatically mean sustainability. Measures that should guarantee the placing in the market only of timber legally logged do not ensure sustainable harvesting practices. Reiterating the point above, a step forward has been made by the EUDR which intends to ensure, through the due diligence and benchmark mechanisms, that timber and other commodities connected with deforestation practices or degradation of forest and exported into the EU (but the same rules apply to commodities originating in the EU) are not only legal but also deforestation-free (produced or harvested in land that has not been subject to deforestation after 2020). Thus, is the combination of the two sets of provisions, those in the FTA and in the EUDR, which potentially can improve the fight against deforestation. Results depend on the extension and the enforcement of the provisions contained in the FTA, and the effective application of the Regulation.

Another possible tool to align European and partner standards are the introduction of provisions in the FTA (so-called mirror clauses) requiring imported products to comply with EU rules on production methods, which, in general terms, condition access to the EU market on compliance with certain essential European standards particularly in the areas of sustainability, the environment, health and animal welfare. However, not only the Commission does not seem persuaded of the solution[78] but the risk is that to counteract this Mercosur Parties may require "rebalancing mechanism", that is compensation when the internal measure of one Party affects trade concessions provided for in the agreement.[79]

The revised TSD chapter with Mercosur has introduced important new elements as regards the fight against deforestation. In the preamble the Parties recognize the "importance of scaling up efforts to protect, conserve, sustainably use, and

[77] An interesting case is that of the verification mechanism in place in Indonesia to ensure that producers put timber on the market upon verification of its legal sources. The Indonesian government proposed to scrap the regulation but it was forced to reintroduce it after internal opposition as the abolition of the regulation would have risked jeopardizing the export of the timber to the Eureopan Union market. https://news.mongabay.com/2020/05/indonesia-svlk-legal-timber-license-eu-vlegal-export/

[78] A commonly referred example is the link of concession of EU trade preferences in the eggs sector to the respect of some animal welfare standards. See Question for written answer E-001973/2023 Introduction of mirror clauses in the free trade agreement with Mercosur. The Commission highlights the preference for an horizontal legislative approach such as the regulation on deforestation as preferable to the inclusion of environmental provisions which risk jeopardizing 20 years of negotiations. See the answer given by Executive Vice-President Dombrovskis on behalf of the European Commission.

[79] The rebalancing mechanism allows the Parties to seek compensation if it considers that the other Party has introduced measures that "nullifies or substantially impairs" the benefit of the agreement (article XX.4 lett. b) of the 2024 revised Dispute settlement provisions). EUDR might be considered—also in the light of WTO complaint—such a measure as its application can have a negative impact on Mercosur's agricultural goods exports. Compensation might be required in this case. The different interpretation of this mechanism by the EU arguing that it does not apply to its environmental measures, could lead to disputes and tensions. Dupré and Kpenou (2025).

sustainably manage and restore all ecosystems, in line with their national capacities and circumstances" (letter e). Ecosystem clearly includes forests. Several articles of the new Annex are related to deforestation reinforcing the commitments of the Parties. One is the provision contained in article 2A, par. 16 where a committment is contained ("shall implement measures") to prevent further deforestation and enhance efforts to stabilize (that is to avoid further reduction of forests) or increase forest cover from 2030. The new Annex specifies that the actions taken to implement the commitments under the agreements will be considered in positive terms for the classification of countries according to the different categories indicated in the EUDR, although this will be only one factor to be considered among "other criteria". This enhanced commitment is balanced by the acknowledgement that the Parties' policies must take into account the social and economic challenges of developing countries and their contribution to global food security. Paragraph 18 refers to the need for enhanced support and investment to achieve these objectives, including through financial resources, technology transfer, capacity-building, and other mechanisms foreseen in this Agreement.

When the FTA with Mercosur encourage "trade in products from sustainably managed forests harvested in accordance with the law of the country of harvest" introduces a higher standard that encompasses more than just legality and align the approach to the one endorsed by the EU with the deforestation regulation (see above on EUDR). The TSD Annex to Mercosur FTAs specifies that "In the context of their due diligence obligations, EU operators and traders may make use of traceability, certification or other third Party verified schemes, the EU shall, upon request from relevant authorities of Mercosur countries, provide support for transparent and independent assessments of traceability, certification or third-Party verification schemes and their alignment with requirements and good practices". All these provisions seem clearly to align the agreement with the EUDR approach.

One can point out the elements of connection.

FTAs' provisions and the EUDR share the objective of combating deforestation and forest degradation, promoting trade in legal and sustainable forest products.

The instruments are complementary: FTAs provide a framework for cooperation and dialogue with partner countries, encouraging the adoption of sustainable forest management policies and practices. The EUDR, on the other hand, establishes binding rules for operators placing forest products on the EU market, requiring them to verify the legality and sustainability of their products. The EUDR introduces a due diligence obligation for operators. This encourages the enforcement of FTA provisions, which on its turn encourage sustainable forest management practices. Both FTA provisions and the EUDR recognize the importance of international cooperation in addressing the problem of deforestation. The EUDR, for example, provides for the possibility of collaborating with third countries to strengthen their control and law enforcement systems.

While the points above highlight synergies and compatibility of aims, there are tensions between traditional trade objectives in FTAs and the EU's deforestation regulation (EUDR). FTAs prioritizes trade liberalization and reduction of barriers. This can incentivize deforestation to produce goods that are demanded on the EU market. The EUDR focuses on environmental protection, imposing strict due diligence requirements. This is perceived as adding costs for traders, and is qualified as a non-tariff trade barriers to trade under the WTO. As for enforcement, EUDR is legally binding for EU operators while FTAs rely on voluntary commitments. So far enforcement mechanisms are excluded as for TSD chapters, even if in perspective this would change as the EU intends to strengthen the enforcement approach of FTAs. This might be difficult to realise as sustainable forest management clauses are not detailed and are formulated as non-binding commitments.

Another issue is the regulatory autonomy of exporting countries that can *de facto* be limited (and resented) as the EU imposes its standard, while the principle of respecting the other Party's regulatory autonomy is clearly spelled out in FTAs.

Finally, it is provided that the inclusion of forest-based local communities and indigenous peoples shall be promoted. Informed consent is also mentioned in the FTA with Mercosur. In the new Annex to the FTA with Mercosur this part is reinforced as in Article A.2, par. 37 where the importance of involving the communities in conservation efforts and respecting their rights is further underlined.

It is to be recalled that the United Nations Declaration on the Rights of Indigenous Peoples requires them to be consulted to obtain prior and informed consent on policies or projects affecting them. The problem is that the provisions are dead letter if there is not a mechanism of monitoring and oversight that are provided for in the countries concerned.

In conclusion, the FTA intends to establish a favourable context for dialogue and cooperation which could ease the tension between unilateral measures and bilateral approach even if one has to consider that EU's model of consumption of goods, production processes, can have unintended negative consequences for the environment, both within and outside its borders.

At the end, the idea is of creating synergy on different levels to tackle the deforestation issues: cooperation and dialogue with partners and binding rules for operators through due diligence and traceability.

3 Sustainable Development and Labour Provisions in Free Trade Agreements of the European Union

3.1 Introduction—Sustainable Development and EU Social Conditionality in Trade Agreements

Following the failure of including a "social" clause within the World Trade Organisation (WTO) legal framework,[80] the European Union (EU) has been increasingly relying on bilateral and regional trade agreements to strengthen the social dimension of its external trade relations.[81] Since the mid-1990s, the majority of EU

[80] Social clause is a term that refers to the linkage of trade concessions to the compliance with ILO labour standards, chiefly core labour standards, see Chan and Ross (2003), pp. 1011–1028.

[81] For a detailed account, see Velluti (2020a), Ch. 5; see also Novitz (2024), Ch. 5.

preferential agreements (PTAs) contain provisions on labour standards and cooperation in social affairs.[82] Marceau et al. note that 'removing labour standards from the WTO's governance did not suppress the issue. Rather, it resulted in the proliferation of regional trade agreements (RTAs) that encouraged and facilitated compliance with labour obligations and international labour commitments.'[83] Changes in the global economy, such as the digitalization of trade, integration of global value chains and climate change has fostered the adoption of deep trade agreements, which encompass a number of disciplines that go beyond traditional trade policy.[84] These can be classified as "WTO plus" ("WTO+") agreements, namely, commitments building on those already agreed to at the multilateral level, e.g. a further reduction in tariffs, and "WTO extra" ("WTO-X"), namely, commitments dealing with issues going beyond the current WTO mandate altogether, e.g. on labour standards.[85]

The EU made a clear commitment to the promotion of social norms with the 2001 Communication on *Promoting Core Labour Standards and Improving Social Governance in the Context of Globalization*, which also signalled a renewed cooperation between the EU and the International Labour Organisation (ILO) to promote Core Labour Standards (CLS) internationally through the EU's external relations policies and development cooperation. The EU's social ambition continues to grow exponentially as exemplified by the increasing number of trade agreements containing social conditionality clauses.[86] To varying degrees and with mixed success, many of the EU's trade agreements (both bilateral and regional) to date include an element of social conditionality, namely social incentive clauses that condition trade concessions and market access on the respect and implementation of internationally recognized human rights, social and environmental standards.

Additionally, since the mid-1990s, sustainable development has become increasingly important in the EU's trade policy and the 2009 Treaty of Lisbon has elevated it to one of the key principles underlying EU external action.[87] Social norms in EU agreements seem to have been included as objectives to be achieved within the broad goal of sustainable development rather than enforce-

[82] For a detailed and up-to-date overview and analysis of labour provisions in trade agreements, see ILO's database, ILO Labour Provisions in Trade Agreements Hub, available at: <https://webapps.ilo.org/LPhub/#home>

[83] Marceau et al. (2023), p. 362.

[84] Laget et al. (2020), pp. 379–410.

[85] Horn et al. (2009).

[86] In this chapter, social conditionality clauses have the same meaning as social clauses, as defined above, see no. 1. Conditionality further emphasises that the objective of inserting social clauses in trade instruments is to improve domestic labour laws and regulations in return of the trade concessions granted to the partner country concerned.

[87] E.g. Article 3(5) TEU and Article 21(2)d TEU; see F. Martines, 'Sustainable Development and the Environment in Free Trade Agreements of the European Union' in this volume, for detailed analysis of trade and sustainable development; for academic discussion, see De Schutter (2015).

able legal commitments as they do not provide for genuine enforcement mechanisms.[88] As Bartels points out 'it is notable that the principle of sustainable development has never been treated as a concrete obligation in itself: none of the agreements admit the possibility of violating the principle of sustainable development.'[89] This is because 'the exact implications of sustainable development for trade agreements are far from clear due to the normative uncertainty surrounding the concept of sustainable development, which has played out differently in varied contexts and is still subject to evolution.'[90] The agreements contain provisions on cooperation and obligations to respect and "strive" to improve multilateral and domestic labour and environmental standards.[91] In particular, a first set of obligations contain minimum obligations to implement certain multilateral obligations and other obligations which require the parties to the agreement not to reduce their levels of protection and encouraging them to raise their levels of protection, subject to a proviso that this is not done for protectionist purposes.[92] With the turn in the 1990s to social trade at the regional and bilateral levels, sustainable development has become increasingly important in the EU's trade policy[93] and the Treaty of Lisbon has elevated it to one of the key principles underlying EU external action.[94]

This overarching legal commitment has been given further effect with the adoption of so-called "new generation" of trade agreements, containing a "trade and sustainable development" (TSD) chapter (both discussed further below), which includes provisions for the respect of labour and environmental standards.[95] Examples of such agreements are the 2011 EU-Korea FTA,[96] the 2012 EU-Central

[88] Velluti (2020a), at p. 234.

[89] Bartels (2013), p. 306.

[90] Durán (2013), p. 126.

[91] For further analysis, see Bartels (2009), pp. 342–366.

[92] Bartels (2013), at 307–309.

[93] The first of the EU's agreements to make reference to the principle of sustainable development was the 1993 EU-Hungary Europe Agreement, see Europe Agreement establishing an association between the European Communities and their Member States, of the one part, and the Republic of Hungary, of the other part OJ L 347, 31/12/1993, p. 0002; see Bartels (2013), 306.

[94] Article 21(2)d and (3) TEU.

[95] For detailed analysis, see Ionel (2022).

[96] Free Trade Agreement between the European Union and its Member States of the one part, and the Republic of Korea of the other part (EU-Korea FTA) *OJ* [2011] L127/6, 14 May 2011, p. 6. It entered into force in July 2011 and it is the EU's first trade agreement with an Asian country. It is also the first completed agreement in a new generation of FTAs launched by the EU in 2007 as part of its strategy to create "deep and comprehensive" free trade agreements (DCFTA) with selective partners following the Doha round stand-still at the WTO. On this point see, Hoffmeister (2014), Ch. 9.

America Agreement[97] and the 2012 EU—Colombia/Peru Agreement.[98] Specifically, in relation to labour issues the agreements require the effective implementation in law and practice of CLS. Hence, with the 2009 Treaty of Lisbon non-trade values have become a staple of FTAs concluded by the EU.[99] In relation to sustainability provisions in FTA's, the Court of Justice of the EU (CJEU) in Opinion 2/15 concerning the EU's FTA with Singapore, clearly held that 'the objective of sustainable development [...] forms an integral part of the Common Commercial Policy'.[100]

In 2017, the Parliamentary Assembly of the Council of Europe issued a resolution in which it called on the EU to ensure that these modern trade agreements were to be 'designed to promote environmental sustainability, human rights and the rule of democratic law, and to facilitate the mutual benefits of trade.'[101] In so doing, it also urged Member States 'to open, as far as possible, negotiations to the scrutiny of democratically elected representatives at both European and national levels and to ensure that such agreements are subject to ratification by national parliaments insofar as they deal with shared competences.'[102]

As of 2011, the EU has been inserting TSD chapters in its FTAs. In a standardized clause, parties affirm their commitments to the 1998 ILO Declaration on Fundamental Principles and Rights at Work and accordingly 'commit to respecting, promoting and realizing, in their laws and practices, the principles concerning the fundamental rights' such as the freedom of association, or eliminating forced and child labour.[103] While the 2013 EU–Central America FTA also specifically lists out the eight ILO conventions that the parties commit to, most EU FTAs typically refer to the 'internationally recognised core labour standards as contained in the fundamental Conventions of the ILO'. Another novel element of the EU's TSD chapter is a commitment for parties to effectively implement the ILO Conventions that they have ratified and to make continued and sustained efforts towards ratifying the fundamental ILO Conventions as well as the other Conventions that are classified as "up-to-date" by the ILO.[104] With regard to the dispute settlement mechanism

[97] Agreement establishing an Association between the European Union and its Member States, on the one hand, and Central America on the other (EU-CAAA) *OJ* [2012] L346/3, 15 December 2012, p. 3.

[98] Trade Agreement between the European Union and its Member States, of the one part, and Colombia and Peru, of the other part *OJ* [2012] L354/3, 21 December 2012, p. 3.

[99] Marín Durán (2020), pp. 1031–1068.

[100] Free Trade Agreement between the European Union and Singapore, 17 October 2014, Authentic text as of May 2015 available at <http://trade.ec.europa.eu/doclib/press/index.cfm?id=961>; Opinion 2/15 *EU-Singapore FTA*, EU:C:2017:376, para 147.

[101] Parliamentary Assembly of the Council of Europe, '"New generation" trade agreements and their implications for social rights, public health and sustainable development', Resolution 2152/2017, para. 8, available at: <https://assembly.coe.int/nw/xml/XRef/Xref-XML2HTML-en.asp?fileid=23489&lang=en&gt>

[102] Idem.

[103] See Article 13.4.3 of the 2011 EU-Korea FTA.

[104] Idem.

(DSM), TSD chapters are not subject to the regular DSM of a trade agreement.[105] In the case of a labour dispute, EU trade agreements foresee a cooperative approach, which relies on dialogue and cooperation between the parties and between government officials and civil society.[106] Specifically, one party can request consultations with the other party with a view to reaching a mutually satisfactory solution. If the issue cannot be resolved in this way, a panel of experts can be established upon request of a party. The panel of experts, after seeking input from various sources, issues a report with its findings and recommendations. The party concerned must inform the other party of the measures it intends to undertake to address the panel's findings. However, there are no sanctions or remedies foreseen should it fail to undertake the needed actions and the complaining party cannot impose tariff increases or any other economic penalties. TSD chapters of modern EU FTAs, therefore, are largely unenforceable legally.[107] The EU-South Korea labour dispute, which precedes the European Commission's 2022 Trade Review mentioned further below, sheds some light on this aspect.[108] In early 2021, the EU initiated consultations with South Korea at the request of the EU Domestic Advisory Group (DAG). The EU's complaint regarding Korean conduct under the FTA was based on two claims. The first one concerned the fact that South Korea had made insufficient efforts to ratify several core ILO Conventions, including those concerning freedom of association (namely, Conventions Nos 87 and 98). The second concerned certain breaches of freedom of association because four provisions of the Korea's Trade Union and Labour Relations Act 1997 (TULRAA) were not in line with the freedom of association. The EU Commission relied on Article 13.4 of the EU-Korea FTA, which required an effect on trade. Starting with the latter claim, in responding to South Korea's counterclaims, the panel of experts concluded that violations of CLS do not need to be connected to trade to be considered unlawful. The Panel of Experts noted that 'the phrase "in a manner affecting trade" of Article 16.2.1(a) of the 2004 Dominican Republic–Central American Free–United States Trade Agreement (CAFTA-DR) does not mean the same thing as "measures affecting trade-related aspects of labour" as set out in Article 13.2.1 of the EU-Korea FTA' and that the "contextual setting" of the provisions in the two FTAs differ.[109]

---

[105] The only exception is Article 203 of the 2008 EU-CARIFORUM EPA, which states that the DSM provisions apply to any dispute concerning the interpretation and application of the agreement; see Economic Partnership Agreement between the CARIFORUM States, of the one part, and the European Community and its Member States, of the other part (OJ [2008] L289, 30/10/2008, p. 3).

[106] E.g. Article 13.15 of the 2011 EU-Korea FTA; the TSD sub-committees can be equated to which parallel the 'labour affairs councils' as specified in US FTAs.

[107] Bronckers and Gruni (2021), pp. 25–51.

[108] For analysis, see S. Peers (2021); for detailed academic commentary, see Novitz, (2022), pp. 3–23; T. Novitz (2024), pp. 241–246.

[109] Panel of Experts Proceeding Constituted under Art. 13.15 of EU-South Korea (2011), paras 90–93. Kübek and Wessel maintain that it still remains unclear 'whether the standard of demonstrating "in a manner affecting trade" established in the *CAFTA-DR* case could be applied in the same way for enforcing non-regression clauses under EU FTAs', see Kübek and Wessel (2024).

Moreover, the expert panel recommended that South Korea should bring its labour legislation in line with the principle of freedom of association. This meant that all workers, including the self-employed, dismissed and unemployed would be included in the notion of "worker". Significantly, in drafting its recommendations, the panel found that certain decisions of relevant ILO supervisory bodies could be taken into account even if South Korea had not ratified the relevant conventions. While interpreting Article 13.4 of the EU-Korea FTA, the panel of experts stated that even in the absence of specific reference to ILO Conventions, the reference to principles concerning fundamental rights was sufficiently precise to invoke a legally binding obligation to implement the principles of freedom of association as expressed in the ILO Conventions 87 and 98.[110] On the issue that South Korea's efforts to ratify the four outstanding conventions had fallen short of the standard of "continued and sustained efforts", the panel of experts disagreed with the EU Commission on grounds that this obligation is one of "best endeavours", so the party should make efforts that go beyond a minimal threshold, but without requiring the use of all means available.[111] This is particularly the case in the absence of explicit targets. In considering South Korea's efforts in this regard, the expert panel found that it had not acted inconsistently with its obligations towards ratification of the core ILO conventions.[112] Some scholars have criticised the lack of assertiveness on the part of the EU Commission,[113] while others have been disappointed by the fact that South Korea's delay in ratifying certain core ILO Conventions has largely not been criticised.[114]

A lengthy review and consultation period was launched in 2022 during which the EU Commission decided to take into account calls from European Parliament and civil society for the better enforcement of EU TSD.[115] This review aimed to identify ways for broadening the EU sustainability agenda to tailor it more closely to the situation in partner countries. It also aimed to strengthen the implementation and enforcement of TSD chapters within trade agreements, including through the potential use of trade sanctions and the extension of the dispute settlement compliance stage to TSD matters, thereby departing from a purely "cooperative" approach to a

[110] See Report of the Panel of Experts (2020) Proceeding constituted under Article 13.15 of the EU–Korea Free Trade Agreement, 25 January 2021, paras 136–141; Panel: Dr Jill Murray (Chairperson), Professor Laurence Boisson de Chazournes and Professor Jaemin Lee; available at: <https://trade.ec.europa.eu/doclib/docs/2021/january/tradoc_159358.pdf>.

[111] Ionel (2022), at p. 10.

[112] Idem.

[113] Nissen (2022), p. 609.

[114] Orbie (2021), p. 199.

[115] European Commission, 'The Power of Trade Partnerships: Together for Green and Just Economic Growth', COM(2022) 409 final; see also European Commission, Feedback and way forward on improving the implementation and enforcement of Trade and Sustainable Development chapters in EU Free Trade Agreements. Non-paper. 26 February 2018, available at: <https://www.politico.eu/wp-content/uploads/2018/02/TSD-Non-Paper.pdf>; European Commission, 'Trade Policy Review—An Open, Sustainable and Assertive Trade Policy', (COM/2021/66 Final); Bronckers and Gruni (2019), pp. 1591–1622.

"sanctions-based" approach for compliance with specific commitments. In particular, the EU Commission announced that it would 'extend the standard state-to-state dispute settlement compliance phase to the TSD chapter of [...] trade agreements' and 'include the possibility to apply, as a last resort, trade sanctions for material breaches of the Paris Climate Agreement and the ILO fundamental labour principles.'[116] The 2024 EU-New Zealand FTA is the first agreement that follows this new approach by the EU Commission.[117] It aligns dispute settlement procedures on sustainability and trade issues under a single horizontal mechanism.[118] However, Kübek and Wessel remain sceptical as in their view the horizontal DSM included in the 2024 EU-New Zealand FTA 'largely incorporates the "specific" procedural rules for settling TSD disputes that were previously set out in the TSD Chapter itself.'[119] Hence, in their view dispute settlement procedures concerning sustainability issues are "specific" to those on pure trade issues and the enforcement of expert panel reports remains largely based on a cooperative approach.[120] Ultimately, the complaining party cannot adopt temporary remedies unless the party complained against does not comply with the final report.[121] By way of exception, temporary remedies are possible if the report of the panel finds that the party complained against either violated the ILO fundamental labour principles or defeated the material object and purpose of the Paris Agreement, and did not sufficiently remedy its behaviour.[122] In particular, it remains unclear, how a party, through its individual conduct, can "materially defeat" the object and purpose of the Paris Agreement.[123] On the other hand, as discussed further below, the 2020 EU–UK TCA is the first EU agreement to expressly allow the suspension of the FTA's trade obligations under Art. 410.3 EU-UK TCA if the expert panel's report is not implemented.

In this chapter we will be evaluating the effectiveness of EU social conditionality and look at the 2019 EUJEPA[124] and the 2020 EU-UK TCA[125] and examine whether the unique features of the "new generation" of trade agreements, con-

[116] European Commission (2022), Sect. 3.6.

[117] Free Trade Agreement between the European Union and New Zealand (OJ L, 2024/866, 25.3. 2024).

[118] Art. 26.2 EU-New Zealand FTA.

[119] Kübek and Wessel (2024); they rely on Article 26.5(3)(b) and 26.6(1)(b) (composition of the panel); or Article 26.13(3) (compliance monitoring) 2024 EU-New Zealand FTA as examples to illustrate their point.

[120] Idem.

[121] Article 26.16 2024 EU-New Zealand FTA has limited application for disputes based on the TSD Chapter (see second paragraph).

[122] Article 26.16(2) 2024 EU-New Zealand FTA.

[123] Kübek and Wessel (2024).

[124] Agreement between the European Union and Japan for an Economic Partnership (OJ L 330, 27.12.2018, p. 3–899).

[125] Trade and Cooperation Agreement between the European Union and the European Atomic Energy Community, of the one part, and the United Kingdom of Great Britain and Northern Ireland, of the other part (OJ L 149, 30.4.2021, p. 10–2539).

tribute to respecting labour and social standards. In particular, we will look at whether—in the absence of actions resulting in sanctions against the other party—they entail an improvement of the implementation-capacity of partner countries to respect and protect labour standards and thus lead to an effective improvement of labour standards internationally. Bazillier and Rana define labour standards broadly as measures that have the purpose of improving labour conditions.[126] They subdivide labour standards into *de jure* and *de facto* standards.[127] *De jure* standards include the ratification of ILO fundamental and governance conventions while the use of the term *de facto* refers to the actual implementation of conventions and recommendations as well as application of labour standards.[128]

At the outset, it should be noted that labour provisions in EU trade agreements vary, ranging from simple political commitments or aspirations to respect labour rights where the parties to the agreement agree to include labour standards provisions without making reference to any legal consequences in case of non-compliance—and, as such, have no legal standing—to legal provisions which are legally binding and thus enforceable.[129]

Particularly insightful is Wang's analytical framework[130] developed to examine and understand the significant heterogeneity and rationales behind trade agreements. He envisages three variables with two indicators each:

breadth (regulatory outreach) with two indicators (WTO-plus and WTO-beyond rules);

depth (regulatory density) with two indicators (regulatory cooperation and coherence, and domestic law changes); and

strength (rule use intensity) with two indicators (state-to-state dispute settlement (SSDS) rules, and SSDS coverage).

Moreover, a major empirical study conducted on the effectiveness of labour provisions in 435 trade agreements between 1958 and 2023 measured quantitatively their effects on various labour standards or labour outcomes in partner countries. Their findings show that overall labour provisions contained in trade agreements have a positive effect on the number of ILO ratifications.[131] As to labour standards violations, the study shows that the inclusion of institutionalised cooperation mechanisms in these labour provisions together with their legal enforceability is pivotal in reducing the number of labour standard violations,[132] even though one should take into account that the institutional design in these labour clauses is diversified

[126] Bazillier and Rana (2025), pp. 1–31, at 3.

[127] Idem.

[128] Idem.

[129] Bazillier and Rana (2025); for detailed analysis about the different types of labour provisions, see Marceau et al. (2023).

[130] Wang (2021), pp. 247–279.

[131] Idem; for further empirical analysis, see also Timini et al. (2022), pp. 2820–2853; Carrère et al. (2022), pp. 1–31.

[132] Bazillier and Rana (2025), at 2.

and that social clauses exhibit heterogeneous patterns with varying degrees of institutional depth.[133] Generally, the evidence to date suggests that labour provisions, now part of the EU FTAs sustainability objectives, do not seem to have a direct positive impact on labour rights violations.[134]

On the basis of these findings, the analysis will now proceed to the examination of two modern EU FTAs, namely, the 2019 EUJEPA and the 2020 EU-UK TCA.

3.2 *Sustainable Development and Labour Provisions in EU Free Trade Agreements: The Case of Middle Power Countries*

Japan and the UK have been chosen as middle power countries, namely states that are neither a superpower or a great power, but nevertheless exert influence and play a significant role in international relations. These countries often possess certain characteristics and capabilities, such as strong economies, advanced technologies and diplomatic influence, that allow them to have a voice in global affairs and act as bridge-builders between larger powers.[135] Middle powers play a key role in the international system promoting multilateralism, cooperation and peaceful resolution of conflicts. Specifically, middle powers help to maintain the international order through coalition-building, by serving as mediators and "go-betweens".[136] Moreover, they are able to leverage their resources and diplomatic skills to advance their national interests while also contributing to global stability and prosperity.[137] Middle power diplomacy can play a particularly vital role in the twenty-first century, particularly in the light of the absence of the US in the international trade order, which started with the first administration of President Donald Trump and is now being completed with a push for isolationism and protectionism.[138] During his second mandate, he has been intentionally ignoring the rules of an open and rules-based international trading system—as exemplified by the World Trade Organisation (WTO)—as well as the norms of the liberal international order—as represented by the rule of law approach, to the extent that he has been threatening the US' long-standing democratic allies with territorial expansion, Canada being a case in point.[139] It is argued that both the UK and Japan can forge a (new) strategic partnership with the EU—itself a middle power economy amid the uncertainty generated by the US trade and foreign policy, the belligerent attitude of Russia,

[133] Ibid. at 4 and Appendix A.

[134] Hradilovà and Svoboda (2018), pp. 1019–1042.

[135] Jordaan (2003), pp. 165–181; see also, Laurence (2023).

[136] Neak (2000).

[137] Hamill and Lee (2001), pp. 33–59.

[138] Morita-Jaeger (2025).

[139] Sharp (2024).

and the rise of China on the global scene, and the security threats that all of these factors pose to the democratic world. Japan has been selected as a middle power country in East Asia where, together with South-East Asia, the EU has been increasingly developing economic and geopolitical interests to gain access to new markets in order to boost the European economy and the competitiveness of EU firms. The UK has been selected as a former EU Member State, which has played a key role in providing the foundations of the liberal international order, particularly in the European context. Both middle power countries are industrialised states with advanced economies, albeit with quite different historical and cultural backgrounds. As such they can leverage their resources and diplomatic capabilities to promote their national interests while, at the same time, contribute to global security and prosperity.

3.3 The EU-Japan Economic Partnership Agreement

3.3.1 Introduction

The EU-Japan Economic Partnership Agreement (EUJEPA)[140] is the largest bilateral trade agreement ever concluded by the EU in terms of market size, covering close to 30% of global gross domestic product (GDP) and 40% of global trade. It establishes an ambitious framework to further liberalise and better organise trade relations between two highly developed economies. This agreement has led to the elimination of 99% of tariffs on European goods entering Japan and 97% of Japanese products in the EU.[141] Moreover, it contains the most up-to-date EU provisions on corporate governance, the mobility of natural persons for business and Intellectual Property Rights (IPR) protection, including trade secrets. As such, it represents a further deepening of the EU's trade treaties, and it represents the joint efforts of the EU and Japan to develop a model for modern trade agreements.[142]

The EUJEPA must be understood in the broader context of an increasingly stronger EU and Japan interregional relationship. It also has to be examined together with the adoption of the 2018 EU-Japan Strategic Partnership Agreement (SPA).[143]

---

[140] The EUJEPA entered into force on 1 February 2019 after nearly 5 years of negotiations; see also Sautter (2016).

[141] European Commission, 'The EU-Japan Economic Partnership Agreement at a Glance', available at: <https://trade.ec.europa.eu/access-to-markets/en/content/eu-japan-economic-partnership-agreement#toc_0>

[142] European Commission, The EU-Japan Economic Partnership Agreement, available at: <https://trade.ec.europa.eu/access-to-markets/en/content/eu-japan-economic-partnership-agreement>

[143] The SPA was signed by the EU and Japan at the 25th EU-Japan summit in Tokyo on 17 July 2018; it is yet to enter into force. However, both the EU and Japan agreed to apply a number of the SPA's articles provisionally pending its full ratification; see Council Decision (EU) 2018/1197 of 26 June 2018 on the signing, on behalf of the European Union, and provisional application of the Strategic Partnership Agreement between the European Union and its Member States, of the one

The SPA is the bilateral framework agreement between the EU and Japan which defines and underlies the overall relationship, enhancing political and sectoral cooperation as well as joint actions on issues of common interest, including on regional and global challenges. With this agreement the EU and Japan have pledged to strengthen the rules-based global order with a joint commitment to defend multilateralism, the rule of law, democracy, respect for human rights, open markets, free and fair trade. The EUJEPA establishes an ambitious framework to further liberalise and better organise trade relations between two highly developed economies that already have substantial trade and investment ties.[144] This FTA belongs to the family of "new generation" EU trade agreements with developed economies.[145] However, the EUJEPA goes somewhat further than these earlier agreements by introducing new commitments in certain areas such as corporate governance and climate change. The predilection for an economic partnership agreement (EPA) as opposed to merely a free trade agreement signifies in itself that this deal is intended to go beyond trade, while highlighting the need to focus on cooperation and the regulation of globalisation.[146] In the first year of implementation, the EPA showed some very encouraging results: European exports to Japan went up to 6.6% in comparison with the previous year, and 6.3% the other way around.[147]

There are several reasons for the adoption of the trade agreement between the EU and Japan. Since 2004, the EU has been considering its relationship with Japan as a strategic partnership, that is, a powerful relationship that plays an increasingly central role in the international system. In spite of the different understanding of and approaches to sustainability, as "middle power" economies, they both have a strong incentive to collaborate, among others, on sustainability issues in order to stabilize and maintain their political stance in international fora.[148] At the same time, the EPA and the SPA have not been agreed with the sole aim of fostering a joint response to the crisis of the liberal world order, but also with the objective of counterweighting the Chinese "Belt and Road Initiative", Beijing's macro-project to invest in infrastructures.[149] Additionally, together with the rise of China, the Russian invasion of

part, and Japan, of the other part (OJ L 216, 24.8.2018, p. 1–3) and Council Decision (EU) 2024/1394 of 22 April 2024 on the conclusion, on behalf of the European Union, of the Strategic Partnership Agreement between the European Union and its Member States, of the one part, and Japan, of the other part (*OJ L, 2024/1394, 21.5.2024*).

[144] Chowdhry et al. (2018), p. 1.

[145] E.g. Comprehensive Economic and Trade Agreement (CETA) between Canada, of the one part, and the European Union and its Member States, of the other part, OJ L 11, 14.1.2017, p. 23–1079 (2017 CETA), the 2015 EUSFTA and the 2011 EUKFTA.

[146] Frenkel and Walter (2017), pp. 358–363.

[147] European Commission, 'Trade: First year of the EU-Japan Economic Partnership Agreement shows growth in EU exports', Press Release, 31 January 2020, available at: <https://ec.europa.eu/commission/presscorner/detail/en/ip_20_161>.

[148] Herman (2023) p. 40.

[149] López (2024), p. 137; Jie and Wallace (2021).

Ukraine, the emergence of a new Cold War between two defining blocs have resulted in mutual interests between the EU and Japan in the Asia-Pacific region.[150]

In the words of López, 'the signing of the EPA and the SPA cannot only be explained by a matrix of economic benefit; it is also the result of the logic of structure (the rise of China and the Russian invasion of Ukraine), the logic of actors (recent changes in their limited actorness), and the logic of the interaction (that is, the institutional context within which this relationship takes place).'[151] This EU strategy has been taking shape with the EU Commission's 2015 Communication *Trade for All—Towards more responsible trade and investment policy*,[152] where priority was given to the conclusion of trade negotiations with Japan and the strengthening of the EU's presence in the Asia-Pacific region.

The EUJEPA enables the EU to set its own rules and standards with a major Pacific economy, in the context of the EU's ongoing negotiations with other Asian economies and also the totality of ASEAN countries[153] as well as ASEAN plus three countries (APT) of which Japan is a member.[154] Recent changes in the EU and Japanese domestic and international environments, namely, global moves towards anti-multilateralism and market disintegration,[155] a sharp decline in levels of imports for both economies,[156] show how both parties' relations have shifted from a period of indifferences and low expectations to a new momentum of cooperation in facing common global challenges.[157] In addition, the EUJEPA has gained heightened geo-

[150] Idem.

[151] López (2024), at 141.

[152] Communication from the Commission of 14 October 2015 on 'Trade for All: Towards a More Responsible Trade and Investment Policy', COM(2015)497 final.

[153] The Association of Southeast Asian Nations (ASEAN) was founded in 1967 and comprises ten countries: Indonesia, Malaysia, Philippines, Singapore, Thailand, Brunei Darussalam, Cambodia, Laos, Myanmar (Burma), and Vietnam; further information is available at: <https://asean.org/>; while both the EU and ASEAN are based on the idea of bringing countries closer together with a strong cultural basis there are some significant differences between the EU and ASEAN. They differ significantly in their levels of integration, decision-making processes, and political systems. The EU is a supranational organization with significant transfers of sovereignty to its institutions, while ASEAN remains an intergovernmental organization with a strong emphasis on consensus-based decision-making and non-interference in Member States' internal affairs. In the ASEAN there's less emphasis on specific political ideologies or democratic standards as a condition for membership. ASEAN's scope of cooperation is more focused on regional security, economic cooperation, and political dialogue; see Koh (2020), pp. 37–41; Camroux (2018); Jochheim (2022).

[154] ASEAN Plus Three (APT) refers to the cooperation framework involving the Association of Southeast Asian Nations (ASEAN) and the People's Republic of China, Japan, and the Republic of Korea. It was established in 1997 and aims to promote regional economic integration and cooperation in various areas such as, for example, trade and investment, technology and innovation, transnational crime, security, agriculture and forestry and tourism; further information is available at: <https://aseanplusthree.asean.org/>. For academic analysis, see Manea (2013); for academic discussion on the relationship between Japan and ASEAN countries, see Yuzawa (2013).

[155] Yoshimatsu (2020), pp. 429–443.

[156] Chowdhry et al. (2018), at p. 7.

[157] López (2024); see also Suzuki (2017), pp. 875–889.

political importance following the withdrawal of the UK from the EU and the end of talks between the EU and the US on the Transatlantic Trade and Investment Partnership (TTIP) agreement.[158] The EUJEPA provides, therefore, a major platform for both the EU and Japan to reinforce their commitment to rules-based trade and deepen their alliance against unilateral and protectionist policies. In the case of Japan, the agreement is an integral component of so-called third arrow (structural reforms) of "Abenomics",[159] that is the economic policies set out for Japan in 2012 when Prime Minister Shinzo Abe of the Liberal Democratic Party (LDP) came into power for a second term. In July 2018, Japan also ratified the Comprehensive and Progressive Agreement for Trans-Pacific Partnership (CPTPP),[160] the successor to the Trans-Pacific Partnership (TPP) agreement,[161] from which the US withdrew in January 2017.

The next section will focus on selected and the most salient aspects of the TSD Chapter of the EUJEPA, which are illustrative of the potential that the labour provisions of this specific chapter may have for the future of trade sustainability in Japan.

3.3.2 The Trade and Sustainable Development Chapter in the EUJEPA

The development of Japan's and the EU's sustainable trade strategy can be considered an example of "value-oriented diplomacy" applied to environmental policy and, more broadly, to trade sustainability.[162] As noted by Kettunen and Alvstam, 'the EU's consecutive agreements with three Asian countries—South Korea, Singapore and Vietnam—show an evolution from vague to more detailed notions of TSD issues in the final texts.'[163] One noticeable difference between the EUJEPA and the FTAs with other Asian countries is that the TSD Chapter is more detailed and con-

---

[158] For academic discussion, see De Ville and Gheyle (2019), pp. 16–30.

[159] Chowdhry et al. (2018), at p. 7.

[160] Text of the CPTPP is available at: <https://www.mfat.govt.nz/en/trade/free-trade-agreements/free-trade-agreements-in-force/cptpp/comprehensive-and-progressive-agreement-for-trans-pacific-partnership-text-and-resources>; the CPTTP is a free trade agreement that was signed on 8 March 2018 in Santiago, Chile. The 11 original signatories were: Australia; Brunei Darussalam; Canada; Chile; Japan; Malaysia; Mexico; New Zealand; Peru; Singapore and Vietnam. The CPTPP has now entered into force for all the above countries. The CPTPP itself builds on, and incorporates, most of the provisions of the original TPP though certain provisions of the TPP were suspended upon entry into force of CPTPP. Those provisions are explicitly identified for suspension in the CPTPP. This means that all chapters contained in the TPP are part of the CPTPP. Certain provisions of the CPTPP are modified for the UK (the latter acceded to this agreement in December 2024) by the accession protocol. This means that the CPTPP should be read together with the accession protocol.

[161] Schott (2018).

[162] Herman (2023), at p. 14; the main novelty of the EUJEPA is that there is an explicit reference to tackling climate change. It is the first EU trade agreement to specifically mention in Article 16.4.4 the commitments of the Parties to effectively implement the 1992 United Nations Framework Convention on Climate Change (UNFCCC) and the 2015 Paris Agreement.

[163] Kettunen and Alvstam, (2020), p. 96.

tains more articles.[164] This might be explained by the fact that both the EU and Japan, albeit differently, have moved to trade sustainability as a means of applying a value-oriented diplomacy and (re)gain prominence on the international plane.

Kettunen and Alvstam further argue that in terms of norm-setting this consistency in approach on the part of the EU and Japan may provide the basis for developing what they define as a process of "multilateralizing regionalism".[165] In a similar vein, by drawing on a case study on the EU-Vietnam FTA,[166] Sicurelli maintains that the EU emerges as an actor able to export regulatory standards.[167] In particular, she posits that the attractiveness of the European market and the global standing of the EU as a standard setter in multiple policy fields enhances cooperation between the EU and the ASEAN region more broadly, envisioning even a future interregional FTA.[168] Sicurelli argues that 'the potential of the EU-sponsored norms to increase the international reputation of its negotiating counterparts within UN venues is a further asset for the EU to perform the role of a normative power in the Southeast Asian region.'[169] At the same time, her research shows that the EU is perceived as an incoherent, divided and intrusive actor, especially by Vietnamese government representatives.

Garcia and Masselot argue that 'the challenges encountered in negotiating with Asian states with fundamentally different conceptions of economic governance and views on how social values are related to trade structures, at a time when the market leverage of the EU may be waning due to rising multipolarity, increasing non-Western activism in economic norm-setting (or resistance to new norms), have led the EU to innovate mutually acceptable solutions for instance, in the form of a "soft" approach to social norms in FTAs.'[170] Nevertheless, this still leaves the question about whether the EU can be considered a norm promoter in its EPA with Japan in relation to sustainable development issues.[171] To address this point, it is important to emphasise that the EUJEPA largely serves to reaffirm and reinforce the commitments made by both the EU and Japan at the multilateral level, and in previous bilateral agreements. Chapter 16 is the dedicated chapter on 'Trade and Sustainable Development.' The TSD chapter maintains intact the Parties' right to regulate and determine their own domestic policies to protect human, animal and plant health. As in the case of other modern FTAs, the chapter calls for upholding existing standards for protecting consumers, labour rights and the environment and also includes non-regression provisions. In the case of labour standards, Article 16.3.3 EUJEPA contains a commitment to continued and sustained efforts to pursue ratification of ILO

[164] Chapter 16 of the EUJEPA contains 19 articles and the TSD chapter in the other FTAs, Chap. 13, contains 17 articles.

[165] Kettunen and Alvstam (2020), at p. 96; see also Kettunen and Alvstam (2018), pp. 13–28.

[166] Free Trade Agreement between the European Union and the Socialist Republic of Viet Nam (OJ L 186, 12.6.2020, p. 3–1400).

[167] Sicurelli (2015), pp. 23–39.

[168] Ibid., at 36.

[169] Idem.

[170] Garcia and Masselot (2015), p. 251.

[171] Kettunen and Alvstam (2020), at 96.

Conventions and other ILO Conventions which each Party considers appropriate to ratify. Japan has ratified seven of the eight ILO core fundamental conventions and hence must make progress on ratification of the remaining one on discrimination in employment and occupation, 1958, (Convention No. 111). Article 16.3.3. EUJEPA, albeit not legally binding, has prompted Japan to ratify the ILO Convention No. 105 on the abolition of forced labour in July 2022, which at the time of the signing of the agreement it was yet to ratify. It should also be pointed out that the signing of the EUJEPA was per se sufficient to propel Japan to do this.

During the Second World War, the Japanese military conscripted into forced labour millions of civilians and prisoners of war, including but only from Korea and Manchuria, for projects such as the Burma Railway.[172] Moreover, so-called "comfort women", mostly from Korea and China, were forced into sexual slavery during the Second World War.[173] Following the end of the conflict, the Japanese Government while officially apologising has also downplayed the claims made against it. The ratification of ILO Convention No. 105, therefore, signifies Japan's departure from this attitude and a strong commitment to the fight against all forms of forced labour. Other provisions that are important are Articles 16.5 and 16.6 EUJEPA as they create a civil society consultation mechanism, which is a novelty in Japan. The country must now engage with the social partners and, more broadly, with both Japanese and European organised civil society representatives to discuss what they do with the provisions of the agreement in terms of domestic policy on climate and labour matters, in the context of an iterative process of policy evaluation and monitoring. Disputes relating to this chapter will be discussed through government consultations, with recourse to an independent panel of experts. The Preamble of the EUJEPA, as the 2017 CETA's Preamble, also reaffirms the Parties' commitments to the principles enshrined in the 1948 Universal Declaration of Human Rights. Even though the reference is in the Preamble to the agreement it is worth pointing out that these are not explicitly mentioned in the 2015 EUSFTA and the 2011 EUKFTA.

3.3.3 Concluding Remarks

Moving forward, the EU should utilise the EPA to push Japan to ratify additional ILO instruments to address the extant gender imbalance in the country, namely, ILO Convention Discrimination (Employment and Occupation) No. 111, the Equal Remuneration Convention No. 100 and the Maternity Protection Convention No. 183. The ratification of these ILO Conventions could help to mitigate the potential adverse effects that the EUJEPA could have and promote gender equality in the application of the EUJEPA in Japan.[174]

---

[172] Duró and Palmer (2024), pp. 311–330.

[173] Vickers and Frost (2021); 'BBC, 'Japan ordered to compensate wartime "comfort women"', 23 November 2023, <https://www.bbc.co.uk/news/world-asia-67512578>.

[174] Sautter (2016).

It is equally important to highlight that the EUJEPA also has significant non-economic implications for both economies in the years to come. As middle power economies, the EU and Japan share the common values of liberal democracies and social market economies. Additionally, they share a deep commitment to the rules-based multilateral system not only in relation to trade but also in other areas, including climate change.[175] Chowdry et al. argue that 'closer economic and political cooperation via the EUJEPA will reinforce their ability to shape the course of global developments in a manner that better reflects their shared interests and values.'[176] This is particularly so at a time when superpowers and illiberal democracies such as China and Russia are applying pragmatic authoritarianism, and the US—until 2025 a close ally of both the EU and Japan—is increasingly reluctant to uphold the rules-based multilateral system that they helped build at the end of the Second World War.[177]

3.4 The EU-UK Trade and Cooperation Agreement

3.4.1 Introduction

On 31 January 2020, the UK officially left the EU.[178] This was a historic moment, which put an end to the wrangles that mired the UK's political and constitutional landscape in the aftermath of the 2016 EU referendum. It also seemingly put an end to the "Brexistential angst"[179] and the unsettling uncertainty that came with it. That said, the Brexit process is ongoing and it entails a "material change in circumstances"[180] in a very fundamental way.[181] As Michael Dougan aptly puts it[182]:

> the UK's decision to leave the European Union marks a fundamental reorientation in UK law and policy: both internally, when it comes to the structures, processes and outputs of our own domestic legal systems; and externally, as regards the UK's place in and relations with the broader European and international legal orders.

Undoubtedly, the withdrawal from the EU has posed a number of formidable challenges for UK employment law. Many UK workers' rights hinge on the substantial body of EU primary law (in addition to the Treaties, the EU Charter of Fundamental Rights (EUCFR)[183] is of particular salience as a living instrument for human rights

---

[175] Chowdhry et al. (2018), at p. 47.

[176] Idem.

[177] Idem.

[178] For analysis and commentary, see Lazowski and Cygan (2022); Fabbrini (2020–2023).

[179] Hay (2019), pp. 187–206.

[180] Sturgeon, 'Scottish independence: Will there be a second referendum?' 22 November 2022, BBC News, available at: <https://www.bbc.co.uk/news/uk-scotland-scotland-politics-50813510>.

[181] Velluti (2020b).

[182] Dougan (2017), p. 1.

[183] Charter of Fundamental Rights of the European Union OJ C 326, 26.10.2012, p. 391–407.

protection) and secondary legislation[184] and their exercise has been strengthened by the jurisprudence of the Court of Justice of the European Union (CJEU). Even though the Court does not always consider social rights its "cherished offspring"[185] and has held at times that EU labour law also applies in the interests of businesses[186] and employers,[187] it has nevertheless delivered some rather bold rulings that have strengthened the level of protection of workers' rights[188] and expanded the scope of social rights.[189] It should also be recalled that EU law offers a higher level of protection because it grants individuals the right to an effective judicial remedy and also requires Member States to ensure adequate protection of EU rights in line with the judgments of the CJEU. More generally, the loss of EU citizenship and the correlated freedom of movement will also affect British citizens and workers, not only EU nationals.[190]

On 30 December 2020, the EU and the UK signed a Trade and Cooperation Agreement (TCA),[191] after almost 10 months of negotiations. The TCA constitutes the cornerstone for the new relationship between the EU and the UK.[192] The UK was a Member State of the EU until 31 January 2020 and (almost all) EU laws applied to the UK until the end of the transition period on 31 December 2020. It is important to point out that the UK is a *sui generis* non-EU country. Both the EU and the UK are middle power economies and are also close and strongly inter-connected and inter-dependent neighbours. For these reasons, the trading relationship between the EU and the UK is fundamentally different from that between the EU and other

---

[184] For a list of EU Labour Law, visit: <https://employment-social-affairs.ec.europa.eu/policies-and-activities/rights-work/labour-law_en>.

[185] Ford (2015).

[186] E.g. Case C-426/11, *Mark Alemo-Herron and Others v Parkwood Leisure Ltd*, ECLI:EU:C:2013:521.

[187] E.g. Case C-80/14, *Union of Shop, Distributive and Allied Workers (USDAW), B. Wilson v WW Realisation 1 Ltd, in liquidation, Ethel Austin Ltd, Secretary of State for Business, Innovation and Skills*, ECLI:EU:C:2015:291.

[188] E.g. Case C-385/11, *Isabel Elbal Moreno v Instituto Nacional de la Seguridad Social (INSS), Tesorería General de la Seguridad Social (TGSS)*, ECLI:EU:C:2012:746.

[189] E.g. Case C-307/05, *Yolanda Del Cerro Alonso v Osakidetza-Servicio Vasco de Salud*, ECLI:EU:C:2007:509.

[190] E.g. Case C-673/20, *EP v Préfet du Gers, Institut national de la statistique et des études économiques (INSEE)*, ECLI:EU:C:2022:449.

[191] Trade and Cooperation Agreement between the European Union and the European Atomic Energy Community, of the one part, and the United Kingdom of Great Britain and Northern Ireland, of the other part, OJ 2021 L149/10; UK Government, 'UK-EU Trade and Cooperation Agreement—Summary', 30 April 2021, available at: <https://assets.publishing.service.gov.uk/government/uploads/system/uploads/attachment_data/file/962125/TCA_SUMMARY_PDF_V1-.pdf>; European Commission, 'EU-UK Trade and Cooperation Agreement: A new relationship, with big changes—Brochure' 24 December 2020, available at: <https://commission.europa.eu/document/5f9a61e8-e0a2-4f4a-8be2-1109bf136a4d_en>; Ioannides (2023); for detailed academic commentary, see Peers (2022), pp. 49–80; Kübek et al. (2024); Fabbrini (2024).

[192] The European Union (Future Relationship) Act 2020 (c. 29) implements the EU-UK TCA in the UK.

countries.[193] The TCA has therefore been designed with a view to ensuring that a level playing-field (LPF) would continue post-Brexit. The ensuing analysis focuses on workers' rights after Brexit and, in particular, on those provisions of the TCA which concern labour and social standards.

3.4.2 The Level Playing Field Provisions Concerning Labour and Social Standards in the TCA

As a starting point, the key chapters for the substantive provisions on labour and social standards are to be found in Chap. 6 on labour and social standards[194] and Chap. 8 on sustainable development.[195]

Title XI of Part Two, entitled 'Trade, Transport, Fisheries and other Arrangements' lays out the LPF provisions. These are designed to ensure fair competition and touch upon a range of areas, among others, labour and social standards, environment and climate, and other instruments for trade and sustainable development.[196] While the standard TSD provisions aim to promote convergence of labour and social standards and environment and climate change policy,[197] the LPF provisions in the TCA aim at avoiding "significant" divergence.[198] Upon entry into force of the TCA the EU and the UK—the latter being a member of the EU for 48 years—already shared the same standards and their economies remain close and substantially interconnected.[199]

The LPF provisions on labour cover three areas: a) general principles and commitments to international treaties and conventions, b) non-regression and rebalancing measures, and c) dispute settlement mechanism. Chapter 1 of Title XI introduces the general provisions that are applicable to all the level playing fields. Significantly, it recognises the common understanding of mutual benefits of the level playing field provisions in preventing distortion of trade or investment and emphasises that the

---

[193] Hallak (2021b).

[194] Chapter 6 of Title XI of Part Two (Articles 386–389) EU-UK TCA.

[195] Chapter 8 of Title XI of Part Two (Articles 397–407) EU-UK TCA.

[196] See Article 355(4) EU-UK TCA where Parties have committed 'to maintain and improve their respective high standards' in the areas covered by the LPF.

[197] For a comparative analysis of the general provisions and commitments contained in the TCA and the new generation of EU FTAs, see Hallak (2021), pp. 5–8.

[198] Ibid. at 2.

[199] Idem. To avoid divergence with adverse effects on fair competition, the 2020 Political Declaration signed between the EU and the UK stated that the parties should uphold the common EU and UK standards prevailing at the end of the transition, making explicit reference to the areas of state aid, competition, social and employment standards, environment, climate change, and relevant tax matters, see *Political declaration setting out the framework for the future relationship between the European Union and the United Kingdom* (2020 OJ C34/1), para. 17. The negotiations on the LPF provisions on labour, social and environmental standards were particularly difficult, for detailed analysis see Kenner (2022), pp. 320–345, Sects 2 and 3.

aim is not to harmonise standards.[200] Chapter 8 of Title XI entitled 'Other Instruments for Trade And Sustainable Development' includes a general commitment to promoting the development of international trade in a way that is conducive to decent work for all, as expressed in the 2008 ILO Declaration on Social Justice for a Fair Globalization and the 2000 ILO Decent Work Agenda, and makes explicit reference to the 1998 ILO Declaration on Fundamental Principles and Rights at Work, it includes a commitment to respecting, promoting and effectively implementing the internationally recognised core labour standards (CLS), to making continued and sustained efforts to ratify the fundamental ILO Conventions if they have not yet done so, to implementing all the ILO Conventions that the UK and the Member States have respectively ratified and the different provisions of the European Social Charter that, as members of the Council of Europe, the Member States and the UK have respectively accepted.[201] In addition, there is also a reference to protecting and promoting social dialogue on labour matters and cooperating on trade-related aspects of labour and the impact of the latter on investment.

The non-regression provisions warrant special attention, particularly the DSM envisaged, as it is more robust than that in other EU FTAs. Article 387(2) of Chap. 6 on 'Labour and Social Standards', provides that 'a Party shall not weaken or reduce, in a manner affecting trade or investment between the Parties, its labour and social levels of protection below the levels in place at the end of the transition period, including by failing to effectively enforce its law and standards.' In addition, Article 389(1) of Chap. 6 provides that 'the Parties shall make all efforts through dialogue, consultation, exchange of information and cooperation to address any disagreement on the application of the Chapter.' Disappointingly, there is no reference to a dynamic alignment with the EU labour standards in Article 387(4) EU-UK TCA to fend off regulatory divergence. Instead, there is 'a feeble promise that the parties shall continue to strive to increase their respective labour and social levels of protection'.[202] In the event of a dispute, the Parties shall have recourse exclusively to the procedures established under Articles 408 (on Consultations), 409 (on the Panel of Experts) and 410 (on the Panel of Experts for non-regression areas) of Chap. 9.[203]

Articles 408–410 of Chap. 9, outline a DSM under which a party may request consultation with the other party regarding any matter arising under Chap. 6. This is in line with the EU's approach in its other recent FTAs. In particular, should parties be unable to address disagreements through consultation and dialogue, a party may request that a panel of three experts be created to examine the case. The panel is required to deliver an interim report no later than 125 days after the establishment of

[200] Article 355(4) EU-UK TCA.

[201] Article 399 EU-UK TCA.

[202] Kenner (2022), at p. 334.

[203] In some specific instances, the TCA links dispute resolutions on labour and environment policy to the horizontal dispute settlement mechanism (HDSM) of Part Six (Dispute settlement and horizontal provisions), Title I (Dispute settlement), instead of the dispute settlement mechanism in Part Two (Trade), Title XI. Worthy of mention here is the cross-referencing to the panel selection procedures, see Article 409(19) and Article 740 EU-UK TCA.

the panel of experts. Each party may make a reasoned request to review particular aspects of the interim report within 25 days, and the other party may comment on that request within 15 days. The panel of experts must deliver the final report within 195 days of the establishment of the panel at the latest, and the report must be made public by parties within 15 days of its delivery. The final report will determine if a party has not respected its obligations, and the parties will discuss the appropriate measures.

An important novelty of the EU-UK TCA is the rebalancing mechanism to be applied to labour and social standards, which Kenner aptly defines as the "nuclear option" under the EU-UK TCA as it is intended to act as a deterrent against future blatant violations of the LPF.[204]

Article 411(2)–(3) envisages the adoption of rebalancing measures in cases where significant divergences arise in relation to labour and social standards, or with respect to subsidy control, and which result in material impacts on trade and investment. In such instances, the parties may enter into consultation upon notification by the party concerned. Should no mutually acceptable solution be reached, the concerned party may adopt strictly necessary and proportionate rebalancing measures to remedy the material impact, unless the other party requests the establishment of an arbitration tribunal.[205] If after 30 days, the arbitration tribunal has not delivered its final ruling, the party concerned may adopt rebalancing measures, and in that case, the other party may take proportionate counter-measures, until the tribunal delivers its decision. Significantly, the party concerned must provide reliable evidence and not 'merely conjecture or remote possibility.'[206] While the EU-UK TCA is silent as to which rebalancing measures the party concerned may adopt, there is the possibility that these may be in the form of the imposition of tariffs.

As pointed out by Hallak, 'the LPF provisions therefore not only provide for a rebalancing mechanism against divergences due to decisions "lowering" standards, but also allow a party to increase their own standards and adopt measures that rebalance the material impact and preserve fair competition.'[207] These rebalancing measures can also be adopted before the arbitration tribunal decision.

3.4.3 Concluding Remarks

As Kenner observes, 'the EU-UK TCA represents a compromise between the parties' positions with strong LPF protections against regression from labour standards, on the one hand and, on the other hand, governance arrangements that, as far as labour matters are concerned, do not involve the CJEU but do require independent arbitration of disputes and allow for unilateral measures to be taken.'[208]

---

[204] Kenner (2022), at p. 339.

[205] Article 739(2) EU-UK TCA.

[206] Article 411(2) EU-UK TCA.

[207] Hallak (2021a), p. 16.

[208] Kenner (2022), at p. 331.

Nevertheless, obligations in relation to labour standards are stricter than those normally contained in other EU FTAs, as most of the provisions are enforceable obligations and Parties can take "temporary remedies", i.e. trade remedies when obligations are breached.[209] The Agreement provides that the UK and EU must not weaken or reduce the level of employment rights in place on 31 December 2020, in a manner that affects trade or investment and to this end the EU-UK TCA commits both sides to maintaining a system for effective domestic labour enforcement. That said, besides the problems already examined in relation to the condition that the changes must affect trade and investment, it should also be stressed that the burden of proof for demonstrating this impact has been set very high[210] as it would be very difficult to prove that "material impacts on trade and investment" between the EU and the UK actually results from a lowering of TSD standards.[211] Moreover, there are some contradictions in the way that certain provisions concerning labour and social standards have been drafted. For example, in defining labour and social levels of protection, Article 386(1) EU-UK TCA excludes social security and pensions.[212]

While the Agreement restricts to some extent the UK's ability to make significant changes to employment law, two points should be made at this juncture. First, Article 356(1) EU-UK TCA provides that the Parties affirm their respective 'right to set their policies and priorities in the areas covered by this Title, to determine the levels of protection it deems appropriate and to adopt or modify its law and policies in a manner consistent with each Party's international commitments, including its commitments under this Title', even though they are subject to rebalancing measures.[213] It should also be pointed out that changes to domestic employment law are not permitted only when this affects trade or investment. An example of what this means would be the removal of working time regulations or agency worker rules altogether, as deregulation would give UK businesses a clear competitive advantage, which is likely to affect trade or investment.[214] As to the LPF, the rational of the EU-UK TCA's non-regression and rebalancing provisions is to create a level playing-field between UK-based and EU-based employers, to avoid scenarios whereby either can compete unfairly through lower and cheaper employment standards. Some contest the very idea of a level playing-field in relation to employment law given that there are no EU minimum standards on wages or dismissal costs or rates for taxation and social security contributions.[215] In broader terms, it can also be questioned whether EU labour laws have in and of themselves established a level playing-field in the first place considering the existing level of diversity between

---

[209] Ares et al. (2021), p. 41.

[210] Morris (2020).

[211] For further analysis, see Bäumler (2024), pp. 359–380.

[212] See Countouris et al. (2021); for critical commentary from the perspective of compliance with ILO standards and the European Social Charter, see also Ewing (2021), pp. 306–343.

[213] Article 411(2) EU-UK TCA.

[214] Leckey and Taylor (2020).

[215] Idem.

Member States employment laws which—it ought to be said—EU law itself permits. Be that as it may, the EU-UK TCA notably makes a provision that the labour and social standards in place on 31 December 2020 will act as a baseline and that significant future divergence could ultimately attract trade retaliation.

The points made above should also be considered in the context of major legislative changes that have taken place at domestic level in the UK since leaving the EU. In particular, the impact that the Retained EU Law (Revocation and Reform) Act 2023[216] will have on EU-derived employment rights. The Act will change the way that EU-derived law is interpreted in the UK, but it will also undermine the existing body of case law, potentially creating doubts about the scope, meaning and application of key EU-derived employment rights.[217] The uncertainty that it will generate is bound to make it difficult for employers to understand their obligations and for employees to understand their rights, which in turn is likely to lead to disputes and litigation.[218]

3.5 Conclusion

The present chapter, together with the preceding contribution by Martines, has provided a detailed examination of two key components of sustainable development contained in the chapters concerning environmental and labour standards of modern EU FTAs. The findings offer a rather mixed and, at times, unsatisfactory picture of the EU's approach to trade sustainability, which overall suggests that the EU is yet to meet its own TEU obligations as outlined in Article 3(5) TEU and Article 21 TEU. The empirical evidence to date indicates that sustainability provisions in modern EU FTAs while (perhaps) increasing ratification of multilateral instruments do not reduce violations of environmental and/or labour standards. This, inevitably, raises the question as to why the EU keeps inserting specific provisions on trade and sustainable development in its trade agreements. This state of affairs provides some sustenance to those who maintain that these provisions act as a legitimacy token for the EU's external action while "conquering" new markets further afield to boost the EU's ailing economies.

As posited by Kübek and Wessel, the 'Union's "new approach" for governing sustainability through trade, launched in 2022, can be seen as a new step in using FTAs to live up to its Treaty brief to "uphold and promote its values and interests" (Article 3(5) TEU) and to "ensure consistency between the different areas of its external action and between these and its other policies" (Article 21(3) TEU).'[219] Since then, the more recent TSD Chapters have a much broader remit covering *inter*

[216] Retained EU Law (Revocation and Reform) Act 2023 (2023 Chap. 28).

[217] Mason (2023).

[218] Idem.

[219] Kübek and Wessel (2024).

alia the promotion of responsible business conduct, deforestation-free supply chains and gender equality. This development is to be welcomed, as it increases the visibility and emphasises the importance of the UN's Sustainable Development Goals (SDGs). While linking trade with the pursuit of sustainability goals can be consequentially good, the evidence suggests that (largely soft) conditionality in EU trade agreements on its own is insufficient and needs to be combined with other measures at all levels of governance. On a more positive note, as Novitz observes, 'what has been interesting in relation to a broader sustainable development agenda has been the ways in which the normative framework of ILO core labour standards, ILO Conventions and a broader notion of "decent work" still operate as a reference point for "sustainable" trade conditionality.'[220] This point can be extended to key international instruments in the field of environmental protection and environmental standards.

References

Adinolfi G (2017) Alla ricerca di un equilibrio tra interessi economici e tutela dell'ambiente nella politica commerciale dell'Unione europea. Eurojus 4:1–6

Adinolfi G (2020) A Cross-cutting Legal Analysis of the European Union Preferential Trade Agreement's Chapters on Sustainable Development. Further Steps towards the Attainment of the Sustainable Development Goals? In: Beverelli C, Kurtz J, Raess D (eds) International Trade, Investment and the Sustainable Development Goals. Cambridge University Press, Cambridge, pp 15–49

Ares E, Carver D, Fella S, Ferguson D, Jozepa I, Seely A, Shalchi A (20 May 2021) The UK-EU Trade and Cooperation Agreement: Level Playing Field. Briefing Paper, No. 9190, https://researchbriefings.files.parliament.uk/documents/CBP-9190/CBP-9190.pdf

Azam M (2022) The TRIPS Agreement Revisited—Time to Open-Up Climate Technologies for Least Developed Countries. Journal of Intellectual Property Rights 27:107–129

Bartels L (2009) Social Issues: Labour, Environment, and Human Rights. In: Lester S, Mercurio B (eds) Bilateral and Regional Trade Agreements: Commentary, Analysis and Case Studies. Cambridge University Press, Cambridge, pp 342–366

Bartels L (2013) Human Rights and Sustainable Development Obligations in EU Free Trade Agreements. Legal Issues of Economic Integration 40:297–313

Bäumler J (2024) Level Playing Field and Sustainable Development. In: Kübek G, Tams CJ, Terhechte JP (eds) EU-UK Trade and Cooperation Agreement: A Handbook. Nomos, Hart, Beck, Baden-Baden/Oxford/Munich, pp 359–380

Bazillier R, Rana AT (2025) Social Clauses in Free Trade Agreements: An Efficient Tool to Improve Labour Standards? World Econ 0:1–31

Bellmann C, Van der Ven C (2020) Greening Regional Trade Agreements on Non-Tariff Measures through Technical Barriers to Trade and Regulatory Co-Operation. OECD Trade and Environment Working Papers, No. 2020/04, OECD Publishing, Paris

Brandi C (2017) Trade Elements in Countries' Climate Contributions under the Paris Agreement. International Centre for Trade and Sustainable Development (ICTSD), Geneva

[220] Novitz (2024), at p. 314.

Bronckers M, Gruni G (2019) Taking the Enforcement of Labour Standards in the EU's Free Trade Agreements Seriously. Common Market Law Review 56:1591–1622. https://doi.org/10.54648/cola2019126

Bronckers M, Gruni G (2021) Retooling the Sustainability Standards in EU Free Trade Agreements. J Int Econ Law 24:25–51. https://doi.org/10.1093/jiel/jgab007

Brown Weiss (1992) Environment and Trade as Partners in Sustainable Development: A Commentary, American Journal of International Law 86:728

Camroux D (Jan 2018) The European Union and ASEAN: Two to Tango?. Notre Europe, https://institutdelors.eu/wp-content/uploads/2018/01/etude65eu-asean-en.pdf

Carrère C, Olarreaga M, Raess D (2022) Labour Clauses in Trade Agreements: Hidden Protectionism? Rev Int Organ 17:1–31

Chan A, Ross RJS (2003) Racing to the Bottom: International Trade Without a Social Clause. Third World Q 24:1011–1028

Charnovitz S (2014) Green Subsidies and the WTO, EUI Working Papers Robert Schuman Centre for Advanced Studies, RSCAS 2014/93

Chowdhry S, Sapir A, Terzi A (Sept 2018) The EU-Japan Economic Partnership Agreement, Study Requested by the INTA Committee, Policy Department for External Relations; Directorate General for External Policies of the Union, EP/EXPO/B/INTA/2018/03—European Parliament

Cima E, Esty DC (2024) Making International Trade Work for Sustainable Development: Toward a New WTO Framework for Subsidies. *J Int Econ Law 27*:1–17

Countouris N, Ewing KD, Hendy J (2021) The EU-UK Trade and Cooperation Agreement and Workers' Rights. ETUI Research Paper—Policy Brief 3/2021

De Schutter O (2015) Trade in the Service of Sustainable Development. Hart, Oxford

De Ville F, Gheyle N (2019) The Unintended Consequences of the Transatlantic Trade and Investment Partnership Negotiations. Int Spect 54:16–30. https://doi.org/10.1080/03932729.2019.1551822

Delimatsis P, Reins L (2021) Trade and Environmental Law. Edgard Publishing

Dougan M (2017) Editor's Introduction. In: Dougan M (ed) The UK after Brexit. Legal and Policy Challenges. Intersentia, Cambridge—Antwerp—Portland, pp 1–12

Dupré M, Kpenou S (2025) Key Insights into the Final EU-Mercosur Agreement, Veblen Institute for Economic Reforms. https://www.veblen-institute.org/Key-Insights-into-the-Final-EU-Mercosur-Agreement.html

Durán GM (2013) Innovations and Implications of the Trade and Sustainable Development Chapter in the EU–Korea Free Trade Agreement. In: Harrison J (ed) The European Union and South Korea. The Legal Framework for Strengthening Trade, Economic and Political Relations. Edinburgh University Press, Edinburgh, pp 124–146

Durel L (2024) Border Carbon Adjustment Compliance and the WTO: The Interactional Evolution of Law. *J Int Econ Law 27*:18–40

Duró Á, Palmer D (2024) Japan's Forgotten Korean Forced Laborers: The Search for Hidden Wartime Graves in Hokkaido. International Labor and Working-Class History 106:311–330. https://doi.org/10.1017/S0147547924000048

European Parliament Research Service (EPRS) (2015) Clean Trade and Investment Partnerships A New Instrument in the EU's Trade Policy Toolbox

Ewing D (2021) The EU-UK Trade and Cooperation Agreement: Implications for ILO Standards and the European Social Charter in the United Kingdom. King's Law J 32:306–343. https://doi.org/10.1080/09615768.2021.1969757

Fabbrini F (2020–2023) The Law & Politics of Brexit: Volumes I-IV. OUP, Oxford

Fabbrini F (2024) The Law & Politics of Brexit: Volume V—The Trade and Cooperation Agreement. OUP, Oxford

Ford M (11 May 2015) USDAW v Ethel Austin in the ECJ. OxHRH Blog, http://humanrights.dev3.oneltd.eu/usdaw-v-ethel-austin-in-the-ecj/

Fournier P Ozinga S (2018) Forests and Forest People in EU Free Trade Agreements. Fern Discussion Paper. https://www.fern.org/fileadmin/uploads/fern/Documents/2018/Fern-Forests-in-EU-FTAs-report.pdf

Francioni F (1998) La tutela dell'ambiente e la disciplina del commercio internazionale. In Diritto e organizzazione del commercio internazionale dopo la creazione della Organizzazione Mondiale del Commercio, Atti del Convegno della Società italiana di diritto internazionale, Editoriale Scientifica, Napoli, pp 147–181

Frenkel M, Walter B (2017) The EU-Japan Economic Partnership Agreement: Relevance, Content and Policy Implications. Intereconomics 52:358–363

Garcia M, Masselot A (2015) EU-Asia Free Trade Agreements as Tools for Social Norm/Legislation Transfer. Asia Europe Journal 13:241–252. https://doi.org/10.1007/s10308-015-0423-0

Gehring MW, Cordonier MC (eds) (2005) Sustainable Development in World Trade Law. Kluwer Law International

Hallak I (Feb 2021a) EU-UK Trade and Cooperation Agreement—An Analytical Overview. EPRS In-depth Analysis, European Parliament, https://www.europarl.europa.eu/thinktank/en/document/EPRS_IDA(2021)679071

Hallak I (Nov 2021b) The Level Playing-Field for Labour and Environment in EU-UK Relations. EPRS, Briefing, European Parliament, https://www.europarl.europa.eu/RegData/etudes/BRIE/2021/690576/EPRS_BRI(2021)690576_EN.pdf

Hamill J, Lee D (2001) A Middle Power Paradox? South African Diplomacy in the Post-apartheid Era. International Relations 15:33–59. https://doi.org/10.1177/004711701015004004

Hay C (2019) Brexistential Angst and the Paradoxes of Populism: On the Contingency, Predictability and Intelligibility of Seismic Shifts. Political Studies 68:187–206. https://doi.org/10.1177/0032321719836356

Herman S (2023) The EUJEPA, Expectations and Realities of a "New-Generation FTA". Implications for EU-Japan Relations on Sustainable Trade and Development, Final year Master thesis—Graduate School of Public Policy, University of Tokyo, Japan; full text, https://www.pp.u-tokyo.ac.jp/wp-content/uploads/2016/02/0fa6177da45e2dc36e03762bd236ff04.pdf

Hickey GM (2004) Regulatory Approaches to Monitoring Sustainable Forest Management. Int For Rev 6(2):89–98

Hoffmeister F (2014) The European Union as an International Trade Negotiator. In: Koops J, Macaj G (eds) The European Union as a Diplomatic Actor. Palgrave Macmillan, London, pp 138–154

Horn H, Mavroidis P, Sapir A (2009) Beyond the WTO? An Anatomy of EU and US Preferential Trade Agreements. Bruegel Blueprint Series, Brussels, Vol. VV, https://www.bruegel.org/system/files/wp_attachments/bp_trade_jan09.pdf

Hradilovà K, Svoboda O (2018) Sustainable Development Chapters in EU Free Trade Agreements: Searching for Effectiveness. Journal of World Trade 52:1019–1042. https://doi.org/10.54648/TRAD2018044

Ioannides I (Aug 2023) The EU-UK Trade and Cooperation Agreement Two Years on: Unpacking Early Evidence. European Implementation Assessment, EPRS, https://www.europarl.europa.eu/thinktank/en/document/EPRS_STU(2023)747433

Ionel Z (Jan 2022) Labour Rights in EU Trade Agreements Towards Stronger Enforcement. EPRS Briefing, European Parliament, https://www.europarl.europa.eu/thinktank/en/document/EPRS_BRI(2022)698800

Jie Y, Wallace J (13 Sept 2021) What is China's Belt and Road Initiative (BRI)?, Chatham House, https://www.chathamhouse.org/2021/09/what-chinas-belt-and-road-initiative-bri

Jochheim U (Dec 2022) ASEAN: The EU's Strategic Partner in Asia. Briefing, EPRS, European Parliament, https://www.europarl.europa.eu/RegData/etudes/BRIE/2021/698807/EPRS_BRI(2021)698807_EN.pdf

Jordaan E (2003) The Concept of a Middle Power in International Relations: Distinguishing between Emerging and Traditional Middle Powers. *Politikon: South African Journal of Political Studies 30*:165–181

Kenner J (2022) Brexit and Workers' Rights: Managing Divergence and Managing Trust. In: Lazowski A, Cygan A (eds) Research Handbook on Legal Aspects of Brexit. Elgar Publishing, Cheltenam, pp 320–345

Kettunen E, Alvstam CG (2018) Free trade agreements and responsible business: examples from the EU's bilateral agreements in East and Southeast Asia in Andreosso-O'Callaghan

B, Jaussaud J, Zolin MB (eds), Asian Nations and Multinationals: Overcoming the Limits to Growth. Palgrave, London, pp. 13–28.
Kettunen E, Alvstam CG (2020) The EU-Japan Economic Partnership Agreement as a Norm Model for Sustainable Development Issues in the Future EU FTAs in Asia. In: Andreosso-O'Callaghan B, Dzever S, Jaussaud J, Taylor R (eds). Wiley, Sustainable Development and Energy Transition in Europe and Asia, pp 93–110. https://doi.org/10.1002/9781119705222.ch5
Kim HE (2011) Green Technology Transfer and IP, in The Role of the Patent System in Stimulating Innovation and Technology Transfer for Climate Change: Including Aspects of Licensing and Competition Law. Nomos Verlagsgesellschaft mbH, pp 57–64
Koh T (2020) ASEAN and EU—Similarities and Differences. In: ASEAN-EU Partnership—The Untold Story, pp 37–41. https://doi.org/10.1142/9789811223112_0004
Kübek G, Wessel RA (2024) Governing Sustainability through Trade in EU External Relations: The 'New Approach' and its Challenges. In: Bergamaschine Mata Diz J (ed) Trade and Sustainable Development: The Foreign Relations of the European Union. https://doi.org/10.2139/ssrn.4941502
Kübek G, Tams CJ, Terhechte JP (2024) EU-UK Trade and Cooperation Agreement: A Handbook. Nomo, Hart, Becks, Baden-Baden/Oxford/Munich
Laget E et al (2020) Deep Trade Agreements and Global Value Chains. Rev Ind Organ 57:379–410. https://doi.org/10.1007/s11151-020-09780-0
Laurence M (Oct 2023) Middle Powers. Oxford Research Encyclopedia of International Studies. https://doi.org/10.1093/acrefore/9780190846626.013.783
Lazowski A, Cygan A (2022) Research Handbook on Legal Aspects of Brexit. Elgar Publishing, Cheltenam
Leckey A, Taylor G (30 Dec 2020) What does the Brexit Trade Deal Mean for Employment Law, https://www.lewissilkin.com/insights/2020/12/30/what-does-the-brexit-trade-deal-mean-for-employment-law
Lonardo L (2018) Common Foreign and Security Policy and the EU's external action objectives: an analysis of Article 21 of the Treaty on the European Union. European Constitutional Law Review 14(3):584–608
López V (2024) The EU–Japan Partnership in the Post-pandemic Order: What Comes Next? Journal of Asian Security and International Affairs 11:122–145. https://doi.org/10.1177/23477970241230376
Manea MG (2013) The Institutional Dimension of EU-ASEAN/ASEAN Plus Three Inter-regional Relations. In: Christiansen T, Kirchner E, Murray P (eds) The Palgrave Handbook of EU-Asia Relations. Palgrave Macmillan, London. https://doi.org/10.1057/9780230378704_20
Marceau G, Walker R, Oeschger A (2023) The Evolution of Labour Provisions in Regional Trade Agreements. Journal of World Trade 57:361–410
Marín Durán G (2020) Sustainable Development Chapters in EU Free Trade Agreements: Emerging Compliance Issues. Common Market Law Review 57:1031–1068
Mason L (4 July 2023) Employment Law and the Retained EU Law Act 2023, https://www.linklaters.com/en/insights/blogs/employmentlinks/2023/july/employment-law-and-the-retained-eu-law-act-2023
McLachlan C (2005) The Principle of Systemic Integration and Article 31(3)(C) of the Vienna Convention. ICLQ 54:279–320
Montini M (2025) L'azione esterna dell'Unione Europea per l'attuazione dello sviluppo sostenibile. Editoriale scientifica, Napoli
Morita-Jaeger (14 Mar 2025) The "New Normal": Can the UK and Other Democratic Middle Powers Play a Pivotal Role?. UKTPO Blog, https://www.uktpo.org/2025/03/14/can-the-uk-democratic-middle-powers-play-a-pivotal-role/

Morris M (Dec 2020) The Agreement on the Future Relationship: A First Analysis. Institute for Public Policy Research, https://ippr-org.files.svdcdn.com/production/Downloads/agreement-on-future-relationship-ippr-assessment-1.pdf

Neak L (14–18 Mar 2000) Middle Powers Once Removed: The Diminished Global Role of Middle Powers and American Grand Strategy. Working Papers, Columbia University, https://ciaotest.cc.columbia.edu/isa/nal01/

Nissen A (2022) Not That Assertive: The EU's Take on Enforcement of Labour Obligations in Its Free Trade Agreement with South Korea. European Journal of International Law 33:607–630. https://doi.org/10.1093/ejil/chac037

Nolte D (2021) The EU's Beef with Mercosur: Geo-economics Versus Climate Diplomacy. Latin America's Environmental Policies in Global Perspective Series Wilson Center, Washington, D.C.

Novitz TA (2022) Sustainable Labour Conditionality in EU Free Trade Agreements? Implications of the EU-Korea Expert Panel Report. European Law Review 47:3–23

Novitz T (2024) Trade, Labour and Sustainable Development. Elgar Publishing, Cheltenham

Orbie J (2021) EU Trade Policy Meets Geopolitics: What about Trade Justice? European Foreign Affairs Review 26:197–202

Peers S (26 Jan 2021) Free Trade v Freedom of Association? The EU/South Korea Free Trade Agreement and the Panel Report on the EU Challenge to South Korean Labour Law. EU Law Analysis Blog, https://eulawanalysis.blogspot.com/2021/01/free-trade-v-freedom-of-association.html

Peers S (2022) So Close, Yet So Far: The EU/UK Trade and Cooperation Agreement. Common Market Law Review 59:49–80

Reinsch WA, Benson E, Puga C (2021) Environmental Goods Agreement A New Frontier or an Old Stalemate? Report of the Center for Strategic and International Studies, https://www.csis.org/analysis/environmental-goods-agreement-new-frontier-or-old-stalemate-

Remondino V (2022) New Generation Free Trade Agreements at a Crossroads. Assessing Environmental Enforcement of the E.U.'s Trade and Sustainable Development Chapters from Global Europe to the Power of Trade Partnerships Communication. University of Bologna Law Review 8:149–186

Sautter T (2016) Trade Sustainability Impact Assessment of the Free Trade Agreement between the European Union and Japan—Final Report. Directorate-General for Trade, Trade Sustainability Impact Assessment, European Commission, Directorate-General for Trade 2016

Schott JJ (2018) The Origins of the TPP. In: Looney RE (ed) *Handbook of International Trade Agreements: Country, regional and global approaches*. Routledge, London

Sharp A (19 Dec 2024) The 51st Star on the U.S. Flag? U.S. President-elect Donald Trump has Bolstered his Tariff Threats with Another Suggestion of Canadian Statehood. Foreign Policy, World Brief

Sicurelli D (2015) The EU as a Norm Promoter through Trade. The Perceptions of Vietnamese Elites. Asia Europe Journal 13:23–39. https://doi.org/10.1007/s10308-014-0407-5

Steinberg RH (2002) Greening of Trade Law. International Trade Organizations and Environmental Issues. Rowman & Littlefield, NewYork

Suzuki H (2017) The New Politics of Trade: *EU-Japan Journal of European Integration 39*(7): 875–889.

Timini J, Cortinovis N, López Vicente F (2022) The Heterogeneous Effects of Trade Agreements with Labour Provisions. World Econ 45:2820–2853

Toenshoff C (2024) Defensive Issue Linkage: Exploring the Origins of Environmental Content in Trade Agreements. Environmental Politics 33(6):953–975

Van Elsuwege P (2010) EU External Action after the Collapse of the Pillar Structure: In Search of a New Balance between Delimitation and Consistency. CMLR 47(4):987–1019

van Gellecum H (2012) Environmental Law in the Context of Article 31(3)(C) of the Vienna Convention on the Law of Treaties: Reconciling Treaty Interpretation and Progressive

Environmental Norms: The Pulp Mills Case and Beyond. https://ssrn.com/abstract=1989468 or https://doi.org/10.2139/ssrn.1989468

Van Hasselt (2021) Trade. In: Lavanya R, Peel J (eds) The Oxford Handbook of International Environmental Law, 2nd edn. Oxford Handbooks, pp 751–767

van Noordwijk M, Leimona B, Minangn P (2025) The European Deforestation-Free Trade Regulation: Collateral Damage to Agroforesters? Curr Opin Environ Sustain 72:1–9

Velluti S (2020a) The Role of the EU in the Promotion of Human Rights and International Labour Standards in Its External Trade Relations. Springer, Cham

Velluti S (16 Apr 2020b) The Potential Impact(s) of Brexit on Employment Rights during the Global Pandemic. DCU Brexit Institute, Blog, https://dcubrexitinstitute.eu/2020/04/the-potential-impacts-of-brexit-on-employment-rights-during-the-global-pandemic/

Vickers E, Frost M (2021) The "Comfort Women" as Public History. Asia-Pacific Journal Japan Focus 19(Special Issue):5542. https://apjjf.org/2021/5/ToC

Wang H (2021) How to Assess Regional Trade Agreements? Deep FTAs v. China's Trade Agreements. The International Lawyer 54:247–279

Wold C, Gaines S (2023) Trade and the Environment. Carolina Academic Press

Yoshimatsu H (2020) The EU-Japan Free Trade Agreement in Evolving Global Trade Politics. Asia Europe Journal 18:429–443

Yuzawa T (2013) ASEAN-Japan Cooperation on Democracy and Human Rights Promotion: Challenges and Opportunities. In: Beyond 2015—ASEAN-Japan Strategic Partnership for Democracy, Peace, and Prosperity in Southeast Asia, Japan Center for International Exchange, Part 14, https://jcie.or.jp/data/media/Publication/14/14_yuzawa.pdf

The Exportation of EU Fundamental Rights to Privacy and Personal Data Protection in the Wider World Through International Agreements

Gabriele Rugani

Contents

Abstract This chapter investigates how the European Union strives to export the fundamental rights to privacy and data protection (enshrined in articles 7 and 8 of the Charter of Nice) in the wider world through its international agreements. Indeed, the EU has inserted—in several bilateral treaties having (at least partially) commercial nature concluded with third countries—provisions which are aimed at increasing the safeguards ensured by its counterparts to the fundamental rights at stake. Given the above, first of all, the contribution examines the articles included in some agreements signed by the EU in the second decade of the twenty-first century, such as the ones with South Korea, Colombia-Peru-Ecuador, Central America, Ukraine, Canada (CETA), Japan (EPA), Singapore and Viet Nam. It also highlights, however,

G. Rugani (✉)
Department of Law, University of Pisa, Pisa, Italy
e-mail: gabriele.rugani@jus.unipi.it

L. Pasquali (ed.), *EU Values and International Law*, European Union and its Neighbours in a Globalized World 35,
https://doi.org/10.1007/978-3-032-20521-6_8

the critical issues raised by the provisions at stake, due mainly to their weak formulation and to the unclear obligational content of certain terms. Then, the analysis focuses on a new and stronger mechanism endorsed by the EU Commission in 2018 in order to overcome the abovementioned critical issues: the so-called "Horizontal provisions for cross-border data flows and for personal data protection", to be inserted in subsequent EU trade agreements in place of "old-fashioned" articles. Therefore, the chapter takes into consideration the agreements currently under negotiation in which the EU is attempting to include the Horizontal provisions—such as the ones with Australia and Tunisia—and, above all, the trade agreements that are already in force in which similar articles have actually been inserted, such as the ones with New Zealand, Chile and United Kingdom. Finally, it is possible to make some evaluations concerning not only the positive effects that such provisions can have in exporting worldwide the fundamental rights to privacy and data protection, but also the limitations that persist.

1 Introduction: The Aim of the EU to Export the Fundamental Rights to Privacy and Personal Data Protection in the Wider World

As well known, in the European Union legal order both privacy and personal data protection are considered as fundamental rights. Indeed, both are enshrined in the Charter of Fundamental Rights of the EU (CFREU), also known as Charter of Nice, which was solemnly proclaimed in 2000 and since 2009 has the same legal value as the Treaties.[1]

It is worth focusing more closely on the content of the two rights and the differences between them. The right to privacy, originally conceived in the US at the end of the XIX century,[2] offers a "static", "negative" kind of protection: indeed, it only consists in preventing others from interfering with one's private life.[3] At international level, such right has been included in various instruments, such as the 1948 Universal Declaration of Human Rights[4] and the 1966 International Covenant on Civil and Political Rights,[5] both adopted by the United Nations General Assembly

[1] Art. 6, para 1, TEU.

[2] Warren and Brandeis (1890).

[3] Rodotà (2009), p. 79.

[4] Art. 12 of the 1948 Universal Declaration of Human Rights (adopted by the United Nations General Assembly) states that: "No one shall be subjected to arbitrary interference with his privacy, family, home or correspondence, nor to attacks upon his honour and reputation. Everyone has the right to the protection of the law against such interference or attacks".

[5] Art. 17 of the 1966 International Covenant on Civil and Political Rights (adopted by the United Nations General Assembly) states that: "1. No one shall be subjected to arbitrary or unlawful interference with his privacy, family, home or correspondence, nor to unlawful attacks on his honour

(UNGA), but also the 1950 Convention for the Protection of Human Rights and Fundamental Freedoms—also known as European Convention on Human Rights (ECHR)—of the Council of Europe (CoE).[6] At EU level, the right to privacy is enshrined in art. 7 CFREU, entitled "Respect for private and family life", according to which: "Everyone has the right to respect for his or her private and family life, home and communications".

The right to protection of personal data, instead, offers a "dynamic", "positive" kind of protection, since it confers on individuals powers of control and intervention which follow the data in all their movements.[7] Such right, introduced by art. 8 of the Charter of Nice, in some respects can be described as an innovative fundamental right,[8] while in some others is not really new[9]: its constitutive elements have their roots in existing instruments, both at EU level and at international level (such as the ones adopted by the Organisation for Economic Co-operation and Development—OECD—and by the CoE).[10] The innovative aspect of the CFREU consists in the fact that such elements become part of a fundamental right deserving protection per se.[11] It is worth clarifying that the qualification of a right as "fundamental" implies particularly stringent conditions on its limitations, which must in any case respect its essence.[12]

At present, in the framework of EU law, the right to protection of personal data frequently complements the right to privacy, and in many contexts the former has replaced almost completely the latter.[13] This is particularly evident in the main EU instrument in the field, i.e. Regulation (EU) 2016/679 "on the protection of natural persons with regard to the processing of personal data and on the free movement of such data", better known as General Data Protection Regulation (GDPR).[14]

---

and reputation. 2. Everyone has the right to the protection of the law against such interference or attacks".

[6] Art. 8 ("Right to respect for private and family life") of the 1950 Convention for the Protection of Human Rights and Fundamental Freedoms (adopted by the Council of Europe) states that: "1. Everyone has the right to respect for his private and family life, his home and his correspondence. 2. There shall be no interference by a public authority with the exercise of this right except such as is in accordance with the law and is necessary in a democratic society in the interests of national security, public safety or the economic well-being of the country, for the prevention of disorder or crime, for the protection of health or morals, or for the protection of the rights and freedoms of others".

[7] Rodotà (2009), pp. 79–80.

[8] Braibant (2001), p. 47.

[9] Bernsdorff (2003), p. 160.

[10] On the point see, for instance: González Fuster (2014), p. 204.

[11] Docquir (2008), p. 41.

[12] On the point see, for instance: Tribe and Dorf (1990); Lenaerts (2019).

[13] González Fuster (2014), pp. 242–245.

[14] Regulation (EU) 2016/679 of the European Parliament and of the Council of 27 April 2016 *on the protection of natural persons with regard to the processing of personal data and on the free movement of such data, and repealing Directive 95/46/EC (General Data Protection Regulation)*, O.J. L 119/1 (2016).

The GDPR, indeed, defines itself as an instrument almost exclusively aimed at safeguarding the right to the protection of personal data,[15] while there are only minor references to the right to privacy.[16] Nevertheless, in EU law, the connection between the right to the protection of personal data and the right to privacy is still very strong, and disentangling them turns out to be completely impossible.[17] Therefore, it is always important to keep both into consideration.

Given the relevance of privacy and personal data protection in the EU legal order, we must not be surprised by the attempt of the EU to export such fundamental rights globally. This is perfectly consistent with the aims of the EU external action: the latter, according to Art. 21 TEU, seeks to advance in the wider world the principles which have inspired the creation, development and enlargement of the Union, such as the universality and indivisibility of human rights and fundamental freedoms.[18]

In pursuing the abovementioned purpose, the EU has included, in several bilateral treaties having (at least partially) a commercial nature concluded with third countries, provisions which are aimed at increasing the safeguards ensured by its counterparts to the fundamental rights to privacy and personal data protection. This chapter, therefore, will take into consideration such provisions and will try to assess whether they are capable of effectively exporting worldwide the rights at stake.

More specifically, first of all, the contribution will investigate the articles included in some agreements concluded by the EU in the second decade of the twenty-first century. It will also highlight, however, the critical issues raised by the provisions at stake, due mainly to their weak formulation and to the unclear obligational content of certain terms. Then, the analysis will focus on a new and stronger mechanism endorsed by the EU Commission in 2018 in order to overcome the abovementioned critical issues: the so-called "Horizontal provisions for cross-border data flows and for personal data protection", to be inserted in subsequent EU trade agreements in place of "old-fashioned" articles. Therefore, the paper will take into consideration the agreements currently under negotiation in which the EU is attempting to include the Horizontal provisions and, above all, the trade agreements that are already in force in which similar articles have actually been inserted. Finally, it will be possible to make some evaluations concerning not only the positive effects that such provisions can have in exporting worldwide the fundamental rights to privacy and data protection, but also the limitations that persist.

---

[15] Art. 1 ("Subject-matter and objectives"), para 2, of Regulation (EU) 2016/679 states that: "This Regulation protects fundamental rights and freedoms of natural persons and in particular their right to the protection of personal data".

[16] Whereas 4 of Regulation (EU) 2016/679 states that: "[...] This Regulation respects all fundamental rights and observes the freedoms and principles recognised in the Charter as enshrined in the Treaties, in particular the respect for private and family life [...]".

[17] González Fuster (2014), pp. 242–245.

[18] Art. 21, para 1, TEU states that "The Union's action on the international scene shall be guided by the principles which have inspired its own creation, development and enlargement, and which it seeks to advance in the wider world: democracy, the rule of law, the universality and indivisibility of human rights and fundamental freedoms, respect for human dignity, the principles of equality and solidarity, and respect for the principles of the United Nations Charter and international law [...]".

2 The "Old-Fashioned" Privacy and Personal Data Protection Provisions in EU International Agreements

As anticipated, the contribution will firstly investigate the privacy and personal data protection articles included in some agreements concluded by the EU in the second decade of the twenty-first century[19]: we refer, for instance, to the Free Trade Agreement (FTA) with South Korea (2010),[20] the Trade Agreement with Colombia-Peru-Ecuador (2012),[21] the two Association Agreements with Central America (2012)[22] and Ukraine (2014),[23] the Comprehensive Economic and Trade Agreement (CETA) with Canada (2016),[24] the Economic Partnership Agreement (EPA) with Japan (2018)[25] and the FTAs with Singapore (2018)[26] and Viet Nam (2019).[27]

The articles in such agreements are formulated as follows. Their first part represents a "data flows commitment", i.e. a commitment to allow the free flow of information between the parties, given the importance of cross-border data transfers in fostering the expansion of international trade. Their second part, instead, is the true "data protection provision", i.e. a provision designed to ensure the rights to privacy and to personal data protection through the obligation to adopt or maintain "adequate safeguards".[28]

It must be pointed out that the articles at stake are usually inserted in the parts of EU agreements concerning the financial services sector and the telecommunication services sector. It is not surprising: the former is one of the most pertinent sectors for digital economy,[29] but it also raises significant issues and the public is particularly concerned about the processing of personal financial data.[30] Similar

---

[19] On the EU's new generation trade agreements, see for instance: Pasquali (2020, 2021).

[20] Free Trade Agreement between the European Union and its Member States, of the one part, and the Republic of Korea, of the other part, 6 October 2010, O.J. L 127/6 (2011).

[21] Trade Agreement between the European Union and its Member States, of the one part, and Colombia and Peru, of the other part, 26 June 2012, O.J. L 354/3 (2012).

[22] Agreement establishing an Association between the European Union and its Member States, on the one hand, and Central America on the other, 29 June 2012, O.J. L 346/3 (2012).

[23] Association Agreement between the European Union and its Member States, of the one part, and Ukraine of the other part, 21 March and 27 June 2014, O.J. L 161/3 (2014).

[24] Comprehensive Economic and Trade Agreement (CETA) between Canada, of the one part, and the European Union and its Member States, of the other part, 30 October 2016, O.J. L 11/23 (2017).

[25] Agreement between the European Union and Japan for an Economic Partnership, 17 July 2018, O.J. L 330/3 (2018).

[26] Free trade Agreement between the European Union and the Republic of Singapore, 19 October 2018, O.J. L 294/3 (2019).

[27] Free Trade Agreement between the European Union and the Socialist Republic of Viet Nam, 30 June 2019, O.J. L 186/3 (2020).

[28] On the point see, for instance: Yakovleva and Irion (2020a).

[29] Burri (2017), p. 83.

[30] Sousa De Jesus (2004), p. 4.

considerations also apply to the latter: its importance for the digital economy is unquestionable, but its intensive use of data increases the demand of an appropriate protection.[31]

In order to better explain the provisions at stake, we will use as an example the ones included in the EU-Canada CETA, given the importance and notoriety of such agreement.

We should start from Chapter Thirteen of the CETA, devoted to "Financial services": its aim is to enable financial institutions and investors in the EU and Canada to benefit from fair, equal access to each other's markets, while applying certain conditions which fully comply with the prudential and regulatory standards in place in the EU and Canada.[32] In this chapter, it is possible to find art. 13.15, concerning "Transfer and processing of information". According to its para 1, "Each Party shall permit a financial institution or a cross-border financial service supplier of the other Party to transfer information in electronic or other form, into and out of its territory, for data processing if processing is required in the ordinary course of business of the financial institution or the cross-border financial service supplier". It is, as evident, a "data flows commitment", as described above. Para 2 of art. 13.15, instead, provides as follows: "Each Party shall maintain *adequate safeguards to protect privacy* [emphasis added], in particular with regard to the transfer of personal information. If the transfer of financial information involves personal information, such transfers shall be in accordance with the legislation governing the protection of personal information of the territory of the Party where the transfer has originated". As anticipated, we are faced with a "data protection provision", which obliges the parties to implement "adequate safeguards" to protect the rights at stake.[33]

It is now possible to move on to Chapter Fifteen of the CETA, entitled "Telecommunications", in which the EU and Canada commit to giving each other's businesses fair and equal access to public telecommunications networks and services and to ensuring competition in the telecommunications market, while guaranteeing the respect of customers' rights. Here the relevant article for our purposes is art. 15.3, concerning "Access to and use of public telecommunications transport networks or services". Its para 3 states the following: "Each Party shall ensure that enterprises of the other Party may use public telecommunications transport networks and services for the movement of information in its territory or across its borders, including for intra-corporate communications of these enterprises, and for access to information contained in data bases or otherwise stored in machine-readable form in the territory of either Party". According to para 4, instead, "[…] notwithstanding paragraph 3, a Party shall take *appropriate measures* [emphasis added] to protect: (a) the security and confidentiality of public telecommunications transport services; and (b) the privacy of users of public telecommunications transport services, subject to the requirement that these measures are not applied in a

[31] On the point see, for instance: Van Der Marel (2015), p. 2.

[32] On the point see, for instance: Mulas (2020), p. 419.

[33] On the point see, for instance: Irion et al. (2016), p. 43; Yakovleva and Irion (2020a), p. 214.

manner that would constitute a means of arbitrary or unjustifiable discrimination or a disguised restriction on trade". Even in this case, it is possible to notice the same structure: a "data flows commitment" followed by a "data protection provision".[34]

As previously mentioned, however, similar articles can also be found in other bilateral treaties having (at least partially) commercial nature concluded by the EU with third countries in the second decade of the twenty-first century. By way of example, in the FTA with South Korea (2010), there is art. 7.43 (on financial services)[35]; in the Trade Agreement with Colombia-Peru-Ecuador (2012), there is art. 157 (on financial services)[36]; in the Association Agreement with Central America (2012), there is art. 198 (on financial services)[37]; in the Association Agreement with Ukraine (2014), there is art. 129 (on financial services)[38]; in the EPA with Japan (2018), there is art. 8.44 (on telecommunication services)[39]; in the FTA with

[34] On the point see, for instance: Irion et al. (2016), p. 43; Yakovleva (2018), p. 493.

[35] Art. 7.43 ("Data processing") of the EU-South Korea FTA states that: "No later than two years after the entry into force of this Agreement, and in no case later than the effective date of similar commitments stemming from other economic integration agreements: (a) each Party shall permit a financial service supplier of the other Party established in its territory to transfer information in electronic or other form, into and out of its territory, for data processing where such processing is required in the ordinary course of business of such financial service supplier; and (b) each Party, reaffirming its commitment to protect fundamental rights and freedom of individuals, shall adopt adequate safeguards to the protection of privacy, in particular with regard to the transfer of personal data".

[36] Art. 157 ("Data processing") of the EU-Colombia-Peru-Ecuador Trade Agreement states that: "1. Each Party shall permit a financial service supplier of another Party to transfer information in electronic or other form, into and out of its territory, for data processing where such processing is required in the ordinary course of business of such financial service supplier. 2. Each Party shall adopt adequate safeguards for the protection of the right to privacy and the freedom from interference with the privacy, family, home or correspondence of individuals, in particular with regard to the transfer of personal data".

[37] Art. 198 ("Data processing") of the EU-Central America Association Agreement states that: "1. Each Party shall permit a financial service supplier of the other Party to transfer information in electronic or other form, into and out of its territory, for data processing where such processing is required in the ordinary course of business of the financial service supplier. 2. Each Party shall adopt or maintain adequate safeguards to the protection of privacy and fundamental rights, and freedom of individuals, in particular with regard to the transfer of personal data".

[38] Art. 129 ("Data processing") of the EU-Ukraine Association Agreement states that: "1. Each Party shall permit a financial service supplier of the other Party to transfer information in electronic or other form, into and out of its territory, for data processing where such processing is required in the ordinary course of business of such financial service supplier. 2. Each Party shall adopt adequate safeguards for the protection of privacy and fundamental rights and the freedom of individuals, in particular with regard to the transfer of personal data".

[39] Art. 8.44 ("Access and use") of the EU-Japan EPA states that: "[…] 3. Each Party shall ensure that service suppliers of the other Party may use public telecommunications transport networks and services for the movement of information within and across the borders of the former Party, including for intra-corporate communications of such service suppliers, and for access to information contained in databases or otherwise stored in machine-readable form in either Party or in any other member of the WTO. 4. Notwithstanding paragraph 3, a Party may take such measures as are necessary to ensure the security and confidentiality of messages subject to the requirement that

Singapore (2018), there are articles 8.26 and 8.27 (on telecommunication services)[40] and art. 8.54 (on financial services)[41]; in the FTA with Viet Nam (2019), there are articles 8.31 and 8.36 (on telecommunication services)[42] and art. 8.45 (on financial services).[43]

All these articles include, on the one hand, a commitment to allow the free flow of information between the parties in the sector at stake; on the other hand, more importantly for our purposes, an obligation to protect individuals' rights by adopting or maintaining "adequate safeguards" (sometimes alternative expressions are used, such as "appropriate safeguards" or "appropriate measures", but "adequate safeguards" is the most frequent).

---

those measures are not applied in a manner which would constitute a means of arbitrary or unjustifiable discrimination or a disguised restriction on trade in services [...]".

[40] Art. 8.26 ("Access to and Use of Public Telecommunications Networks and Services") of the EU-Singapore FTA states that: "[...] 3. Each Party shall ensure that all service suppliers of the other Party may use public telecommunications networks and services for the movement of information in its territory or across its borders, including for intra-corporate communications of such service suppliers and for access to information contained in databases or otherwise stored in machine-readable form in the territory of either Party. Any new or amended measures of a Party significantly affecting such use shall be notified to the other Party and shall be subject to consultations". Art. 8.27 ("Confidentiality of Information") of the EU-Singapore FTA, instead, states that: "Each Party shall ensure the confidentiality of telecommunications and related traffic data by means of any public telecommunications network or service, without restricting trade in services".

[41] Art. 8.54 ("Data processing") of the EU-Singapore FTA states that: "1. Each Party shall, subject to appropriate safeguards on privacy and confidentiality, permit a financial service supplier of the other Party to transfer information in electronic or other form, into and out of its territory, for data processing, where such processing is required in the ordinary course of business of such financial service supplier. 2. Each Party shall adopt or maintain appropriate safeguards to protect privacy and personal data, including individual records and accounts, as long as these safeguards are not used to circumvent the provisions of this Agreement".

[42] Art. 8.31 ("Access to and Use of Public Telecommunications Networks and Services") of the EU-Viet Nam FTA states that: "[...] 3. Each Party shall ensure that all service suppliers of the other Party may use public telecommunications networks and services for the movement of information in its territory or across its borders, including for intra-corporate communications of such service suppliers and for access to information contained in databases or otherwise stored in machine-readable form in the territory of either Party. Any new or amended measures of a Party significantly affecting such use shall be notified to the other Party and shall be subject to consultations". Art. 8.36 ("Confidentiality of Information") of the EU-Viet Nam FTA, instead, states that: "Each Party shall ensure the confidentiality of telecommunications and related traffic data by means of a public telecommunications network and publicly available telecommunications services without restricting trade in services".

[43] Art. 8.45 ("Data processing") of the EU-Viet Nam FTA states that: "1. Each Party shall adopt or maintain appropriate safeguards to protect personal data and privacy, including individual records and accounts. 2. No later than two years from the date of entry into force of this Agreement, each Party shall permit financial service suppliers of the other Party to transfer information in electronic or other form, into and out of its territory, for data processing where such processing is required in the ordinary course of business of such financial service suppliers. 3. Nothing in this Article restricts the right of a Party to protect personal data and privacy, so long as such right is not used to circumvent this Agreement".

3 The Critical Issues Raised by the "Old-Fashioned" Provisions in EU International Agreements

The provisions illustrated so far, however, raise relevant critical issues, which risk undermining their capacity to effectively export the rights to privacy and personal data protection worldwide.

Such critical issues mainly depend on the weak formulation of such articles and on the unclear obligational content of certain terms. First of all, the obligation to adopt safeguards is often diminished by the fact that such measures must comply with several limits and conditions. It is the case of art. 15.3 CETA, according to which (as already seen) the implementation of safeguards is "subject to the requirement that these measures are not applied in a manner that would constitute a means of arbitrary or unjustifiable discrimination or a disguised restriction on trade". It is also the case, however, of art. 8.27 of the EU-Singapore FTA and art. 8.36 of the EU-Viet Nam FTA, which state that the adoption of the safeguards must happen "without restricting trade in services". In addition, we can even mention art. 8.54 of the EU-Singapore FTA and art. 8.45 of the EU-Viet Nam FTA, under which the measures cannot be used to circumvent the provisions of the agreements concerned.[44] It is immediately clear that the respect of the commitments to allow data flows, which are essential for international trade, remains the priority compared to the protection of privacy and personal data.[45]

A further consideration must be made in relation to the fact that the abovementioned safeguards must be "adequate" (sometimes equivalent expressions are used, such as "appropriate", but "adequate" is the most common"). The same term can also be found in the GDPR, notably in art. 45, pursuant to which transfers of personal data to a third country may take place where an "adequacy decision" has been adopted, i.e. where the EU Commission has decided that the third country ensures an "adequate" level of protection of privacy and personal data.[46] Moreover, the meaning of the word "adequate" was better clarified by the case law of the Court of Justice of the European Union (CJEU): according to the latter, such term must be understood as requiring the third country to ensure a level of protection that is "essentially equivalent" to that guaranteed within the EU by virtue of the relevant legal framework read in the light of the Charter of Nice.[47] In other words, through

---

[44] On the point, with particular reference to art. 8.54 of the EU-Singapore FTA, see for instance: Wessel (2018).

[45] On the point see, for instance: Yakovleva (2018), p. 495.

[46] Art. 45 ("Transfers on the basis of an adequacy decision"), para 1, of Regulation (EU) 2016/679 states that: "A transfer of personal data to a third country or an international organisation may take place where the Commission has decided that the third country, a territory or one or more specified sectors within that third country, or the international organisation in question ensures an adequate level of protection. Such a transfer shall not require any specific authorisation".

[47] Case C-362/14 *Maximillian Schrems v. Data Protection Commissioner* [2015] ECLI:EU:C:2015:650, para 73, according to which: "[...] the term 'adequate level of protection' must be understood as requiring the third country in fact to ensure, by reason of its domestic law

the valorisation of the previously addressed articles 7 and 8 of the CFREU, the Court elevates the standard of "adequacy" into one of "essential equivalence" to EU safeguards, giving priority to the protection of individuals at the expense of free data flows.[48]

At this stage, one might think that the word "adequate" in EU international agreements has the same meaning of the word "adequate" in the GDPR, which ensures an extremely high level of protection due to the fact that the CJEU reads it in the light of the Charter, as just explained.

However, a more nuanced analysis paints a less positive picture. Indeed, the settlement of the disputes concerning the interpretation of trade agreements does not obviously fall in the jurisdiction of the CJEU, but in the one of the supranational bodies established by such agreements: the latter, in case of a dispute on the matter, are not obliged at all to read the "adequate safeguards" in the light of the CFREU.[49]

What has just been stated is certainly true with reference to the bodies tasked with settling disputes *between the parties*, which are established in all the agreements examined so far in a rather similar manner. To give an example, we can once again consider the EU-Canada CETA, where the articles concerning the "Dispute settlement" between the parties are inserted in Chapter Twenty-Nine: its art. 29.17, entitled "General rule of interpretation", merely states that the provisions of the agreement shall be interpreted in accordance with customary rules of interpretation of public international law, including those set out in the Vienna Convention on the Law of Treaties, also taking into account the relevant interpretations of WTO bodies.

Moreover, the same argument can be repeated with regard to the bodies tasked with the resolution of disputes *between investors and States*. On the matter, it must be highlighted that not all EU trade agreements contain Investor-State Dispute Settlement (ISDS) mechanisms, but some of them do. In particular, an ISDS mechanism is provided by Section F of Chapter Eight of the EU-Canada CETA itself, even if it is not provisionally applied.[50] Now then, art. 8.31, governing the "Applicable law and interpretation" in the framework of such procedures, only refers to the need for the bodies at stake to apply the agreements as interpreted in accordance with the

or its international commitments, a level of protection of fundamental rights and freedoms that is essentially equivalent to that guaranteed within the European Union by virtue of Directive 95/46 read in the light of the Charter [...]"; Case C-311/18 *Data Protection Commissioner v. Facebook Ireland Ltd and Maximillian Schrems* [2020] ECLI:EU:C:2020:559, para 94, according to which: "[...] the term 'adequate level of protection' must [...] be understood as requiring the third country in fact to ensure, by reason of its domestic law or its international commitments, a level of protection of fundamental rights and freedoms that is essentially equivalent to that guaranteed within the European Union by virtue of the regulation, read in the light of the Charter [...]".

[48] On the point see, for instance: Pollicino and Bassini (2016).

[49] On the point, with reference to art. 13.15 of the EU-Canada CETA, see: Wessel (2016a).

[50] Council Decision (EU) 2017/38 of 28 October 2016 *on the provisional application of the Comprehensive Economic and Trade Agreement (CETA) between Canada, of the one part, and the European Union and its Member States, of the other part*, O.J. L 11/1080 (2017), art. 1, para 1, let. a.

Vienna Convention on the Law of Treaties and other rules and principles of international law applicable between the parties.[51]

As seen, in none of the aforementioned procedures the supranational bodies are required to interpret the agreement in accordance with the Charter of Nice or the case law of the Court of Justice of the EU.

Therefore, the word "adequate" enshrined in the data protection provisions of EU international trade agreements, since it does not mean "essentially equivalent" to EU standards, has no precise obligational content,[52] and requires a lower protection than the term "adequate" as interpreted by the CJEU.[53] The further consequence of the weakness of the articles in question is that it seems highly unlikely that they can effectively export worldwide the EU fundamental rights to privacy and personal data protection.

4 The Endorsement of the New "Horizontal Provisions" to Be Inserted in Subsequent EU International Agreements

In truth, the issues described above have not been completely neglected, and the need to improve the data protection provisions in EU international trade agreements has been underlined not only by scholars, but also at institutional level. For example, in 2016 the European Parliament, in its recommendations to the Commission on the negotiations for the (never concluded) Trade in Services Agreement (TiSA), has suggested using a different and more robust wording in order to better protect privacy and personal data.[54]

Therefore, following similar exhortations, in 2018 the European Commission—thanks to the work carried out by a project team led by First Vice-President Timmermans—endorsed a new instrument: the so-called "Horizontal provisions for cross-border data flows and for personal data protection", to be inserted in subsequent EU international trade agreements in place of "old-fashioned" provisions,[55] in order to make such agreements as consistent as possible with the high protection standards established by the GDPR.[56] Such horizontal clauses were published on the Commission's website in May 2018[57] and, in July of the same year, they were made

[51] On the point, allow me to refer to: Rugani (2025).

[52] Yakovleva (2018), p. 495.

[53] Wessel (2016a); see also: Wessel (2016b).

[54] European Parliament resolution of 3 February 2016 *containing the European Parliament's recommendations to the Commission on the negotiations for the Trade in Services Agreement (TiSA) (2015/2233(INI))*.

[55] European Commission (2018).

[56] On the point see, for instance: Yakovleva and Irion (2020b).

[57] The "Horizontal provisions for cross-border data flows and for personal data protection", in their May 2018 version, can be found on the dedicated page of the European Commission's website, accessible at the following link: https://ec.europa.eu/newsroom/just/items/627665/en.

available in a further revised version in the framework of the negotiations for a Free Trade Agreement with Indonesia (negotiations which were finalised on 23 September 2025).[58]

The first feature of the clauses to highlight is that, as suggested by their name, they are "horizontal": this means that they cover all economic sectors and are not limited to specific fields such as financial or telecommunication services.[59]

With regard to the structure of the provisions, it is actually quite similar to that of the "old-fashioned" articles: on the one hand, there is a "data flows commitment" and, on the other, a "data protection provision". There is also an additional article, devoted to cooperation on regulatory issues with regard to digital trade.

Examining in detail the content of the clauses, the first article is devoted to "Cross-border data flows" and commits the parties to ensure them to facilitate trade in the digital economy.[60] To that end, such flows shall not be restricted between the parties through the use of specific techniques, which are listed in detail (para 1).[61] A mechanism for reviewing the implementation of the provision in question is also envisaged (para 2).

However, the most significant article for our purposes is certainly the second one, dedicated to "Protection of personal data and privacy".[62] In particular, its para 1 states as follows: "Each Party recognises that *the protection of personal data and*

[58] The horizontal clauses, in their July 2018 version, can be found at the following link: https://circabc.europa.eu/ui/group/09242a36-a438-40fd-a7af-fe32e36cbd0e/library/363b4081-c535-4d7c-9365-84a64f9dc582/details.

[59] On the point see, for instance: Velli (2019), p. 892.

[60] Art 1 ("Cross-border data flows") of the Horizontal provisions states that: "1. The Parties are committed to ensuring cross-border data flows to facilitate trade in the digital economy. To that end, cross-border data flows shall not be restricted between the Parties by: (a) requiring the use of computing facilities or network elements in the Party's territory for processing, including by imposing the use of computing facilities or network elements that are certified or approved in the territory of the Party; (b) requiring the localisation of data in the Party's territory for storage or processing; (c) prohibiting storage or processing in the territory of the other Party; (d) making the cross-border transfer of data contingent upon use of computing facilities or network elements in the Party's territory or upon localisation requirements in the Party's territory. 2. The Parties shall keep the implementation of this provision under review and assess its functioning within three years of the entry into force of this Agreement. A Party may at any time propose to the other Party to review the list of restrictions listed in the preceding paragraph. Such request shall be accorded sympathetic consideration".

[61] On the point see, for instance: Yakovleva and Irion (2020a), p. 219; Geraets and Vander Schueren (2018), par. 2.

[62] Art 2 ("Protection of personal data and privacy") of the Horizontal provisions states that: "1. Each Party recognises that the protection of personal data and privacy is a fundamental right and that high standards in this regard contribute to trust in the digital economy and to the development of trade. 2. Each Party may adopt and maintain the safeguards it deems appropriate to ensure the protection of personal data and privacy, including through the adoption and application of rules for the cross-border transfer of personal data. Nothing in this agreement shall affect the protection of personal data and privacy afforded by the Parties' respective safeguards. 3. Each Party shall inform the other Party about any safeguard it adopts or maintains according to paragraph 2. 4. For the purposes of this agreement, "personal data" means any information relating to an identified or

privacy is a fundamental right [emphasis added] and that high standards in this regard contribute to trust in the digital economy and to the development of trade". There are also other relevant provisions. According to para 2, each party "may adopt and maintain the safeguards it deems appropriate to ensure the protection of personal data and privacy" and nothing in the agreement "shall affect the protection of personal data and privacy" ensured by the parties' respective safeguards.[63] Para 3 enshrines an obligation for each party to inform the other party about any safeguard it adopts or maintains according to para 2. Para 4 clarifies that "personal data" means any information relating to an identified or identifiable natural person: a definition that is identical to the one contained in the GDPR.[64] Furthermore, according to para 5, the issues concerning data flows and the protection of personal data and privacy are excluded from the jurisdiction of the (eventual) Investment Court System (ICS), leaving possible violations to be resolved only between the parties.[65]

Finally, we must not forget the third and last article of the Horizontal provisions, concerning "Cooperation on regulatory issues with regard to digital trade".[66] The first two paragraphs, which provide for a dialogue on regulatory issues raised by digital trade, are nothing new: indeed, similar provisions can already be found in previously negotiated trade agreements (we can cite, for example, art. 8.52 of the EU-Viet Nam FTA).[67] Para 3, instead, is the truly innovative aspect: for greater

---

identifiable natural person. 5. For greater certainty, the Investment Court System does not apply to the provisions in Articles 1 and 2".

[63] On the point see, for instance: Yakovleva and Irion (2020a), pp. 219–220.

[64] Art. 4 ("Definitions") of Regulation (EU) 2016/679 states that: "For the purposes of this Regulation: (1) 'personal data' means any information relating to an identified or identifiable natural person ('data subject'); an identifiable natural person is one who can be identified, directly or indirectly, in particular by reference to an identifier such as a name, an identification number, location data, an online identifier or to one or more factors specific to the physical, physiological, genetic, mental, economic, cultural or social identity of that natural person [...]".

[65] On the point see, for instance: Velli (2019), pp. 892–893.

[66] Art X ("Cooperation on regulatory issues with regard to digital trade") of the Horizontal provisions states that: "1. The parties shall maintain a dialogue on regulatory issues raised by digital trade, which shall inter alia address the following issues: a. the recognition and facilitation of interoperable cross-border electronic trust and authentication services; b. The treatment of direct marketing communications; c. The protection of consumers in the ambit of electronic commerce; and d. any other issue relevant for the development of digital trade. 2. Such cooperation shall focus on exchange of information on the Parties' respective legislation on these issues as well as on the implementation of such legislation. 3. For greater certainty, this provision shall not apply to a Party's rules and safeguards for the protection of personal data and privacy, including on cross-border data transfers of personal data".

[67] Art. 8.52 ("Regulatory Cooperation on Electronic Commerce") of the EU-Viet Nam FTA states that: "1. The Parties shall maintain a dialogue on regulatory issues raised by electronic commerce, which shall, inter alia, address the following issues: (a) the recognition of certificates of electronic signatures issued to the public and the facilitation of cross-border certification services; (b) the liability of intermediary service providers with respect to the transmission or storage of information; (c) the treatment of unsolicited electronic commercial communications; (d) the protection of consumers in the ambit of electronic commerce; and (e) any other issue relevant for the development of electronic commerce. 2. This dialogue may take the form of exchange of information on

certainty, it explicitly excludes from cooperation on digital trade regulation the "rules and safeguards for the protection of personal data and privacy", in order to prevent negotiations aimed at weakening the protection of such rights.[68]

It cannot be ignored that, in truth, the main aim of the Horizontal clauses is to allow the European Union to maintain and apply *its own* privacy and data protection rules, ensuring that trade agreements cannot be used by counterparts to challenge these strong rules on the grounds that they might result in limitations of data flows.[69] This is particularly clear from para 2 of the second article: as just seen, according to this provision, each party "may adopt and maintain the *safeguards it deems appropriate* [emphasis added] to ensure the protection of personal data and privacy" and nothing in the agreement "shall affect the protection of personal data and privacy" ensured by the parties' respective safeguards. However, the clauses can also play a role in exporting the rights to privacy and personal data protection worldwide, thanks to other provisions: among these, para 1 of the second article, which (as previously mentioned) expressly recognises the rights at stake as "fundamental".

5 The New "Horizontal Provisions" in Practice: Successes and Failures

As anticipated, the "Horizontal provisions for cross-border data flows and for personal data protection" have been designed to be inserted in subsequent EU international trade agreements in place of "old-fashioned" provisions.

The EU is attempting to include similar clauses in several agreements which are currently under negotiation.[70] Among these, we can cite the agreement with Australia, whose negotiations were authorised on 22 May 2018; and the Deep and Comprehensive Free Trade Agreement with Tunisia, whose negotiations were launched on 13 October 2015.[71]

Moreover, the EU is also seeking to integrate the Horizontal provisions in its relations with countries that are already covered by existing trade agreements, by incorporating the clauses into separate Digital Trade Agreements[72]: in this regard, it is worth mentioning the cases of Singapore (negotiations concluded on 25 July 2024, entry into force on 1 February 2026) and South Korea (negotiations

---

the Parties' respective laws and regulations on the issues referred to in paragraph 1 as well as on the implementation of such laws and regulations".

[68] On the point see, for instance: Velli (2019), p. 893; Yakovleva and Irion (2020a), p. 219.

[69] On the point, allow me to refer to: Rugani (2024), pp. 167–179.

[70] Updates on the agreements currently under negotiation by the EU can be found on the dedicated page of the European Commission's website, accessible at the following link: https://policy.trade.ec.europa.eu/eu-trade-relationships-country-and-region/negotiations-and-agreements_en.

[71] On the point see, for instance: Brännström (2023), Burri (2023), and Fahey (2023).

[72] On Digital Trade Agreements see, for instance: Burri and Chander (2023) and Burri and Kugler (2024).

concluded on 10 March 2025),[73] which were also welcomed by the European Data Protection Supervisor (EDPS).[74]

There is more. Similar provisions, above all, have actually been included in the final text of certain EU trade agreements that are already in force. In particular, we refer to the FTA with New Zealand,[75] signed on 9 July 2023 and entered into force on 1 May 2024,[76] and namely to its articles 12.4 ("Cross-border data flows and personal data protection")[77] and 12.5 ("Protection of personal data and privacy")[78]; and

[73] Information on Digital Trade Agreements with Singapore and South Korea can be found on the dedicated page of the European Commission's website, accessible at the following link: https://policy.trade.ec.europa.eu/help-exporters-and-importers/accessing-markets/goods-and-services/digital-trade/digital-trade-agreements_en.

[74] European Data Protection Supervisor Opinion 18/2023 of 15 May 2023 *on the Recommendation for a Council Decision authorising the opening of negotiations for digital trade disciplines with the Republic of Korea and with Singapore.*

[75] Free Trade Agreement between the European Union and New Zealand, 9 July 2023, O.J. L 2024/866 (2024).

[76] On the EU-New Zealand FTA, see for instance: Burri et al. (2024).

[77] Art. 12.4 ("Cross-border data flows and personal data protection") of the EU-New Zealand FTA states that: "1. The Parties are committed to ensuring cross-border data flows to facilitate trade in the digital economy and recognise that each Party may have its own regulatory requirements in this regard. 2. To that end, a Party shall not restrict cross-border data flows taking place between the Parties in the context of an activity that is within the scope of this Chapter, by: (a) requiring the use of computing facilities or network elements in its territory for data processing, including by requiring the use of computing facilities or network elements that are certified or approved in the territory of the Party; (b) requiring the localisation of data in its territory; (c) prohibiting storage or processing of data in the territory of the other Party; or (d) making the cross-border transfer of data contingent upon the use of computing facilities or network elements in its territory or upon localisation requirements in its territory. 3. For greater certainty, the Parties understand that nothing in this Article prevents the Parties from adopting or maintaining measures in accordance with Article 25.1 (General exceptions) to achieve the public policy objectives referred to therein, which, for the purposes of this Article, shall be interpreted, where relevant, in a manner that takes into account the evolutionary nature of the digital technologies. The preceding sentence does not affect the application of other exceptions in this Agreement to this Article. 4. The Parties shall keep the implementation of this Article under review and assess its functioning within three years after the date of entry into force of this Agreement unless the Parties agree otherwise. A Party may also at any time propose to the other Party to review this Article. Such proposal shall be accorded sympathetic consideration [...]".

[78] Art. 12.5 ("Protection of personal data and privacy") of the EU-New Zealand FTA states that: "1. Each Party recognises that the protection of personal data and privacy is a fundamental right and that high standards in this regard contribute to enhancing consumer confidence and trust in digital trade. 2. Each Party may adopt or maintain measures it deems appropriate to ensure the protection of personal data and privacy, including through the adoption and application of rules for the cross-border transfer of personal data. Nothing in this Agreement shall affect the protection of personal data and privacy afforded by the Parties' respective measures. 3. Each Party shall inform the other Party about any measures referred to in paragraph 2 that it adopts or maintains. 4. Each Party shall publish information on the protection of personal data and privacy that it provides to users of digital trade, including: (a) how individuals can pursue a remedy for a breach of protection of personal data or privacy arising from digital trade; and (b) guidance and other information regarding compliance of businesses with applicable legal requirements protecting personal data and privacy".

also to the Interim Trade Agreement with Chile,[79] signed on 13 December 2023 and entered into force on 1 February 2025, and in particular to its articles 19.5 ("Cross-border data flows")[80] and 19.6 ("Protection of personal data and privacy").[81] The abovementioned provisions, indeed, correspond quite faithfully to the Horizontal clauses endorsed by the EU Commission in 2018.

However, despite such encouraging examples, there are still reasons to doubt that the Commission will actually be able to include the Horizontal provisions in all future trade agreements negotiated with third countries.

Preliminarily, it is worth remembering that some of the previously analysed agreements were signed *after* the endorsement of the clauses: it is the case of the EU-Viet Nam FTA. The provisions could have been included in its final text, but this did not happen. On the contrary, as someone pointed out, the "EU-Vietnam trade agreement contains weak safeguards for data protection [...]. This is all the more frustrating as the EU commission knows how to do better [...]".[82]

Furthermore, it is even more concerning that some articles included in recent agreements, despite being seemingly inspired by the Horizontal clauses, depart from them in the most important aspects.

The most significant example is probably the Trade and Cooperation Agreement (TCA) between the EU and the United Kingdom,[83] signed on 30 December 2020 and entered into force on 1 May 2021. In this agreement, there are two provisions that should correspond to the first and second articles of the Horizontal clauses, i.e. art. 201, concerning "Cross-border data flows",[84] and art. 202, concerning

[79] Interim Agreement on trade between the European Union and the Republic of Chile, 13 December 2023, O.J. L 2024/2953 (2024).

[80] Art. 19.5 ("Cross-border data flows") of the EU-Chile Interim Trade Agreement states that: "The Parties are committed to ensuring cross-border data flows to facilitate digital trade. To that end, a Party shall not restrict cross-border data flows between the Parties by: (a) requiring the use of computing facilities or network elements in the territory of that Party for processing, including by imposing the use of computing facilities or network elements that are certified or approved in the territory of that Party; (b) requiring the localisation of data in the territory of that Party for storage or processing; (c) prohibiting storage or processing in the territory of the other Party; or (d) making the cross-border transfer of data contingent upon the use of computing facilities or network elements in the territory of that Party or upon localisation requirements in the territory of that Party".

[81] Art. 19.6 ("Protection of personal data and privacy") of the EU-Chile Interim Trade Agreement states that: "1. Each Party recognises that the protection of personal data and privacy is a fundamental right and that high standards in that regard contribute to trust in the digital economy and to the development of trade. 2. Each Party may adopt and maintain the measures it deems appropriate to ensure the protection of personal data and privacy, including the adoption and application of rules for the cross-border transfer of personal data. Nothing in this Agreement shall affect the protection of personal data and privacy afforded by the measures of a Party".

[82] Wessel (2020).

[83] Trade and Cooperation Agreement between the European Union and the European Atomic Energy Community, of the one part, and the United Kingdom of Great Britain and Northern Ireland, of the other part, 30 December 2020, O.J. L 149/10 (2021).

[84] Art. 201 ("Cross-border data flows") of the EU-UK TCA states that: "1. The Parties are committed to ensuring cross-border data flows to facilitate trade in the digital economy. To that end, cross-

"Protection of personal data and privacy".[85] However, while art. 201 is largely consistent with the first article of the Horizontal provisions, the same cannot be said for art. 202, which deviates from the second article of the clauses in extremely important points. In particular, it is true that para 1 enshrines the "right to the protection of personal data and privacy", but it does not refer to such right as "fundamental". Moreover, even if para 2 affirms the possibility for a party to adopt or maintain "measures on the protection of personal data or privacy", the words "it deems appropriate" are not included, and the measures are conditioned on providing for "instruments enabling transfers". Such different formulation, less attentive to the protection of privacy and personal data, has been deeply criticised by the European Data Protection Supervisor.[86]

It should be noted that something very similar can be repeated with regard to the EU-Japan deal on data flows, signed on 28 October 2023 and entered into force on 1 July 2024,[87] that amended the abovementioned EU-Japan EPA. The "new" articles 8.81, on "Cross-border transfer of information by electronic means",[88] and 8.82, on

---

border data flows shall not be restricted between the Parties by a Party: (a) requiring the use of computing facilities or network elements in the Party's territory for processing, including by imposing the use of computing facilities or network elements that are certified or approved in the territory of a Party; (b) requiring the localisation of data in the Party's territory for storage or processing; (c) prohibiting the storage or processing in the territory of the other Party; or (d) making the cross-border transfer of data contingent upon use of computing facilities or network elements in the Parties' territory or upon localisation requirements in the Parties' territory. 2. The Parties shall keep the implementation of this provision under review and assess its functioning within three years of the date of entry into force of this Agreement. A Party may at any time propose to the other Party to review the list of restrictions listed in paragraph 1. Such a request shall be accorded sympathetic consideration".

[85] Art. 202 ("Protection of personal data and privacy") of the EU-UK TCA states that: "1. Each Party recognises that individuals have a right to the protection of personal data and privacy and that high standards in this regard contribute to trust in the digital economy and to the development of trade. 2. Nothing in this Agreement shall prevent a Party from adopting or maintaining measures on the protection of personal data and privacy, including with respect to cross-border data transfers, provided that the law of the Party provides for instruments enabling transfers under conditions of general application for the protection of the data transferred. 3. Each Party shall inform the other Party about any measure referred to in paragraph 2 that it adopts or maintains".

[86] European Data Protection Supervisor Opinion 3/2021 of 22 February 2021 *on the conclusion of the EU and UK trade agreement and the EU and UK exchange of classified information agreement.*

[87] Information on the entry into force of the EU-Japan deal on data flows can be found on the dedicated page of the European Commission's website, accessible at the following link: https://policy.trade.ec.europa.eu/news/eu-japan-deal-data-flows-enters-force-2024-07-01_en.

[88] Art. 8.81 ("Cross-border transfer of information by electronic means") of the EU-Japan EPA, as amended by the EU-Japan deal on data flows, states that: "1. The Parties are committed to ensuring the cross-border transfer of information by electronic means where this activity is for the conduct of the business of a covered person. 2. To that end, a Party shall not adopt or maintain measures which prohibit or restrict the cross-border transfer of information set out in paragraph 1 by: (a) requiring the use of computing facilities or network elements in the territory of the Party for information processing, including by requiring the use of computing facilities or network elements that are certified or approved in the territory of the Party; (b) requiring the localisation of information in the territory of the Party for storage or processing; (c) prohibiting storage or processing of infor-

"Protection of Personal Data",[89] should correspond to the Horizontal provisions. However, also in this case, the second article shows significant differences from the original text of the clauses (for example, just like in the EU-UK TCA, the right to the protection of personal data and privacy is not defined as "fundamental"). This has led, once again, to strong criticism from the EDPS.[90]

---

mation in the territory of the other Party; (d) making the cross-border transfer of information contingent upon use of computing facilities or network elements in the territory of the Party or upon localisation requirements in the territory of the Party; (e) prohibiting the transfer of information into the territory of the Party; or (f) requiring the approval of the Party prior to the transfer of information to the territory of the other Party. 3. Nothing in this Article shall prevent a Party from adopting or maintaining measures inconsistent with paragraphs 1 and 2 to achieve a legitimate public policy objective, provided that the measure: (a) is not applied in a manner which would constitute a means of arbitrary or unjustifiable discrimination between countries where like conditions prevail, or a disguised restriction on trade; and (b) does not impose restrictions on transfers of information that are greater than necessary to achieve the objective. 4. Nothing in this Article shall prevent a Party from adopting or maintaining measures on the protection of personal data and privacy, including with respect to cross-border transfers of information, provided that the law of the Party provides for instruments enabling transfers under conditions of general application for the protection of the information transferred. 5. This Article does not apply to cross-border transfer of information held or processed by or on behalf of a Party. 6. A Party may at any time propose to the other Party to review the measures listed in paragraph 2".

[89] Art. 8.82 ("Protection of Personal Data") of the EU-Japan EPA, as amended by the EU-Japan deal on data flows, states that: "1. The Parties recognise that individuals have a right to the protection of their personal data and privacy as provided for by the laws and regulations of each Party and that high standards in this regard contribute to trust in the digital economy and to the development of trade. Each Party recognises the right of the other Party to determine the appropriate level of the protection of personal data and privacy, to be provided for by their respective measures. 2. Each Party shall endeavour to adopt measures that protect individuals, without discrimination based on grounds such as nationality or residence, from personal data protection violations occurring within its jurisdiction. 3. Each Party shall adopt or maintain a legal framework that provides for the protection of personal data related to electronic commerce. In the development of its legal framework for the protection of personal data and privacy, each Party should take into account the principles and guidelines of relevant international bodies. The Parties also recognise that high standards of privacy and data protection as regards government access to privately held data, such as those outlined in the OECD Principles for Government Access to Personal Data held by Private Sector Entities, contribute to trust in the digital economy. 4. Each Party shall publish information on the protection of personal data and privacy it provides to users of electronic commerce, including: (a) how individuals can pursue remedies for a breach of the protection of personal data or privacy arising from digital trade; and (b) guidance and other information regarding compliance of businesses with applicable legal requirements for the protection of personal data and privacy".

[90] European Data Protection Supervisor Opinion 3/2024 of 10 January 2024 *on the signing and conclusion on behalf of the European Union, of the Protocol amending the Agreement between the European Union and Japan for an Economic Partnership regarding free flow of data.*

6 Concluding Remarks: Positive Effects and Persistent Limitations of Privacy and Data Protection Provisions in EU International Agreements

This chapter investigated how the European Union strives to export the fundamental rights to privacy and data protection (enshrined in articles 7 and 8 of the Charter of Nice) in the wider world through its international agreements. To this end, it took into consideration the privacy and data protection provisions included by the EU in several bilateral treaties having (at least partially) commercial nature concluded with third countries.

First of all, the contribution examined the articles inserted in some trade agreements signed by the EU in the second decade of the twenty-first century, such as the ones with South Korea, Colombia-Peru-Ecuador, Central America, Ukraine, Canada (CETA), Japan (EPA), Singapore and Viet Nam. However, it highlighted that, due to their weak formulation and to the unclear meaning of the word "adequate", they do not seem able to achieve the objective stated above.

Then, the research focused on a new and stronger mechanism endorsed by the EU Commission in 2018 in order to overcome the abovementioned critical issues: the so-called "Horizontal provisions for cross-border data flows and for personal data protection", to be inserted in subsequent EU trade agreements in place of "old-fashioned" articles. Therefore, the paper considered the agreements currently under negotiation in which the EU is attempting to include the Horizontal provisions—such as the ones with Australia and Tunisia—and, above all, the trade agreements that are already in force in which similar articles have actually been inserted, such as the ones with New Zealand, Chile and UK.

After this analysis, it is now possible to make some evaluations concerning the capacity of the Horizontal provisions to effectively export the fundamental rights to privacy and personal data protection worldwide.

On the one hand, compared to the "old-fashioned" clauses, the new ones undeniably represent a clear step forward. The former articles merely refer to the obligation of the parties to adopt or maintain "adequate safeguards" to protect privacy and personal data; however, the word "adequate" does not have the same meaning assigned by the CJEU, i.e. "essentially equivalent" to EU standards: therefore, such a term has no precise obligational content and does not necessarily require a high level of protection. The latter provisions, instead, clearly define the rights to privacy and to the protection of personal data as "fundamental": a qualification that implies particularly stringent conditions on their limitations, which must in any case respect their essence. Moreover, the Horizontal clauses also contain other significant provisions: for example, the one that excludes the matter from the jurisdiction of the (eventual) Investment Court System, and the one that prevents negotiations aimed at weakening the protection of the rights at stake, since they are both intended to shelter privacy and personal data protection from negative influences.

Furthermore, it is particularly encouraging that the EU is not only attempting to insert similar clauses in agreements currently under negotiation, but has also succeeded in including them in the final text of certain agreements that are already in force: in particular, the FTA with New Zealand and the Interim Trade Agreement with Chile, both of which contain articles that closely correspond to the Horizontal clauses endorsed by the EU Commission in 2018.

However, it is also necessary to highlight some persistent critical aspects.

First of all, precisely because of the high level of protection required, it is by no means guaranteed that the EU's counterparts will always and unconditionally accept the text of the Horizontal provisions without modifications. The cases of the EU-UK TCA and of the EU-Japan deal on data flows are emblematic: the articles included in these agreements, despite being seemingly inspired by the Horizontal clauses, depart from them in extremely important aspects. It is noteworthy that this occurs in relation to two States – the UK and Japan – both of which maintain strong ties with the EU, the former having previously been a Member State in particular: this underscores that, in the field of privacy and personal data protection, significant divergences of approach exist even with countries regarded as "close", and that risks to the aforementioned rights may also arise from such States. Moreover, as someone pointed out, such cases can be considered as "revealing of the limited influence of the EU position".[91]

There is also another aspect that must be remembered. In truth, as mentioned above, the main purpose of the Horizontal provisions is to allow the EU to maintain and apply *its own* privacy and data protection rules, ensuring that agreements cannot be used by counterparts to challenge these strong rules on the grounds that they might result in limitations of data flows. This is particularly clear from para 2 of the second article, according to which each party "may adopt and maintain the *safeguards it deems appropriate* [emphasis added] to ensure the protection of personal data and privacy" and nothing in the agreement "shall affect the protection of personal data and privacy" ensured by the parties' respective safeguards.

What has just been said allows us to state that the main instruments through which the EU strives to export the fundamental rights to privacy and data protection in the wider world are *not international agreements*, but rather *unilateral* mechanisms.

One of these is the already mentioned "adequacy decision" of art. 45 GDPR, pursuant to which transfers of personal data to a third country may take place where the EU Commission has decided that the third country ensures an "adequate" level of protection of privacy and personal data; in this case, the word "adequate" must be read as "essentially equivalent" to EU standards, according to the case law of the CJEU. By virtue of such instrument, if non-EU countries wish to allow entities within their territories (in particular companies) to receive personal data from the EU and to have access to the EU market, they will have to adopt and implement EU-conformant laws that ensure a high level of protection to privacy and personal

[91] Brännström (2023).

data.[92] Moreover, there are also other unilateral mechanisms: one is art. 3 of the GDPR itself, concerning the territorial scope of the Regulation,[93] that requires the single foreign entities that target the EU market to respect the GDPR in its entirety.[94]

This is what the author Anu Bradford defines as "Brussels effect", an expression that indicates the ability of the EU to *unilaterally* influence third countries' regulations through its central position in the global economy.[95] A strategy that has already accomplished significant outcomes: according not only to the Commission,[96] but also to important authors, the EU internal legal framework on the matter really emerged as a key reference point at international level, and inspired a great number of third countries in the introduction of their privacy and data protection rules.[97]

In conclusion, it can be said that the European Union attempts to export the fundamental rights to privacy and data protection in the wider world through several instruments, that are mainly unilateral and that have already achieved important results. The privacy and personal data protection provisions included by the EU in the international agreements concluded with third countries are certainly part of this broader strategy, even more so after the endorsement of the Horizontal provisions, that are a clear improvement compared to the "old-fashioned" articles. However, in the effort to pursue the aforementioned aim, they do not represent the most relevant tool, nor the most effective one: this is because it is not guaranteed that the EU's counterparts will always accept the text of the clauses without modifications, but also because such provisions are primarily focused on different objectives.

---

[92] On the point see, for instance: Höglund (2018), p. 26.

[93] Art. 3 ("Territorial scope") of Regulation (EU) 2016/679 states that: "1. This Regulation applies to the processing of personal data in the context of the activities of an establishment of a controller or a processor in the Union, regardless of whether the processing takes place in the Union or not. 2. This Regulation applies to the processing of personal data of data subjects who are in the Union by a controller or processor not established in the Union, where the processing activities are related to: (a) the offering of goods or services, irrespective of whether a payment of the data subject is required, to such data subjects in the Union; or (b) the monitoring of their behaviour as far as their behaviour takes place within the Union. 3. This Regulation applies to the processing of personal data by a controller not established in the Union, but in a place where Member State law applies by virtue of public international law".

[94] On the point see, for instance: Gstrein and Zwitter (2021).

[95] Bradford (2012, 2020).

[96] Communication from the Commission to the European Parliament and the Council of 24 June 2020 *Data protection as a pillar of citizens' empowerment and the EU's approach to the digital transition—two years of application of the General Data Protection Regulation COM(2020)264final*.

[97] On the point see, for instance: Casoria and Alsarraf (2019), Greenleaf (2019, 2020, 2021, 2022, 2023).

References

Bernsdorff N (2003) Kapitel II, Freiheiten: Artikel 6 Bis 19. In: Meyer J (ed) Kommentar zur Charta der Grundrechte der Europäischen Union. Nomos Verlagsgesellschaft, Baden-Baden, pp 135–262
Bradford A (2012) The Brussels effect. Northwest Univ Law Rev 107(1):1–68
Bradford A (2020) The Brussels effect: how the European Union rules the world. Oxford University Press, Oxford
Braibant G (2001) La Charte des Droits fondamentaux de l'Union européenne. Editions du Seuil, Paris
Brännström L (2023) Global inequality and the EU international law position on cross-border data flows. Nordic J Int Law 92:119–137
Burri M (2017) The governance of data and data flows in trade agreements: the pitfalls of legal adaptation. Univ Calif Davis Law Rev 51:65–132
Burri M (2023) Cross-border data flows and privacy in global trade law: has trade trumped data protection? Oxf Rev Econ Policy 39(1):85–97
Burri M, Chander A (2023) What are digital trade and digital trade law? AJIL Unbound 117:99–103
Burri M, Kugler K (2024) Regulatory autonomy in digital trade agreements. J Int Econ Law 27(3):397–423
Burri M, Kugler K, Ker AD (2024) Digital trade in the EU-New Zealand free trade agreement: an appraisal. Legal Issues Econ Integr 51(1):11–46
Casoria M, Alsarraf EM (2019) The impact of the GDPR on extra-EU legal systems: the case of the Kingdom of Bahrain. In: Tzanou M (ed) Personal data protection and legal developments in the European Union. IGI Global, Hershey, pp 224–237
Docquir B (2008) Le droit à la vie privée. De Boeck-Larcier, Bruxelles
European Commission (2018) European Commission endorses provisions for data flows and data protection in EU trade agreements. Press Release
Fahey E (2023) Does the EU's digital sovereignty promote localisation in its model digital trade clauses? Eur Papers 8(2):503–511
Geraets D, Vander Schueren P (2018) Exporting the EU privacy regime through trade instruments? Mayer Brown
González Fuster G (2014) The emergence of personal data protection as a fundamental right of the EU. Springer, Dordrecht
Greenleaf G (2019) Global data privacy laws 2019: 132 national laws & many bills. Privacy Laws & Business International Report
Greenleaf G (2020) Ends a decade of 62 new data privacy laws. Privacy Laws & Business International Report
Greenleaf G (2021) Global data privacy laws 2021: despite COVID delays, 145 laws show GDPR dominance. Privacy Laws & Business International Report
Greenleaf G (2022) Now 157 countries: twelve data privacy laws in 2021/22. Privacy Laws & Business International Report
Greenleaf G (2023) Global data privacy laws 2023: 162 national laws and 20 Bills. Privacy Laws & Business International Report
Gstrein OJ, Zwitter AJ (2021) Extraterritorial application of the GDPR: promoting European values or power? Internet Policy Rev 10(3):1–30
Höglund W (2018) Exporting data protection law. The extraterritorial reach of the GDPR. Umeå Universitet, Umeå
Irion K, Yakovleva S, Bartl M (2016) Trade and privacy: complicated bedfellows? How to achieve data protection-proof free trade agreements. Institute for Information Law (IViR), Amsterdam
Lenaerts K (2019) Limits on limitations: the essence of fundamental rights in the EU. German Law J 20(6):779–793
Mulas L (2020) Il Comprehensive Economic and Trade Agreement (CETA): tra liberalizzazione e regolamentazione prudenziale. Diritto Comun Degli Scambi Int 2:415–449

Pasquali L (2020) Il contributo dell'accordo UE – Mercosur alla governance internazionale dell'ambiente. Nomos 20(3):179–200
Pasquali L (2021) The EU-MERCOSUR agreement as source of development of specific global norms and standards. In: García Segura C, Ibáñez J, Pareja P (eds) Actores Regionales y Normas Globales: la Unión Europea y los BRICS como Actores Normativos. Tirant lo Blanch, Valencia, pp 131–142
Pollicino O, Bassini M (2016) La Carta dei diritti fondamentali dell'Unione europea nel reasoning dei giudici di Lussemburgo. In: Resta G, Zeno-Zencovich V (eds) La protezione transnazionale dei dati personali: dai "Safe Harbour Principles" al "Privacy Shield". Roma TrE-Press, Roma, pp 73–112
Rodotà S (2009) Data protection as a fundamental right. In: Gutwirth S, Poullet Y, De Hert P, De Terwangne C, Nouwt S (eds) Reinventing data protection? Springer, New York, pp 77–82
Rugani G (2024) La regolamentazione dei flussi di dati personali dall'UE verso Paesi terzi. Alla ricerca di un bilanciamento tra espansione del commercio internazionale e *personal data protection*. G. Giappichelli Editore, Torino
Rugani G (2025) The actual ability of Investor-State Dispute Settlement (ISDS) mechanisms included in EU international agreements to sufficiently safeguard Human Rights: the specific case of privacy and data protection. In: Crespo Navarro E, González Serrano A (eds) Los Derechos Humanos como elementos de interacción en el Derecho internacional público. Marcial Pons – Ediciones Jurídicas y Sociales, Madrid, pp 131–146
Sousa De Jesus A (2004) Data protection in EU financial services, ECRI research report No. 6. European Credit Research Institute
Tribe LH, Dorf MC (1990) Levels of generality in the definition of rights. Univ Chicago Law Rev 57(4):1057–1108
Van Der Marel E (2015) Disentangling the flows of data: inside or outside the multinational company? ECIPE Occasional Paper No. 7. European Centre for International Political Economy
Velli F (2019) The issue of data protection in EU trade commitments: cross-border data transfers in GATS and bilateral free trade agreements. Eur Papers 4(3):881–894
Warren SD, Brandeis LD (1890) The right to privacy. Harv Law Rev 4:193–220
Wessel A (2016a) CETA will harm our privacy. Foundation for a Free Information Infrastructure (FFII) Blog
Wessel A (2016b) CETA: ISDS and data protection. Foundation for a Free Information Infrastructure (FFII) Blog
Wessel A (2018) EU-Singapore trade agreement not compatible with EU data protection. Foundation for a Free Information Infrastructure (FFII) Blog
Wessel A (2020) Weak data protection in EU-Vietnam trade agreement. Blog Van Vrijschrift
Yakovleva S (2018) Should fundamental rights to privacy and data protection be a part of the EU's international trade 'deals'? World Trade Rev 17(3):477–508
Yakovleva S, Irion K (2020a) Pitching trade against privacy: reconciling EU governance of personal data flows with external trade. Int Data Privacy Law 10(3):201–221
Yakovleva S, Irion K (2020b) Toward compatibility of the EU trade policy with the general data protection regulation. AJIL Unbound 114:10–14

Upholding and Promoting Human Rights and the Rights of Persons Belonging to Minorities in EU Free Trade Agreements: New Developments and Persistent Challenges

Miriam Schettini

Contents

Abstract This chapter examines how the European Union upholds and promotes human rights, including the rights of persons belonging to minorities, through its new generation trade agreements. It begins by setting out the relevant framework with a brief overview of the evolution of human rights integration into the EU's common commercial policy. The second part examines how human rights are promoted in the context of EU new generation trade agreements. In particular, it highlights that human rights are not confined to the "essential elements" clause but are

M. Schettini (✉)
Department of Law, University of Pisa, Pisa, Italy
e-mail: miriam.schettini@jus.unipi.it

L. Pasquali (ed.), *EU Values and International Law*, European Union and its Neighbours in a Globalized World 35,
https://doi.org/10.1007/978-3-032-20521-6_9

also embedded in some "new generation" provisions of the agreements. However, it highlights that the mechanisms for operationalizing these commitments remain weak. The third part focuses on the specific dimension of the rights of persons belonging to minorities. In particular, it discusses the recent EU-New Zealand Free Trade Agreement, which introduces innovative elements that could serve as a useful model for future bilateral and multilateral agreements. The chapter concludes with some brief reflections on the extent to which EU new generation trade agreements represent progress in the international protection of human rights and their potential to shape future developments in the international legal order. It also highlights the inherent shortcomings of the current EU approach.

1 Introduction

The European Union's efforts to uphold and promote human rights in the world are characterized by a multifaceted and occasionally contentious nature.[1] On the one hand, the EU's actions are seen by some as an attempt to impose a specific model on the world, arguing that the 1948 Universal Declaration of Human Rights, while establishing the basic principles of human rights doctrine in terms of universality, interdependence, indivisibility and interrelatedness,[2] reflects a "Eurocentric" perspective.[3] On the other hand, the real willingness and ability of the European Union to effectively promote human rights beyond mere political rhetoric is often questioned.[4] Indeed, the EU would seem to apply a "double standard" between its internal and external policies.[5] Moreover, the Treaties would not have effectively provided the Union with all the necessary means to emerge as a "global protector" of human rights, since the EU has not been endowed with a general competence in the field of human rights.[6]

---

[1] On this point, see among others de Búrca (2011), pp. 649–693; Borlini (2016), pp. 93–132; Velluti (2016), pp. 342–366; Wouters and Ovádek (2021), pp. 539–645; Tuominen (2022), pp. 935–950.

[2] As recognized in the Vienna Declaration and Programme of Action, adopted by consensus at the World Conference on Human Rights in Vienna on 25 June 1993, art. 5.

[3] This is a rather old idea; for example, see Pollis and Schwab (1979). Along the same lines, see among others Mickelson (1998), pp. 19–48, Walz (2002), pp. 437–448, Donnely (2007), pp. 281–306. An interesting analysis aimed at arguing against this position from a philosophical perspective can be found in Suárez Müller (2012), pp. 279–293. For a critique of the Western attempt to define an "intercultural" approach to human rights as opposed to a "multicultural" one, see Berry (2018), pp. 441–471. Conversely, on the role of intercultural dialogue in developing a non-ethnocentric conception of human rights, see Flinn (2014). For an interesting analysis aimed at deconstructing the criticism of the universality of human rights, see Viola (2006), pp. 155–187.

[4] See the 2024 Human Rights Watch report at this link: https://www.hrw.org/world-report/2024/country-chapters/european-union. Accessed 14 March 2025.

[5] See Williams (2004).

[6] See in particular the argument advanced in Cannizzaro (2015), pp. 1097–1098.

This chapter seeks to contribute to the ongoing debate on the role of the European Union in promoting human rights in its external relations by focusing on a particular tool, namely the "new generation" free trade agreements (FTAs) that the EU concludes bilaterally with third countries and regional organizations.[7] This analytical approach provides a lens through which to assess whether these efforts amount to little more than an attempt to "export values" or whether they reflect a commitment to asserting the EU's role as a "responsible global actor" in the promotion of human rights worldwide.[8] In particular, this chapter aims to examine how human rights considerations have been embedded in EU new generation FTAs in order to determine whether they represent a qualitative advancement in EU action in this area and to identify possible improvements. A further element of originality in this analysis lies in its emphasis on a dimension of the EU's commitment to human rights: the protection of the rights of persons belonging to minorities. Indeed, Article 2 of the Treaty on European Union (TEU), which lists the EU's fundamental values, explicitly includes the rights of persons belonging to minorities as a specific component of the broader human rights protection.

The chapter is organized into three main sections. The first section provides an analysis of the EU's human rights commitments in its external action, focusing on its common commercial policy. The second section analyses the protection of human rights in EU new generation FTAs. It highlights that not all of these agreements contain a human rights clause. However, it shows how human rights considerations are intrinsically embedded in the "new generation" provisions of EU FTAs. It also assesses the mechanisms established in the agreements for the effective implementation of human rights commitments, questioning whether they are robust enough to ensure compliance. The third section examines the protection of the rights of persons belonging to minorities. In particular, it analyses the innovative provisions of the recent EU-New Zealand FTA[9] aimed at integrating Māori—the indigenous people of New Zealand—into trade relations while protecting their rights. The chapter concludes with an evaluation of the extent to which new generation FTAs represent an advance in the international protection of human rights and their potential to influence future developments in the international legal order.

---

[7] On EU new generation trade agreements, see among others Ruotolo (2016), pp. 392–354; von Danwitz (2018), pp. 201–207; Fernández Rozas (2019), pp. 1–59; Barthesaghi et al. (2019), pp. 447–477; Adinolfi (2021); Blanc Altemir (2020), pp. 93–132; Maillo (2021); Vincent (2021); Pasquali (2024a, 2024b), pp. 199–249. For a comprehensive analysis of the post-Lisbon common commercial policy, with insightful discussions on EU new generation trade agreements, see Hahn and Van der Loo (2021).

[8] A detail review of the literature on the EU's role as global actor can be found in Velluti (2020), pp. 11–38. For an analysis aimed at understanding whether and how the EU positions itself as a "good global actor" in international relations, see Fahey and Mancini (2022).

[9] Free Trade Agreement between the European Union and New Zealand, O.J. L 2024/866 (2024).

2 Human Rights in EU Common Commercial Policy

The European Union's commitment to uphold and promote its values worldwide—and, in the specific case of our interest, human rights—is enshrined in the Treaties. In particular, Article 3(5) TEU states that:

> In its relations with the wider world, the Union shall uphold and promote its values and interests and contribute to the protection of its citizens. It shall contribute to peace, security, the sustainable development of the Earth, solidarity and mutual respect among peoples, free and fair trade, the eradication of poverty, and the protection of human rights, in particular the rights of the child, as well as to the strict observance and development of international law, including respect for the principles of the United Nations Charter.

The values that the EU is called upon to promote globally are those listed in Article 2 TEU, namely, respect for human dignity, freedom, democracy, equality, rule of law, and respect for human rights, including the rights of persons belonging to minorities.[10] There is an important point to be drawn even from this first remark. Through Article 3(5), the Treaty defines the existence of a connection between EU values and the maintenance of the international order. In other words, Article 3(5) TEU frames the promotion of EU values as an instrument for ensuring the observance and development of international law, with a view to safeguarding international peace and security.[11] The dimensions of sustainable development, solidarity, mutual respect among peoples, free and fair trade, poverty eradication, and human rights protection all contribute to this objective, in full accordance with the underlying logic of the United Nations Charter.[12] The promotion of human rights by the EU can thus be seen as having a dual dimension: (a) a distinct value of the European Union to be upheld and promoted within the Union itself and in its external relations; (b) an essential contribution that the EU is called upon to make to the maintenance of the international order.

This framework is further specified in Article 21 TEU, which relates to the Union's external action. Article 21 states that the Union's action on the international scene "*shall be guided by the principles which have inspired its own creation, development and enlargement, and which it seeks to advance in the wider world*", including "*democracy, the rule of law, the universality and indivisibility of human rights and fundamental freedoms, respect for human dignity, the principles of equality and solidarity, and respect for the principles of the United Nations Charter and international law*". Furthermore, paragraph 2 of the same article clarifies that the Union

[10] Peraldi Leneuf (2020). See also the contribution of Elena Crespo Navarro in this volume.

[11] For a focused analysis of the European Union's contribution to international peace and security, see Marquardt and Blockmans (2023). The authors note that the EU is not only "an intra-European peace project based on the values set out in Article 2 TEU", but also, according to Arts. 3(5) and 21(2)(c) TEU, "an external peace project", ibid. p. x.

[12] It is well known that the UN Charter is based on three pillars: peace and security, human rights, and economic and social development. Indeed, the drafters of the Charter were well aware that ensuring international peace and security required more than just prohibiting the use of force in international relations; it also required addressing the root causes of conflicts.

"*shall work for a high degree of cooperation in all fields of international relations, in order... to consolidate and support democracy, the rule of law, human rights and the principles of international law*".[13] A combined reading of Article 21 TEU and Article 205 of the Treaty on the Functioning of the European Union (TFEU) further underlines how the Union's external action has been conceived: the Union should position itself as a global actor committed to the maintenance of the international order through the promotion of the fundamental values that have shaped its creation. The Union's common commercial policy is undoubtedly one of the most effective instruments to this end. Article 207 TFEU confirms this by stating that "*the common commercial policy shall be conducted in the context of the principles and objectives of the Union's external action*", thus establishing an inextricable link with Article 21 TEU. Indeed, the European Union's market is one of the largest in the world[14] and the prospect of access to it undeniably has the potential to act as an incentive for third countries to take steps to comply with certain values. This dynamic must be understood within the logic of a "cost-benefit analysis" on the part of the trading partner: the greater the perceived benefits of access to the EU market, the more likely it is that the partner will be willing to make commitments beyond the purely commercial sphere. For this reason, the EU common commercial policy is an appropriate instrument to support the EU's promotional efforts in the field of human rights.

2.1 GSP Schemes

The integration of the promotion of human rights into the European Union's common commercial policy is not a recent development.[15] One tool the EU uses to this end is the Generalized System of Preferences (GSP), a mechanism created in 1971 to promote economic growth of developing countries by granting their products

[13] For a clear and thorough analysis of the nature and effect of the combined provisions of Articles 3(5) and 21, highlighting both their objectives and their inherent limitations, see Cannizzaro (2021), pp. 3–18.

[14] As reported by EUROSTAT: "*The EU is one of the world's largest players in global trade being the second largest exporter of goods in the world after China and the third largest importer after the United States and China. Moreover, the EU is the world's number one trader of services*"; see EUROSTAT website at: https://ec.europa.eu/eurostat. Accessed 15 February 2025.

[15] The Court of Justice of the EU recognised a considerable time ago that the common commercial policy could address issues beyond the scope of purely commercial matters and include other objectives. For example, in the 1987 judgment *Tariff preferences*, the Court, referring to Opinion 1/78 of 4 October 1979, stated that: "*The Court has already acknowledged that the existence of a link with development problems does not cause a measure to be excluded from the sphere of the common commercial policy as defined by the Treaty. it considered that it would no longer be possible to carry on any worthwhile common commercial policy if the community were not in a position to avail itself also of means of action going beyond instruments intended to have an effect only on the traditional aspects of external trade. A "commercial policy" understood in that sense would be destined to become negatory in the course of time*", Case 45/86 *Commission of the European Communities v Council of the European Communities* (EU:C:1987:163), par. 20.

more favourable market access conditions.[16] This system is an exception to the most-favoured-nation clause that generally governs multilateral trade relations.[17] It is based on the unilateral definition of conditions by the granting party; consequently, it will not be addressed further, as it does not align with the broader discussion pursued in this chapter. Indeed, the chapter aims to explore the possibility that the EU, through its trade agreements, can outline a new approach to achieving common solutions that allow for a broader protection of human rights, thereby contributing to the advancement of international law in this area.

2.2 *The Origin of the "Essential Elements" Clauses in EU International Agreements*

References to human rights were first included in EU trade and aid agreements with the African, Caribbean and Pacific (ACP) countries. In particular, art. 5 of the Fourth Lomé Convention of 1989 with the ACP countries was the first to include such a reference, highlighting the link between development policy and cooperation and the respect for and enjoyment of fundamental human rights.[18] The 1990 agreement between the EU and Argentina[19] was the first to include an article which stated that "*ties between the Community and Argentina and this Agreement in its entirety are based on respect for democratic principles and human rights*".[20] Similar clauses

[16] The EU has introduced special conditionalities in its relations with developing countries, linking preferential market access conditions to compliance with core human rights standards. This system underwent a major reform in 2005, leading to the establishment of a three-tier framework: the General Arrangement (GSP), the Special Incentive Arrangement for Sustainable Development and Good Governance (GSP+), and the Everything But Arms (EBA) scheme. Such framework was further strengthened by the 2012 reform. Developing countries eligible for the GSP+ must apply individually, unlike the standard GSP and EBA schemes, for which eligibility is determined on the basis of lists drawn up by United Nations bodies according to economic criteria. When applying for the GSP+, countries must declare that they have ratified, effectively implemented and complied with the monitoring requirements of 27 international conventions on human rights and labour rights, good governance and environmental protection. See Regulation (EU) No. 978/2012 of the European Parliament and of the Council of 25 October 2012 applying a scheme of generalised tariff preferences and repealing Council Regulation (EC) No. 732/2008, O.J. L303/1 (2012). The regulation, based on art. 207 TFEU, was due to expire in 2023. However, the Council and the European Parliament signed an amendment to the existing Regulation for the period 2024–2027. On the topic, see Velluti (2016), pp. 342–366; Hachez and Marx (2021), pp. 652–662.

[17] General Agreement on Tariffs and Trade (GATT 1947), art. 1. See Martines (2005), pp. 287–316; Bartels (2007), pp. 869–886.

[18] Fourth ACP-EEC Convention signed at Lomé on 15 December 1989, O.J. L 229/3 (1991), art. 5.

[19] Framework Agreement for trade and economic cooperation between the European Economic Community and the Argentine Republic, O.J. L295/67 (1990).

[20] Ibid., art. 1.1.

were subsequently included in EU agreements with Chile,[21] Uruguay,[22] Paraguay,[23] Macao,[24] and Mongolia.[25]

The proposal to sanction human rights violations was made in a Communication of the Commission.[26] Subsequently the Council explicitly supported the inclusion of conditionality clauses in all Cooperation and Association Agreements between the Community and its partners of the Conference on Security and Cooperation in Europe (CSCE).[27]

The first formulation of this clause—known as the "Baltic clause" because it was introduced in agreements with the Baltic States[28]—provided for the immediate suspension of the agreement in the event of a violation of any of its essential provisions, including those relating to human rights. However, a less stringent version was subsequently adopted, known as "Bulgarian clause", so named because it was first included in the EU-Bulgaria agreement.[29] This version provided for the adoption of "appropriate measures" in the event of a violation of the essential provisions of the agreement, favouring dialogue and making suspension of the agreement a measure of last resort.[30] Thus, since 1995, the EU has included a political

[21] Framework Agreement for cooperation between the European Economic Community and the Republic of Chile, O.J. L79/2 (1991), art. 1.

[22] Framework Cooperation Agreement between the European Economic Community and the Eastern Republic of Uruguay, O.J. L 94/2 (1992), art. 1.

[23] Framework Agreement for cooperation between the European Economic Community and the Republic of Paraguay, O.J. L 313/72 (1992), art. 1.

[24] Agreement for trade and cooperation between the European Economic Community and Macao, O.J. L 404/27 (1992), art. 1.

[25] Agreement on trade and economic cooperation between the European Economic Community and Mongolia, O.J. L 41/46 (1993), art. 1.

[26] Commission Communication to the Council and the Parliament, Human rights, democracy and development cooperation policy, SEC (61) 91 of 25 March 1991, p. 6: "*Although the fourth Lomé Convention contains no express sanctions clause in the case of human rights violations, the spirit of the Conventional lows certain consequences to be drawn as regards the management of cooperation if Article 5 is breached*".

[27] Council statement on respect for democratic principles, human rights and principles of the market economy, Bull. EC (1992) 5, 1.2.13.

[28] Agreement between the European Economic Community and the Republic of Estonia on Trade and Commercial and Economic Cooperation, O.J. L 403/7 (1992), Art. 21; Agreement between the European Economic Community and the Republic of Latvia on Trade and Commercial and Economic Cooperation, O.J. L 403/16 (1992), Art. 21; Agreement between the European Economic Community and the European Atomic Energy Community, of the one part, and the Republic of Lithuania, of the other part, on trade and commercial and economic cooperation, O.J. L 403/25 (1992), Art. 21. A similar clause was introduced also in agreements with Albania and Slovenia.

[29] Agreement establishing an association between the European Communities and their Member States, of the one part, and the Republic of Bulgaria, of the other part, O.J. L 233/24 (1994), Art. 118. On this point, see among others Horng (2003), pp. 677–701.

[30] Communication from the Commission on the inclusion of respect for democratic principles and human rights in Agreements between the Community and third Countries, COM(95) 216 final, p. 8: "*The difference between the two formulas resides in the degree of sensitivity allowed for. The "Baltic clause" is more severe in that it provides only for extreme cases warranting immediate*

conditionality based on the Bulgarian clause—commonly referred to as the "non-execution clause"—in trade and cooperation agreements.[31] In particular, such provisions can be found in the Economic Partnership Agreements concluded with the ACP countries in accordance with the provisions of the Cotonou Agreement of 2000, which succeeded the Lomé Convention.[32] The Cotonou Agreement has been replaced by the Post-Cotonou Agreement, also known as the Samoa Agreement. This agreement established the new general framework for relations between the EU and the ACP countries for the next two decades, reaffirming and extending commitments on human rights.[33]

2.3 *Trade and Human Rights: The European Approach*

In 2009, the Treaty of Lisbon strengthened the integration of human rights considerations into EU trade policy,[34] especially by increasing the role of the European Parliament in the conclusion of trade agreements.[35] Indeed, the Treaty of Lisbon provides that Parliament must give its consent to the conclusion of international agreements, giving it the power to veto over such agreements at the ratification stage.[36] Another key innovation that strengthened Parliament's role and enabled it to exert pressure for the inclusion of human rights considerations in trade agreements was the introduction of the "duty of information", which obliges the Commission to report to Parliament on the progress of negotiations.[37]

---

suspension without consultation of any kind. The "Bulgarian clause" not only provides for a conciliation procedure and a range of different options but is also designed to keep the agreement operational wherever possible. It asserts that immediate suspension should be envisaged only in cases of special urgency".

[31] For a thorough analysis of the conditionality clause in European Union agreements, see, Bartels (2005); Lochak (2012), pp. 539–549; Martines (2016), pp. 37–62; Martines (2020), pp. 97–180.

[32] Articles 96 and 97 of the Cotonou Agreement establish the principle of conditionality on respect for fundamental rights, democracy and the rule of law.

[33] See Partnership Agreement between the European Union and its Member States, of the one part, and the Members of the Organisation of African, Caribbean and Pacific States, of the other part, O.J. L 2023/2862 (2023). For a further analysis of the Samoa Agreement, see Lillo (2024), pp. 271–298. For an analysis of the promotion of human rights in the negotiations of the Samoa Agreement from a TWAIL perspective, see Carbone (2024), pp. 1314–1331.

[34] On this point, see Marrella (2011, 2014) insightful analyses.

[35] As argued by Velluti (2016), p. 47: "*The ToL [Treaty of Lisbon] has given the EU Parliament a stronger role in relation to the conclusion of international agreements, which is of great significance given that it constitutes a formally independent voice for EU citizens and that it is a strong human rights advocate. This flows from its ongoing commitment to the protection of human rights generally as well as its democratic legitimation function that may be said to be independent and separate from that of the Member States*".

[36] TFEU, Article 218(6)(a).

[37] TFEU, Article 207(3).

This has led to a special approach in the negotiation of international agreements, which aims to ensure that trade does not compromise human rights.[38] It is worth considering that the relationship between human rights and trade has long been the subject of scholarly debate, with conflicting views.[39] Some argue that international trade may have a negative impact on the protection of human rights.[40] On the one hand, this concern stems from the economic rationale of trade, which prioritize the maximization of aggregate benefits over individual well-being and may therefore remain indifferent to the impact on human rights at the individual level. On the other hand, increased trade opportunities risk to incentivize governments to weaken labour protections or lower the threshold for the enjoyment of other rights in order to develop comparative advantages over the trading partner and attract investment and capital. From another perspective, however, international trade—if properly managed—can have the reverse effect of improving human rights conditions.[41] Trade fosters interactions and reciprocal influences. Countries can learn from trading partners with higher standards of protection, and individuals can gain greater awareness of their conditions. In addition, human rights considerations can be integrated into trade negotiations and become a factor to be weighed when concluding trade agreements. Indeed, a partner with higher standards of protection may have an interest in ensuring that its counterpart complies with similar standards (e.g. on labour rights) in order to maintain a level playing field. At the same time, there may be an interest in ensuring that trade does not compromise consumer safety, i.e. allowing the import of food products from the partner with lower safety standards. It is worth noting that the European Union adopts integrated assessments—which are conducted at different stages of the negotiation process and subsequent agreement implementation—to evaluate the impact of trade agreements on different dimensions, including human rights.[42] Such impact assessments are undoubtedly a

---

[38] See European Commission, Guidelines on the analysis of human rights impacts in impact assessments for trade-related policy initiatives, 2015.

[39] See Cottier et al. (2005).

[40] For an overview of these positions, see Ibrahim (2013), pp. 321–337.

[41] See the position of former WTO Director-General Pascal Lamy, 'Towards shared responsibility and greater coherence: human rights, trade and macroeconomic policy' (speech at the Colloquium on Human Rights in the Global Economy, Co-organized by the International Council on Human Rights and Realizing Rights, Geneva, 13 January 2010).

[42] Four integrated assessments are conducted at various stages of the negotiation process and subsequent agreement implementation. Firstly, an Impact Assessment is conducted as a prerequisite for entering into negotiations. This examines the potential impact of the trade agreement, taking into account economic, social and environmental dimensions, as well as, where relevant, its impact on human rights. Secondly, a Sustainability Impact Assessment (SIA) is conducted during the negotiation process to provide the Commission with a more detailed insight into the impact of the future agreements. Thirdly, an assessment is conducted after the main elements of the agreement have been finalised, focusing on the economic impact. Finally, an *ex post* evaluation is undertaken once the agreement has entered into force and a sufficient period of time has passed to allow a comprehensive assessment of its impact. See https://policy.trade.ec.europa.eu/analysis-and-assessment/policy-evaluation_en. Accessed 10 February 2025.

valuable—albeit improvable—tool for breaking the vicious circle that can arise between trade liberalization and negative impacts on human rights.[43]

Nevertheless, in addition to preventing trade from having a negative impact on human rights, the European Union's trade policy, as outlined in the Treaties, is required to promote improvements in the protection of human rights at the global level. The EU has explicitly reaffirmed this commitment in several key documents adopted since 2011.

2.3.1 The EU Action Plans on Human Rights and Democracy

The Joint Communication of the European Commission and the High Representative of the European Union for Foreign Affairs and Security Policy, "Human Rights and Democracy at the Heart of EU External Action—Towards a More Effective Approach",[44] states that "*The protection and promotion of human rights is a 'silver thread' running through all EU action, both at home and abroad*".[45] The Communication recognizes that the EU has a crucial role to play in addressing global risks to human rights protection, including the violation of fundamental norms under the pretext of cultural differences, challenges to the domestic implementation of internationally accepted standards by third countries and the risks posed by globalization.[46] Against this background, the EU is called upon to commit itself "*to promoting and protecting freedom, dignity, equality and justice for all as a key foreign policy priority*".[47] Indeed, trade policy has been identified as one of the key instruments to achieve this objective. This communication was followed by the "EU Strategic Framework and Action Plan on Human Rights and Democracy",[48] which reaffirms that "*the European Union is founded on a shared determination to promote peace and stability and to build a world based on respect for human rights, democracy and the rule of law*".[49] A key development of this strategic framework, in line with the discussion in this chapter, is the recognition of bilateral relations with third countries as an effective tool for strengthening human rights. These

[43] For a broad analysis of human rights impact assessments of trade agreements, see Walker (2009).

[44] *Human rights and democracy at the heart of EU external action—Towards a more effective approach.* Joint communication from the Commission and the High Representative of the European Union for Foreign Affairs and Security Policy to the European Parliament and to the Council. COM (2011) 886 final, 12 December 2011.

[45] Ibid., p. 4.

[46] Ibid., p. 6.

[47] Ibid., p. 7.

[48] Council of the European Union, *EU Strategic Framework and Action Plan on Human Rights and Democracy*, 25 June 2012, 11855/12.

[49] Ibid., p. 1. It is worth noting that the document clarifies that human rights are "universally applicable legal norms", whereas democracy is a "universal aspiration". This distinction is important: while democracy remains an evolving construct, not yet endowed with the attribute of universality, human rights must be upheld as universal norms.

relations must be based on dialogue, as "*While firmly based on universal norms, the EU's policy on human rights will be carefully designed for the circumstances of each country*".[50] In addition, point 11 of the Action Plan specifically addresses the objective of "*making trade work in a way that helps human rights*". It outlines six key actions, including developing methodologies to assess human rights conditions in third countries prior to trade or investment agreements, strengthening human rights dialogues with FTAs partners, ensuring that EU investment policy is consistent with human rights principles, and reviewing regulations on trade in goods that could be used for the death penalty or torture. The latest Action Plan, the "EU Action Plan on Human Rights and Democracy 2020–2024",[51] which has been extended to 2027, underlines that the EU will "*continue to widen and deepen bilateral partnerships and build new cross-regional coalitions*" and "*also intensify its efforts to promote a positive narrative underlining the multiple benefits that the advancement of human rights and democracy brings to all stakeholders in support of sustainable development, peace and security, and the advancement of equal, diverse, pluralistic and inclusive societies*".[52] This approach is in line with the provisions of the Treaties and confirms the ambition of promoting values with a view to strengthening international law.

2.3.2 The "Trade for All" Strategy and Its Development

The framework outlined above outlines a path for defining a responsible trade policy that seeks not only to protect the interests of the European Union, but also to uphold and promote its values. This approach is fully reflected in the "Trade for All" strategy, which sets a new direction for EU trade policy.[53] Following the Commission's Communication "Global Europe: Competing in the World",[54] the European Union had set a new course for its trade policy by introducing a new type of FTAs, the so-called "new generation" free trade agreements,[55] which follow the so-called "deep trade" approach.[56] Accordingly, such FTAs contain provisions that go beyond trade itself to cover additional policy areas. In a context where the

[50] Ibid., p. 3.

[51] European Commission, Joint Communication to the European Parliament and the Council, *EU Action Plan on Human Rights and Democracy 2020–2024*, JOIN/2020/5 final.

[52] Ibid.

[53] European Commission: Directorate-General for Trade and Economic Security, *Trade for all—Towards a more responsible trade and investment policy*, Publications Office, 2014, https://data.europa.eu/doi/10.2781/1753. Accessed 10 February 2025.

[54] See Communication from the Commission to the Council, the European Parliament, the European Economic and Social Committee and the Committee of the Regions—Global Europe—Competing in the world—A contribution to the EU's Growth and Jobs Strategy, COM/2006/0567 final.

[55] Supra note 7.

[56] See Melo Araujo (2016).

multilateral trading system is at an impasse,[57] the conclusion of bilateral agreements allows for the introduction of WTO-plus provisions, namely measures that go beyond those established in the WTO framework. "Trade for All", in particular, introduces commitments related to the promotion of values. Among these, the European Union commits to introduce elements aimed at "*the development of poorer countries, high social and environmental standards, and respect for human rights*".[58] As stated in "Trade for All", "*one of the EU's objectives is to ensure that economic growth goes hand in hand with social justice, respect for human rights, high labour and environmental standards, and health and safety protection*".[59] Thus, a key aspect is the growing link between the protection of human rights and the broader objective of sustainable development.[60] The Commission Communication "The Power of Trade Partnerships: Working together for green and fair economic growth" reinforces these EU commitments.[61] It is structured around six policy priorities, namely (1) a more pro-active approach to working with partners; (2) a strengthened country-specific approach; (3) the objective of integrating the principle of sustainability into all aspects of the agreements; (4) enhanced monitoring of the implementation of trade and sustainable development commitments; (5) a strengthened role for civil society; (6) enhanced enforcement of sustainable development provisions through the use of trade sanctions as a last resort.

[57] As is well known, the failure of the Doha Round has brought the WTO negotiations to a standstill. The only achievement so far has been the conclusion of the 2022 Agreement on Fisheries Subsidies, reached after 21 years of negotiations. However, this agreement remains underdeveloped and raises concerns about its enforceability. On this point, see Auld et al. (2024), pp. 25–49. It should also be noted that current geopolitical landscape, in particular the positions of the newly elected US President Trump, pose new risks to the functioning of the multilateral trading system.

[58] Trade for all—Towards a more responsible trade and investment policy, cit., p. 22.

[59] Ibid.

[60] The relationship between human rights and sustainable development remains a matter of debate. The question is whether the 2030 Agenda should be adopted as a common framework, given its broader and more ambitious scope, or whether the established human rights conventions should be used instead. Indeed, the former is a soft law instrument, while the latter are legally binding. However, an analysis of the 2030 Agenda shows that its Sustainable Development Goals (SDGs) are consistent with human rights norms enshrined in binding international conventions. Thus, rather than introducing a separate framework, the 2030 Agenda provides a common structure that integrates human rights within the overarching goal of sustainable development. On this point, see the guide prepared by the Danish Institute for Human Rights, which provides an analysis of the Sustainable Development Goals and related targets and links them to existing international human rights obligations; the guide is available at the following link: https://sdg.humanrights.dk/. Accessed 12 March 2025.

[61] Communication from the Commission to the European Parliament, the Council, the European Economic and Social Committee and the Committee of the Regions, *The power of trade partnerships: together for green and just economic growth*, Brussels, 22.6.2022, COM(2022) 409 final.

3 Upholding and Promoting Human Rights Through EU New Generation Trade Agreements

The European Union has so far concluded new generation FTAs with South Korea,[62] Colombia/Peru/Ecuador,[63] the Central American Association,[64] Canada (CETA),[65] Japan,[66] Singapore,[67] Vietnam,[68] Chile,[69] Kenya,[70] and New Zealand.[71] In addition, political agreements have been reached on new generation FTAs with Mercosur[72] and Mexico.[73] Negotiations are also underway for similar agreements with

[62] Free Trade Agreement between the European Union and its Member States, of the one part, and the Republic of Korea, of the other part, O.J. L 127/6 (2011).

[63] Trade Agreement between the European Union and its Member States, of the one part, and Colombia and Peru, of the other part, O.J. L 354/3 (2012). On 1 January 2017, Ecuador also joined the agreement, see Protocol of Accession to the Trade Agreement between the European Union and its Member States, of the one part, and Colombia and Peru, of the other part, to take account of the accession of Ecuador, O.J. L 356/3 (2016).

[64] Agreement establishing an Association between the European Union and its Member States, on the one hand, and Central America on the other, O.J. L 346/3 (2012).

[65] Comprehensive Economic and Trade Agreement (CETA) between Canada, of the one part, and the European Union and its Member States, of the other part, O.J. L 11/23 (2017).

[66] Agreement between the European Union and Japan for an Economic Partnership, O.J. L 330/3 (2018).

[67] Free trade Agreement between the European Union and the Republic of Singapore, O.J. L 294/3 (2019).

[68] Free Trade Agreement between the European Union and the Socialist Republic of Viet Nam, O.J. L 186/3 (2020).

[69] Interim Agreement on trade between the European Union and the Republic of Chile, O.J. L 2024/2953 (2024). It is important to clarify that this agreement reflects only the trade pillar of a broader advanced framework agreement that will govern future bilateral relations between the EU and Chile. This agreement will include a political and cooperation pillar and a trade and investment pillar. Once this agreement will enter into force, the Interim Agreement will expire, as clarified in its art. 33.15.

[70] Economic Partnership Agreement between the European Union, of the one part, and the Republic of Kenya, Member of the East African Community, of the other part, O.J. L 2024/1648 (2024).

[71] Supra note 9.

[72] On 17 January 2026 the EU and Mercosur signed the Partnership Agreement and the Interim Trade Agreement.

[73] Bilateral relations between the EU and Mexico are actually governed by the 2000 "Global Agreement"; Economic Partnership, Political Coordination and Cooperation Agreement between the European Community and its Member States, of the one part, and the United Mexican States, of the other part, O.J. L 276/45 (2000). On 17 January 2025, EU and Mexico concluded the negotiations for a modernised Global Agreement which contains elements of new generation FTAs. The texts of the EU-Mexico Agreement in principle, which, as clarified on the official website of the Commission, "*are published for information purposes only and may undergo further modifications including as a result of the process of legal revision*" and "*will be final upon signature and will become binding on the parties under international law only after completion by each party of its internal legal procedures necessary for the entry into force of the agreement (or its provisional application)*", are available at: https://policy.trade.ec.europa.eu/eu-trade-relationships-country-

Australia,[74] Eastern and Southern Africa (ESA 5),[75] India,[76] Indonesia[77] and Thailand.[78] This chapter focuses on these agreements only and does not include the association agreements with candidate countries such as Moldova,[79] Georgia[80] and Ukraine.[81] Although these agreements also contain new generation provisions, they fall outside the scope of our analysis. The reason for this is that candidate countries, by seeking EU membership, are required to align themselves fully with its values and thus become part of the EU framework.[82] The present analysis, by contrast, is driven by an alternative objective: namely, to explore the potential for promoting values, with a particular focus on human rights, in third countries that do not aspire to accede to the Union, thereby exerting influence on the broader international system. It is evident that, despite the bilateral nature of these agreements, the EU is establishing a network of agreements with the potential to serve as both an alternative to and a reinforcement of the multilateral system. Similarly, the agreement with the United Kingdom will not be examined in detail, as although it is no longer a member of the EU, it remains a country with deep ties to the Union.[83]

and-region/countries-and-regions/mexico/eu-mexico-agreement/agreement-principle_en. Accessed 20 February 2025.

[74] The reports of the negotiation rounds and the EU's initial text proposal are available at: https://policy.trade.ec.europa.eu/eu-trade-relationships-country-and-region/countries-and-regions/australia/eu-australia-agreement/documents_en. Accessed 20 February 2025.

[75] The reports of the negotiation rounds and the EU's initial text proposal are available at: https://policy.trade.ec.europa.eu/eu-trade-relationships-country-and-region/countries-and-regions/eastern-and-southern-africa-esa/eu-eastern-and-southern-africa-agreement-documents_en. Accessed 20 February 2025.

[76] The reports of the negotiation rounds and the EU's initial text proposal are available at: https://policy.trade.ec.europa.eu/eu-trade-relationships-country-and-region/countries-and-regions/india/eu-india-agreement/documents_en. Accessed 20 February 2025.

[77] The reports of the negotiation rounds and the EU's initial text proposal are available at: https://policy.trade.ec.europa.eu/eu-trade-relationships-country-and-region/countries-and-regions/indonesia/eu-indonesia-agreement_en. Accessed 20 February 2025.

[78] The reports of the negotiation rounds and the EU's initial text proposal are available at: https://policy.trade.ec.europa.eu/eu-trade-relationships-country-and-region/countries-and-regions/indonesia/eu-indonesia-agreement_en. Accessed 20 February 2025.

[79] Association Agreement between the European Union and the European Atomic Energy Community and their Member States, of the one part, and the Republic of Moldova, of the other part, O.J. L 260/4 (2014).

[80] Association Agreement between the European Union and the European Atomic Energy Community and their Member States, of the one part, and Georgia, of the other part, O.J. L 261/4 (2014).

[81] Association Agreement between the European Union and the European Atomic Energy Community and their Member States, of the one part, and Ukraine, of the other part, O.J. L 161/3 (2014).

[82] Article 49 TEU clearly states that "*Any European State which* respects the values referred to in Article 2 and is committed to promoting them *may apply to become a member of the Union*" (emphasis added).

[83] Trade and Cooperation Agreement between the European Union and the European Atomic Energy Community, of the one part, and the United Kingdom of Great Britain and Northern Ireland, of the other part, O.J. L 149/10 (2021). For a detailed analysis of this agreement, see Adinolfi et al. (2022), Kübek et al. (2024).

3.1 *Human Rights Conditionality in EU New Generation Trade Agreements*

In the first place, the preamble of all the above-mentioned FTAs makes reference to the Universal Declaration of Human Rights. It is worth noting, however, that only some of the EU new generation FTAs contain a clause which considers the respect for human rights to be an essential element of the agreement and provides for the possibility of adopting "appropriate measures" in the event of a violation.[84] These agreements are those with Colombia, Peru and Ecuador[85] and with the Central American Association.[86] Furthermore, the Agreement with Kenya specifies that it builds on the acquis of the Cotonou Agreement and its successor.[87] A conditionality clause is also included in the future Advanced Framework Agreement with Chile[88] and in the Partnership Agreement with Mercosur.[89] The agreements with Korea, Vietnam, New Zealand and Singapore must also be taken into account. The reason for this is that while these agreements do not contain a specific human rights clause, such provisions can be found in the existing Framework and Cooperation Agreements (FCA) between the EU and these countries.[90] Indeed, each of the four FTAs mentioned contains an article stating that the agreement is an integral part of the broader relationship between the EU and the countries concerned and is integrated into the common institutional framework established by the FCAs they concluded with the EU.[91] It is worth noting that this approach follows a policy guideline set by the Council of the European Union. Indeed, it has emphasized the preference to first

[84] Following the provisions of Article 60 of the Vienna Convention on the Law of Treaties (1969), United Nations, Treaty Series, vol. 1155, p. 331.

[85] EU-Colombia-Peru-Ecuador FTA, art. 1 and art. 8(3).

[86] EU-Central America Agreement, art. 1 and art. 355(2). It is worth noting that this is an "Association agreement with a strong trade component".

[87] EU-Kenya PA, art. 4(a).

[88] Supra note 67.

[89] The clause is also complemented by two additional commitments that constitute an "essential element" of the agreement itself: the commitment to remain a party to the UNFCCC and its Paris Agreement in good faith; the provisions on weapons of mass destruction.

[90] Framework Agreement between the European Union and its Member States, on the one part, and the Republic of Korea, on the other part, O.J. L 20/2 (2013), art. 1 and art. 45; Framework Agreement on Comprehensive Partnership and Cooperation between the European Union and its Member States, of the one part, and the Socialist Republic of Viet Nam, of the other part, O.J. L 329/8 (2016), art. 1 and art. 57; Partnership and cooperation agreement between the European Union and its member states, of the one part, and the Republic of Singapore, of the other part, not yet in force, art. 1 and art. 44; Partnership Agreement on Relations and Cooperation between the European Union and its Member States, of the one part, and New Zealand, of the other part, O.J. L 321/3 (2016), art. 2 and art. 54.

[91] EU-Korea FTA, Art. 15.14(2); EU-Vietnam FTA, Art. 17.22(2); EU-New Zealand FTA, Art. 1.5(2); EU-Singapore FTA, Art. 16.8.

conclude a framework agreement with partner countries, defining the overarching structure for cooperation in key areas, including political dialogue, and then to proceed with sector-specific agreements, such as trade agreements.[92] This strategy follows a clear logic. Partner countries may be unwilling to incorporate a conditionality clause directly into trade agreements, whereas they may be more open to linking the trade agreement to a political agreement that includes such a clause. What is particularly significant, however, is that this linkage effectively extends the non-execution clause to the trade agreements, thus linking trade relations to fundamental human rights commitments. In this context, it is worth noting that CETA and the EU-Japan EPA are not technically linked to the respective FCAs with the EU, which contain a human rights clause.[93]

The clause refers generally to the obligation to respect human rights as enshrined in the Universal Declaration of Human Rights. As is well known, these rights have achieved the status of customary international law and are therefore binding on all members of the international community. Significantly, some agreements also refer to "*other relevant international human rights instruments to which the Parties are Contracting Parties*", thereby broadening and deepening the scope of protection. In particular, this suggests an open-ended nature of the clause, which could also encompass future international instruments related to the protection of human rights.[94] In any case, it is clear that the inclusion of a conditionality clause does not represent a substantial innovation in the EU's approach. As noted above, the EU introduced its system of conditionality well before the conclusion of new generation FTAs. Admittedly, these agreements extend conditionality to a wider range of partners and link it to trade deals that offer significant economic benefits. However, they do not fundamentally change the conditionality itself, leaving its inherent weaknesses unaddressed.[95] In particular, the conditionality clause states that if one party fails to comply with the "essential elements" of the agreement, the other party "*may immediately adopt appropriate measures*". These measures must be "*proportionate*" to the violation and should prioritize options that least disturb the functioning of the agreement. This wording inherently allows for the possibility that the clause may never be used, as the provision clearly states that a party "*may*" take action, rather than being required to do so. Moreover, if it is used, it is more likely that the parties will opt for political dialogue, with potentially unsatisfactory outcomes. This highlights the inherent tension between the EU's ambition to promote its values and the economic objectives of its trade policy. As noted above, not all agreements

---

[92] Such an approach was outlined by the Council in COREPER on 3 June 2009. The document is partially declassified by Council doc. 10491/1/09 of 25 April 2013, available at: https://data.consilium.europa.eu/doc/document/ST-7008-2009-INIT/en/pdf. Accessed 25 February 2025.

[93] Strategic Partnership Agreement between the European Union and its Member States, of the one part, and Canada, of the other part, O.J. L 329/45 (2016), Art. 2; Strategic Partnership Agreement between the European Union and its Member States, of the one part, and Japan, of the other part, O.J. L 216/4 (2018), Art. 2 and Art. 43.

[94] See Van Elsuwege and De Coninck (2022), p. 19.

[95] Ibid, p. 7.

contain a conditionality clause, and it seems unlikely that its application would lead to significant disruptions in trade with an important trading partner.

3.2 Human Rights Included in FTA's "New Generation" Provisions

The promotion of human rights in EU new generation FTAs is not limited to the human rights clause. Indeed, FTAs contain provisions that relate to specific categories of human rights. This should not be seen as unnecessary duplication. The human rights clause is deliberately broad in scope, while the agreements address specific rights which are directly linked to trade and are framed within the broader objective of sustainable development. This is relevant for two main reasons. First, it ensures the protection of some categories of human rights even in agreements that do not contain a conditionality clause. Second, it represents the real innovation of these trade agreements, shaping a new evolutionary path. In this way, human rights are not just a general underlying principle of the agreement, but become an integral part of the FTA itself, directly linked to trade. This integration allows human rights to be more effectively embedded into the framework of reciprocal obligations between partners. In this respect, an important point to note is that there have been significant developments in EU new generation FTAs. The latest agreements contain additional and even more detailed provisions, following the European Commission's 2022 Communication "The Power of Trade Partnerships: Together for Green and Just Economic Growth.[96]

Looking at the agreements, it is clear that human rights are promoted in the agreements' chapter on trade and sustainable development, which is one of the main innovations and can be found in all EU new generation FTAs.[97] Sustainable development encompasses the social, environmental and economic dimensions. It recognizes that these dimensions are interconnected and mutually reinforcing.[98] Consequently, a key category of rights addressed in the EU FTAs in the framework

---

[96] Supra note 61.

[97] See EU-South Korea FTA, Chapter 13; EU-Colombia/Peru/Ecuador FTA, Title IX; EU-Central American Association agreement, Title VIII; CETA, Chapters 22, 23, and 24; EU-Japan EPA, Chapter 16; EU-Singapore FTA, Chapter 12; EU-Vietnam FTA, Chapter 13; EU-Chile Interim Agreement, Chapter 16; EU-Kenya PA, Annex V; EU-New Zealand FTA, Chapter 19. Rules on trade and sustainable development are included in the future agreement with Mercosur and Mexico and in the proposals EU has made for future agreements with Australia, ESA 5, India, Indonesia and Thailand.

[98] Report of the World Summit on Sustainable Development, Johannesburg, South Africa, 26 August–4 September 2002 (United Nations publication, Sales No. E.03.II.A.1 and corrigendum), chap. I, resolution 1, annex. On the topic of sustainable development, analysed from a legal perspective, see among others Freestone and Boyle (1999); Schrijver (2008); Barral (2012); Juste Ruiz et al. (2018); Buonfrate and Uricchio (2023).

of sustainable development relates to *labour*.[99] Parties commit to respect, promote and effectively implement internationally recognised core labour standards as defined in the ILO fundamental conventions. These include freedom of association and the effective recognition of the right to collective bargaining; the elimination of all forms of forced and compulsory labour; the abolition of child labour; elimination of discrimination in respect of employment and occupation. Only some of the agreements also refer to the right to a safe and healthy working environment.[100] Of particular importance is the commitment of the parties to ratify the fundamental ILO Conventions to which they are not yet parties and to exchange information regularly on their progress in ratifying ILO Conventions or Protocols. Parties also commit not to lower the level of protection of workers' rights in order to attract trade and investment and, conversely, not to use labour standards as a disguised restriction on trade.

Furthermore, within the broader framework of trade and sustainable development, a specific category of human rights is implicitly included: the so-called "third generation" human rights.[101] All agreements contain provisions on trade and the environment in the section on trade and sustainable development.[102] In these provisions, the parties commit themselves to effectively implement the Multilateral Environmental Agreements (MEAs) to which they are parties and to exchange information on their respective situation with respect to MEAs or their protocols. Particular attention is given, albeit with varying degrees of intensity, to the fight against climate change and to the Parties' commitment to comply with the Paris Agreement's emission reduction targets.[103] Indeed, meeting these commitments is

[99] EU-South Korea FTA, art. 13.4; EU-Colombia/Peru/Ecuador FTA, Art. 269; EU-Central American Association agreement, Art. 286; CETA, Chapter 23; EU-Japan EPA, Art. 16.3; EU-Singapore FTA, Chapter 12, Section B; EU-Vietnam FTA, Chapter 13.4; EU-Chile Interim Agreement, Chapter 16, Section C; EU-Kenya PA, Annex V, art. 3; EU-New Zealand FTA, Art. 19.3. See the contribution of Samantha Velluti in this volume.

[100] CETA, Art. 23.3(2)(a); EU-Chile, Art. 26.16(4)(e); EU-Kenya PA, Art. 2(3)(c). In the EU-New Zealand FTA, a transitional provision is included in Art. 19.3(4), which provides for a future amendment to Art. 19.3(3) to include the right to a safe and healthy environment.

[101] "Third generation" human rights, also known as "solidarity" rights, are both individual and collective rights belonging to all individuals and all peoples. International cooperation is crucial to give them effect and they can only be realized through the concerted efforts of all actors of the international community. Examples of such rights include the right to a healthy environment, access to clean water, clean air, the right to peace; see Vasak (1974), pp. 344–345.

[102] EU-South Korea FTA, Art. 13.5; EU-Colombia/Peru/Ecuador FTA, Art. 270; EU-Central American Association agreement, Art. 287; CETA, Chapter 24; EU-Japan EPA, Art. 16.4; EU-Singapore FTA, Chapter 12, Section C; EU-Vietnam FTA, Chapter 13.5; EU-Chile Interim Agreement, Chapter 16, Section B; EU-Kenya PA, Annex V, Art. 5; EU-New Zealand FTA, Art. 19.5. See the contribution of Francesca Martines in this volume.

[103] In this respect, the most ambitious agreements are the most recent ones, namely the EU-Chile Interim Agreement, Art. 26.10; the EU-Kenya Partnership Agreement, Art. 6; the EU-New Zealand Agreement, Art. 19.6. The EU-Kenya Partnership Agreement explicitly states that in the event of a violation by one Party of the obligation to refrain from any act or omission that materially defeats the object and purpose of the Paris Agreement, the other Party may take "*appropriate measures in accordance with the procedure set out in Article 96 of the Cotonou Agreement or the corresponding provisions of any successor agreement*"; Art. 6(4). In addition, as noted above, the recent political agreement on the partnership with Mercosur includes compliance with the Paris Agreement commitments in the conditionality clause.

essential to ensure the *right to a safe, clean, healthy and sustainable environment* for present and future generations.[104] By including these provisions in its agreements, the European Union can contribute to making this right operational and consolidating it in the international legal order.

Some of the EU new-generation trade agreements also contain provisions relating to third-generation human rights that are not included in the trade and sustainable development section. For example, some agreements include provisions on cooperation between the parties to facilitate the transition to "sustainable food systems".[105] This term refers to "*a food system which ensures access to safe, nutritious and sufficient food all year round, in a way that does not compromise the economic, social, cultural and environmental basis for food security and nutrition for future generations*".[106] This system is thus functional for the *right to food*, another third-generation human right.[107] Indeed, it is based on principles of intra- and inter-generational solidarity and aim to make food systems more accessible and resilient. In this perspective, such provisions are also in line with the principles underpinning the UN Declaration on the Rights of Peasants and Other People Working in Rural Areas, adopted by the General Assembly in 2018.[108] Essential to this objective is cooperation between the Parties, coordinated by a Sustainable Food Systems Committee, which is composed of representatives of each Party and co-chaired at the appropriate level by representatives of both Parties.

Similarly, some agreements include a commitment by the parties to the transition to a circular economy,[109] which has the potential to exercise an impact on human rights by promoting equitable resource distribution and supporting healthier environments. Indeed, the circular economy is a system of production and consumption that contrasts with the currently dominant linear economic model. The latter follows a pattern in which materials are "exploited, extracted, processed, consumed, and

---

[104] On 8 October 2021, the United Nations Human Rights Council adopted a resolution recognising a human right to a "safe, clean, healthy and sustainable environment"; UN Doc A/HRC/RES/48/13. This right was subsequently recognised by the UN General Assembly on 28 July 2022; UN Doc A/76/L.75. In addition, the Parliamentary Assembly of the Council of Europe has proposed the adoption of an additional protocol to the European Convention on Human Rights concerning the right to a "safe, clean, healthy and sustainable environment"; Resolution 2396 (2021). It is worth mentioning Human Rights Council resolution 48/14, which established the mandate for a Special Rapporteur on the protection and promotion of human rights in the context of climate change. On this topic, see Castellaneta (2000), pp. 913–964; Theil (2021).

[105] EU-Chile Interim Agreement, Chapter 7; EU-New Zealand FTA, Chapter 7. EU proposes to insert similar provisions in agreement with Indonesia, India, Thailand.

[106] EU-New Zealand FTA, art. 7.3.

[107] Committee on Economic, Social and Cultural Rights, General Comment No. 12 on the right to adequate food, E/C.12/1999/5. On this topic, see Söllner (2007), pp. 391–415.

[108] Resolution adopted by the General Assembly on 17 December 2018, United Nations Declaration on the Rights of Peasants and Other People Working in Rural Areas, A/RES/73/165.

[109] EU-Kenya PA, Art. 3(5)(a), Art. 6(5); EU-Chile Interim Agreement, Art. 26.10(2); EU-New Zealand FTA, Art. 19.5(5). Similar provisions can also be found in the agreement in principle with Mexico, the one with Mercosur and the proposals presented by the EU for agreements with Australia, ESA 5, India and Thailand.

discarded", making it unsustainable in the long term. The circular economy seeks to break this cycle by implementing a model that optimises product use, minimises waste and reduces the need to extract natural resources. Accordingly, EU-New Zealand FTA contains provisions aimed at "*facilitating trade and investment between the Parties to promote, develop and increase the production of energy from renewable sources and the sustainable production of raw materials, including through the use of green technologies*".[110] Particular attention is given to research, development and innovation activities to improve efficiency, sustainability and competitiveness in the energy and raw materials sectors.

Some agreements, particularly the more recent ones, also address the issue of *gender equality*—which is, *inter alia*, another EU value—in connection with trade and as a dimension of sustainable development. The issue has received attention at the international level, with the WTO showing increasing sensitivity to gender issues.[111] To date, however, no WTO agreement contains explicit provisions relating to gender. Nevertheless, gender issues are addressed in several regional trade agreements (RTAs). Of the 353 RTAs in force and notified to the WTO, 101 contain at least one explicit reference to gender issues.[112] The European Union's trade agreements, particularly the more recent ones, address this issue in a more comprehensive way. Whereas in the early new generation FTA gender issues were mainly addressed in the context of labour rights and within the broader objective of "working together on trade and sustainable development", more recent EU agreements now include a specific chapter on the issue.[113] In this chapter, the Parties undertake to ensure that their laws and policies promote and protect equal rights, treatment and opportunities. They also commit to improving these frameworks, while retaining the right to define their own scope and levels of protection for gender equality, provided that they are consistent with their international obligations. A key aspect of this commitment is to raise public awareness of the economic impact of gender equality policies. Accordingly, the Parties reaffirm their obligations under relevant

---

[110] EU-New Zealand FTA, Art. 13.1.

[111] In 2017, the Buenos Aires Declaration was adopted on the margin of the WTO Ministerial Conference and endorsed by 118 WTO members and observer countries. The Declaration aims to promote cooperation among WTO members to ensure that gender considerations are included in trade and development. See Joint Declaration on Trade and Women's Economic Empowerment on the Occasion of the WTO Ministerial Conference in Buenos Aires in December 2017. On 23 September 2020, an Informal Working Group on Trade and Gender was established to intensify efforts to increase women's participation in international trade. In addition, since 2016, the WTO Secretariat has been working to integrate gender considerations in accordance with the 2017–2020 Action Plan on Trade and Gender and the subsequent 2021–2026 plan.

[112] See Database on gender provisions in RTAs, available at the following link: https://www.wto.org/english/tratop_e/womenandtrade_e/gender_responsive_trade_agreement_db_e.htm. Accessed 27 February 2025.

[113] EU-Kenya PA, art. 4 of Annex V on Trade and Sustainable Development, EU-New Zealand FTA, art. 19.4 of Chapter 19 on Trade and Sustainable Development, EU-Chile Agreement, Chapter 27. The EU proposes to insert chapter on trade and gender in the future agreement with ESA 5, India, Thailand.

United Nations conventions, including the Convention on the Elimination of All Forms of Discrimination against Women. They also recognize their obligations under labour law, in particular with regard to the effective implementation of the ILO Conventions on gender equality and the elimination of discrimination in respect of employment and occupation.[114]

An innovative aspect of EU new generation FTAs is the inclusion of civil society mechanisms.[115] These are composed of Domestic Advisory Groups in each partner and a Joint Civil Society Forum, which brings together members of the Domestic Advisory Groups and other civil society representatives. Their main function is to monitor the implementation of the chapter on trade and sustainable development. In recent agreements, particularly those with Chile and New Zealand, their role has been strengthened as they are now involved in the implementation of the agreement beyond the trade and sustainable development chapter. This reflects a clear policy direction from the European Commission, promoted by the aforementioned Commission Communication "The power of trade partnerships: together for green and inclusive economic growth".[116] These mechanisms have the potential to make a significant contribution to the protection and promotion of human rights. However, their effectiveness remains to be fully assessed.[117]

The EU new generation FTAs also address another category of human rights which are linked to the risks connected with the digital environment, by including provisions on privacy and personal data protection.[118]

Another aspect that is addressed in recent EU FTAs concerns trade, responsible business conduct and supply chain management. The parties commit to promoting and complying with relevant international soft law instruments such as the OECD Guidelines for Multinational Enterprises, the ILO Tripartite Declaration of Principles concerning Multinational Enterprises and Social Policy, the UN Global Compact and the UN Guiding Principles on Business and Human Rights.

We also find more traditional trade-related provisions linked to human rights, such as intellectual property rights and sanitary and phytosanitary measures.

---

[114] Such as ILO, C100—Equal Remuneration Convention, 1951; ILO C111—Discrimination (Employment and Occupation) Convention, 1958; ILO C156—Workers with Family Responsibilities Convention, 1981; ILO C183—Maternity Protection Convention, 2000; ILO C190—Violence and Harassment Convention, 2019.

[115] EU-South Korea FTA, Art. 13.12 and Art. 13.13; EU-Colombia/Peru/Ecuador FTA, Art. 282; EU-Central American Association agreement, Art. 295; CETA, Art. 22.5; EU-Japan EPA, Art. 16.15 and Art. 16.16; EU-Chile Interim Agreement, Art. 33.5, Art. 33.6 and Art. 33.7; EU-Kenya PA, Art. 108; EU-New Zealand FTA, Art. 24.6 and Art. 24.7.

[116] Supra note 61.

[117] See Drieghe et al. (2022), pp. 581–596. It should also be noted that in some agreements, such as those with Vietnam and Singapore, there has been political resistance to the inclusion of such mechanisms. These agreements do not even mention the term "civil society", instead using the broader term "stakeholders": EU-Singapore FTA, Art. 12.15; EU-Vietnam FTA, Art. 13.15. On this point, see Thu and Schweißhelm (2020).

[118] See the contribution of Gabriele Rugani in this volume.

Finally, a concern for human rights can also be seen in the European Union's attempt to reform the investor-state dispute settlement mechanism, which is also being pursued through its trade agreements with third countries.[119] In fact, by promoting a more predictable and fairer system, it also aims to avoid the so-called "chilling effect", i.e. a disincentive for governments to adopt legitimate domestic regulations in the public interest because of the risk of exposing themselves and their taxpayers to liability under an investment treaty.

In the light of the above, it is clear that the European Union's new generation trade agreements address human rights beyond the conditionality clause. However, it is worth considering that the mechanisms provided in the majority of the agreements to ensure compliance with such provisions do not appear to be sufficient to ensure their enforcement. Indeed, in cases of non-compliance with sustainable development provisions, the vast majority of agreements provide for an ad hoc dispute settlement mechanism, which lacks a binding outcome and is distinct from the general mechanism provided for the commercial part. This undoubtedly weakens the human rights provisions embedded in the sustainable development section, relegating them to the realm of goodwill statements. However, it should be noted that there is a continuous evolution in this regard, in line with the objectives of the Commission Communication "The Power of Trade Partnerships: Working together for green and fair economic growth".[120] Indeed, this Communication proposes that sustainable development provisions should also be covered by the general dispute settlement mechanism, with the possibility of resorting to the imposition of trade sanctions as a last resort. A further observation is that, as noted above, human rights are also embedded in norms relating to more strictly commercial aspects. The extent to which they prove effective is both the challenge and the opportunity for trade agreements to make a real contribution in this area.

4 Upholding and Promoting the Right of Persons Belonging to Minorities in EU New Generation Trade Agreements

The analysis of how the European Union promotes the rights of persons belonging to minorities in its trade agreements requires a separate discussion. As noted above, the Treaty on European Union explicitly states that respect for human rights, one of the core values of the Union, includes the rights of persons belonging to

[119] CETA, Section F, arts. 8.18–8.45; EU-Singapore Investment Protection Agreement (not yet in force); EU-Vietnam Investment Protection Agreement (not yet in force); EU-Mexico Agreement (not yet in force); EU-Chile Advanced Framework agreement. On this subject, see the contribution of Francisco Pascual-Vives in this volume. See also the in-depth analysis by Pasquali (2024a, 2024b), pp. 383–435.

[120] Supra note 61.

minorities.[121] This protection is in line with the fundamental principles that characterise European society, as set out in Article 2 TEU: "*pluralism, non-discrimination, tolerance, justice, solidarity and equality between women and men*". Furthermore, Article 10 TFEU states: "*In defining and implementing its policies and activities, the Union shall aim to combat discrimination based on sex, racial or ethnic origin, religion or belief, disability, age or sexual orientation*".

Some of the European Union's new generation FTAs, which are the subject of our analysis, contain horizontal reservations in the lists of commitments related to establishment, allowing each party to adopt or maintain any measure granting rights or preferences to economically or socially disadvantaged minorities.[122] The EU-Central America Agreement—which is a comprehensive agreement that goes beyond the economic sphere and is based on three pillars, political dialogue, cooperation and trade—contains specific provisions on cooperation to promote the protection of the rights of indigenous peoples and minorities. In particular there is a commitment to respect the social, economic and cultural identity of these groups and promote their participation in key areas such as natural resource management, environmental protection, education and health care.[123] In any case, what characterizes the attention paid to minorities in EU FTAs is the attempt to protect them from the effects of trade, while no specific provision is included for their active participation in trade relations.

4.1 A Case of Study: EU-New Zealand FTA

The EU-New Zealand FTA shows the most innovative features. It is in fact the first EU FTA to include a specific chapter on indigenous peoples, in particular Māori, the indigenous population of "Aotearoa New Zealand".[124] In this regard, it is worth noting that indigenous peoples have specific characteristics that often associate them with the concept of "minority", even though there is not a perfect overlap between the two.[125] Indeed, although there is no internationally accepted definition, according to Capotorti, a minority is understood as a "*group numerically inferior to the rest of the population of a State, in a non-dominant position, whose members—being nationals of the State—possess ethnic, religious or linguistic characteristics differing from those of the rest of the population and show, if only implicitly, a sense*

[121] On the topic of minority protection within the European Union, see Bilgin (2019), pp. 92–115; Carta (2019), pp. 128–134. Regarding the interaction between EU and international law on protecting minorities, see Tóth (2022).

[122] Provisions of this kind can be found in CETA, Central America Association Agreement, EU-Colombia-Perù-Ecuador FTA, EU-South Korea.

[123] EU-Central America Association agreement, Art. 43 and Art. 45.

[124] EU-New Zealand FTA, Chapter 20.

[125] Castellino and Doyle (2018).

of solidarity, directed towards preserving their culture, religion or language".[126] On the contrary, indigenous peoples are those who "*on account of their descent from the populations which inhabited the country, or a geographical region to which the country belongs, at the time of conquest or colonisation or the establishment of present state boundaries and who, irrespective of their legal status, retain some or all of their own social, economic, cultural and political institutions*".[127] Thus, the fundamental difference lies in the fact that minorities share the element of nationality with the majority population of the country, whereas indigenous peoples, often numerically inferior, have an historical peculiarity: they have experienced a process of superimposition by the group that later became the majority. The protection of the rights of indigenous peoples can thus be included in the protection of minority rights if their role as a minority is recognized,[128] as in the case of the Māori in New Zealand. However, it is important to acknowledge the unique status of the Māori, who, as an Indigenous people, cannot be fully assimilated into a minority group.[129] For the purposes of this study, however, the provisions contained in the FTA may serve as a reference point for identifying a potential virtuous model that could be replicated in future agreements, albeit with necessary adaptations to the specific context.

In examining the EU-New Zealand agreement, it is immediately clear that Māori interests play a significant role. This is also due to the active participation of Māori organizations in the negotiations that led to its conclusion.[130] As evidence of this increased attention, the word "Māori" appears approximately 80 times throughout the agreement, which constitutes, with the exception of the New Zealand-United Kingdom FTA,[131] a real innovation.[132]

The relationship between indigenous peoples and trade is a subject of ongoing discussion and interest.[133] So far, however, these two agreements remain unique in their characteristics.

The agreement between the EU and New Zealand contains in the first place more "classical" provisions. In particular, it contains a clause that allows New Zealand to take any necessary measures to provide more favourable treatment to Māori in

[126] Capotorti (1979) Special Rapporteur of the Sub-Commission on Prevention of Discrimination and Protection of Minorities, Study on the rights of persons belonging to ethnic, religious and linguistic minorities, E/CN.4/Sub.2/384/Rev.1.

[127] ILO, C169—Indigenous and Tribal Peoples Convention, 1989, Art. 1.

[128] Cf. Kugelmann (2007), p. 239.

[129] Charters (2024), p. 470.

[130] See https://www.mfat.govt.nz/en/trade/free-trade-agreements/free-trade-agreements-in-force/new-zealand-european-union-free-trade-agreement/maori-interests#bookmark4.

[131] Free Trade Agreement between the United Kingdom of Great Britain and Northern Ireland and New Zealand signed on 28 February 2022, available at the following link: https://www.mfat.govt.nz/assets/Trade-agreements/UK-NZ-FTA/NZ-UK-Free-Trade-Agreement.pdf.

[132] For a comparison between the EU-New Zealand FTA and the UK-New Zealand FTA, see Riffel (2024), pp. 445–468.

[133] See Borrows and Schwartz (2020).

matters covered by the Agreement, including in fulfilling its obligations under the Treaty of Waitangi,[134] provided that such measures do not constitute a disguised restriction on trade.[135] It also explicitly states that the interpretation of the Treaty of Waitangi is not subject to the dispute settlement mechanism of the Agreement. Indeed, the Union may request the establishment of a panel only to determine whether a measure is capable of impairing its rights under the agreement.[136] The agreement also recognizes New Zealand's right to regulate for the promotion and protection of Māori rights, interests, duties and responsibilities.[137]

Turning to the more innovative aspects of the FTA, it is evident that it contains provisions that demonstrate a clear intention to respect Māori cultural rights.[138] In the chapter on "Economic and Trade Cooperation with Māori" of the EU-New Zealand FTA, the parties commit to base their trade cooperation on respect for "*te ao Māori*", namely the Māori worldview which takes a holistic approach that recognizes the close relationship between humans and nature. The parties also agree to give due consideration to "*tikanga Māori*"—Māori protocols, customs and traditional practices—and "*mātauranga Māori*"—traditional Māori knowledge related to *te ao Māori*. For example, manuka is considered a separate category of goods as it is a product that is culturally important to Māori as a *taonga* (*taonga* means the connection between Māori, their ancestors and the land) and is a traditional medicine for them.[139] This is significant. It represents an openness to understanding a different cultural approach, embracing its complexity and establishing a common ground for cooperation and dialogue. This mutual understanding is also important for another reason. Indigenous peoples tend to have a closer relationship with nature and their traditional practices often offer valuable lessons on sustainability. Their role should therefore be recognized and enhanced, especially when the objective is to use trade as a tool to achieve sustainable development.

Another indigenous people right covered by the Agreement is the right of participation. Chapter 24 provides for the inclusion of Māori representatives in domestic advisory groups and civil society forums.[140] The participation of Māori will ensure that their interests and perspectives are incorporated into the overall implementation of the FTA. Further attention to Māori rights is given in the chapter on digital trade,

[134] The Treaty of Waitangi (te Tiriti o Waitangi) is fundamental to understand the relationship between New Zealand and Māori. Signed in 1840 between the chiefs of the indigenous tribes and the British Crown, the Treaty continues to govern the relationship between the Māori and the New Zealand government, recognising Māori sovereignty over their lands, the protection of their culture and the right to self-determination.

[135] EU-New Zealand FTA, Art. 25.6(1).

[136] EU-New Zealand FTA, Art. 25.6(2).

[137] EU-New Zealand FTA, Art. 10.1; Art. 12.3.

[138] As recognised by the 2007 UN Declaration on the Rights of Indigenous Peoples, Official Records of the General Assembly, Sixty-first Session, Supplement No. 53 (A/61/53), part one, chap. II, sect. A.

[139] EU-New Zealand FTA, Art. 20.4.

[140] EU-New Zealand FTA, Art. 24.6 and Art. 24.7.

which explicitly provides for Māori participation in the possible revision of provisions on personal data flows and data protection.[141] In addition, the article on trade and gender equality commits the parties to ensure that *wāhine Māori* (Māori women) have access to and benefit from the opportunities created by the FTA.[142]

Given the above, it is evident that this agreement introduces significant innovations in the protection of Māori rights and could serve as a model for future trade agreements, both bilateral and multilateral.

5 Final Remarks

The European Union's effort to uphold and promote human rights in the world, as provided for in the Treaties, is pursued in diverse ways. This chapter has examined these promotional efforts in the context of the "new generation" trade agreements recently concluded by the European Union. These agreements are characterized by the fact that, in addition to provisions dealing specifically with trade issues, they contain clauses that go beyond the WTO system and incorporate broader considerations, including non-commercial aspects. Such agreements have the potential to serve as a privileged instrument for promoting EU values by favouring mutually acceptable solutions. The very nature of these agreements facilitates the convergence of the interests of the parties and enables them to reach a compromise, usually after lengthy negotiations. In this context, the European Union can take advantage of its privileged position as one of the world's largest players in global trade. At the same time, this dialectical process ensures that the discussion goes beyond the mere "imposition" of values. The analysis in the second section has highlighted that the new generation FTAs address human rights beyond the non-execution clause and thus represent an innovation in this regard. They provide a replicable example of how human rights considerations can be integrated into trade and linked to the broader objective of sustainable development. However, it is also worth noting that this inclusion remains largely limited to the sustainable development sections (which, in the case of the majority of agreements, are not covered by the binding dispute settlement mechanism), although the agreements include provisions linked to human rights considerations in the trade section. One interesting aspect concerns the promotion of the rights of persons belonging to minorities. In particular, the European Union has recently adopted an innovative approach in its FTA with New Zealand. This approach entails a more active involvement of the Māori in trade relations while ensuring the protection of their cultural identity. It is considered desirable that this should serve as a model for bilateral and multilateral trade agreements in the future.

[141] EU-New Zealand FTA, Art. 12.4.

[142] EU-New Zealand FTA, Art. 19.4(7).

Another consideration that can be drawn from the analysis in this chapter is that the new generation of FTAs reflects the European Union's strategy of positioning itself as a responsible global leader committed to strengthening the international system, rather than as an actor seeking to "export" its values. The FTAs consistently refer to instruments adopted at the international level, including very recent ones, with the aim of contributing to their implementation through the agreements themselves. This could also serve as an interesting model that could be applied in the wider multilateral context as well.

However, a less positive evaluation can be made of the mechanisms put in place in the vast majority of EU FTAs to ensure compliance with these provisions. Both in terms of the enforcement of the conditionality clause in agreements that include it, and in terms of the protection of human rights linked to specific provisions within these agreements, there remains a risk that the commitments made will amount to little more than goodwill statements. This in turn underlines the continuing challenge of ensuring a coherent and consistent EU approach in this area. The EU could, for example, choose not to fully enforce such provisions in order to prevent its current and future trading partners from being lured away by other economic powers, such as China, which do not require the same standards. Thus, whether the EU will fully commit to enforcing these provisions, or whether economic considerations will ultimately prevail, remains to be seen.

References

Adinolfi G (2021) Gli accordi preferenziali di nuova generazione dell'Unione europea. Giappichelli, Torino

Adinolfi G, Malatesta A, Vellano M (2022) L'accordo sugli scambi commerciali e la cooperazione tra l'Unione Europea e il Regno Unito. Giappichelli, Torino

Auld K, Del Savio L, Feris L (2024) An environmental agreement in a trade court – is the WTO's agreement on fisheries subsidies enforceable? World Trade Rev:25–49

Barral V (2012) Sustainable development in international law: nature and operation of an evolutive legal norm. EJIL 23:377–400

Bartels L (2005) Human rights conditionality in the EU's international agreements. Oxford University Press, Oxford

Bartels L (2007) The WTO legality of the EU's GSP+ arrangement. J Int Econ Law 10:869–886

Barthesaghi I, De Maria Calvelo N, Melgar Alassio N, Pereira ME (2019) La nueva generación de acuerdos de la Unión Europea y sus implicancias en el sistema internacional. In: Tremolada Álvarez E (ed) Gobernanza, cooperación internacional y valores democráticos communes. Universidad Externado de Colombia, Bogotà, pp 447–477

Berry S (2018) Aligning interculturalism with international human rights law: 'living together' without assimilation. Hum Rights Law Rev 18:441–471

Bilgin A (2019) Minority protection in the European Union. Int J Minority Group Rights 26:92–115

Blanc Altemir A (2020) La Unión Europea, promotora del libre comercio. Análisis e impacto de los principales Acuerdos comerciales. Thomson Reuters Aranzadi, Cizur Menor

Borlini L (2016) L'Unione Europea: attore 'globale' nella protezione e promozione dei diritti umani? Limiti e prospettive. DPCE Online:93–132

Borrows J, Schwartz R (2020) Indigenous peoples and international trade. Building equitable and inclusive international trade and investment agreements. Cambridge University Press, Cambridge

Buonfrate A, Uricchio A (2023) Trattato breve di diritto dello sviluppo sostenibile. CEDAM, Milano

Cannizzaro E (2015) The EU's human rights obligations in relation to policies with extraterritorial effects: a reply to Lorand Bartels. EJIL 25:1093–1099

Cannizzaro E (2021) The value of the EU international values. In: Douma WT, Eckes C, Van Elsuwege P, Kassoti E, Ott A, Wessel RA (eds) The evolving nature of EU external relations law. T.M.C. Asser Press, The Hague, pp 3–18

Capotorti F (1979) Study on the rights of persons belonging to ethnic, religious and linguistic minorities, E/CN.4/Sub.2/384/Rev.1.

Carbone M (2024) Beyond the Heaven-Hell binary and the one-way traffic paradigm: the European Union, Africa and contested human rights in the negotiations of the Samoa agreement. JCMS 62:1314–1331

Carta MC (2019) La tutela delle minoranze: i principi ispiratori della risoluzione del Parlamento Europeo del 13 novembre 2018. Ordine Int Diritti Umani:120–134

Castellaneta M (2000) L'individuo e la protezione dell'ambiente nel diritto internazionale. Rivista Diritto Int:913–964

Castellino J, Doyle C (2018) Who are 'indigenous peoples'? An examination of concepts concerning group membership in the UNDRIP. In: Hohmann J, Weller M (eds) The UN declaration on the rights of indigenous peoples: a commentary. Oxford University Press, Oxford, pp 7–37

Charters C (2024) A deeper understanding of the constitutional status of Māori and their rights required: a reply to Christian Riffel. Eur J Int Law:469–478

Cottier T, Pauwelyn J, Bürgi E (2005) Human rights and international trade. Oxford University Press, Oxford

de Búrca M (2011) The road not taken: the European Union as a global human rights actor. AJIL 105:649–693

Donnely J (2007) The relative universality of human rights. Hum Rights Quart:281–306

Drieghe L, Orbie J, Potjomkina D, Shahin J (2022) Participation of civil society in EU trade policy making: how inclusive is inclusion? New Polit Econ:581–596

Fahey E, Mancini I (2022) Understanding the EU as a good global actor. Ambitions, values and metrics. Edward Elgar Publishing, Cheltenham, UK

Fernández Rozas JC (2019) Permanencia y expansión del bilateralismo: los acuerdos comerciales de "Nueva Generación" entre la Unión Europea y terceros países. La Ley Unión Eur:1–59

Flinn J (2014) Reframing the intercultural dialogue on human rights. A philosophical approach. Abingdon, Routledge, New York

Freestone A, Boyle D (1999) International law and sustainable development: past achievements and future challenges. Oxford University Press, Oxford

Hachez N, Marx A (2021) EU trade policy and human rights. In: Wouters J, Ovádek M (eds) The European Union and human rights - law and policy. Oxford University Press, Oxford, pp 365–385

Hahn M, Van der Loo G (2021) Law and practice of the common commercial policy. The first 10 years after the Treaty of Lisbon. Brill, Leiden-Boston

Horng DC (2003) The human rights clause in the European Union's external trade and development agreements. Eur Law J:677–701

Ibrahim A (2013) International trade and human rights: an unfinished debate. German Law J 14:321–337

Juste Ruiz J, Bou Franch V, Pereira Coutinho F (2018) Desarrollo sostenible y derecho internacional. Dykinson, Valencia

Kübek G, Tams C, Terhechte JP (2024) EU-UK Trade and Cooperation Agreement - A Handbook. Bloomsbury Publishing, Beck/Hart/Nomos

Kugelmann D (2007) The protection of minorities and indigenous peoples respecting cultural diversity. In: von Bogdandy A, Wolfrum R (eds) Max Planck yearbook of UN law, vol 11. Brill, Leiden-Boston, pp 233–263

Lillo J (2024) La dimensione istituzionale e la condizionalità nell'Accordo di Samoa. Uno studio retrospettivo per comprendere il futuro delle relazioni UE-ACP. Studi Sull'integrazione Eu XIX:271–298

Lochak D (2012) Les droits de l'homme dans les accords d'association et de coopération conclus par l'Union européenne. In: Benlolo-Carabot M, Candas U, Cujo E (eds) Union européenne et droit international. En l'honneur de Patrick Daillier. Editions A. Pedone, Paris, pp 539–549

Maillo J (2021) Acuerdos comerciales UE de "Nueva Generación": origen, rasgos y valoración. Fundación Universitaria San Pablo CEU

Marquardt S, Blockmans S (2023) The European Union's contribution to international peace and security: Liber Amicorum in honour of Gert-Jan van Hegelsom. Brill, Leiden-Boston

Marrella F (2011) Verso una nuova politica commerciale internazionale dell'Ue dopo il Trattato di Lisbona? Alcune riflessioni. Lavoro e Diritto 25:89–103

Marrella F (2014) Unione Europea, Commercio internazionale e diritti umani. In: Treu T, Garofoli R (eds) Treccani, Il libro dell'anno del diritto 2014. Istituto dell'Enciclopedia Italiana Treccani, Roma, pp 747–750

Martines F (2005) Sistemi di preferenze generalizzate, la normativa comunitaria e il diritto dell'OMC. Il diritto dell'Unione Europea:287–316

Martines F (2016) Human rights clauses in EU Agreement. CLEER Papers:37–62

Martines F (2020) EU political conditionality as a tool for the promotion and protection of non-trade values in non-EU countries. In: Velluti S (ed) The role of the EU in the promotion of human rights and international labour standards in its external trade relations. Springer, Cham, pp 97–180

Melo Araujo B (2016) The EU deep trade agenda: law and policy. Oxford University Press, Oxford

Mickelson K (1998) How universal is the universal declaration? Univ New Brunswick Law J 47:19–48

Pasquali L (2024a) La contribución del acuerdo Unión Europea-México a la gobernanza medioambiental internacional. In: Petrucci A, Gómez Alcalá R (eds) Uniformación, internacionalización y regionalismo en el Derecho (con énfasis en el Derecho Privado). Editorial Tirant Lo Blanch México, pp 199–249

Pasquali L (2024b) La protección de las inversiones en el tratado comercial entre la Unión Europea y México. In: Petrucci A, Gómez Alcalá R (eds) Uniformación, internacionalización y regionalismo en el Derecho (con énfasis en el Derecho Privado). Editorial Tirant Lo Blanch México, pp 383–435

Peraldi Leneuf F (2020) Les Valeurs de l'Union européenne. Pedone, Paris

Pollis A, Schwab P (1979) Human rights? A western construct with limited applicability. In: Pollis A, Schwab P (eds) Human rights? Cultural and ideological perspectives. Praeger, New York, pp 1–18

Riffel C (2024) Constitutional law-making by international law: the indigenization of free trade agreements. EJIL 35:445–468

Ruotolo G (2016) Gli accordi commerciali di ultima generazione dell'Unione europea e i loro rapporti col sistema multilaterale degli scambi. Studi Sull'integrazione Eur:329–354

Schrijver NJ (2008) The evolution of sustainable development in international law: inception, meaning and status. Brill, Leiden-Boston

Söllner S (2007) Interpretation of the human right to food. Max Planck Yearbook of United Nations Law Online, pp 391–415

Suárez Müller F (2012) Eurocentrism, human rights, and humanism. Int J Appl Philos 26:279–293

Theil S (2021) Towards the environmental minimum: environmental protection through human rights. Cambridge University Press, Cambridge

Thu MH, Schweißhelm E (2020) Labour rights and civil society empowerment in the EU-Vietnam Free Trade Agreement. In: IPE working papers 135/2020. School of Economics and Law, Institute for International Political Economy (IPE), Berlin

Tóth N (2022) European Union law and international minority rights law. In: Malloy T, Vizi B (eds) Research handbook on minority politics in the European Union. Edward Elgar Publishing, Cheltenham

Tuominen H (2022) Effective human rights promotion and protection? The EU and its member states at the UN human rights council. J Common Market Stud 61(4):935–950

Van Elsuwege P, De Coninck J (2022) The effectiveness of human rights clauses in EU Trade Agreements: challenges and opportunities. Policy report. Ghent European Law Institute (GELI)

Vasak K (1974) Le droit international des droits de l'homme. In: Collected courses of The Hague Academy of International Law - recueil des cours, vol 140

Velluti S (2016) Human rights conditionality in the EU GSP scheme: a focus on those in need or a need to refocus? In: Ferreira N, Kostakopoulou D (eds) The human face of the European Union. Are EU law and policy humane enough? Cambridge University Press, Cambridge, pp 342–366

Velluti S (2020) The role of the EU in the promotion of human rights and international labour standards in its external trade relations. Springer, Cham

Vincent P (2021) Les nouveaux accords commerciaux conclus par l'Union Européenne. Cahiers de Science Politique de l'Université de Liège, pp 54–76

Viola F (2006) L'universalità dei diritti umani: un'analisi concettuale. In: Botturi F, Totaro F (eds) Universalismo ed etica pubblica. Vita e Pensiero, Milano, pp 155–187

von Danwitz T (2018) Les accords externes de l'Union européenne en matière commerciale et la contribution de la Cour de justice. Rev Droit l'Union Eur:201–207

Walker S (2009) The future of human rights impact assessments of trade agreements. Intersentia, Antwerp, Portland

Walz S (2002) Reclaiming and rebuilding the history of the universal declaration of human rights. Third World Quarterly 23:437–448

Williams A (2004) EU human rights policies: a study in Irony. Oxford University Press, Oxford

Wouters J, Ovádek M (2021) Human rights in EU external action. In: Wouters J, Ovádek M (eds) The European Union and human rights - law and policy. Oxford University Press, Oxford, pp 539–645

The International Investment Agreements Concluded by the European Union: Moving Toward an Institutionalization of International Investment Law

Francisco Pascual-Vives

Contents

Abstract This chapter examines how the EU is contributing to the ISDS reform. It analyses how the new international agreements concluded by the EU with third States (Canada, Chile, Singapore, and Vietnam) may promote a progressive institutionalization of ISDS in international investment law. It further analyses the practice of the EU within the codification process undertaken by UNCITRAL

This chapter has been also prepared within the framework of the project "Toward a New Legal Framework for Socially Responsible and Sustainable Investments: International Law and European Union Responses" (Ref. PID2023-149020NB-I00).

F. Pascual-Vives (✉)
School of Law, University of Alcalá, Alcalá de Henares - Madrid, Spain
e-mail: f.pascualvives@uah.es

L. Pasquali (ed.), *EU Values and International Law*, European Union and its Neighbours in a Globalized World 35,
https://doi.org/10.1007/978-3-032-20521-6_10

Working Group III, with the objective of comparing if the proposals that the EU has made in this multilateral forum to address the general concerns identified are consistent with the EU agreements already concluded. The chapter focuses on the procedural mechanisms proposed by the EU to enhance the consistency, coherence, predictability, and correctness of arbitral decisions, in particular through the creation of an appellate body and a standing mechanism to settle investment claims as well as through the avoidance of both frivolous claims and the disruptive effects of multiple proceedings.

1 Introduction

The initiatives undertaken by the European Union (EU) in the field of foreign direct investment (FDI) protection since the Treaty of Lisbon came into force can be classified in diverse categories.

First, the EU has adopted secondary law to systematize different aspects of its competence on FDI. In this vein, it has established[1] and updated[2] the legal regime on FDI screening.[3] And it has also adopted a framework for managing financial responsibility linked to investor-to-state dispute settlement (ISDS) tribunals established by international agreements to which the EU is a party.[4]

Secondly, the Court of Justice of the EU (CJEU) has rendered judgments in several cases dealing with the compatibility between EU law and international

[1] Regulation (EU) 2019/452 of the European Parliament and of the Council of 19 March 2019 establishing a framework for the screening of foreign direct investments into the Union (OJ L 79 I, 21 March 2019, p. 1).

[2] Commission Delegated Regulation (EU) 2020/1298 of 13 July 2020 amending the Annex to Regulation (EU) 2019/452 of the European Parliament and of the Council establishing a framework for the screening of foreign direct investments into the Union (OJ L 304, 18 September 2020, p. 1); Commission Delegated Regulation (EU) 2021/2126 of 29 September 2021 amending the Annex to Regulation (EU) 2019/452 of the European Parliament and of the Council establishing a framework for the screening of foreign direct investments into the Union (OJ L 432, 3 December 2021, p. 1).

[3] In addition, the EU is undertaking ambitious reforms with the aim of expanding this legal framework: see Proposal for a Regulation of the European Parliament and the Council on the screening of foreign investments in the Union and repealing Regulation (EU) 2019/452 of the European Parliament and of the Council, COM(2024), 23 final, 24 January 2024; White Paper on Outbound Investments, COM(2024), 24 final, 24 January 2024; White Paper on Export Controls, COM(2024), 25 final, 24 January 2024; Proposal for a Council Recommendation on enhancing research security, COM(2024), 26 final, 24 January 2024; White Paper on options for enhancing support for research and development involving technologies with dual-use potential, COM(2024), 27 final, 24 January 2024.

[4] Regulation (EU) No. 912/2014 of the European Parliament and of the Council of 23 July 2014 establishing a framework for managing financial responsibility linked to investor-to-state dispute settlement tribunals established by international agreements to which the European Union is party (OJ L 257, 28 August 2014, p. 121).

investment law.[5] In some cases, the CJEU has adopted a pragmatic stance. This approach advocates for the recognition of the principle of autonomy of EU law.[6] However, it puts the harmony between international law and EU law in check.[7]

Thirdly, the EU is actively participating in the modernization of the ISDS.[8] This task is undertaken in several multilateral fora, including the International Centre for Settlement of International Investment Disputes (ICSID)[9] and the United Nations Commission on International Trade Law (UNCITRAL).[10]

And fourthly, the EU has negotiated international trade agreements with third States that include provisions regulating the protection of foreign investments and a new ISDS system.[11] These are not traditional bilateral investment treaties (BITs). They encompass diverse areas. But they all contain a chapter devoted to the promotion and protection of foreign investments envisaging a new ISDS.

---

[5] Judgment 3 March 2009, *Commission v. Republic of Austria*, C-205/06, ECLI:EU:C:2009: 118; Judgment 3 March 2009, *Commission v. Kingdom of Sweden*, C-249/06, ECLI: EU: C:2009: 119; Judgment 19 November 2009, *Commission v. Republic of Finland*, C-118/07, ECLI: EU:C:2009:715; Judgment 15 September 2011, *Commission v. Slovak Republic*, C-264/09, ECLI:EU:C:2011:580; Opinion 16 May 2017, *Free Trade Agreement between the European Union and the Republic of Singapore*, 2/15, ECLI:EU:C:2017:376; Opinion 30 April 2019, *Comprehensive Economic and Trade Agreement between Canada, of the one part, and the European Union and its Member States, of the other part (CETA)*, 1/17, ECLI:EU:C:2019:341; Judgment 2 September 2021, *Republic of Moldova v. Komstroy LLC*, C-741/19, ECLI:EU:C:2021:655; Judgment 20 October 2021, *Republic of Poland v. PL Holdings S.à r.l.*, C-109/20, ECLI:EU:C:2021:875; Opinion 16 June 2022, *Draft modernised Energy Charter Treaty*, 1/20; ECLI:EU:C:2022:485.

[6] Contartese (2017), pp. 1627–1672; Hindelang (2019), pp. 383–400; Scheu and Nikolov (2019), pp. 474–504; van Rossem (2020), 35–68; Pascual-Vives (2022), pp. 669–693.

[7] Judgment 6 March 2018, *Slovak Republic v. Achmea BV*, C-284/16, ECLI:EU:C:2018:158; Judgment 14 March 2024, *Commission v. United Kingdom*, C-516/22, ECLI:EU:C:2024:231.

[8] In 2013 the United Nations Conference on Trade and Development (UNCTAD) made some proposals to reform the ISDS system based on five points "Promoting alternative dispute resolution; Tailoring the existing system through individual IIAs; Limiting investor access to ISDS; Introducing an appeals facility; Creating a standing international investment court": see UNCTAD (2013) Reform of Investor-State Dispute Settlement: In Search of a Roadmap.

https://unctad.org/system/files/official-document/webdiaepcb2013d4_en.pdf. Accessed 10 December 2024.

[9] Council Decision (EU) 2022/438 of 14 March 2022 on the position to be adopted on behalf of the European Union within the Administrative Council of the International Centre for Settlement of Investment Disputes (OJ L 89, 17 March 2022, p. 8).

[10] A/CN.9/WG.III/WP.145, 12 December 2017; A/CN.9/WG.III/WP.159, 24 January 2019; A/CN.9/WG.III/WP.159/Add.1, 24 January 2019; A/CN.9/WG.III/WP.231, 26 July 2023; A/CN.9/WG.III/WP.235, 20 November 2023.

[11] The EU has provided some guidance to the conventional activity developed on this subject by its member States before and after the latter attributed this competence to the former: see Regulation (EU) No. 1219/2012 of the European Parliament and of the Council of 12 December 2012 establishing transitional arrangements for bilateral investment agreements between Member States and third countries (OJ L 351, 20 December 2012, p. 40); Non-Paper on Annotations to the Model Clauses for negotiation or re-negotiation of Member States' Bilateral Investment Agreements with third countries, 21 September 2023.

This chapter examines how the EU is contributing to the ISDS reform. It analyses how the new international agreements concluded by the EU with third States may promote a progressive institutionalization of ISDS.[12]

In particular, the international agreements concluded with Canada,[13] Chile,[14] Singapore,[15] and Vietnam[16] are used as evidence. We further analyse the practice of the EU within UNCITRAL Working Group III (WG III), with the objective of comparing if the proposals that the EU has made in this multilateral forum to address the general concerns identified[17] keep in tune with the conventional practice of the EU with third States.

The chapter is divided in three sections. In Sect. 2 we delve into the procedural mechanisms designed to enhance consistency, coherence, predictability, and correctness of the decisions adopted by arbitral tribunals. In Sect. 3 we examine the way frivolous claims are being discouraged within the ISDS reform. And finally, in Sect. 4 we study the tools developed to mitigate the disruptive effects of multiple proceedings.

2 Promoting Consistency, Coherence, Predictability and Correctness of Arbitral Decisions

Arbitral decisions constitute a very heterogeneous body of caselaw because of the decentralised nature of investment arbitration[18] and the challenges arising from treaty shopping.[19] The EU is promoting the use procedural instruments designed to overcome such heterogeneity. Although in a reactive manner,[20] these tools enhance the consistency, coherence, predictability, and correctness of arbitral decisions.

---

[12] This trend erodes the bilateral and decentralized nature that has traditionally characterized the ISDS system: see Vadi (2018), pp. 14–15.

[13] Signed on 30 October 2016.

[14] Signed on 13 December 2023.

[15] Signed on 15 October 2018.

[16] Signed on 30 June 2019.

[17] A/CN.9/WG.III/WP.159/Add.1, 24 January 2019, para. 6.

[18] As shown by the interpretation given by investment tribunals to the state of necessity defence in several cases against Argentina: see Zarra (2018), pp. 137–185.

[19] Foote (2022) pp. 31–46.

[20] Proactive measures (such as preliminary rulings before the CJEU) would also lessen this challenge: see Schreuer (2007).

2.1 Heterogeneity as an Integral Part of the Current ISDS System

The EU has highlighted before UNCITRAL WG III that each arbitral decision is issued by an investment tribunal composed by different members, responding to particular facts and circumstances and within a diverse legal context. All these factors may condition their consistency, coherence, predictability, and correctness.[21]

The way in which arbitral tribunals have addressed the relationship between EU law and the Energy Charter Treaty serves as an example.[22] Though arbitral tribunals have noted the need to make a harmonious interpretation of both legal sectors, they have taken diverse roads toward achieving this objective.

In *Electrabel*, an arbitral tribunal found the inexistence of "a general principle of international law compelling the harmonious interpretation of different treaties. This may be a desirable outcome; but the end does not establish the means to that end".[23] Conversely, the arbitral tribunal in *RREEF Infrastructure* found that "in case two treaties are [...] applicable, they must be interpreted in such a way as not to contradict each other".[24]

In other cases, the seat of the arbitration has conditioned the result of the dispute. When the seat of the arbitration has been an EU member State, jurisdiction over certain investment claims brought against EU member States has been rejected,[25] or the enforcement of an award favourable to the foreign investor has been stayed considering the primacy of EU law.[26]

---

[21] A/CN.9/WG.III/WP.145, 12 December 2017, para. 22–25.

[22] Signed on 17 December 1994. On 30 May 2024, having obtained the European Parliament's consent, the Council agreed on the EU and Euratom's withdrawal from the Energy Charter Treaty: see Council Decision (EU) 2024/1638 of 30 May 2024 on the withdrawal of the Union from the Energy Charter Treaty (OJ L, 5 June 2024); Council Decision (EU) 2024/1677 of 30 May 2024 on the approval of the withdrawal of the European Atomic Energy Community from the Energy Charter Treaty (OJ L, 13 June 2024). The withdrawal of the EU and the Euratom from the Energy Charter Treaty was notified to the depositary of the treaty on 27 June 2024.

[23] *Electrabel S.A. v. Hungary* (ICSID Case No. ARB/07/19, Decision 30 November 2012, para. 4.130).

[24] *RREEF Infrastructure (G.P.) Limited and RREEF Pan-European Infrastructure Two Lux S.à r.l. v. Kingdom of Spain* (ICSID Case No. ARB/13/30, Decision 6 June 2016, para. 76).

[25] *Green Power Partners K/S and SCE Solar Don Benito APS v. Kingdom of Spain* (SCC Case No. 2016/135, Award 16 June 2022, para. 474–477).

[26] *Greentech Energy Systems A/S, NovEnergia II Energy & Environment (SCA) SICAR, and NovEnergia II Italian Portfolio SA v. Italian Republic* (SCC Case No. 2015/095, Award 23 December 2018); Svea Court of Appeal, Division 2, Section 020102, Case No. T 3229–19, Judgment 28 March 2019. To the contrary, in an arbitration whose seat was in Switzerland the international award was upheld: see Tribunal Fédéral de Suisse, ârret du 23 février 2021, 4A_187/2020.

Investment claims administered by ICSID tribunals, also involving EU member States, have been more favourable to the interests[27] of foreign investors acting as claimants,[28] since ICSID awards are considered binding international decisions pursuant to Article 54 of the ICSID Convention.[29]

It is important to note that these investment claims have different objects. Though they all involve the interpretation and application of the same international investment agreement (the Energy Charter Treaty[30]).

This nuance is relevant because on occasions, the decisions adopted by investment tribunals arise from the interpretation and application of diverse international

---

[27] At least in the case of Spain: see *Masdar Solar & Wind Cooperatief U.A. v. Kingdom of Spain* (ICSID Case No. ARB/14/1, Award 16 May 2018); *Antin Infrastructure Services Luxembourg S.à r.l. and Antin Energia Termosolar B.V. v. Kingdom of Spain* (ICSID Case No. ARB/13/31, Award 15 June 2018); *NextEra Energy Global Holdings B.V. and NextEra Energy Spain Holdings B.V. v. Kingdom of Spain* (ICSID Case No. ARB/14/11, Award 12 March 2019); *9REN Holding S.à r.l v. Kingdom of Spain* (ICSID Case No. ARB/15/15, Award 31 May 2019); *Cube Infrastructure Fund SICAV and others v. Kingdom of Spain* (ICSID Case No. ARB/15/20, Award 15 July 2019); *SolEs Badajoz GmbH v. Kingdom of Spain* (ICSID Case No. ARB/15/38, Award 31 July 2019); *InfraRed Environmental Infrastructure GP Limited and others v. Kingdom of Spain* (ICSID Case No. ARB/14/12, Award 2 August 2019); *OperaFund Eco-Invest SICAV PLC and Schwab Holding AG v. Kingdom of Spain* (ICSID Case No. ARB/15/36, Award 6 September 2019); *RREEF Infrastructure (G.P.) Limited and RREEF Pan-European Infrastructure Two Lux S.à r.l. v. Kingdom of Spain* (ICSID Case No. ARB/13/30, Award 11 December 2019); *Watkins Holdings S.à r.l. and others v. Kingdom of Spain* (ICSID Case No. ARB/15/44, Award 21 January 2020); *The PV Investors v. Spain* (PCA Case No. 2012–14, Award 28 February 2020); *Hydro Energy 1 S.à r.l. and Hydroxana Sweden AB v. Kingdom of Spain* (ICSID Case No. ARB/15/42, Award 5 August 2020); *STEAG GmbH v. Kingdom of Spain* (ICSID Case No. ARB/15/4, Award 8 September 2020); *RWE Innogy GmbH and RWE Innogy Aersa S.A.U. v. Kingdom of Spain* (ICSID Case No. ARB/14/34, Award 18 December 2020); *BayWa r.e. Renewable Energy GmbH and BayWa r.e. Asset Holding GmbH v. Kingdom of Spain* (ICSID Case No. ARB/15/16, Award 25 January 2021); *Eurus Energy Holdings Corporation v. Kingdom of Spain* (ICSID Case No. ARB/16/4, Decision 17 March 2021); *Aharon Naftali Biram, Gilatz Spain SL, Redmill Holdings Ltd and Sun-Flower Olmeda GmbH v. Kingdom of Spain* (ICSID Case No. ARB/16/17, Award 22 June 2021); *STEAG GmbH v. Kingdom of Spain* (ICSID Case No. ARB/15/4, Award 17 August 2021); *Infracapital F1 S.à r.l. and Infracapital Solar B.V. v. Kingdom of Spain* (ICSID Case No. ARB/16/18, Decision 13 September 2021); *JGC Holdings Corporation v. Kingdom of Spain* (ICSID Case No. ARB/15/27, Award 9 November 2021); *RENERGY S.à r.l. v. Kingdom of Spain* (ICSID Case No. ARB/14/18, Award 6 May 2022); *Cavalum SGPS, S.A. v. Kingdom of Spain* (ICSID Case No. ARB/15/34, Award 29 September 2022); *EDF Energies Nouvelles S.A. v. Kingdom of Spain* (PCA Case No. AA613, Award 11 April 2023); *Cordoba Beheer B.V., Cross Retail S.L., Sevilla Beheer B.V., Spanish project companies v. Kingdom of Spain* (ICSID Case No. ARB/16/27, Award 22 May 2023); *Frank Schumm, Joachim Kruck, Jürgen Reiss and others v. Kingdom of Spain* (ICSID Case No. ARB/15/23, Award 6 October 2023).

[28] *A contrario*: see *Sapec, S.A. v. Kingdom of Spain* (ICSID Case No. ARB/19/23, Award 11 October 2024); *European Solar Farms A/S v. Kingdom of Spain* (ICSID Case No. ARB/18/45, Award 11 October 2024).

[29] Article 54 of the ICSID Convention provides: "(1) Each Contracting State shall recognize an award rendered pursuant to this Convention as binding and enforce the pecuniary obligations imposed by that award within its territories as if it were a final judgment of a court in that State".

[30] Signed on 17 December 1994.

investment agreements. And these treaties may well have a different wording, because of the dispositive nature of public international law. In other words, States may agree their investment commitments asymmetrically, considering the specific circumstances of each case.

In this context, the consistency, coherence, predictability, and correctness of arbitral decisions is in no way favoured by the decentralisation of international investment law as well as by the plurality of legal instruments containing these international obligations.[31]

This legal ecosystem, to the contrary, promotes heterogeneity. The existence of diverse provisions agreed upon by States in different international treaties can lead to divergent interpretations. We can label this phenomenon, which seems integral to investment arbitration, as proper heterogeneity.

As UNCITRAL WG III has pointed out:

> different factors might lead to different arbitral decisions (for example, the rules of treaty interpretation required a tribunal to consider more than the ordinary meaning to be given to the terms of a treaty provision when interpreting it, the manner and the extent to which relevant evidence were presented, and how disputing parties made their arguments).[32]

But this differs completely from what we could label as improper heterogeneity, meaning, that various arbitral tribunals interpret substantive[33] or procedural[34] obligations within the same international investment agreement in different ways.

Improper heterogeneity erodes the consistency, coherence, predictability, and correctness of arbitral decisions. The current legal framework in international investment law is not equipped with sufficient tools to fix the dysfunctions arising from the latter phenomenon.[35] For this and other reasons, the EU has proposed various measures to promote consistency, coherence, predictability, and correctness.

---

[31] According to the UNCTAD Division on Investment and Enterprise there are currently 2242 BITs and 417 treaties with investment provisions in force.

[32] A/CN.9/964, 6 November 2018, para. 28.

[33] A/CN.9/WG.III/WP.150, 28 August 2018, para. 16.

[34] Ibid, para. 17.

[35] "Under the ICSID system, annulment is only available to correct a very limited set of errors. Article 52 of the ICSID Convention only provides for annulment in limited circumstances. These do not touch upon the substantive correctness of the award. Similarly, domestic arbitration laws or the New York Convention on the Recognition and Enforcement of Foreign Arbitral Awards limit the grounds on which recognition and enforcement of an award can be refused": see A/CN.9/WG.III/WP.145, 12 December 2017, para. 28.

2.2 *Judicial Mechanisms Fostering a "Jurisprudence Constante"*

Notwithstanding that the *stare decisis* principle is not applicable in public international law, international courts and tribunals have developed a "*jurisprudence constante*"[36] that is persuasive, and which provides some predictability to the system of international justice. Several proposals have been made in international investment law with the aim of fostering this "*jurisprudence constante*".

Amongst these proposals we can highlight, firstly, the creation of an appeals tribunal in charge of supervising factual or legal errors. And secondly, the creation of a multilateral investment court (or standing mechanism). Both initiatives may contribute to combat improper heterogeneity.

2.2.1 An Appeals Tribunal: A Top-Down Mechanism to Combat Improper Heterogeneity

The EU has firmly advocated for the creation of an appellate mechanism in international investment law, since it first negotiated the agreement with Canada.[37] However, Article 53.1 of the ICSID Convention sets forth an obstacle. This provision envisages that the awards rendered under the ICSID Convention "shall not be subject to any appeal or to any other remedy except those provided for in this Convention". In other words, the ICSID Convention does not allow the appeal of arbitral awards.

To overcome this hurdle all (or at least some) of the States parties to the ICSID Convention should agree to change the content of that provision. Through such modification, concluded pursuant to Article 41.1 of the Vienna Convention on the Law of Treaties (VCLT), an appeals mechanism could be implemented.[38] It is not surprising that, due to the interest generated by this issue,[39] UNCITRAL WG III has devoted part of its discussions to searching for formulas for the creation of an appellate mechanism by means of an international agreement.[40]

---

[36] Devaney (2022), pp. 641–659.

[37] Article 8.28.1.

[38] Article 41.1 of the VCLT provides: "Two or more of the parties to a multilateral treaty may conclude an agreement to modify the treaty as between themselves alone if: (a) the possibility of such a modification is provided for by the treaty; or (b) the modification in question is not prohibited by the treaty and: (i) does not affect the enjoyment by the other parties of their rights under the treaty or the performance of their obligations; (ii) does not relate to a provision, derogation from which is incompatible with the effective execution of the object and purpose of the treaty as a whole".

[39] Sauvant (2008); Platt (2013), pp. 531–560; Nilsson and Englesson (2013), pp. 561–579; Ngangjoh-Hodu and Ajibo (2015) pp. 308–331; Feldman (2017), pp. 528–544; van den Berg (2019), pp. 156–189; Kucik and Puig (2023) pp. 562–583; Chaisse (2024), pp. 443–465.

[40] A/CN.9/WG.III/WP.202, 12 November 2020; A/CN.9/WG.III/WP.224, 17 November 2022; A/CN.9/1130, 7 February 2023, pp. 18–24.

The appellate tribunal would be competent to hear appeals based on the following grounds: "error of law (including serious procedural shortcomings) or manifest errors in the appreciation of the facts". The appeals tribunal, on the contrary, could not make "a *de novo* review of the facts".[41]

In this vein, the EU has also promoted the establishment of an appeal mechanism in the international agreements already concluded with third States. In fact, the agreements with Canada,[42] Chile,[43] Singapore[44] and Vietnam[45] foresee such a possibility. In all of them, three grounds of appeal are established: a) that the tribunal erred in the application or interpretation of the applicable law; b) that the tribunal manifestly erred in the appreciation of the facts; and c) those provided for in Article 52 of the ICSID Convention, in so far as they are not covered by subparagraphs (a) and (b).

This initiative merits at least three general considerations. Firstly, the EU proposes including the actual grounds of annulment established under Article 52 of the ICSID Convention[46] amongst the grounds that might trigger the jurisdiction of the appellate tribunal.

Arbitral practice developed within the ICSID framework has been very blunt when underlining the exceptional character of annulment proceedings,[47] and as to how the grounds of annulment established under Article 52 of the ICSID Convention[48] should be interpreted. An annulment committee:

---

[41] A/CN.9/WG.III/WP.159/Add.1, 24 January 2019, para. 14.

[42] Article 8.28.1.

[43] Article 17.55.1.

[44] Article 3.19.1.

[45] Article 3.54.1.

[46] Article 52.1 of the ICSID Convention provides: "Either party may request annulment of the award by an application in writing addressed to the Secretary-General on one or more of the following grounds: (a) that the Tribunal was not properly constituted; (b) that the Tribunal has manifestly exceeded its powers; (c) that there was corruption on the part of a member of the Tribunal; (d) that there has been a serious departure from a fundamental rule of procedure; or (e) that the award has failed to state the reasons on which it is based".

[47] *Tulip Real Estate and Development Netherlands B.V. v. Republic of Turkey* (ICSID Case No. ARB/11/28, Decision 30 December 2015, para. 43); *Antoine Abou Lahoud and Leila Bounafeh-Abou Lahoud v. Democratic Republic of the Congo* (ICSID Case No. ARB/10/4, Decision 29 March 2016, para. 108); *Venoklim Holding v. Bolivarian Republic of Venezuela* (ICSID Case No. ARB/12/22, Decision 2 February 2018, para. 183–184); *Churchill Mining PLC and Planet Mining Pty Ltd v. Republic of Indonesia* (ICSID Case No. ARB/12/14 and 12/40, Decision 18 March 2019, para. 188); *Cube Infrastructure Fund SICAV and others v. Kingdom of Spain* (ICSID Case No. ARB/15/20, Decision 28 March 2022, para. 92); *Cyprus Popular Bank Public v. the Hellenic Republic* (ICSID Case No. ARB/14/16, Decision 30 November 2022, para. 180); *OperaFund Eco-Invest Sicav Plc and Schwab Holding AG v. Kingdom of Spain* (ICSID Case No. ARB/15/36, Decision 2 March 2023, para. 71).

[48] *Mr. Tza Yap Shum v. Republic of Peru* (ICSID Case No. ARB/07/6, Decision 12 February 2015, para. 112); *SAUR International SA v. Republic of Argentina* (ICSID Case No. ARB/04/4, Decision 19 December 2016, para. 160); *Tenaris S.A. and Talta - Trading e Marketing Sociedade Unipessoal Lda. v. Bolivarian Republic of Venezuela* (ICSID Case No. ARB/12/23, Decision 28 December

> is not a court of appeal and [...] its competence extends only to annulment based on one or other of the grounds expressly set out in Article 52 of the ICSID Convention.[49]

It seems that the EU agreements would allow this appellate mechanism to exercise both functions (appeal and annulment).[50] The basic objective of this dual system of review would be to reinforce consistency, coherence, predictability, and correctness.

Secondly, it is worth highlighting the role of EU law. As EU law is considered within the EU agreements as an issue of fact (not a legal issue),[51] its invocation before the appeal mechanism should be limited to "manifest errors in the appreciation of the facts".

Finally, to avoid abuses of the appeals mechanism, the EU suggests, amongst other measures, "requiring security for cost to be paid".[52] While the agreement with Canada allows the Joint Committee to define this issue,[53] other international agreements have regulated it expressly.

The agreement with Chile proposes requiring the appellant party to pay a bond to cover the costs of the appeal.[54] Whereas the agreements with Singapore[55] and Vietnam[56] would allow the appellate tribunal some discretion to determine "a reasonable amount" considering the circumstances of each case.

To conclude, the appeal mechanism is intended to provide more coherence to international investment law. We understand that its inclusion in the new ISDS system will not impede the use of other post award remedies (such as rectification, supplementation, and interpretation of the award), since they each have a different legal nature and serve diverse purposes. In any case, as its inclusion depends upon the consent of States expressed in an international agreement, it is a solution that guarantees more homogeneity only for those States concluding such an agreement.

2018, para. 43); *Standard Chartered Bank (Hong Kong) Limited v. Tanzania Electric Supply Company Limited* (ICSID Case No. ARB/10/20, Decision 22 August 2019, para. 59); *Hydro S.r.l. and others v. Republic of Albania* (ICSID Case No. ARB/15/28, Decision 2 April 2021, para. 107).

[49] *Compañía de Aguas del Aconquija S.A. and Vivendi Universal S.A. v. Argentine Republic* (ICSID Case No. ARB/97/3, Decision 3 June 2002, para. 62); *CMS Gas Transmission Company v. Argentine Republic* (ICSID Case No. ARB/01/8, Decision 25 September 2007, para. 43); *Bernhard von Pezold et 50 al v. Republic of Zimbabwe* (ICSID Case No. ARB/10/15, Decision 21 November 2018, para. 239).

[50] ICSID (2004) Possible Improvements of the Framework for ICSID Arbitration. https://icsid.worldbank.org/sites/default/files/publications/Possible%20Improvements%20of%20the%20Framework%20of%20ICSID%20Arbitration.pdf. Accessed 11 December 2024.

[51] Opinion 30 April 2019, *Comprehensive Economic and Trade Agreement between Canada, of the one part, and the European Union and its Member States, of the other part (CETA)*, 1/17, ECLI:EU:C:2019:341, para. 131.

[52] A/CN.9/WG.III/WP.159/Add.1, 24 January 2019, para. 15.

[53] Article 8.28.7.

[54] Article 17.55.6.

[55] Article 3.19.5.

[56] Article 3.54.6.

2.2.2 A Multilateral Investment Court: A Bottom-Up Mechanism to Combat Improper Heterogeneity

The creation of a multilateral investment court (or standing mechanism) is a much more ambitious and complex alternative. However, UNCITRAL is making a genuine effort to reach a general agreement (*consensus*) on this topic.[57]Transition toward a standing mechanism implies a radical change in the current ISDS system. A permanent tribunal needs to be codified in an international agreement. In addition, it would be necessary to reach a general agreement among States for its functioning to be fully operational. As some States have declared in the debates of UNCITRAL WG III, a:

> critical mass of States need[s] to participate in any permanent structure for it to function properly and be financially and logistically viable.[58]

There is also the possibility that the degree of adhesion to the international agreement establishing the multilateral investment court would initially be scarce, and that many States would prefer to remain out of it for diverse reasons.

The latter States would continue resolving their investment disputes through investment arbitration, in application of the criteria that regulate successive treaties relating the same subject matter.[59] All of this without prejudice to their recurring to this body as an appellate mechanism, if they so deem it.[60]

From the perspective of the coherence and consistency of the ISDS system, the potential cross-fertilization between decisions of the standing mechanism and (past and future) decisions issued by *ad hoc* tribunals remains to be explored. If the multilateral investment court is finally created, it will be interesting to study its interplay with *ad hoc* investment tribunals.

This would be relevant in proceedings involving the same State before different forums as it could lead to the situation in which a State (State A) concludes an international investment agreement with another State (State B) recognising the jurisdiction of the standing mechanism. And, at the same time, such permanent jurisdiction is not foreseen in an international investment agreement concluded between State A and another State (State C).

If State A is involved in two different investment claims with regards to foreign investors based on State B and State C, these disputes will have to be settled before different forums. The former before the standing mechanism, and the latter before an *ad hoc* investment tribunal.

---

[57] Sornarajah (2016).

[58] A/CN.9/1050, 17 March 2021, para. 20.

[59] Article 30.4 of the VCLT provides: "When the parties to the later treaty do not include all the parties to the earlier one: (a) as between States Parties to both treaties the same rule applies as in paragraph 3; (b) as between a State party to both treaties and a State party to only one of the treaties, the treaty to which both States are parties governs their mutual rights and obligations".

[60] Dutta (2021), pp. 244–245.

In any case, States joining the standing mechanism, once that body is designed through the corresponding international agreement,[61] will need to develop transitional legal mechanisms between the ISDS regime currently in place and the new regime established by the standing mechanism.

For this reason, the agreements concluded by the EU promote the cooperation between the parties toward obtaining "the establishment of a multilateral investment tribunal and appellate mechanism for the resolution of investment disputes".[62] The agreement with Vietnam exceptionally includes a more stringent language, as it indicates that the parties:

> shall enter into negotiations for an international agreement providing for a multilateral investment tribunal in combination with, or separate from, a multilateral appellate mechanism applicable to disputes under this Agreement.[63]

In 2018 the EU published negotiation directives toward the conclusion of an international agreement creating a multilateral investment court. These directives include, amongst other issues, that this body should have an appellate system and that the proceedings should be conducted under the UNCITRAL Transparency Rules.[64]

The EU additionally promotes the proposal of a multilateral investment court within UNCITRAL WG III.[65] In our opinion, it is the adequate forum to advocate for this initiative. Even when there may be resistance from some States,[66] and these may obstruct an initial *consensus*.

3 Restricting Frivolous Claims

Other mechanisms implemented to reform the ISDS system aim at restricting the presentation of frivolous investment claims. The creation of both an appeal and a standing mechanism to settle investment claims has the primary objective of promoting consistency, coherence, predictability, and correctness.But the EU has stated that these judicial mechanisms have additional objectives. Particularly, in its submissions before UNCITRAL WG III the EU has argued that a "consistent case-law both at the first and appeal level will allow a stable understanding of provisions to develop and hence reduce 'adventurous' claims".[67]

---

[61] Bungenberg and Reinisch (2020), pp. 175–196; Funk (2022), pp. 227–250.

[62] Article 8.29 (Canada); Article 17.37 (Chile); Article 3.12 (Singapore).

[63] Article 3.41.

[64] Doc. 12,981/17 ADD 1, 20 March 2018, para. 10 and 13.

[65] A/CN.9/WG.III/WP.213, 8 December 2021.

[66] A/CN.9/1004/Add.1, 28 January 2020, para. 88–92; A/CN.9/1050, 17 March 2021, para. 19.

[67] A/CN.9/WG.III/WP.159/Add.1, 24 January 2019, para. 42.

3.1 A Brief Characterisation of Frivolous Claims in ISDS

Frivolous claims can surface for formal (or jurisdictional) and substantive reasons.[68] An example of this type of claims can take place when the foreign investor brings a claim once the term established in the international investment agreement has elapsed. In this case, that claim would be extemporary and manifestly lacking legal merit. This was the conclusion reached in *AFC Investment Solutions*, a case in which the investor presented the claim past the 3 years established under Article 10.5 of the BIT between Spain and Colombia.[69] The investment tribunal considered that the investor had not complied with a requirement envisaged in Article 10 of the BIT:

> for the claim [...] to be subjected to arbitration, which leads this Tribunal to consider that the Claimant's claim is manifestly lacking legal merit.[70]

In other cases, such as *Global Trading Resource*, the claim presented by the investor was based on purely commercial (sale and purchase) transactions that did not have the consideration of "investments" under Article 25 of the ICSID Convention. As they could not be considered as investments, they were not protected under the ICSID Convention. The investment tribunal therefore held that it lacked jurisdiction over a claim based solely on commercial transactions.[71]

Finally, investors may base their claims on arguments that are manifestly unfounded. It so happened in *Trans-Global Petroleum*, where the claimant attempted to invoke a right that Article VIII of the BIT between the United States of America and Jordan[72] had granted to the parties to the agreement (and not to the investor). The investment tribunal found that:

> whilst the Respondent bears an obligation thereunder to consult with the USA as its "Contracting Party", it is obvious the Respondent owes no similar obligation to the Claimant. The Claimant clearly has no legal rights under Article VIII. [...] Accordingly, the essential legal basis for this claim is entirely missing under the BIT.[73]

As it is highlighted by these cases, there is sufficient evidence in arbitral practice demonstrating the need to allow States to establish defence mechanisms against speculative or frivolous claims.

---

[68] A/CN.9/WG.III/WP.245, 8 July 2024, para. 15.

[69] Signed on 31 March 2005.

[70] *AFC Investment Solutions S.L. v. Republic of Colombia* (ICSID Case No. ARB/20/16, Award 24 February 2022, para. 244) (own translation).

[71] *Global Trading Resource Corp. and Globex International, Inc. v. Ukraine* (ICSID Case No. ARB/09/11, Award 1 December 2010, para. 55–57).

[72] Signed on 2 July 1997.

[73] *Trans-Global Petroleum, Inc. v. The Hashemite Kingdom of Jordan* (ICSID Case No. ARB/07/25, Decision 12 May 2008, para. 118–119).

3.2 *Summary Dismissal as a Deterrent Measure Against Frivolous Claims*

The UNCITRAL WG III discussions have attempted to systematise legal tools that allow States (usually acting as the respondent party in investment claims) to combat frivolous claims. UNCITRAL WG III is debating a proposal based on Rule 41.5 of the ICSID Arbitration Rules.[74] This rule establishes the possibility that the respondent State may file an objection that a claim is manifestly without legal merit.[75] This procedural tool was included in the ICSID Arbitration Rules in 2006 precisely to reduce frivolous claims.[76]

In this vein, the proposal by UNCITRAL establishes an expedited proceeding allowing any of the disputing parties to "object that a claim is manifestly without legal merit".[77] If this objection is not accepted by the investment tribunal, the objecting party could "raise a plea that the Tribunal does not have jurisdiction or to argue subsequently in the proceeding that the claim is without legal merit".[78]

The conventional practice of the EU has already used this solution. In fact, the agreement with Canada allows the disputing parties to object against "claims manifestly without legal merit"[79] as well as "claims unfounded as a matter of law".[80] This mechanism foresees a "double layer of protection".[81] It allows for the expeditious dismissal of unfounded or abusive claims.

The first objection against manifestly unfounded claims can be raised at the very beginning of a case, no later than 30 days after the constitution of the division of the tribunal, and in any event before its first session. Whereas a second defense against legally unfounded claims can be raised also at a later stage of the proceedings, and no later than the date the tribunal fixes for the respondent to submit its counter-memorial.

The system of summary dismissal proposed in the international agreements concluded by the EU is flexible. It allows for the possibility to object at a later stage of

---

[74] A/CN.9/WG.III/WP.245, 8 July 2024, para. 15.

[75] Rule 41.5 of the ICSID Arbitration Rules provides: "Unless the parties have agreed to another expedited procedure for making preliminary objections, a party may, no later than 30 days after the constitution of the Tribunal, and in any event before the first session of the Tribunal, file an objection that a claim is manifestly without legal merit. The party shall specify as precisely as possible the basis for the objection. The Tribunal, after giving the parties the opportunity to present their observations on the objection, shall, at its first session or promptly thereafter, notify the parties of its decision on the objection. The decision of the Tribunal shall be without prejudice to the right of a party to file an objection pursuant to paragraph (1) or to object, in the course of the proceeding, that a claim lacks legal merit".

[76] Luttrell (2019), p 1190.

[77] A/CN.9/WG.III/WP.244, 8 July 2024, Draft Provision 4.

[78] Ibid, Draft Provision 4, para. 7.

[79] Article 8.32. See also Article 17.42 (Chile); Article 3.14 (Singapore); Article 3.44 (Vietnam).

[80] Article 8.33. See also Article 17.43 (Chile); Article 3.15 (Singapore); Article 3.45 (Vietnam).

[81] A/CN.9/WG.III/WP.244, 8 July 2024, p. 6.

the proceedings, and at the same time contributes to eradicate "unmeritorious"[82] claims in ISDS.[83] Finally, three issues must be considered while assessing this mechanism of summary dismissal.

Firstly, both disputing parties have the right to be heard by the investment tribunal.[84] The tribunal must decide considering all the relevant information presented by the parties. To be clear, this objection cannot become an escape route from investment arbitration.

Secondly, this system establishes a high threshold[85] to conclude that a claim presented by the investor constitutes a claim manifestly without legal merit.[86] But if the objection is accepted, the proceedings would automatically end with a decision dismissing the claim.

And thirdly, this objection is based on indeterminate legal categories. Though arbitral tribunals have been fine tuning when a claim "is manifestly without legal merit", it is also true that this concept can progressively evolve through arbitral practice.[87]

4 Facing the Challenges Arising From Multiple Proceedings

Another objective pursued by the EU is to reduce the disruptive effects of multiple proceedings. Before examining the tools proposed by the EU to achieve this goal, it is important to examine the notion of multiple proceedings in international investment law.

4.1 The Notion of Multiple Proceedings in International Investment Law

Multiple proceedings can be defined as the presentation of various claims against a State, based on the same facts, but before diverse forums. The nature of ISDS makes this phenomenon possible in, at least,[88] three circumstances.

Firstly, a claim may be presented simultaneously before different international courts (such as a human rights tribunal and an investment tribunal). The most

[82] A/CN.9/WG.III/WP.245, 8 July 2024, para. 14.

[83] Nguyen (2022), pp. 240–254.

[84] Brown and Puig (2011), pp. 227–259.

[85] *RSM Production Corporation and others v. Grenada* (ICSID Case No. ARB/10/6, Award 10 December 2010, para. 6.1.1–6.1.2).

[86] Chatterjee (2012) pp. 486–501.

[87] Potestà and Sobat (2012) pp. 137–168.

[88] A/CN.9/964, 6 November 2018, para. 42–44.

significant precedent in this category is *Yukos*. In this case, a company argued that the Russian authorities had illegally expropriated its assets.

The company (Yukos) brought a claim before the European Court of Human Rights (ECtHR), alleging a violation of the rights to due process and to own property envisaged in the European Convention on Human Rights.[89] While the main shareholders of Yukos initiated three arbitrations against the Russian Federation before the Permanent Court of Arbitration (PCA) alleging violations of the Energy Charter Treaty.[90] The international responsibility of the Russian Federation was established in these proceedings,[91] although the ECtHR and the three investment tribunals fixed different compensations.[92]

Secondly, a foreign investor can initiate proceedings both in commercial and investment arbitration. This means that the same set of facts could give rise to discuss non-compliance of contractual and conventional obligations.[93] As the annulment committee in *Vivendi* noted:

> where "the fundamental basis of the claim" is a treaty laying down an independent standard by which the conduct of the parties is to be judged, the existence of an exclusive jurisdiction clause in a contract between the claimant and the respondent state or one of its subdivisions cannot operate as a bar to the application of the treaty standard. At most, it might be relevant—as municipal law will often be relevant—in assessing whether there has been a breach of the treaty.[94]

[89] *Case of OAO Neftyanaya Kompaniya Yukos v. Russia*, No. 14902/04, ECtHR 2011.

[90] *Hulley Enterprises Limited (Cyprus) v. Russian Federation* (PCA Case No. 2005–03/AA226, Award 18 July 2014); *Yukos Universal Limited (Isle of Man) v. Russian Federation* (PCA Case No. 2005–04/AA227, Award 18 July 2014); *Veteran Petroleum Limited (Cyprus) v. Russian Federation* (PCA Case No. 2005–05/AA228, Award 18 July 2014).

[91] This case may also serve as an example of other categories of multiple proceedings identified in this section. In fact, minority investors in Yukos initiated investment and commercial arbitration proceedings, respectively, against the Russian Federation and Rosneft, a company to which the Russian Federation had transferred certain Yukos assets after the expropriation: see *RosInvestCo UK Ltd. v. The Russian Federation* (SCC Case No. V079/2005, Award 12 September 2010); *Renta 4 S.V.S.A., Ahorro Corporación Emergentes F.I., Ahorro Corporación Eurofondo F.I., Rovime Inversiones SICAV S.A., Quasar de Valors SICAV S.A., Orgor de Valores SICAV S.A., GBI 9000 SICAV S.A. v. The Russian Federation* (SCC No. 24/2007, Award 20 July 2012); *Yukos Capital S.à r.l. v. OJSC Rosneft Oil Company* (ICC Case).

[92] The ECtHR awarded EUR 1,866,104,634 as compensation: see *Case of OAO Neftyanaya Kompaniya Yukos v. Russia*, No. 14902/04, ECtHR 2014. The investment tribunals awarded compensations worth of USD 50,020,867,798: see *Hulley Enterprises Limited (Cyprus) v. Russian Federation* (PCA Case No. 2005–03/AA226, Award 18 July 2014, Annex C, Table T1); *Yukos Universal Limited (Isle of Man) v. Russian Federation* (PCA Case No. 2005–04/AA227, Award 18 July 2014, Annex C, Table T1); *Veteran Petroleum Limited (Cyprus) v. Russian Federation* (PCA Case No. 2005–05/AA228, Award 18 July 2014, Annex C, Table T1).

[93] Shany (2005), pp. 835–851.

[94] *Compañía de Aguas del Aconquija S.A. and Vivendi Universal S.A. v. Argentine Republic* (ICSID Case No. ARB/97/3, Decision 3 July 2002, para. 101).

Société Générale de Surveillance still today constitutes one of the more significant precedents.[95] In this case, Pakistan unsuccessfully objected against an investment arbitration based on the BIT between Switzerland and Pakistan,[96] alleging that the controverted measures were being addressed in a pending commercial arbitration.

The investment tribunal admitted that it had "jurisdiction to pass upon and determine the claims of violation of provisions of the Swiss-Pakistan BIT raised by the Claimant".[97] It further added that such jurisdiction "would to any degree [not] be shared by the PSI Agreement arbitrator".[98]

And thirdly, legal or natural persons related to an investment can initiate claims against the same State based on different international investment agreements. *Orascom* stands out as a significant precedent. In this case, two investment claims were brought against Algeria based on the BIT between Algeria and Egypt (*Orascom Telecom Holding*)[99] and the BIT between Algeria and the Belgium-Luxembourg Economic Union (*Orascom TMT Investments*), respectively.[100]

The first of these arbitrations (*Orascom Telecom Holding*) was settled[101] by the parties in 2015. Thus, the investment tribunal in *Orascom TMT Investments* considered that the agreement reached by the parties in 2015 also served to end the second dispute. Both proceedings had been initiated by companies belonging to the same group:

> the Claimant cannot bring claims in this arbitration that OTH decided to settle, as the settlement clearly resolved the dispute that the Claimant has brought before this Tribunal as is shown by the comparison of the notices of disputes above. The existence of a settlement agreement does not change the Tribunal's conclusions in relation to the OTH Arbitration, as the settlement stands in lieu of the investment treaty tribunal's award which would have been forthcoming in that arbitration. The settlement agreement puts an end to the dispute arising from Algeria's measures in the same manner as the award would have ended the dispute. In the absence of harm which it incurred itself to the exclusion of OTH, the Claimant cannot take over the dispute that OTH has settled. In this respect, the content of the settlement, whether beneficial or detrimental to OTH/OTA, is irrelevant. What matters is that the claims arising from Algeria's measures have ceased to exist due to the settlement agreement.[102]

---

[95] *SGS Société Générale de Surveillance S.A. v. Islamic Republic of Pakistan* (ICSID Case No. ARB/01/13).

[96] Signed on 11 July 1995.

[97] *SGS Société Générale de Surveillance S.A. v. Islamic Republic of Pakistan* (ICSID Case No. ARB/01/13, Decision 3 August 2003, para. 155).

[98] Ibid.

[99] Signed on 29 March 1997.

[100] Signed on 24 April 1991.

[101] *Orascom Telecom Holding S.A.E v. People's Democratic Republic of Algeria* (PCA Case No. 2012–20, Consent Award 12 March 2015).

[102] *Orascom TMT Investments S.à r.l. v. People's Democratic Republic of Algeria* (ICSID Case No. ARB/12/35, Award 31 May 2017, para. 524).

As this case demonstrates, multiple proceedings can generate disruptive effects in investment arbitration. They may lead to situations of abuse of process, inconsistent decisions, and double recovery.

4.2 *Reducing the Disruptive Effects of Multiple Proceedings*

UNCITRAL WG III has debated about the necessity of implementing measures to "promote procedural efficiency, reliability and legitimacy".[103] These measures would further allow for the reduction of the disruptive effects of multiple proceedings "through joinder of cases, consolidation, stay of proceedings or even dismissal of cases".[104]

Amongst the proposals discussed by UNCITRAL WG III,[105] this chapter focuses on the waiver of rights to initiate dispute resolution proceedings (also known as a "No-U-turn clause").[106] This measure implies that, before initiating an investment arbitration, the foreign investor must waive its right to initiate any claim or proceeding under domestic or international law and, if already initiated, the foreign investor must withdraw or discontinue any existing proceeding before a tribunal or court under domestic or international law with respect to a measure alleged to constitute a breach referred to in its investment claim.[107] In conclusion, if such rights have not been waived by the claimant,[108] the investment arbitration cannot proceed.[109]

The foreign investor continues to have domestic and international litigation options available to defend its rights, but if it chooses to initiate an investment arbitration, it must definitively waive other dispute settlement mechanisms. The definitive (unqualified and unconditional) character of the waiver has been recognised in practice.[110]

The EU has included the waiver of claims in the international agreements concluded with third States, though in different ways. The agreement with Canada envisages that:

> "An investor may only submit a claim pursuant to Article 8.23 if the investor:
> [...]

[103] A/CN.9/964, 6 November 2018, para. 48.

[104] A/CN.9/WG.III/WP.159/Add.1, 24 January 2019, para. 56.

[105] A/CN.9/WG.III/WP.244, 8 July 2024.

[106] UNCTAD (2014) Investor-State Dispute Settlement: A Sequel. https://unctad.org/system/files/official-document/diaeia2013d2_en.pdf. Accessed 10 December 2024.

[107] A/CN.9/WG.III/WP.244, 8 July 2024, Draft Provision 15.

[108] Boisson de Chazournes (2019), pp. 331–361.

[109] Bahmany (2023), pp. 219–224.

[110] *Bacilio Amorrortu v. Republic of Peru* (PCA Case No. 2020–11, Partial Award 5 August 2022, para. 225).

(f) withdraws or discontinues any existing proceeding before a tribunal or court under domestic or international law with respect to a measure alleged to constitute a breach referred to in its claim; and

(g) waives its right to initiate any claim or proceeding before a tribunal or court under domestic or international law with respect to a measure alleged to constitute a breach referred to in its claim".[111]

Whereas the agreement with Singapore sets forth:

"A claim may be submitted under this Section only if:

[...]

(f) the claimant:

(i) withdraws *any* pending claim submitted to the Tribunal, or to *any* other domestic or international court or tribunal under domestic or international law, concerning the same treatment as alleged to breach the provisions of Chapter Two (Investment Protection);

(ii) declares that it will not submit such a claim in the future; and

(iii) declares that it will not enforce any award rendered pursuant to this Section before such award has become final, and will not seek to appeal, review, set aside, annul, revise or initiate any other similar procedure before an international or domestic court or tribunal, as regards an award pursuant to this Section".[112]

Though the difference between both provisions is subtle, the latter places emphasis on the definitive character of the waiver in using the word "any". This formula has been employed by other international investment agreements and is built on the interpretation made by the investment tribunal in *Renco Group*.[113]

Finally, it is worth mentioning that the conventional practice of the EU[114] also envisages the waiver of claims for those proceedings in which the foreign investor initiates an investment arbitration claiming for the damages suffered in the host State by a local company in which it is a shareholder.[115]

---

[111] Article 8.22.1.

[112] Article 3.7.1 (emphasis added). See also Article 17.29.1 (Chile); Article 3.34.1 (Vietnam). In the agreement with Vietnam, Annex 12 further establishes a higher restriction for investors from the EU who "Notwithstanding paragraph 1 of Article 3.34 (Other Claims), [...] shall not submit to the Tribunal under Section B (Resolution of Disputes between Investors and Parties) of Chapter 3 (Dispute Settlement) a claim that Viet Nam has breached a provision referred to in Article 2.1 (Scope) if the investor has submitted a claim alleging a breach of that same provision referred to in Article 2.1 (Scope) in proceedings before a court or administrative tribunal of Viet Nam or any international arbitration".

[113] *The Renco Group, Inc. v. Republic of Peru* (ICSID Case No. UNCT/13/1, Partial Award 15 July 2016, para. 79–83).

[114] Article 8.22.2. See also Article 17.29.3 (Chile); Article 3.7.2 (Singapore); Article 3.34 (Vietnam).

[115] A/CN.9/WG.III/WP.244, 8 July 2024, Draft Provision 18.

5 Final Remarks

The tension between the private and public features that underlie in international investment law remains in those agreements recently concluded by the EU with third States. One can assert that these agreements erode private traits of investment arbitration and reinforce its public dimension.

From a procedural standpoint, this argument is manifested through the creation of institutional dispute settlement bodies (such an appellate tribunal and a standing mechanism) designed to promote consistency, coherence, predictability, and correctness of arbitral decisions.

Despite assuming a less decentralised nature, the ISDS system designed in the EU international investment agreements will be administered by separate investment tribunals (one tribunal per agreement), until a standing mechanism is established. As each agreement creates a different tribunal, there is no reason that its members would coincide, so heterogeneity still may be a factor. Therefore, beyond the harmonizing work that the appellate tribunal would develop, it remains to be seen in which way this new ISDS system will create a body of "*jurisprudence constante*" that may reduce improper heterogeneity.

The consistency, coherence, predictability, and correctness of arbitral decisions is also promoted through the avoidance of both frivolous claims and the disruptive effects of multiple proceedings. Restricting the options of international litigation offered to foreign investors by ISDS is problematic, given the consensual character of investment arbitration. But these restrictions may be effective if they are implemented with the purpose of avoiding an abuse of process, inconsistent decisions, and double recovery.

The EU is actively contributing to the development of ISDS in UNCITRAL WG III. Its conventional activity is serving as a benchmark to institutionalize investment arbitration from a procedural standpoint. The coherence between the conventional practice of the EU and its activities within UNCITRAL contributes to strengthen the role of the EU as a prominent actor in the United Nations system. It further serves as a precedent that illuminates how to undertake future codification processes of international law where the interests of the EU and its member States are at stake.

References

Bahmany L (2023) Double recovery in investment arbitration: toward a principled treatment of double compensation. Brill/Nijhoff, Leiden/Boston

van den Berg AJ (2019) Appeal mechanism for ISDS awards: interaction with the New York and ICSID conventions. ICSID Rev 34:156–189

Boisson de Chazournes L (2019) Parallel and overlapping proceedings in international economic law: towards an ordered co-existence. In: Ruiz Fabri H (ed) International law and litigation. Nomos, Baden-Baden, pp 331–361

Brown C, Puig S (2011) The power of ICSID tribunals to dismiss proceedings summarily: an analysis of rule 41(5) of the ICSID arbitration rules. Law Pract Int Courts Trib 10:227–259

Bungenberg M, Reinisch A (2020) From bilateral arbitral tribunals and investment courts to a multilateral investment court. In: Options regarding the institutionalization of investor-state dispute settlement, 2nd edn. Springer, Berlin
Chaisse J (2024) The appeal in international investment arbitration. In: Fach Gómez K, Titi C (eds) The award in international investment arbitration. Oxford University Press, Oxford, pp 443–465
Chatterjee C (2012) A critical examination of rule 41(5) of the ICSID arbitration rules, 2006. J World Inv Trade 13:486–501
Contartese C (2017) The autonomy of the EU legal order in the ECJ's external relations case-law: from the 'essential' to the 'specific characteristics' of the union and Back again. Common Market Law Rev 54:1627–1672
Devaney JG (2022) The role of precedent in the jurisprudence of the international court of justice: a constructive interpretation. Leiden J Int Law 35:641–659
Dutta S (2021) The quest for "consistency" in international investment jurisprudence and the idea of a multilateral investment court. In: Galvao Teles P, Almeida Riberio M (eds) Case-law and the development of international law contributions by international courts and tribunals. Brill/Nijhoff, Leiden/New York, pp 230–245
Feldman M (2017) Investment arbitration appellate mechanism options: consistency, accuracy, and balance of power. ICSID Rev 32:528–544
Foote S (2022) The Bona fide investor: corporate nationality and treaty shopping in investment treaty law. Kluwer Law International, Alphen aan den Rijn
Funk L (2022) Reforming ISDS through an opt-in treaty—the case of a multilateral investment court. In: Scheu J, Schöttmer L (eds) Creation and implementation of a multilateral investment court. Nomos, Baden-Baden, pp 227–250
Hindelang S (2019) Conceptualisation and application of the principle of autonomy of EU law: the CJEU'S judgment in Achmea put in perspective. Eur Law Rev 3:383–400
Kucik J, Puig S (2023) Towards an effective appellate mechanism for ISDS tribunals. World Trade Rev 22:562–583
Luttrell S (2019) Particular Procedures. In: Fouret J, Gerbav R, Álvarez GM (eds) The ICSID convention, regulations and rules: a practical commentary. Edward Elgar Publishing Limited, Cheltenham, pp 1139–1224
Ngangjoh-Hodu Y, Ajibo CC (2015) ICSID annulment procedure and the WTO appellate system: the case for an appellate system for investment arbitration. J Int Dispute Settl 6:308–331
Nguyen TTA (2022) Provisions on frivolous claims in the European Union—Vietnam investment protection agreement—would they be benefits to Vietnam? J Int Trade Law Pol 21:240–254
Nilsson A, Englesson O (2013) Inconsistent awards in investment treaty arbitration: is an appeals court needed? J Int Arb 30:561–579
Pascual-Vives F (2022) El principio de autonomía y el arbitraje de inversión ante el Tribunal de Justicia de la Unión Europea: A propósito de Polonia c. PL Holdings. Cuadernos Derecho Transnacional 14:669–693
Platt R (2013) The appeal of appeal mechanisms in international arbitration: fairness over finality? J Int Arb 30:531–560
Potestà M, Sobat M (2012) Frivolous claims in international adjudication: a study of ICSID rule 41(5) and of procedures of other courts and tribunals to dismiss claims summarily. J Int Disp Settl 3:137–168
van Rossem JW (2020) Pushing limits: the principle of autonomy in the external relations case law of the European court of justice. In: Andenas M, Pantaleo L, Happold M, Contartese C (eds) EU external action in international economic law: recent trends and developments. TMC Asser, The Hague, pp 35–68
Sauvant KP (2008) Appeals mechanism in international investment disputes. Oxford University Press, New York

Scheu J, Nikolov P (2019) The incompatibility of intra-EU investment treaty arbitration with European Union law—assessing the scope of the ECJ's Achmea judgment. German Yb Int Law 62:475–504

Schreuer CH (2007) Preliminary rulings in investment arbitration. Transnational Dispute Management 6

Shany Y (2005) Contract claims v. treaty claims: mapping conflicts between ICSID decisions on multi-sourced investment claims. Am J Int Law 99:835–851

Sornarajah M (2016) An international investment court: panacea or purgatory? Columbia FDI Perspectives, p 180

Vadi C (2018) Proportionality, reasonableness and standards of review in international investment law and arbitration. Edward Elgar Publishing Limited, Cheltenham

Zarra G (2018) The issue of incoherence in investment arbitration: is there a need for a systemic reform. Chin J Int Law 17:137–185

Respect for the Principles of the UN Charter and Observance of International Law

Matteo Del Chicca

Contents

Abstract This chapter examines how the new generation international trade agreements concluded by the EU with third Parties uphold and promote the respect for some principles of the UN Charter and the observance of international law. Firstly, this chapter surveys the norms of such agreements which could be interpreted as a way for the EU to sustain and foster the third principle of UN Charter. Secondly, the provisions of such agreements which look to enhance the seventh principle of UN Charter have been taken into consideration. Since UN principles are related to the purposes of the UN Charter, this chapter examines also the provisions included in the new generation international trade agreements concluded by the EU with third Parties which seem to uphold and promote respect for some purposes of UN Charter. Moreover, the provisions of such agreements which expressly refer to the observance of international law have been surveyed.

M. Del Chicca (✉)
Department of Law, University of Pisa, Pisa, Italy
e-mail: matteo.delchicca@unipi.it

L. Pasquali (ed.), *EU Values and International Law*, European Union and its Neighbours in a Globalized World 35,
https://doi.org/10.1007/978-3-032-20521-6_11

1 Introduction

Article 3, Paragraph 5, of the Treaty of the European Union states that "In its relations with the wider world, the Union shall uphold and promote its values and interests and contribute to the protection of its citizens"; the same Paragraph 5 adds that European Union (hereinafter 'EU') shall contribute *inter alia* "to the strict observance and the development of international law, including respect for the principles of the United Nations Charter".

It should be preliminary noted that, from many points of views, the international agreements concluded by EU with third Parties demand themselves the strict observance of international law (and could potentially contribute to its development): for example, their adoption procedures, their interpretation, their effects are all regulated by international law.

This looks to be corroborated by Article 21, Paragraph 1, of the Treaty of the EU, which states that "The Union's action on the international scene shall be guided by the principles which have inspired its own creation, development and enlargement, and which it seeks to advance in the wider world": among such principles, the same Paragraph 1 includes also the "respect for the principles of the United Nations Charter and international law".

The principles of the Charter of the United Nations are notoriously listed at Article 2 of the Charter,[1] and they are evidently related to the purposes of the United Nations (hereinafter 'UN'), listed instead at Article 1 of the UN Charter.[2]

[1]Article 2 of the Charter of the United Nations states what follows: "The Organization and its Members, in pursuit of the Purposes stated in Article 1, shall act in accordance with the following Principles.

1. The Organization is based on the principle of the sovereign equality of all its Members.

2. All Members, in order to ensure to all of them the rights and benefits resulting from membership, shall fulfil in good faith the obligations assumed by them in accordance with the present Charter.

3. All Members shall settle their international disputes by peaceful means in such a manner that international peace and security, and justice, are not endangered.

4. All Members shall refrain in their international relations from the threat or use of force against the territorial integrity or political independence of any state, or in any other manner inconsistent with the Purposes of the United Nations.

5. All Members shall give the United Nations every assistance in any action it takes in accordance with the present Charter, and shall refrain from giving assistance to any state against which the United Nations is taking preventive or enforcement action.

6. The Organization shall ensure that states which are not Members of the United Nations act in accordance with these Principles so far as may be necessary for the maintenance of international peace and security.

7. Nothing contained in the present Charter shall authorize the United Nations to intervene in matters which are essentially within the domestic jurisdiction of any state or shall require the Members to submit such matters to settlement under the present Charter; but this principle shall not prejudice the application of enforcement measures under Chapter VII".

[2]Article 1 of the UN Charter so states: "The Purposes of the United Nations are:

1. To maintain international peace and security, and to that end: to take effective collective measures for the prevention and removal of threats to the peace, and for the suppression of acts of

Firstly, it must be reminded that in the preambles of many new generation international trade agreements concluded by the EU with third Parties the agreement Parties explicitly reaffirm their commitment to the UN Charter. For example, such reaffirmation is included in the preambles of the following agreements: the Free Trade Agreement between the EU and New Zealand, the Free Trade Agreement between the EU and the Socialist Republic of Viet Nam (hereinafter 'Viet Nam'), the Free Trade Agreement between the EU and the Republic of Singapore (hereinafter 'Singapore'), the Agreement between the EU and Japan for an Economic Partnership, the Trade Agreement between the EU and its Member States, of the one part, and Colombia and Peru, of the other part (hereinafter 'Trade Agreement between the EU, Colombia and Peru'), the Free Trade Agreement between the EU and its Member States, of the one part, and the Republic of Korea, of the other part (hereinafter 'Free Trade Agreement between the EU and Korea'). Such commitments are never specifically referred to the principles of the UN Charter, being instead always related to the UN Charter in general.[3]

---

aggression or other breaches of the peace, and to bring about by peaceful means, and in conformity with the principles of justice and international law, adjustment or settlement of international disputes or situations which might lead to a breach of the peace;

2. To develop friendly relations among nations based on respect for the principle of equal rights and self-determination of peoples, and to take other appropriate measures to strengthen universal peace;

3. To achieve international cooperation in solving international problems of an economic, social, cultural, or humanitarian character, and in promoting and encouraging respect for human rights and for fundamental freedoms for all without distinction as to race, sex, language, or religion; and

4. To be a center for harmonizing the actions of nations in the attainment of these common ends".

[3] For example, "Reaffirming their commitment to the Charter of the United Nations signed in San Francisco on 26 June 1945 [...]", included in the preamble of the following agreements: Free Trade Agreement between the EU and New Zealand, OJ L 2024/866, 25.3.2024; Free Trade Agreement Between the EU and the Socialist Republic of Viet Nam, OJ L 186, 12.6.2020; Free Trade Agreement between the EU and the Republic of Singapore, OJ L 294, 14.11.2019; Free Trade Agreement between the EU and its Member States, of the one part, and the Republic of Korea, of the other part, OJ L 127, 14.5.2011. The preamble of a few agreements states more synthetically "Reaffirming their commitment to the Charter of the United Nations [...]", in: Agreement between the EU and Japan for an Economic Partnership, OJ L 330, 27.12.2018; Trade Agreement between the EU and its Member States, of the one part, and Colombia and Peru, of the other part, OJ L 354, 21.12.2012. It seems that only one provision of all the new generation international trade agreements concluded by the EU with third States refers explicitly to the principles of UN Charter, i. e. Article 768, Paragraph 1, of Trade and Cooperation Agreement between the EU and the European Atomic Energy Community, of the one part, and the United Kingdom of Great Britain and Northern Ireland, of the other part, OJ L 149, 30.04.2021, which so states: "The Parties shall cooperate at the bilateral, regional and international levels to prevent and combat acts of terrorism in all its forms and manifestations in accordance with international law, including, where applicable, international counterterrorism-related agreements, international humanitarian law and international human rights law, as well as in accordance with the principles of the Charter of the United Nations".

However, several provisions of certain new generation international trade agreements concluded by the EU with third States pertain to some particular principles and purposes of UN Charter and the strict observance of international law.

From a methodological point of view, it must be premised that some of the principles and of the purposes of the UN are mostly related to peace and security: since both such values are surveyed in another chapter of this book, they will not be examined here.[4] Analogously, they will be taken into consideration only the principles and the purposes of UN Charter that the new generation international trade agreements concluded by the EU with third Parties seem in some way to recall to a slightly greater extent.

For all such reasons, the references to the third principle of UN Charter—in the part which states that "All Members shall settle their international disputes by peaceful means [...]"—will be firstly surveyed in such agreements.[5] The seventh principle of UN Charter will be then considered in such agreements, only in the part which affirms that "Nothing contained in the present Charter shall authorize the United Nations to intervene in matters which are essentially within the domestic jurisdiction of any state or shall require the Members to submit such matters to settlement under the present Charter [...]".[6] Thirdly, the second purpose of UN Charter will be examined in such agreements, in the part which highlights the developing of friendly relations among nations based on respect for the principle of equal rights.[7] Thereafter, the third purpose of UN Charter will be taken into consideration in such agreements, in the part which states the aim "to achieve international cooperation in solving international problems of an economic, social, cultural, or humanitarian character [...]".[8] Lastly, they will be appraised the provisions of the new generation international trade agreements concluded by the EU with third Parties which somewhat recall an observance of international law.[9]

---

[4] For the same reasons, Article 21, Paragraph 2, and Article 41, Paragraph 1, of the Treaty of the EU are only peripherally mentioned herein: Paragraph 2 of Article 21 affirms that "The Union shall define and pursue common policies and actions, and shall work for a high degree of cooperation in all fields of international relations, in order to", among other things, what stated at Letter C, i.e. "preserve peace, prevent conflicts and strengthen international security, in accordance with the purposes and principles of the United Nations Charter [...]"; Article 42, Paragraph 1, states that "The common security and defence policy shall be an integral part of the common foreign and security policy. It shall provide the Union with an operational capacity drawing on civilian and military assets. The Union may use them on missions outside the Union for peace-keeping, conflict prevention and strengthening international security in accordance with the principles of the United Nations Charter. The performance of these tasks shall be undertaken using capabilities provided by the Member States".

[5] *Infra* par. 2.

[6] *Infra* par. 3.

[7] *Infra* par. 4.

[8] *Infra* par. 5. The second part of such purpose is related to human rights and fundamental freedoms, which are analyzed in another chapter of this book: for such reason they will not be taken into consideration in this chapter.

[9] *Infra* par. 6.

2 The UN Charter Principle of Settling International Disputes by Peaceful Means

As noted above,[10] the third principle of the UN Charter imposes among other things that "All Members shall settle their international disputes by peaceful means [...]". On this regard, it must be underscored that a part of all the new generation international trade agreements concluded by the EU with third Parties is always consistently dedicated to a dispute settlement system.[11] As stated, for example, by Article 31.1 of the Interim Agreement on Trade between the EU and the Republic of Chile (hereinafter 'Chile'), the objective of such part is "to establish an effective and efficient mechanism for avoiding and settling any dispute between the Parties concerning the interpretation and application of" the agreement "with a view to reaching a mutually agreed solution".[12] The dispute settlement systems included in all the new generation international trade agreements concluded by the EU with third Parties generally apply with respect to any dispute between the agreement Parties

[10] *Supra* par. 1.

[11] See Interim Agreement on Trade between the EU and the Republic of Chile, OJ L 2024/2953, 20.12.2024, Chapter 31; Economic Partnership Agreement between the EU, of the one Part, and the Republic of Kenya, Member of The East African Community, of the other Part, OJ L 2024/1648, 1.7.2024, Title II; Free Trade Agreement between the EU and New Zealand, Chapter 26; Trade and Cooperation Agreement between the EU and the European Atomic Energy Community, of the one part, and the United Kingdom of Great Britain and Northern Ireland, of the other part, Title XIII; Free Trade Agreement between the EU and Viet Nam, Chapter 15; Free Trade Agreement between the EU and Singapore, Chapter 14; Agreement between the EU and Japan for an Economic Partnership, Chapter 21; Comprehensive Economic and Trade Agreement (CETA) between Canada, of the one part, and the EU and its Member States, of the other part, OJ L 11, 14.1.2017, Chapter 29; Agreement establishing an Association between the EU and its Member States, on the one hand, and Central America on the other, OJ L 346, 15.12.2012, Title X; Trade Agreement between the EU, Colombia and Peru, Title XII; Free Trade Agreement between the EU and Korea, Chapter 14.

[12] Article 31.1 of the Interim Agreement on Trade between the EU and Chile precisely states what follows: "The objective of this Chapter is to establish an effective and efficient mechanism for avoiding and settling any dispute between the Parties concerning the interpretation and application of this Agreement with a view to reaching a mutually agreed solution". Analogous provisions are included in almost all the new generation international trade agreements concluded by the EU with third Parties; see, for example: Article 26.1 of Free Trade Agreement between the EU and New Zealand; Article 695 of Trade and Cooperation Agreement between the EU and the European Atomic Energy Community, of the one part, and the United Kingdom of Great Britain and Northern Ireland, of the other part; Article 15.1 of Free Trade Agreement between the EU and Viet Nam; Article 14.1 of Free Trade Agreement between the EU and Singapore; Article 21.1 of Agreement between the EU and Japan for an Economic Partnership; Article 308 of Agreement establishing an Association between the EU and its Member States, on the one hand, and Central America on the other; Article 298 of Trade Agreement between the EU, Colombia and Peru; Article 14.1 of Free Trade Agreement between the EU and Korea.

concerning the interpretation and application of the provisions of that agreement, with the exception of some parts.[13]

Such dispute settlement systems usually state foremost a consultations phase, where the agreement Parties shall endeavor to resolve any dispute referred to the scope of the dispute settlement system by entering into consultations in good faith with a view to reaching a mutually agreed solution.[14] Such consultations could be followed by an arbitration procedure, which is always accurately detailed in all the new generation international trade agreements concluded by the EU with third Parties.[15] On this regard it must be pointed out that almost all such agreements—with the only exception of the Trade and Cooperation Agreement between the EU and the European Atomic Energy Community, of the one part, and the United Kingdom of Great Britain and Northern Ireland, of the other part (hereinafter 'Trade and Cooperation Agreement between the EU and UK')—state that the arbitration panels shall interpret the provisions referred to the scope of the dispute settlement

[13] About the exceptions see for example the following provisions included in some recent new generation international trade agreements concluded by the EU with third Parties: Articles 5.5, 5.8, 12.8, 23.6, 24.8, 29.13, 30.4 of Interim Agreement on Trade between the EU and Chile; Article 26.2, Paragraph 2, of Free Trade Agreement between the EU and New Zealand; Article 696, Paragraph 2, of Trade and Cooperation Agreement between the EU and the European Atomic Energy Community, of the one part, and the United Kingdom of Great Britain and Northern Ireland, of the other part.

[14] On this regard see, for example: Article 31.4 of Interim Agreement on Trade between the EU and Chile; Article 110 of Economic Partnership Agreement between the EU, of the one Part, and the Republic of Kenya, Member of The East African Community, of the other Part; Article 26.3 of Free Trade Agreement between the EU and New Zealand; Article 698 of Trade and Cooperation Agreement between the EU and the European Atomic Energy Community, of the one part, and the United Kingdom of Great Britain and Northern Ireland, of the other part; Article 15.3 of Free Trade Agreement between the EU and Viet Nam; Article 14.3 of Free Trade Agreement between the EU and Singapore; Article 21.5 of Agreement between the EU and Japan for an Economic Partnership; Article 29.4 of Comprehensive Economic and Trade Agreement (CETA) between Canada, of the one part, and the EU and its Member States, of the other part; Article 310 of Agreement establishing an Association between the EU and its Member States, on the one hand, and Central America on the other; Article 301 of Trade Agreement between the EU, Colombia and Peru; Article 14.3 of Free Trade Agreement between the EU and Korea.

[15] See, for example: Interim Agreement on Trade between the EU and Chile, Chapter 31, Section C; Economic Partnership Agreement between the EU, of the one Part, and the Republic of Kenya, Member of The East African Community, of the other Part, Title II; Free Trade Agreement between the EU and New Zealand, Chapter 26, Section C; Free Trade Agreement between the EU and Viet Nam, Chapter 15, Section C; Free Trade Agreement between the EU and Singapore, Chapter 14; Agreement between the EU and Japan for an Economic Partnership, Chapter 21, Section C; Comprehensive Economic and Trade Agreement (CETA) between Canada, of the one part, and the EU and its Member States, of the other part, Chapter 29, Section C; Agreement establishing an Association between the EU and its Member States, on the one hand, and Central America on the other, Title X, Chapter 3; Trade Agreement between the EU, Colombia and Peru, Title XII, Chapter 3; Free Trade Agreement between the EU and Korea, Chapter 14, Section C.

system in accordance with customary rules of interpretation of public international law, including those codified in the 1969 Vienna Convention on the Law of Treaties.[16]

For such reasons too, it should be considered that all such dispute settlements provisions uphold and promote not only the respect of the cited third principle of UN Charter, but also the strict observance of international law, particularly the rules of international law related to the interpretation of the treaties.[17]

In addition, it could be highlighted that all such agreements—still with the only exception of the Trade and Cooperation Agreement between the EU and UK—provide also a mediation mechanism to facilitate the finding of a mutually agreed solution through a comprehensive and expeditious procedure with the assistance of a mediator.[18]

3 The UN Charter Principle of Domestic Jurisdiction

As aforementioned in paragraph 1, another principle of UN Charter—relevant for this chapter—could be the seventh principle, which so states (in the part here pertinent): "Nothing contained in the present Charter shall authorize the United Nations to intervene in matters which are essentially within the domestic jurisdiction of any

[16] For example, Article 26.22, Paragraph 1, of Free Trade Agreement between the EU and New Zealand states what follows: "The panel shall interpret the covered provisions in accordance with customary rules of interpretation of public international law, including those codified in the Vienna Convention on the Law of Treaties, done at Vienna on 23 May 1969". Analogous provisions are included also in the following agreements: Interim Agreement on Trade between the EU and Chile, Article 31.23, Paragraph 1; Economic Partnership Agreement between the EU, of the one Part, and the Republic of Kenya, Member of The East African Community, of the other Part, Article 123, Paragraph 1; of Free Trade Agreement between the EU and Viet Nam, Article 15.21; Free Trade Agreement between the EU and Singapore, Article 14.18; Agreement between the EU and Japan for an Economic Partnership, Article 21.16; Comprehensive Economic and Trade Agreement (CETA) between Canada, of the one part, and the EU and its Member States, of the other part, Article 29.17; Agreement establishing an Association between the EU and its Member States, on the one hand, and Central America on the other, Article 322, Paragraph 1 (which anyway does not mention the 1969 Vienna Convention on the Law of Treaties); Trade Agreement between the EU, Colombia and Peru, Article 317; Free Trade Agreement between the EU and Korea, Article 14.16.

[17] On this regard see *infra* par. 6.

[18] See, for example: Interim Agreement on Trade between the EU and Chile, Chapter 31, Section D; Economic Partnership Agreement between the EU, of the one Part, and the Republic of Kenya, Member of The East African Community, of the other Part, Article 111; Free Trade Agreement between the EU and New Zealand, Chapter 26, Section D, and Annex 26-C; Free Trade Agreement between the EU and Viet Nam, Article 15.4; Free Trade Agreement between the EU and Singapore, Chapter 15 Agreement between the EU and Japan for an Economic Partnership, Article 21.6; Comprehensive Economic and Trade Agreement (CETA) between Canada, of the one part, and the EU and its Member States, of the other part, Article 29.5 and Annex 29-C; Agreement establishing an Association between the EU and its Member States, on the one hand, and Central America on the other, Title XI; Trade Agreement between the EU, Colombia and Peru, Article 322 and Annex XIV; Free Trade Agreement between the EU and Korea, Annex 14-A.

state or shall require the Members to submit such matters to settlement under the present Charter [...]".[19]

There is no room in this chapter to properly articulate the concept of domestic jurisdiction: we just assume here that the principle of UN Charter now recalled could be also interpreted as a general recognition that occasionally some matters could be not regulated by international law. Following such assumption, for the purposes of this chapter we just highlight here some provisions—included in certain new generation international trade agreements concluded by the EU with third Parties—which acknowledge the power of the Parties to regulate some matters in their domestic law as they deem appropriate, with no interference by any provision of such agreements.

For example, in relation to the part of such agreements dedicated to the regulatory cooperation, sometimes it stated that—fully respecting each Party's right to regulate this matter—nothing in that part shall be construed as obliging a Party to modify its import requirements, to deviate from domestic procedures on the preparation and adoption of regulatory measures, to take action that would undermine or impede the public policy objective of a particular regulatory measure or the timely adoption of regulatory measures to achieve public policy objectives, or to adopt any particular regulatory outcome.[20] On this regard, the Trade and Cooperation Agreement between the EU and UK adds also that nothing in that part shall affect the right of a Party to define or regulate its own levels of protection in pursuit or furtherance of its public policy objectives in many areas as, for example, public

[19] The latter part of this principle has been omitted because it is more properly relative to peace and security, which are EU values surveyed in another chapter of this book.

[20] For example, Article 22.1 of the Free Trade Agreement between the EU and New Zealand (included in Chapter 22 of such agreement, titled "Good Regulatory Practices and Regulatory Cooperation") states what follows: "1. Each Party shall be free to determine its approach to good regulatory practices and regulatory cooperation under this Agreement in a manner consistent with its own legal framework, practice and fundamental principles underlying its regulatory management system. 2. Nothing in this Chapter shall be construed as to require a Party to: (a) deviate from domestic procedures for preparing and adopting regulatory measures; (b) take actions that would risk compromising or undermining the public policy objective of a particular regulatory measure; (c) take actions that would undermine or impede the timely adoption of regulatory measures to achieve its public policy objectives; or (d) achieve any particular regulatory outcome. 3. Each Party shall be free to identify its regulatory priorities and to prepare and adopt regulatory

measures to address those regulatory priorities ensuring the levels of protection that the Party considers appropriate". The wording of Article 340, Paragraphs 1 and 2, of the Trade and Cooperation Agreement between the EU and UK (included in Title X of such agreement, also titled "Good Regulatory Practices and Regulatory Cooperation") is very similar to Article 22.1, Paragraphs 1 and 2, of the Free Trade Agreement between the EU and New Zealand. Article 7.10, Paragraph 3, of Interim Agreement on Trade between the EU and Chile (included in Chapter 7 of such agreement, entitled "Cooperation on Sustainable Food Systems"), analogously states that "Fully respecting each Party's right to regulate, nothing in this Chapter shall be construed as obliging a Party to: (a) modify its import requirements; (b) deviate from domestic procedures on the preparation and adoption of regulatory measures; (c) take action that would undermine or impede the timely adoption of regulatory measures to achieve public policy objectives; or (d) adopt any particular regulatory outcome".

health, human, animal or plant life and health, animal welfare, occupational health and safety, labor conditions.[21]

Furthermore, many new generation international trade agreements concluded by the EU with third Parties include quite identical "specific exceptions" to a part of those agreements usually dedicated to trade in services and electronic commerce. Such specific exceptions state that nothing in that part shall be construed as preventing a Party, including its public entities, from exclusively conducting or providing in its territory activities or services forming part of a public retirement plan or statutory system of social security, or for the account, or with the guarantee or using the financial resources of the Party, or its public entities, except when those activities may be carried out, as provided by the Party's domestic laws and regulations, by financial service suppliers in competition with public entities or private institutions.[22]

In addition, there are a few other provisions in some new generation international trade agreements concluded by the EU with third Parties which could be also in

[21] Article 340, Paragraph 3, of the Trade and Cooperation Agreement between the EU and UK more widely states that "Nothing in this Title shall affect the right of a Party to define or regulate its own levels of protection in pursuit or furtherance of its public policy objectives in areas such as: (a) public health; (b) human, animal or plant life and health, and animal welfare; (c) occupational health and safety; (d) labour conditions; (e) environment including climate change; (f) consumer protection; (g) social protection and social security; (h) data protection and cybersecurity; (i) cultural diversity; (j) integrity and stability of the financial system, and protection of investors; (k) energy security; and (l) anti-money laundering.

For greater certainty, for the purposes of in particular point (c) and (d) of the first subparagraph, the different models of industrial relations, including the role and autonomy of social partners, as provided for in the law or national practices of a Party, shall continue to apply, including laws and practices concerning collective bargaining and the enforcement of collective agreements".

[22] For example, Article 8.46, Paragraph 1, of Free Trade Agreement between the EU and Viet Nam (included in Chapter 8 of such agreement, titled "Liberalisation of investment, trade in services and electronic commerce") states that "Nothing in this Chapter shall be construed as preventing a Party, including its public entities, from exclusively conducting or providing in its territory activities or services forming part of a public retirement plan or statutory system of social security, except when those activities may be carried out, as provided by the Party's domestic laws and regulations, by financial service suppliers in competition with public entities or private institutions", whereas Paragraph 4 of the same Article 8.46 states that "Nothing in this Chapter shall be construed as preventing a Party, including its public entities, from exclusively conducting or providing in its territory activities or services for the account, or with the guarantee or using the financial resources of the Party, or its public entities, except when those activities may be carried out, as provided by the Party's domestic laws and regulations, by financial service suppliers in competition with public entities or private institutions". Almost identical provisions are included, for example, in Article 8.55, Paragraphs 1 and 3, of Free Trade Agreement between the EU and Singapore (included in Chapter 8 of such agreement, titled "Services, establishment and electronic commerce"), as well as in Article 199, Paragraphs 1 and 3, of the Agreement establishing an Association between the EU and its Member States, on the one hand, and Central America on the other (included in Title III of such agreement, named "Establishment, trade in services and electronic commerce"), and in Article 159, Paragraphs 1 and 3, of the Trade Agreement between the EU, Colombia and Peru (included in Title IV of such agreement, named "Trade in services, establishment and electronic commerce").

some way seen as means to sustain and foster the seventh principle of UN Charter, with the meaning considered in this chapter. For example, Article 13.7, Paragraph 2, of the Free Trade Agreement between the EU and Viet Nam, which recognizes the sovereign rights of States over their natural resources, and that the authority to determine access to their genetic resources rests with their respective governments and is subject to their domestic law[23]; or Article 10.22, Paragraph 1, of the Free Trade Agreement between the EU and Singapore, which specifies that the conditions for import, export and commercialization of some products (referred to in the section of such agreement dedicated to geographical indications) in the territory of a Party shall be governed by the domestic law of that Party.[24]

It could be eventually reminded that, in some new generation international trade agreements concluded by the EU with third States, the Parties of such agreements recognize the right of each Party to determine its sustainable development policies and priorities, as well as to establish its own levels of domestic labor and environmental protection (including social protection) that it deems appropriate and its own labor and environmental priorities, and to adopt or modify its law and policies related to labor and environment accordingly. Even if sometimes with slightly different wording, that is stated, for example, in the following agreements: Interim Agreement on Trade between the EU and Chile[25]; Economic Partnership Agreement between the EU, of the one Part, and the Republic of Kenya, Member of The East African Community, of the other Part (hereinafter 'Economic Partnership Agreement between the EU and Kenya')[26]; Free Trade Agreement between the EU and New Zealand[27]; Free Trade Agreement between the EU and Viet Nam[28]; Agreement between the EU and Japan for an Economic Partnership[29]; Agreement establishing an Association between the EU and its Member States, on the one hand, and Central America on the other (hereinafter 'Agreement establishing an Association between the EU and Central America')[30]; Trade Agreement between the EU, Colombia and Peru.[31] Anyway, it must be noted that such agreements point also out that such levels, law and policies shall be consistent with each Party's commitment to the

---

[23] Indeed, Article 13.7, Paragraph 2, of the Free Trade Agreement between the EU and Viet Nam states that "The Parties recognise, in accordance with Article 15 of the CBD, the sovereign rights of states over their natural resources, and that the authority to determine access to their genetic resources rests with their respective governments and is subject to their domestic law […]".

[24] More precisely, Article 10.22, Paragraph 1, of the Free Trade Agreement between the EU and Singapore states what follows: "The conditions for import, export and commercialisation of the products referred to in Sub-Section C (Geographical Indications) in the territory of a Party shall be governed by the domestic law of that Party".

[25] See Article 26.2, Paragraph 1, of such agreement.

[26] See Annex V, Article 2, Paragraph 1, of such agreement.

[27] See Article 19.2, Paragraph 1, of such agreement.

[28] See Article 13.2, Paragraph 1, of such agreement.

[29] See Article 16.2, Paragraph 1, of such agreement.

[30] See Article 285, Paragraph 1, of such agreement.

[31] See Article 268 of such agreement.

internationally recognized standards and agreements to which it is Party.[32] Additionally, in some agreements the Parties stress also that weakening the levels of protection in environmental or labor areas is detrimental to the objectives of that related part of the agreement and that it is inappropriate to encourage trade and investment by weakening the levels of protection afforded in domestic environmental or labor law.[33] From these points of view, such last provisions do not entirely look to uphold and promote the seventh principle of UN Charter, in the sense assumed in this chapter.

4 The UN Charter Purpose of Developing Friendly Relations Among Nations

As premised in paragraph 1, the principles of UN Charter are inevitably interlinked with the purposes of the same Charter. The second of such purposes—i.e. developing friendly relations among nations based on respect for the principle of equal rights—looks particularly relevant for this chapter. Indeed, the new generation international trade agreements concluded by the EU with third Parties include several provisions which could sustain and foster such purpose.

Firstly, it must be underlined that, even if with different intensities, the preambles of most such agreements recall the purpose of developing the relations between the Parties, with an eye to sustainable development.[34] For example, in the preamble of

[32] For example, Article 26.2, Paragraph 2, of Interim Agreement on Trade between the EU and Chile states what follows: "The levels of protection, law and policies referred to in paragraph 1 shall be consistent with each Party's commitment to the multilateral environmental agreements ('MEAs') and multilateral labour standards and agreements, as referred to in this Chapter, to which it is party". Similarly, the second part of Annex V, Article 2, Paragraph 1, of Economic Partnership Agreement between the EU and Kenya states that "[...] Such levels, law and policies shall be consistent with each Party's commitment to the internationally recognised standards and agreements referred to in this Annex". Analogous provisions are included, for example, in: Article 19.2, Paragraph 1, of Free Trade Agreement between the EU and New Zealand; Article 13.2, Paragraph 1, Letter C, of Free Trade Agreement between the EU and Viet Nam; Article 16.2, Paragraph 1, of Agreement between the EU and Japan for an Economic Partnership; Article 285, Paragraph 2, of Agreement establishing an Association between the EU and Central America; Article 268 of Trade Agreement between the EU, Colombia and Peru.

[33] For example, Article 13.3, Paragraph 1, of the Free Trade Agreement between the EU and Viet Nam states that "The Parties stress that weakening the levels of protection in environmental or labour areas is detrimental to the objectives of this Chapter and that it is inappropriate to encourage trade and investment by weakening the levels of protection afforded in domestic environmental or labour law". Similarly, Article 291, Paragraph 1, of Agreement establishing an Association between the EU and Central America states what follows: "The Parties recognise that it is inappropriate to encourage trade or investment by lowering the levels of protection afforded in domestic environmental and labour laws".

[34] Sustainable development is sometimes highlighted as a key element of the relations between Parties not only in the preamble: for example, Article 16.1 Paragraph 2, of Agreement between the EU and Japan for an Economic Partnership states that "The Parties further recognise that the pur-

Interim Agreement on Trade between the EU and Chile the Parties desire "to strengthen their economic relations, in particular their trade and investment relations, by strengthening and improving market access, and contributing to economic growth, while remaining mindful of the need to raise awareness of the economic and social impact of environmental damage, unsustainable patterns of production and consumption and their associated impact on human well-being", moreover "reaffirming their commitment to promote sustainable development in its economic, social and environmental dimensions, their commitment to the development of international trade in such a way as to contribute to sustainable development in those three dimensions [...]". Similar desires and convictions are expressed in the preamble of most of the new generation international trade agreements concluded by the EU with third Parties; for example, in the preamble of the following agreements: Free Trade Agreement between the EU and New Zealand,[35] Free Trade Agreement between the EU and Viet Nam,[36] Free Trade Agreement between the EU and Singapore,[37] Agreement between the EU and Japan for an Economic Partnership,[38] Agreement establishing an Association between the EU and Central America,[39] Trade Agreement

pose of this Chapter is to strengthen the trade relations and cooperation between the Parties in ways that promote sustainable development, and is not to harmonise the environment or labour standards of the Parties" (such Article is included in Chapter 16, titled "Trade and sustainable development").

[35] "Resolved to strengthen their economic relations, and expand bilateral trade and investment [...] Determined to strengthen their economic, trade, and investment relations in accordance with the objective of sustainable development, in its economic, social and environmental dimensions, and to promote trade and investment that are consistent with the aims for high levels of environmental and labour protection and with relevant internationally recognised standards and agreements to which they are a party", in preamble of Free Trade Agreement between the EU and New Zealand.

[36] "Desiring to further strengthen their economic relationship as part of, and in a manner coherent with, their overall relations, and convinced that this Agreement will create a new climate for the development of trade and investment between the Parties [...] Determined to strengthen their economic, trade and investment relationship in accordance with the objective of sustainable development, in its economic, social and environmental dimensions, and to promote trade and investment under this Agreement in a manner mindful of high levels of environmental and labour protection and relevant internationally recognised standards and agreements", in preamble of Free Trade Agreement between the EU and Viet Nam.

[37] The wording of the preamble of such agreement is almost identical to that of Free Trade Agreement between the EU and Viet Nam (*ibidem*).

[38] "Recognising the importance of strengthening their economic, trade and investment relations, in accordance with the objective of sustainable development in the economic, social and environmental dimensions, and of promoting trade and investment between them [...]", in preamble of Agreement between the EU and Japan for an Economic Partnership.

[39] "Desiring to strengthen their economic relations, particularly trade and investment, strengthening and improving the current level of access of the Republics of the CA Party to the European Union market, thus contributing to economic growth in Central America and the reduction of asymmetries between the two regions; Convinced that this Agreement will create a climate conducive to growth in sustainable economic relations between them, more particularly in the trade and investment sectors which are essential to the realisation of the economic and social development and technological innovation and modernisation [...] Highlighting their commitment to working together in pursuit of the objectives of poverty eradication, job creation, equitable and sustainable development", in preamble of Agreement establishing an Association between the EU and Central America.

between the EU, Colombia and Peru,[40] Free Trade Agreement between the EU and Korea.[41] In all such preambles, the friendly relations among Parties are particularly substantiated,[42] sometimes also on the basis of a previous Partnership and Cooperation Agreement between them.[43]

---

[40] "Determined to strengthen those links by building on the existing mechanisms that govern relations between the European Union and its Member States and the signatory Andean Countries [...] Committed to implementing this Agreement in accordance with the objective of sustainable development, including, the promotion of economic progress, the respect for labour rights and the protection of the environment, in accordance with the international commitments adopted by the Parties", in preamble of Trade Agreement between the EU, Colombia and Peru.

[41] "Desiring to further strengthen their close economic relationship as part of and in a manner coherent with their overall relations, and convinced that this Agreement will create a new climate for the development of trade and investment between the Parties [...] Reaffirming their commitment to sustainable development and convinced of the contribution of international trade to sustainable development in its economic, social and environmental dimensions, including economic development, poverty reduction, full and productive employment and decent work for all as well as the protection and preservation of the environment and natural resources", in preamble of Free Trade Agreement between the EU and Korea.

[42] "Considering the strong cultural, political, economic and cooperation ties which unite them", in preamble of Interim Agreement on Trade between the EU and Chile. "Conscious of their longstanding and strong partnership based on common principles and values, and of their important economic, trade and investment relationship", in preamble of Agreement between the EU and Japan for an Economic Partnership. "Considering the traditional historical, cultural, political, economic and social links between the Parties and the desire to strengthen their relations based on common principles and values, building on the existing mechanisms that govern relations between the Parties, as well as the desire to consolidate, deepen and diversify bi-regional links in areas of common interest in a spirit of mutual respect, equality, non-discrimination, solidarity and mutual benefit; Considering the positive development in both regions during the last two decades, which has enabled the furtherance of common goals and interests to enter into a new stage of relations, deeper and more modern and permanent, in order to establish a bi-regional association that responds to the current internal challenges as well as new international realities", in preamble of Agreement establishing an Association between the EU and Central America. "Considering the importance of the historical and cultural links and the special links of friendship and cooperation between the European Union and its Member States and the signatory Andean Countries, and their wish to promote the economic integration between the Parties", in preamble of Trade Agreement between the EU, Colombia and Peru.

[43] "Recognising their longstanding and strong partnership based on the common principles and values reflected in the Partnership Agreement on Relations and Cooperation between the European Union and its Member States, of the one part, and New Zealand, of the other part, done at Brussels on 5 October 2016, and their important economic, trade and investment relationship", in preamble of Free Trade Agreement between the EU and New Zealand. "Recognising their longstanding and strong partnership based on the common principles and values reflected in the Partnership and Cooperation Agreement, and their important economic, trade and investment relationship", in preamble of Free Trade Agreement between the EU and Viet Nam. "Recognising their longstanding and strong partnership based on the common principles and values reflected in the Partnership and Cooperation Agreement, and their important economic, trade and investment relationship", in preamble of Free Trade Agreement between the EU and Singapore. The previous agreement among EU and Korea is a Framework Agreement: "Recognising their longstanding and strong partnership based on the common principles and values reflected in the Framework Agreement", in preamble of Free Trade Agreement between the EU and Korea.

Moreover, such relations are included among the objectives of some new generation international trade agreements concluded by EU with third Parties: for example, Article 2, Paragraph 1, Letter G of Economic Partnership Agreement between the EU and Kenya lists among the objectives of such agreement to "strengthen the existing relations between the Parties on the basis of solidarity and mutual interest [...]".[44] It could be also reminded, for example, that Article 1 of the Trade and Cooperation Agreement between the EU and UK—titled "Purpose"—states clearly that such "[...] Agreement establishes the basis for a broad relationship between the Parties, within an area of prosperity and good neighbourliness characterised by close and peaceful relations [...]".

Furthermore, it could be noted that in many new generation international trade agreements concluded by EU with third Parties, the Parties recognize the importance of two key elements in their relations: regional integration,[45] and free and undistorted competition.[46] From this point of view, such two elements look like significant means for EU to uphold and promote the second purpose of UN Charter, i.e. developing friendly relations among nations, at least in the context of trade relations.

5 The UN Charter Purpose of Achieving International Cooperation to Solve International Problems

The third purpose of UN Charter is "to achieve international cooperation in solving international problems of an economic, social, cultural, or humanitarian character, and in promoting and encouraging respect for human rights and for fundamental

---

[44] Analogously, Article 2 of Agreement establishing an Association between the EU and Central America—titled "Objectives"—lists among them also "strengthen and consolidate the relations between the Parties [...]" (at Letter A), and "reinforce good neighbourly relations [...]" (at Letter F).

[45] For example, Article 10, Paragraph 1, of Trade Agreement between the EU, Colombia and Peru—titled "Regional integration"—states what follows: "The Parties recognise the importance of regional integration in furthering the economic and social development of the signatory Andean Countries and of the European Union, enabling to strengthen the relations between the Parties and to contribute to the objectives of this Agreement". On this regard see also, for example, Article 2, Letter E, Article 13, Paragraph 2, Article 24, Paragraph 2, Letter E, of Agreement establishing an Association between the EU and Central America.

[46] See, for example: Article 23.1 of Interim Agreement on Trade between the EU and Chile, Article 15.1 of Free Trade Agreement between the EU and New Zealand, Article 358 of Trade and Cooperation Agreement between the EU and UK, Article 10.1 of Free Trade Agreement between the EU and Viet Nam, Article 11.1 of Free Trade Agreement between the EU and Singapore, Article 17.2 of Comprehensive Economic and Trade Agreement (CETA) between Canada, of the one part, and the EU and its Member States, of the other part, Article 278 of Agreement establishing an Association between the EU and Central America, Article 11.1, Paragraph 1, of Free Trade Agreement between the EU and Korea.

freedoms for all without distinction as to race, sex, language, or religion".[47] As noted above,[48] since human rights and fundamental freedoms are surveyed in another chapter of this book, only the aspect of international cooperation will be taken here into consideration.

On a larger perspective, the new generation international trade agreements concluded by EU with third Parties are by themselves a way for EU to sustain a promote international cooperation: even just negotiating and ratifying them is already in itself an expression of that. Additionally, cooperation in solving international problems of various character, especially those related to economic matters, is the *ratio* which imbues all the provisions included in such agreements. And besides that, such agreements include also several provisions which distinctly enhance the overarching aspect of the cooperation.

Indeed, such aspect is not only affirmed in the preambles of such agreements,[49] but sometimes, for example, it is explicitly included even among the objectives of the whole agreement: for example, Article 2, Paragraph 1, of the Economic Partnership Agreement between the EU and Kenya contains among the general objectives of such agreement also to promote "economic cooperation" in the East African Community Partner States, and to deep "cooperation in all areas relevant to trade and investment" as well.[50] Similarly, also the Agreement establishing an Association between the EU and Central America and the Trade Agreement between the EU, Colombia and Peru expressly include the cooperation among their overall objectives.[51]

Furthermore, numerous new generation international trade agreements concluded by EU with third Parties explicitly sets cooperation more particularly among

---

[47] *Supra* footnote 2.

[48] *Supra* footnote 8.

[49] See, for example, what affirmed in the following preambles: "Affirming their commitment to strengthen cooperation on bilateral, regional and global issues of common concern and to use all available tools to promote activities designed to develop an active and reciprocal international cooperation", in preamble of Interim Agreement on Trade between the EU and Chile; "Recognising the importance of global cooperation to address issues of shared interest", in preamble of Free Trade Agreement between the EU and New Zealand; "Contributing to the harmonious development and expansion of world and regional trade, and offering a catalyst for international cooperation", in preamble of Trade Agreement between the EU, Colombia and Peru.

[50] Article 2, Paragraph 1, of Economic Partnership Agreement between the EU and Kenya *inter alia* states that the objectives of that agreement are to "[....] promote regional integration, economic cooperation and good governance in the EAC Partner State(s)" (at Letter B), and "strengthen the existing relations between the Parties on the basis of solidarity and mutual interest. To this end, consistent with their WTO rights and obligations, this Agreement shall enhance commercial and economic relations, support a new trading dynamic between the Parties by means of the progressive, asymmetrical liberalisation of trade between them and reinforce, broaden and deepen cooperation in all areas relevant to trade and investment" (at Letter G).

[51] See Article 2, Letters A and C, of Agreement establishing an Association between the EU and Central America, and Article 4, Letter K, of Trade Agreement between the EU, Colombia and Peru.

the objectives of several specific parts of such agreements.[52] Just as one example, the Interim Agreement on Trade between the EU and Chile indicates cooperation as one of the objectives of many peculiar essential parts of that agreement, particularly those related to sanitary and phytosanitary measures,[53] to cooperation on sustainable food systems,[54] to energy and raw materials,[55] to the technical barriers to trade,[56] to environment and trade,[57] to trade and gender equality.[58] Cooperation is not only among the objectives of such parts, but it also permeates more widely all those parts, as well as many other parts of all new generation international trade agreements concluded by EU with third Parties.[59]

Moreover, cooperation is distinctly a key element in many parts of all such agreements: for example, the parts of those agreements typically dedicated to the rules of origin and to origin procedures of the products contain often an article—usually titled "Administrative cooperation"—which *inter alia* imposes to the Parties to cooperate with each other, through their respective customs authorities, in order to verify the originating status of a product or whether the other requirements set out in that part have been met.[60] It should be underlined that the agreements which do

[52] On this regard see, for example, the following provisions included in some recent new generation international trade agreements concluded by EU with third Parties: Articles 22, 58, 82, 98 of Economic Partnership Agreement between the EU and Kenya; Articles 8.1 and 19.1 of Free Trade Agreement between the EU and New Zealand; Articles 101, 494, 522, 527, 564, 580, 656 of Trade and Cooperation Agreement between the EU and UK; Articles 8.50 and 13.1 of Free Trade Agreement between the EU and Viet Nam; Article 7.1 of Free Trade Agreement between the EU and Singapore.

[53] See Article 6.1 of Interim Agreement on Trade between the EU and Chile.

[54] See Article 7.1 *ibidem*.

[55] See Article 8.1 *ibidem*.

[56] See Article 9.1 *ibidem*.

[57] See Article 26.8 *ibidem*.

[58] See Article 27.1 *ibidem*.

[59] See, just as an example, the parts of the Agreement between the EU and Japan for an Economic Partnership dedicated to the following matters: trade in goods, trade in services, customs matters and trade facilitation, investment liberalization, electronic commerce, government procurement, competition policy, intellectual property, trade and sustainable development, transparency, good regulatory practices, agriculture, small and medium-sized enterprises. As an additional example see the parts of, *ex plurimis*, the Comprehensive Economic and Trade Agreement (CETA) between Canada, of the one part, and the EU and its Member States, of the other part dedicated to the following matters: national treatment and market access for goods, technical barriers to trade, customs and trade facilitation, intellectual property, regulatory cooperation, trade and sustainable development, trade and labor, trade and environment, bilateral dialogues, administrative and institutional provisions, transparency, dispute settlement, motor vehicle regulations.

[60] See, for example, Article 3.23 of Interim Agreement on Trade between the EU and Chile, Article 16 of Economic Partnership Agreement between the EU and Kenya, Article 3.24 of Free Trade Agreement between the EU and New Zealand, Article 62 of Trade and Cooperation Agreement between the EU and UK, Section 6 of Free Trade Agreement between the EU and Singapore, Article 3.22 of Agreement between the EU and Japan for an Economic Partnership, Article 2.17 of Free Trade Agreement between the EU and Korea.

not include such article anyway establish a complex control system on these matters, still focused on cooperation.[61]

In addition, cooperation is extensively emphasized in numerous other norms of such agreements, sometimes specifically as a way to solve international problems of various character, i.e. properly with the meaning of the third purpose of UN Charter. For example, international cooperation is frequently underscored in relation to employment and labor affairs, as a response of the international community to economic, employment and social challenges.[62] Similarly, Parties of such agreements often agree to promote the development of electronic commerce between them, sometimes specifying that it should be made in particular by cooperating on the issues raised by electronic commerce.[63]

Lastly, it could be noted that in such agreements cooperation among Parties looks many times connected to the relations between them, so recalling a sort of link between the third and the second purpose of UN Charter (the latter taken into consideration in the previous paragraph). For example, such link appears in the general objectives of some new generation international trade agreements concluded by EU with third Parties: for instance, Article 2, Paragraph 1, Letter G, of Economic Partnership Agreement between the EU and Kenya includes among the objectives of such agreement to "enhance commercial and economic relations, support a new trading dynamic between the Parties by means of the progressive, asymmetrical liberalisation of trade between them and reinforce, broaden and deepen cooperation

[61] See, for example: Article 4.16, Protocol 1 and 2 of Free Trade Agreement between the EU and Viet Nam; Protocol on rules of origin and origin procedures of Comprehensive Economic and Trade Agreement (CETA) between Canada, of the one part, and the EU and its Member States, of the other part; Annex II of Agreement establishing an Association between the EU and Central America; Article 68 and Annex II of Trade Agreement between the EU, Colombia and Peru.

[62] For example, Article 23.1, Paragraph 1, of Comprehensive Economic and Trade Agreement (CETA) between Canada, of the one part, and the EU and its Member States, of the other part, states what follows: "The Parties recognise the value of international cooperation and agreements on labour affairs as a response of the international community to economic, employment and social challenges and opportunities resulting from globalisation. They recognise the contribution that international trade could make to full and productive employment and decent work for all and commit to consulting and cooperating as appropriate on trade-related labour and employment issues of mutual interest". See also, for example, Article 286, Paragraph 1, of Agreement establishing an Association between the EU and Central America, and Article 13.4, Paragraph 1, of Free Trade Agreement between the EU and Korea.

[63] For example, Article 8.50 of Free Trade Agreement between the EU and Viet Nam states what follows: "The Parties, recognising that electronic commerce increases trade opportunities in many sectors, shall promote the development of electronic commerce between them, in particular by cooperating on the issues raised by electronic commerce […]". See also, for example, Article 8.57, Paragraph 2, of Free Trade Agreement between the EU and Singapore; Article 16.2, Paragraph 1, of Comprehensive Economic and Trade Agreement (CETA) between Canada, of the one part, and the EU and its Member States, of the other part; Article 16.2, Paragraph 1, of Trade Agreement between the EU, Colombia and Peru; Article 7.48, Paragraph 1, of Free Trade Agreement between the EU and Korea.

in all areas relevant to trade and investment".[64] Such link between cooperation and the relations among Parties appears also in some specific objectives of certain parts of such agreements: just as an example, among the objectives of the part of Interim Agreement on Trade between the EU and Chile dedicated to labor and trade, there is also the Parties aim to cooperate on trade-related labor issues of mutual interest in order to strengthen the broader relationship between themselves.[65] As an additional example, this time on trade and gender equality matter, it could be cited that the Parties of Economic Partnership Agreement between the EU and Kenya "aim to strengthen their trade relations and cooperation in ways that effectively provide equal opportunities and treatment for women and men to benefit from the provisions [...]" of such agreement.[66]

6 The Observance of International Law

In addition to what have been already preliminary highlighted above on this regard,[67] they could be indicated in this paragraph some provisions—included in certain international agreements concluded by EU with third Parties—which explicitly recall the observance of international law, in various matters.

For example, a large number of such agreements comprises provisions related to territorial application: such provisions often point out among other things that the agreement applies, with respect to the Party of the agreement which is not the EU,

[64] More widely, Article 2, Paragraph 1, Letter G, of Economic Partnership Agreement between the EU and Kenya states what follows: "strengthen the existing relations between the Parties on the basis of solidarity and mutual interest. To this end, consistent with their WTO rights and obligations, this Agreement shall enhance commercial and economic relations, support a new trading dynamic between the Parties by means of the progressive, asymmetrical liberalisation of trade between them and reinforce, broaden and deepen cooperation in all areas relevant to trade and investment". See also, for example, Article 2, Letter A, of Agreement establishing an Association between the EU and Central America, which includes among the objectives of the agreement also the following: "strengthen and consolidate the relations between the Parties through an association based on three interdependent and fundamental parts: political dialogue, cooperation and trade [...]".

[65] See Article 26.15, Paragraph 3, of Interim Agreement on Trade between the EU and Chile. Analogous provisions on the same matter are included in other new generation international trade agreements concluded by EU with third Parties: see, for instance, Article 22.1, Paragraph 3, Letter B, of Comprehensive Economic and Trade Agreement (CETA) between Canada, of the one part, and the EU and its Member States, of the other part, and Article 13.1, Paragraph 3, of Free Trade Agreement between the EU and Korea.

[66] More precisely, Article 4, Paragraph 2, of Annex V of Economic Partnership Agreement between the EU and Kenya states what follows: "The Parties aim to strengthen their trade relations and cooperation in ways that effectively provide equal opportunities and treatment for women and men to benefit from the provisions of this Agreement, including in matters of employment and occupation, in accordance with their international commitments". On the same regard see also, for example, Article 27.1, Paragraph 10, Letter A, of Interim Agreement on Trade between the EU and Chile.

[67] *Supra* par. 1.

to the land, maritime, and air space under its sovereignty, and the exclusive economic zone and the continental shelf within which it exercises sovereign rights and jurisdiction "in accordance with international law",[68] sometimes expressly recalling the application of the United Nations Convention on the Law of the Sea.[69]

Moreover, many international agreements concluded by EU with third Parties contain specific provisions about the fulfilment of the obligations, imposing to each Party to take any general or specific measures required to fulfil its obligations under the agreement.[70] Additionally, if either Party considers that the other Party has failed to fulfil any of the obligations that are described as essential elements in certain norms of the agreement, such provisions often state that it may take appropriate measures: in that case, it is sometimes underlined that such appropriate measures shall be taken in full respect of international law.[71] It could be noted that the Agreement establishing an Association between the EU and Central America, for example, clarifies that such appropriate measures could be carried out only after submitting to the Association Council[72] all the relevant information required for a thorough examination of the situation with a view to seeking a solution acceptable

[68] See, for example, Article 1.4 of Free Trade Agreement between the EU and New Zealand, and Article 360, Paragraph 3, of Agreement establishing an Association between the EU and Central America.

[69] See, for example, Article 33.8 of Interim Agreement on Trade between the EU and Chile, and Article 1.3, Paragraph 2, of Agreement between the EU and Japan for an Economic Partnership.

[70] See, for example, Article 1.6 of Interim Agreement on Trade between the EU and Chile, Article 132 of Economic Partnership Agreement between the EU and Kenya, Article 27.4 of Free Trade Agreement between the EU and New Zealand, Article 772 of Trade and Cooperation Agreement between the EU and UK, Article 17.18 of Free Trade Agreement between the EU and Viet Nam, Article 16.15 of Free Trade Agreement between the EU and Singapore, Article 1.7 of Agreement between the EU and Japan for an Economic Partnership, Article 355 of Agreement establishing an Association between the EU and Central America, Article 8 of Trade Agreement between the EU, Colombia and Peru, Article 15.12 of Free Trade Agreement between the EU and Korea.

[71] For example, Article 1.6, Paragraph 2, of Interim Agreement on Trade between the EU and Chile states what follows: "If either Party considers that the other Party has failed to fulfil any of the obligations that are described as essential elements in Article 1.2(2) or 2.2(1) of the Advanced Framework Agreement, it may take appropriate measures. Appropriate measures shall be taken in full respect of international law and shall be proportionate to the failure to fulfil the obligations referred to in this paragraph. Priority must be given to those measures which least disturb the functioning of this Agreement. For the purposes of this paragraph, 'appropriate measures' may include the suspension, in part or in full, of this Agreement". As an additional example, Article 772, Paragraph 3, of Trade and Cooperation Agreement between the EU and UK similarly states that "The measures referred to in paragraph 1 shall be in full respect of international law and shall be proportionate. Priority shall be given to the measures which least disturb the functioning of this Agreement and of any supplementing agreements".

[72] The Association Council—composed by representatives of the EU and of each of the States of the Central America at ministerial level—oversees the fulfilment of the objectives of the Agreement establishing an Association between the EU and Central America and supervises its implementation: see, for example, Part I, Title II, of Agreement establishing an Association between the EU and Central America.

to the Parties.[73] However, such submission is not mandatory in cases of special urgency, that are cases of material breach of such agreement: in this respect, the agreement specifies that a case of material breach could be also a repudiation of such agreement not sanctioned by general rules of international law.[74] Analogous provisions are included in other international agreements concluded by EU with third Parties, such as, for example, the Free Trade Agreement between the EU and New Zealand, Free Trade Agreement between the EU and Viet Nam, the Trade Agreement between the EU, Colombia and Peru, and the Free Trade Agreement between the EU and Korea.[75]

Furthermore, as surveyed above,[76] it could be reminded that almost all the new generation international trade agreements concluded by the EU with third Parties which detail an arbitration procedure state clearly that the arbitration panels shall interpret the provisions referred to the scope of the dispute settlement system in accordance with customary rules of interpretation of public international law, including those codified in the 1969 Vienna Convention on the Law of Treaties.[77]

Other provisions frequently included in the new generation international trade agreements concluded by the EU with third Parties, which in some way refer to the observance of international law, are those titled "no direct effect". Such provisions emphasize that nothing in the agreement shall be construed as conferring rights or imposing obligations on persons, other than rights or obligations created between the Parties under public international law.[78]

---

[73] Analogous provisions are included in other international agreements concluded by EU with third Parties, even if with no specific reference to Association Council (which is a peculiar institution of the Agreement establishing an Association between the EU and Central America). The reference in the other agreements is sometimes to the relevant norms related to a Joint Committee of the Partnership Agreement previously ratified by the Parties. See, for example, Article 27.4, Paragraph 3, of Free Trade Agreement between the EU and New Zealand, which so states: "This Agreement forms part of the common institutional framework referred to in Article 52(1) of the Partnership Agreement. A Party may take appropriate measures relating to this Agreement in the event of a particularly serious and substantial violation of any of the obligations described in Article 2(1) or Article 8(1) of the Partnership Agreement as essential elements, which threatens international peace and security so as to require an immediate reaction. A Party may also take such appropriate measures relating to this Agreement in the event of an act or omission that materially defeats the object and purpose of the Paris Agreement. Those appropriate measures shall be taken in accordance with the procedure set out in Article 54 of the Partnership Agreement". See also, for example, Article 17.18, Paragraph 2, of Free Trade Agreement between the EU and Viet Nam.

[74] Article 355, Paragraph 4, Letter A, of Agreement establishing an Association between the EU and Central America.

[75] About the Free Trade Agreement between the EU and New Zealand, and the Free Trade Agreement between the EU and Viet Nam, see *supra* footnote 73. For the other agreements see, for example, Article 8, Paragraph 3, of Trade Agreement between the EU, Colombia and Peru, and Article 15.12, Paragraph 2, of Free Trade Agreement between the EU and Korea.

[76] *Supra* par. 2.

[77] *Supra* footnote 16.

[78] See, for example, these Articles—always titled "No direct effect" (with the only exception of Article 23.5 of Agreement between the EU and Japan for an Economic Partnership, which is titled "No direct effect on persons")—included in the following new generation international trade

Lastly, it could be mentioned that interesting specific references to the observance of international law—in relation to two different matters—could be found in the Interim Agreement on Trade between the EU and Chile, and in the Trade Agreement between the EU, Colombia and Peru.

Indeed, the latter agreement—with regard to protection of biodiversity and traditional knowledge—states that the Parties shall cooperate, subject also to international law, to ensure that intellectual property rights are supportive of, and do not run counter to, their rights and obligations under the 1992 Convention on Biological Diversity, in so far as genetic resources and associated traditional knowledge of the indigenous and local communities located in their respective territories are concerned.[79]

Regarding instead the Interim Agreement on Trade between the EU and Chile, the Parties acknowledge in the preamble the importance of a strong and effective multilateral system, based upon international law, in also tackling common challenges. Such acknowledgement seems therefore to uphold and to promote both the observance of international law and the third purpose of UN Charter as well.[80]

7 Concluding Remarks

The new generation international trade agreements concluded by the EU with third Parties include several provisions which could be also seen as means for the EU to uphold and promote the respect for some principles and purposes of the UN Charter and the observance of international law.

For example, a part of all such agreements is always widely dedicated to a dispute settlement system, therefore representing a way for the EU to sustain and foster the third principle of UN Charter, related to the settlement of international disputes by peaceful means.[81]

As an additional example, some of such agreements include norms which acknowledge the exclusive power of the Parties to regulate various topics in their domestic law as they deem appropriate, with no possible interference by any provision of the agreement, so following up in some way the seventh principle of UN Charter.[82]

Furthermore, about the purposes of the UN Charter, it could be for instance reminded that a part of the second of such purposes envisages the development of

---

agreements concluded by the EU with third Parties: Article 27.6, Paragraph 1, of Free Trade Agreement between the EU and New Zealand, Article 17.20 of Free Trade Agreement between the EU and Viet Nam, Article 16.16 of Free Trade Agreement between the EU and Singapore, Article 23.5 of Agreement between the EU and Japan for an Economic Partnership.

[79] See Article 201, Paragraph 6, of Trade Agreement between the EU, Colombia and Peru.

[80] About the third purpose of UN Charter see *supra* par. 5.

[81] *Supra* par. 2.

[82] *Supra* par. 3.

friendly relations among nations: on this regard, such development among the agreement Parties is not only desired in the preambles of most new generation international trade agreements concluded by the EU with third Parties, but also inserted in the general objectives of a few such agreements.[83]

As another example, many provisions in such agreements uphold and promote the part of the third purpose of UN Charter aimed to achieve international cooperation to solve international problems of different character.[84] Cooperation is indeed not only recognized in the preambles of many such agreements, but it is often expressly included amidst the peculiar objectives of several specific parts of them, or sometimes even among the general objectives of the whole agreement. It is evidently also a crucial component in multiple parts of all such agreements, sometimes explicitly as a means to solve international problems in various fields, such as electronic commerce, as well as economic, employment and social challenges resulting from globalization.[85]

It must be also highlighted that in some agreements examined in this chapter cooperation among Parties seems occasionally linked to the relations between them, so evoking a connection among the third and the second purpose of UN Charter.[86] Moreover, in the new generation international trade agreements concluded by the EU with third Parties both the cooperation as well as the relations between the Parties are not established *ex novo*, but they are often instead strengthened, reinforced, enhanced[87]: from this point of view too, these agreements turn out to be a way for EU to uphold and promote such purposes of UN Charter.

Additionally, some provisions in such agreements expressly recall the observance of international law in a variety of matters, such as territorial application, the fulfilment of the obligations, the interpretation of agreements themselves, the direct effect of the norms of the agreements on persons, as well as the protection of biodiversity and traditional knowledge.[88]

From a larger perspective, it could be mentioned that every new generation international agreement concluded by the EU with third Parties, examined in this chapter, could represent by itself—considered as a whole—a way for EU to uphold and promote the observance of international law in wider world. In this respect, it could be noted that, for example, the procedures followed to adopt such agreements, the rules applicable for their interpretation and for implementing their effects too, are all regulated by international law. Similarly, each such agreements—still overall observed, beyond the single provisions—could be itself appraised as a whole as a means for EU to sustain and foster also some principles and purposes of UN Charter,

[83] *Supra* par. 4.

[84] *Supra* par. 5.

[85] *Ibidem*.

[86] *Ibidem*.

[87] *Supra* parr. 4 and 5.

[88] *Supra* par. 6.

such as the settlement of international disputes by peaceful means,[89] the development of friendly relations among nations,[90] as well as the international cooperation to solve international problems.[91]

References

Acconci P (2023) Investimenti stranieri sostenibili. Diritto e *governance* internazionale e dell'Unione europea. Editoriale Scientifica, Napoli

Adinolfi G (ed) (2021) Gli accordi preferenziali di nuova generazione dell'Unione europea. Giappichelli, Torino

Adriaensen J, Postnikov E (eds) (2022) A geo-economic turn in trade policy? EU trade agreements in the Asia-Pacific. Palgrave Macmillan, Cham

Alvarez JE (2005) International organizations as law-makers. Oxford University Press, Oxford

Alvarez JE (2017) The impact of international organizations on international law. Brill/Nijhoff, Leiden/Boston

Aral I, d'Aspremont J (eds) (2024) International law and universality. Oxford University Press, Oxford

Arangio-Ruiz G (1979) The United Nations declaration on friendly relations and the system of the sources of international law with an appendix on the concept of international law and the theory of international organisation. Sijthoff & Noordhoff, Alphen aan den Rijn

Arangio-Ruiz G (1990) Le domaine réservé. L'organisation international et le rapport entre droit international et droit interne. In: Recueil des cours de l'Académie de droit international de La Haye, Tome, p 225

Arato J (2013) Treaty interpretation and constitutional transformation: informal change in international organizations. Yale J Int Law:289–357

Blum G (2008) Bilateralism, multilateralism, and the architecture of international law. Harv Int Law J:323–379

Boisson de Chazournes L, Romano C, Mackenzie R (eds) (2002) International organizations and international dispute settlement: trends and prospects. Transnational Publishers, Ardsley

Bretherton C, Vogler J (2006) The European Union as a global actor, 2nd edn. Routledge, New York

Brownlie I (2009) The peaceful settlement of international disputes. Chin J Int Law:267–283

Cannizzaro E (ed) (2002) The European Union as an actor in international relations. Kluwer Law International, The Hague

Cannizzaro E, Palchetti P, Wessel RA (eds) (2012) International law as law of the European Union. Brill/Nijhoff, Leiden/Boston

Chamon M, Govaere I (eds) (2020) EU external relations post-Lisbon. The law and practice of facultative Mixity. Brill/Nijhoff, Leiden/Boston

Costa O, Soler i Lecha E, Vlaskamp MC (eds) (2025) EU foreign policy in a fragmenting international order. Palgrave Macmillan, Cham

Cremona M (ed) (2018) Structural principles in EU external relations law. Hart Publishing, Oxford/Portland

Cremona M, Thies A, Wessel RA (eds) (2020) The European Union and international dispute settlement. Hart Publishing, Oxford/Portland

Czuczai J, Naert F (eds) (2017) The EU as a global actor—bridging legal theory and practice. Liber Amicorum in honour of Ricardo Gosalbo bono. Brill/Nijhoff, Leiden/Boston

[89] *Supra* par. 2.

[90] *Supra* par. 4.

[91] *Supra* par. 5.

De Waele H, Kuipers J-J (eds) (2013) The European Union's emerging international identity. Views from the global arena. Brill/Nijhoff, Leiden/Boston

Dominguez R (2024) EU foreign policy towards Latin America, 2nd edn. Palgrave Macmillan, Cham

Droubi S, d'Aspremont J (eds) (2020) International organisations, non-state actors, and the formation of customary international law. Manchester University Press, Manchester

Fahey E, Mancini I (eds) (2022) Understanding the EU as a good global actor. Edward Elgar, Cheltenham

Falk R, Lopez-Claros A (eds) (2024) Global governance and international cooperation. Managing global catastrophic risks in the 21st century. Routledge, Oxford

Fassbender B (2018) What's in a name? The international rule of law and the United Nations charter. Chin J Int Law:761–797

Frederking B, Diehl PF (eds) (2015) The politics of global governance: international organizations in an interdependent world, 5th edn. Lynne Rienner Publishers, Boulder

Gross L (1993) Selected essays on international law and organization. Martinus Nijhoff, Dordrecht/Boston/London

Hahn M, Van der Loo G (eds) (2021) Law and practice of the common commercial policy. The first 10 years after the treaty of Lisbon, Brill/Nijhoff, Leiden/Boston

Houben P-H (1967) Principles of international law concerning friendly relations and co-operation among states. Am J Int Law:703–736

Jacobs FG, Roberts S (eds) (1987) The effect of treaties in domestic law. Sweet & Maxwell, London

Joerges C, Petersmann E-U (eds) (2011) Constitutionalism, multilevel trade governance and international economic law. Hart Publishing, Oxford/Portland

Klabbers J (2008) Treaty conflict and the European Union. Cambridge University Press, Cambridge

Larik J (2014) The Kadi Saga as a tale of 'strict observance' of international law: obligations under the UN charter, targeted sanctions and judicial review in the European Union. Netherland Int Law Rev:23–42

Ligustro A (1996) Le controversie tra Stati nel diritto del commercio internazionale: dal GATT all'OMC. CEDAM, Padova

Lippold M (2024) The interrelationship of the sources of public international law. Nomos, Baden-Baden

Martin Martinez MM (1996) National Sovereignty and international organizations. Kluwer Law International, The Hague/Boston/London

McKeever D (2015) Evolving interpretation of multilateral treaties: 'acts contrary to the purposes and principles of the United Nations' in the refugee convention. Int Comp Law Quart:405–444

Melin P (2020) The external dimension of EU social security coordination. Towards a common EU approach. Brill/Nijhoff, Leiden/Boston

Merrills J, De Brabandere E (2022) International dispute settlement, 7th edn. Cambridge University Press, Cambridge

Muldoon JP (2004) The architecture of global governance. An introduction to the study of international organizations. Routledge, New York

Murphy CF (1977) The world court and the peaceful settlement of disputes. Georgia J Int Comp Law:551–578

Nagy CI (ed) (2020) World trade and local public interest. Trade liberalization and National Regulatory Sovereignty. Springer, Cham

Pasquali L (2024) La protección de las inversiones en el tratado comercial entre la Unión Europea y México. In: Petrucci A, Alcalá RG (eds) Uniformación, internacionalización y regionalismo en el Derecho con énfasis en el Derecho Privado. Tirant Lo Blanch, Ciudad de México, pp 381–433

Pauwelyn J (2003) Conflict of norms in public international law. How WTO law relates to other rules of international law. Cambridge University Press, Cambridge

Pauwelyn J, Wessel R, Wouters J (eds) (2012) Informal international lawmaking. Oxford University Press, Oxford
Pease K-KS (2019) International organizations. In: Perspectives on global governance, 6th edn. Routledge, New York
Pietrobon A (2016) Il giudizio nell'arbitrato fra Stati. Editoriale Scientifica, Napoli
Pietrobon A, Gazzini T (2020) Reconsidering multilingualism in EU trade and investment agreements in light of the 'relocation case'. Eur J Legal Stud:43–78
Prinssen JM, Schrauwen A (eds) (2002) Rethinking a classic of EC legal doctrine. Europa Law Publishing, Groningen
Rajan MS (1959) United Nations and domestic jurisdiction. Longmans, New York/London/Toronto
Rasch M (2009) The European Union at the United Nations. The functioning and coherence of EU external representation in a state-centric environment. Brill/Nijhoff, Leiden/Boston
Romanin Jacur F, Bonfanti A, Seatzu F (eds) (2015) Natural resources grabbing: an international law perspective. Brill/Nijhoff, Leiden/Boston
Rosanò A (2019) At the frontier: values and Borders in the EU'S external relations. In: Natoli T, Riccardi A (eds) Borders, legal spaces and territories in contemporary international law—within and beyond. Springer, Cham, pp 237–262
Ruotolo GM (2016) Gli accordi commerciali di ultima generazione dell'Unione europea e i loro rapporti col sistema multilaterale degli scambi. Studi Sull'integrazione Europea:329–354
Šahović M (1972) Codification des principes du droit international des relations amicales et de la coopération entre les Etats
Sarooshi D (2005) International organizations and their exercise of sovereign powers. Oxford University Press, Oxford
Schultz T, Ortino F (eds) (2020) The Oxford handbook of international arbitration. Oxford University Press, Oxford
Sciso E, Baratta R, Morviducci C (a c d) (2016) I valori dell'Unione Europea e l'azione esterna. Giappichelli, Torino
Sola NF (2012) The European Union as a regional organization within the meaning of the UN charter. Polish Yearbook Int Law:259–269
Tanaka Y (2018) The peaceful settlement of international disputes. Cambridge University Press, Cambridge
Treves T, Seatzu F, Trevisanut S (eds) (2014) Foreign investment, international law and common concerns. Routledge, London/New York
Trujillo del Arco A (2021) The 50th anniversary of the declaration on friendly relations and its role in the jurisprudence of the international court of justice. Anuario Español De Derecho Internacional:251–277
Verwey DR (2004) The European Community, the European Union and the international law of treaties—a comparative legal analysis of the community and union's external treaty-making practice. T.M.C. Asser Press, The Hague
Viñuales JE (ed) (2020) The UN friendly relations declaration at 50. An assessment of the fundamental principles of international law. Cambridge University Press, Cambridge
Virzo R, Ingravallo I (eds) (2015) Evolutions in the law of international organizations. Brill/Nijhoff, Leiden/Boston
Von Bogdandy A, Smrkolj M (2010) European Community and union law and international law. The max Planck encyclopedia of public international law. Oxford University Press, Oxford
Vylegzhanin AN, Potier T, Torkunova EA (2020) Towards cementing international law through renaissance of the United Nations charter. Moscow J Int Law:6–25
Wallace-Bruce NL (1998) The settlement of international disputes. The contribution of Australia and New Zealand. Martinus Nijhoff, The Hague/Boston/London

Weiss TG (2018) The United Nations and changing world politics. Routledge, London/New York
White ND (2006) The ties that bind: the EU, the UN and international law. Netherland Yearbook Int Law:57–107
Winand P, Benvenuti A, Guderzo M (eds) (2015) The external relations of the European Union. Historical and contemporary perspectives. Peter Lang, Brussels
Wouters J, Nollkaemper A, de Wet E (eds) (2008) The Europeanisation of international law—the status of international law in the EU and its member states. T.M.C. Asser Press, The Hague
Zarra G (2016) Parallel proceedings in investment arbitration. Eleven/Giappichelli, The Hague/Torino

The Challenge of Promoting EU Values to the Candidate Countries (and Member States)

Teresa Russo

Contents

Abstract The objective of this chapter is to contemplate the significance of the Union's values for the candidate countries and their implementation in the different agreements regarding the "rapprochement" of Third Countries with the European Union and its legislation. The goal is to demonstrate how difficult it is for both the accession states and the member states themselves to effectively conform with the EU values, which is viewed as a "constant" in the process of European integration.

T. Russo (✉)
Department of Legal Sciences (School of Law), University of Salerno, Fisciano, Italy
e-mail: trusso@unisa.it

L. Pasquali (ed.), *EU Values and International Law*, European Union and its Neighbours in a Globalized World 35,
https://doi.org/10.1007/978-3-032-20521-6_12

1 Introductory Considerations on the Relevance of the Union's Values to the Candidate Countries

The values of the European Union take on multiple meanings *vis-à-vis* the candidate countries, carrying significantly more weight than towards the existing Member States.[1] This is due to the fact that their respect informs all stages of the enlargement process, determining when it advances, slows down and/or stalls. Membership status is acquired, in fact, at the end of an articulated inter-institutional and intergovernmental procedure that is not governed by the Treaty on European Union (TEU) and is made up of a series of stages that have developed in practice and that have progressively made the values of the Union, the so-called backbone of enlargement[2]: respect for them informs the eligibility conditions or economic and political criteria for becoming a Member State. This maturation in the weight of principles (former Art. 6 TEU), now values (current Art. 2 TEU), has also occurred as a consequence of their emergence in the various 'waves' of enlargement, making it a broad and profound process of political and economic transformation of the countries involved and of the Union itself. This has resulted in the affirmation of a value dimension of membership of the Union that marks its identity with repercussions also on the Member States themselves, especially in terms of the obligations arising

[1] As is well known, respect for the values of Art. 2 TEU, former principles of Art. 6 TEU, concerns, first and foremost, the Member States. Nevertheless, the current debate on the so-called democratic backsliding in some of the more recently acceded States, with specific reference to respect for the rule of law, has had clear repercussions on the enlargement process and on the obligations of the candidate States from the pre-accession phase and for the transition to any subsequent phase, as well as in terms of economic conditionality. See Ágh (2010), Emerson and Blockmans (2022), Mendelski (2015), Müller (2015), and Szente (2017). See also Regulation (EU) 2021/1529 of the European Parliament and of the Council *establishing the Instrument for Pre-Accession Assistance (IPA III)*, in OJ L 330, (2021), which, in recital 40, in contrast to IPA II, provided that: 'As the respect for democracy, human rights and the rule of law is essential for sound financial management and effective Union funding as referred to in the Financial Regulation, assistance could be suspended in the event of the degradation of democracy, human rights or the rule of law by a beneficiary'. Similarly to this, Regulation (EU, Euratom) 2020/2092 of the European Parliament and of the Council on a general regime of conditionality for the protection of the Union budget, in OJ L 433I (2020), was tasked with protecting the rule of law by the Member States due to the challenges in implementing Art. 7 TEU. This regulation established a general system of conditionality to protect the Union budget from financial risks associated with widespread deficiencies in the rule of law in the Member States. This system makes the disbursement of Union funds contingent on adherence to the common values enshrined in Art. 2 TEU, specifically the rule of law.

[2] For the Commission's approach of addressing fundamentals first prioritises reforms related to rule of law and fundamental rights, economic governance and improving economic competitiveness, and strengthening democratic institutions, see Communication from the Commission to the European Parliament, the Council, the European Economic and Social Committee and the Committee of the Regions Enlargement *Strategy and Main Challenges 2014-15*, COM/2014/0700 final (2014).

from membership.[3] This was not the case in the first enlargements: it became so with the so-called Big Bang of the eastward enlargement and the entry of ten States with different political-economic and cultural backgrounds.[4] Enlargement has, therefore, extended the obligations of 'reciprocity' between the Union and the acceding States within the framework of the accession process. On the one hand, the Union supports and prepares them for the gradual approximation of their national legislation to comply with its principles/values,[5] on the other hand, the acceding States adopt the necessary reforms to ensure the effective application of Union law. On the one hand, the Union favours their integration/absorption as new Member States, also by providing for transitional derogations or special arrangements. On the other hand, the States benefit from this favour because they pledge to achieve full legal integration by taking on all of the Union's obligations both before and after they become new Members. However, this reciprocity has faltered, particularly in the post-accession phase, with clear implications for the enlargement process to the Western Balkans. The values of the Union, above and beyond the various aspects assumed in the accession of new Member States and which will be recalled in the following paragraphs, represent, or at least should represent, a *sic et simpliciter* constant of the European integration process to be safeguarded, also and above all among the Member States themselves.

2 The Respect of Values for the Eligibility of a Third State as a Candidate State

According to the Lisbon reform, which was the most recent revision to the Treaties,[6] Art. 49 TEU now reads as follows: 'Any European State which respects the values referred to in Art. 2 and is committed to promoting them may apply to become a

[3]The connection between enlargement and membership is emphasised by Russo (2024), who stresses how enlargement has progressively defined the characteristics of membership and how, in turn, membership has conditioned the various enlargement processes, dictating their criteria, timing and conditions, as well as how a series of discrepancies have emerged between the accession and post-accession phases.

[4]Sedelmeier (2005).

[5]According to Hillion (2011a, 2011b), the recognition, by the Copenhagen European Council in 1993, that the post-communist countries of Central and Eastern Europe had a vocation to become Members of the Union marked the beginning of a development of the enlargement rules that translate a vigorous commitment of the Union to preparing candidates for membership, thus making enlargement a policy of creating Member States.

[6]The first rules were Art. 98 of the Treaty Establishing the Economic Coal and Steel Community (ECSC), which merely required that it be a 'European' country willing to join the Treaty. The appropriate procedure was carried out by the Organisation itself, via the Council and in collaboration with the then-High Authority. There was no mention of Member States or international agreements. Then, Art. 237 of the Treaty of European Economic Community (EEC) and Art. 205 of the Treaty of the European Community of Nuclear Energy (EURATOM), on the other hand, repre-

member of the Union'. The values referred to are human dignity, freedom, democracy, equality, the rule of law and respect for human rights, including the rights of persons belonging to minorities. According to the text, these values are common to the Member States in a society characterised by pluralism, non-discrimination, tolerance, justice, solidarity and equality between women and men. Respect for the values in question, which are viewed as expressions of European society's homogeneity,[7] is thus a prerequisite for applying or a condition of eligibility. Indeed, the Treaty of Amsterdam had already stated that 'any European State which respects the principles set forth in Article F(1) TEU may apply to become a member of the Union'. It also renumbered the articles (from Art. F to Art. 6 TEU) and added para. 1, which stated: 'The Union is founded on the principles of liberty, democracy, respect for human rights and fundamental freedoms, and the rule of law, principles which are common to the Member States'.

As a prerequisite for candidacy, respect for the Union's principles and values has already expanded the list of viable applicants, allowing for the removal of the geographic restrictions included in the 'European State' regulatory provision.[8] In fact, the European Commission specified in 1992 that the term 'European' has not been officially defined, combining geographical, historical and cultural elements which all contribute to the European identity. It also considers that the shared experience of proximity, ideas, values, and historical interaction could not be condensed into a simple formula but had to be subject to revision each successive generation. Therefore, it concluded that it was neither possible nor appropriate to establish the borders of the European Union whose contours would be shaped over many years to come.[9] Enlargement Commissioner Rehn also stated in a speech in 2005 that it is the values of the Union that determine its borders. Specifically, he pointed out that the conditions for membership went beyond the provisions of the Treaty, identifying certain pre-conditions that a country must fulfil in order to gain the acceptance of European public opinion and governments: *i.e.*, having a European vocation, measured by the willingness of its citizens to join; respecting European values and, above all, being able to maintain respect for them; having the capacity to fulfil the

sented a shift from the method initially intended in the ECSC Treaty, particularly in terms of the responsibility assigned to Member States, as seen by subsequent changes up to Art. 49 TEU today. Furthermore, this article does not formalise either the prerequisites for accession or the procedures for enlargement.

[7] In this sense, see Mangiameli (2012), Blanke and Mangiameli (2013).

[8] Even among academics, the quality of a European State was associated with social, political, and geographic adherence to the shared values of the European integration project. In this sense, Fois (1965), p. 1719, held that the precise meaning of the adjective must be determined by taking into account not only a geographical element, but also historical, cultural, economic and political components. In his reasoning, the requirement of a European state can be recognised to the states of Western Europe bound together not only by a simple geographical continuity, but also by ties of a different nature and by common ideals.

[9] See the Report presented by the Commission to the Lisbon European Council of 26 and 27 June 1992, *Europe and the Challenges of Enlargement*, in Bull. EC, 1992, suppl. 3, 11.

duties of membership and not only exploiting its benefits.[10] Subsequently, the Commission returned to the issue when, in assessing also the Union's capacity to take in other members, it confirmed that the adjective 'European' encompasses a series of geographical, historical and cultural factors, all of which contribute together to the construction of the European identity, reaffirming that the sharing of ideas and values and the common experience of historical interaction cannot be condensed into a simple eternal and immutable formula, but are instead subjected to the scrutiny of each new generation.[11]

This geographical extension of eligible States based on principles/values is also a result of enlargement processes marked by the changeability of the political frame of reference built around individual applicant states and/or groups of states. Although some traces were already discernible in the first enlargements to the states of Western and Northern Europe,[12] the Union experienced different approaches to enlargement following the dissolution of the Soviet bloc and the democratic transition of the states of Central and Eastern Europe from neighbourhood and mere prospect of membership to candidate, then acceding and finally Member States. This approach has been even more evident with the group of Western Balkans, which have also moved from the mere prospect of accession, to the status of potential candidates (this is still the case for Kosovo) to becoming candidate States (five out of six) and acceding States (four out of six) precisely because of the difficulties in implementing reforms that respect the values of the Union, and specifically the rule of law, democracy and respect for human rights and minorities in particular.[13] The defence of one's own principles and the international order against Russia's

[10] Rehn (2005), Member of the European Commission and responsible for enlargement from 2004 to 2010 in his speech to civil society entitled 'Values define Europe, not borders'.

[11] See the Communication from the Commission to the European Parliament and the Council *Enlargement Strategy and Main Challenges 2006–2007 including a special report on the EU's capacity to integrate new members*, COM/2006/649 final (2006), in which the Commission also pointed out that the legal basis of the enlargement process, as set out in Art. 49 TEU, does not imply that all European countries have to apply for membership, nor that the Union is obliged to accept all applications. The European Union is defined first and foremost on the basis of its values.

[12] In this sense, all enlargement processes have led to the search for new unity in diversity and greater depth, promoting the 'value-based' integration of the *acquis* of the Union and its identity, *e. g.* with liberal economic principles in the accession of Denmark, Ireland and the United Kingdom. In the enlargement to include Greece, Portugal and Spain, on the other hand, the principles of pluralist democracy and respect for human rights constituted the common heritage of the peoples of the states in the European Communities and the essential elements of Community membership. In its opinion of 19 April 1994 on the membership applications of Austria, Finland, Norway and Sweden, the Commission emphasised that one of the objectives of the Union was the desire of the Member States to deepen solidarity between their peoples while respecting their history, culture and traditions. See Russo (2024), p. 69.

[13] In the accession process of the Western Balkans, however, enlargement policy focused mainly (and almost exclusively) on respect for the rule of law, linking it to democratic governance and respect for human rights. See, among others, Takács and Jančić (2016).

territorial and political claims,[14] in the end, made Ukraine,[15] Moldova, and Georgia eligible for the Union's new eastern or geopolitical enlargement under association agreements that already acknowledged them as European nations with a common history and values with Member States.

3 Their Application in the European Partnerships with the CEECs, in the Stabilisation Agreements with the Western Balkans...

Therefore, the observance and promotion of principles and values become crucial in the process of bringing third States closer to the Union and their transition to candidate status with the conclusion of various types of association and/or pre-accession agreements that are anchored to precise and increasingly elaborate conditions (Copenhagen criteria and subsequent additions).[16] As a result, a regulatory framework consisting of various political and legal tools that vary from one state to the next is emerging. The CEECs use the Europe Association Agreements,[17] which were based on then-Art. 238 TEC, together with the Accession Partnership, which was enacted based on Art. 235 TEC,[18] and an agreed-upon approach plan, also known as the pre-accession strategy.[19] The list of principles, priorities, intermediate objectives, and conditions that each candidate state had to focus on in order to meet the criteria was included in this partnership. These were subsequently translated into a variety of indicators and gradually outlined in short-, medium-, and long-term priorities that each country had to meet in order to be considered for final accession. By publishing annual reports, the Commission also started to provide a thorough evaluation of each candidate's implementation performance at the European Council's request. The Council used these reports to decide how quickly to proceed with negotiations. The partnership additionally instituted a mechanism that would

---

[14] Schimmelfennig (2023).

[15] Bosse (2022).

[16] According to Cremona (2004), p. 7: 'As the European Council claimed in the Laeken Declaration, the European Union's one boundary is democracy and human rights. The Union is open only to countries which uphold basic values such as free elections, respect for minorities and respect for the rule of law. The aim is to create – or maybe rather to assert – a Union identity which is based on inclusion (sharing common values) rather than exclusion'.

[17] See, among others, Maresceau (1993), Hanf and Dengler (2005), Van Elsuwege and Chamon (2019).

[18] See Council Regulation (EC) 622/98 *on assistance to the applicant States in the framework of the pre-accession strategy, and in particular on the establishment of Accession Partnerships*, in OJ L 85 (1998). See, among others, Grabbe (1999). Furthermore, see Maresceau (2003), Nicolaides (2003).

[19] See Annex IV to the Conclusions containing the Council's Report to the European Council (Essen) on the Strategy to Prepare for the Accession of the Associated Countries of Central and Eastern Europe.

allow the Council to evaluate financial support based on progress, upon a request from the Commission. It also provided for the introduction of benchmarks and the identification of key priorities to be addressed during the pre-negotiation and then negotiation phases, thus leading to the transition from a one-size-fits-all approach to a tailor-made approach, whereby country-specific conditions were defined.

With regard to the Western Balkans, on the other hand, the Union contributes to the implementation of the Paris/Dayton peace agreements and to the realisation of an area of political stability and economic prosperity, including by supporting the process of political and economic reforms and respect for democratic principles and human and minority rights.[20] However, the instability in the region and the countries' inability to cooperate bilaterally, multilaterally and regionally led the European Commission to propose the development of a Stabilisation and Association Process (SAP)[21] that would offer greater incentives to the countries concerned, but with stricter political and economic conditions and the need to intensify regional cooperation. Thus, the Stabilisation and Association Agreements (SAAs) were adopted as a new type of *sui generis*[22] category of contractual relations, taking into account the specific situation of each country, with a view to accession to the Union and subject to compliance with the Copenhagen criteria.

These mixed agreements play an important role in the full integration of the States of the area into the community of democratic nations, as well as their gradual rapprochement with the European Union, eventually prolonging the pre-accession phase rather than the actual accession phase. The latter starts with the negotiating framework being approved, and then the individual negotiating chapters are opened in accordance with a process based on the results of the Commission's screening process for the identification of key priorities. In the case of the Balkans, these priorities centre on the establishment of the structures required to ensure the rule of law, such as judicial and administrative capacity and structures for fighting corruption and fraud (Chapters 23 and 24). The advancement of the accession negotiations is also anchored on progress in the areas covered by these chapters, which are, among other things, further subordinated to intermediate or provisional benchmarks.[23] This is true even after the introduction of the so-called revised methodol-

[20] In general, on the enlargement process to the Balkans, see Blockmans (2007), Rizzo (2011), Blockmans and Łazowski (2014), Balfour and Stratulat (2015), Dabrowski and Mychenkova (2018), Selulić (2020), Deana (2022).

[21] *Cf.* Pippan (2004), Gordon (2010), O'Brennan (2016), Hitaj (2018).

[22] Communication from the Commission to the Council and the European Parliament *on the stabilisation and association process for countries of South-Eastern Europe—Bosnia and Herzegovina, Croatia, Federal Republic of Yugoslavia, former Yugoslav Republic of Macedonia and Albania*, COM/99/0235 final (1999).

[23] See Communication from the Commission to the European Parliament and the Council *Enlargement Strategy and Main Challenges 2006–2007. Including annexed special report on the EUs capacity to integrate new members*, COM/2006/649 final (2006), in which the Commission states that: 'Benchmarks are a new tool introduced as a result of lessons learnt from the fifth enlargement. Their purpose is to improve the quality of the negotiations, by providing incentives for the candidate countries to undertake necessary reforms at an early stage. Benchmarks are mea-

ogy, which was based on a stronger political orientation at the highest level and political dialogue through regular EU-Western Balkans summits and intensified ministerial contacts.[24] This approach grouped the chapters of the negotiations into so-called clusters, placing not only the aforementioned Chapters 23 and 24, but also Chapter 5 on public procurement, Chapter 18 on statistics, and Chapter 32 on financial control—under Cluster 1 on fundamentals. Essentially, the screening process for all of the *acquis*'s chapters lays out the requirements that the candidate nation must fulfil both before negotiations on each chapter can start and in order to temporarily close the chapter. These requirements may include reopening previously closed chapters or suspending negotiations in the event of a significant and ongoing violation of the rule of law, democracy, liberty, and respect for human rights and fundamental freedoms.

3.1 … and in the Deep and Comprehensive Association Agreements with Ukraine, Moldova and Georgia

Even in relations with the three former Soviet States, the promotion of principles and values serves as the foundation for relations with the Union. The latter had expressed an interest in preserving good neighbourly relations in order to promote its values, export its political and economic standards, and bind partners to its 'conditionality'.[25] After the partnership and cooperation agreements, the Union includes them in the European Neighbourhood Policy (ENP)[26] and, later, the Eastern Partnership,[27] with no chance of admission, as far as is known.[28] It does, however,

surable and linked to key elements of the *acquis* chapter. In general, opening benchmarks concern key preparatory steps for future alignment (such as strategies or action plans), and the fulfilment of contractual obligations that mirror *acquis* requirements. Closing benchmarks primarily concern legislative measures, administrative or judicial bodies, and a track record of implementation of the *acquis*. For chapters in the economic field, they also include the criterion of being a functioning market economy'.

[24] Communication from the Commission to the European Parliament, the Council, the European Economic and Social Committee and the Committee of Regions *2020 Communication on EU enlargement policy* COM/2020/660 final (2020). According to Hillion (2010), a creeping process of nationalisation of the procedure, not in accordance with the rules and principles of the Treaty, would have occurred.

[25] Since the 1990s, the European Union has promoted relationships with its neighbours under the belief that, if democratically inspired and well-governed, they can contribute to regional stability. On this point, see Blockmans and Łazowski (2006), p. 3 ff.

[26] As part of the larger European Security Strategy of December 2003, the ENP, which has been in development since 2003, is then implemented through regional partnerships to create privileged relations with neighbouring countries in Eastern Europe, the southern shores of the Mediterranean, and the Southern Caucasus. Regarding the features of this policy, refer to Bartoloni (2022).

[27] Costea (2011), Nielsen and Vilson (2014).

[28] Petrov et al. (2015), Van der Loo (2016).

demonstrate a willingness to establish a *sui generis* relationship by entering into a different type of political association and economic integration agreement based on Arts. 217 and 218 TFEU, subject to a commitment to the common values of democracy, the rule of law, and respect for human rights and fundamental freedoms.[29] The swift transition to enlargement in their perspective was made possible by the advancements made by these nations under these agreements, which since 2014 have already allowed for substantial political and economic integration and the harmonisation of their national laws with the EU *acquis* in a number of areas.

Thus, reciprocity, as embodied in a legally enforceable agreement, has been determined to be appropriate in the pre-accession phase. Conditionality and progress based on a candidate's merits towards achieving the pre-accession criteria are key components of the Union's enlargement strategy. Furthermore, the broad formulation of their goals, which aim for gradual and partial integration into the internal market, has made it easier to adjust to the pre-accession and accession procedures. The preambles to the three agreements also acknowledge that the common values that underpin the Union, namely democracy, respect for human rights and fundamental freedoms, and the rule of law, are likewise vital to political association and economic integration. Indeed, issues of political dialogue, foreign and security policy and internal reforms in the areas of justice and home affairs cooperation precede trade issues, emphasising the need to promote the rule of law, democracy and human rights.

However, the respect of principles and values is also relevant in the progressive approximation of national legislation to that of the Union, as a specific form of 'market access' conditionality, subject to strict monitoring based on progress reporting, which is a common practice within the pre-accession strategy, but also through on-the-spot missions, with the participation of EU institutions, bodies and agencies, non-governmental bodies, supervisory authorities, independent. In association agreements, the latter option is a tool designed specifically to guarantee that legislative approximation extends beyond a formal adaptation of national legislation.[30] Therefore, as stated, they are part of the so-called integration-oriented agreements since they involve EU law principles, concepts, and regulations that must be construed and applied as if the third state were a member of the EU.[31] Finally, the extensive program of political, socioeconomic, legal, and institutional reforms required to effectively implement these agreements, as well as the States' commit-

[29] Ghazaryan (2015).

[30] In accordance with Art. 475(1) of Association Agreement between the European Union and its Member States, of the one part, and Ukraine, of the other part: 'Monitoring shall mean the continuous appraisal of progress in implementing and enforcing measures covered by this Agreement'. See also Art. 419(3) of the Association Agreement between the European Union and the European Atomic Energy Community and their Member States, of the one part, and Georgia, of the other part, in OJ L 261 (2014), and, with some differences, Arts. 450, 451(2) and 419(3) of the Association Agreement between the European Union and the European Atomic Energy Community and their Member States, of the one part, and the Republic of Moldova, of the other part, and Art. 419(3).

[31] Maresceau (2013).

ment to decisively support these reforms based on the Union's democratic values, closely align with the conditions for accession.

However, these agreements are only one component of the enlargement policy framework defined by the European Council and the Council, which also includes other instruments such as European Parliament resolutions, Commission communications, and joint communications between the Commission and the High Representative of the European Union for Foreign Affairs and Security Policy. This is especially true in Ukraine, where the demands for reconstruction and accession overlap. As stated in the preamble of Regulation (EU) 2024/792 establishing the Instrument for Ukraine, it is a single, exceptional medium-term tool that brings together the Union's bilateral support for Ukraine from 2024 to 2027 to address Ukraine's financing, recovery, reconstruction, and modernisation needs, while also supporting Ukraine's reform efforts on its path to EU membership.[32] This means Ukraine's willingness to embrace the Union's principles, to respect and defend them both internationally and domestically by energetically pursuing the required reforms in the interests of its people, making it an important choice as a future member of the Union.

4 The Effective Alignment to the Criteria/Values of National Legal Systems: The Precedent of the Cooperation and Verification Mechanism (CVM) and the Case *Asociația Inițiativa pentru Justiție v. Commission*

As a result, national legal systems must ensure adaptation to the Union's criteria/values through long-term changes capable of assuring the right and effective application of Union law, also considering the Court of Justice's interpretation that makes a distinction between adaptation and derogation.[33] However, the most serious challenges have arisen at the national level, as adaptation to the criteria does not address States' effective competence to adopt appropriate policies for transposing and enforcing such a large and complex Union *acquis*. In practice, the necessary institutions and laws should be precisely established during the pre-accession, negotiation,

[32] Regulation (EU) 2024/792 of the European Parliament and of the Council *establishing the Ukraine Facility*, in OJ L, 2024/792 (2024).

[33] *Cf.* Court of Justice, *European Parliament v. Council*, C-413/04 (28 November 2006), paras. 67–68, as well as the Court of Justice, *European Parliament v. Council*, C-414/04 (28 November 2006), para. 28 ff. in which the Court was asked to evaluate the legal foundation (Art. 57 of the Act of Accession) for the additional derogations adopted for Estonia and Slovenia, respectively, in the energy sector. They were distinguished from 'adaptations' because their only goal was to temporarily postpone the effective implementation of a community act for a new Member State without adding to the *acquis* it must respect, meaning that the Union would have jurisdiction after the transitional period was over. See also Court of Justice, *Ziolkowski and Szeja*, C-424/10 and C-425/10 (21 December 2011), para. 56.

and actual accession stages—which include signing the relevant treaty and obtaining membership status after it has been ratified by both the applicant State and the Member States—and a thorough track record of implementation history should be established to ensure permanent or at least long-lasting reforms.[34] However, the number of reforms needed to align with the *acquis* has been perceived as a 'package' that is not always transferable, has significant cultural and social costs in addition to economic ones, and has minimal involvement from future citizens. Furthermore, the reforms are frequently insubstantial and formal, meaning they are not connected to a social transformation of the state, which regains some degree of autonomy following membership. The Court of Justice itself has confirmed that the adoption of safeguard clauses in the accession treaties with the provision, in the so-called post-accession phase, of transitional derogations necessary to balance the particular interests of the new State with the general interest of the Community has also been a defining feature of gaining membership status. These provisions ensure respect for the principles of equality, fairness, or solidarity between the current and future Member States.[35]

However, in the case of some CEECs, particularly Bulgaria and Romania, these deviations were excessive. Apart from the aforementioned safeguard clauses, their accession treaties actually called for the creation of a Cooperation and Verification Mechanism (CVM) as a transitional measure to help the two nations address deficiencies in the areas of judicial reform, the fight against corruption, and (as far as Bulgaria is concerned) the fight against organised crime.[36] This meant that the post-accession phase would last much longer than the customary 3-year period. Due to their inability to comply with the Commission's report requirements based on this system, Romanian judges were able to specifically claim the defence of their independence from the pressure and meddling of the political classes that emerged after the enlargement. As a means of 'judicial self-defence', these judges had, after some initial hesitancy, demonstrated a tendency to think more 'systemically', going beyond the text of the national law and basing their decisions on the Union's laws

[34] Before achieving full membership status, the candidate country must first meet a number of conditions. Furthermore, in practice, it has been discovered that the conditions to be met in order for a country to advance to the next stage with the acquisition of the relevant status vary depending on the applicant country, and that the decisions to proceed in this process are based on political considerations rather than the objective fulfilment of predetermined criteria. So, Hillion (2011a, 2011b), p. 208.

[35] See *supra* note 33.

[36] See Commission Decision 2006/928/EC *establishing a mechanism for cooperation and verification of progress in Romania to address specific benchmarks in the areas of judicial reform and the fight against corruption*, in OJ L 354 (2006); Commission Decision (EU) 2023/1785 *repealing Decision 2006/929/EC establishing a mechanism for cooperation and verification of progress in Bulgaria to address specific benchmarks in the areas of judicial reform and the fight against corruption and organised crime*, in OJ L 229 (2023). Both decisions are no longer in force as of 8 October 2023. See the considerations of Toneva-Metodieva (2014), who deems it necessary to review the post-enlargement mechanisms. However, there are significant concerns about admitting governments that do not meet the fundamental requirements for membership, which are now necessary for any advancement in the Western Balkans' accession process.

and values.[37] The Court of Justice, for its part, had made it clear that, based on the combined provisions of Arts. 2 and 49 TEU, the decision implementing that mechanism fell within the scope of the Accession Treaty until it was repealed. It was mandatory in all its elements, meaning that Romania was required to take all necessary steps to fulfil the requirements compulsory to fully join the Union.

On closer examination, this situation has led to the emergence of criticalities resulting from members not being fully integrated on the 'fundamentals' of the Union, in addition to creating a gap with other states that have joined and future members regarding whom these conditions are strictly applied and monitored. Furthermore, this mechanism's existence created such a 'reliance' on its role as a guarantee for the rule of law's protection in Romania's judicial system that a professional association of Romanian prosecutors challenged the Commission's decision to abolish it, arguing that doing so would directly impact its members and expose them to more illegal disciplinary action.[38] Although the Tribunal of the EU ruled that the action was inadmissible due to a lack of standing, missing a direct and individual prejudice to the legal position of the prosecutors and the association, the *Asociația Inițiativa pentru Justiție v. Commission*[39] case seems significant because it expresses concerns regarding the alignment of national legislation with the parameters of magistrate independence. In fact, the Court of Justice has had occasion to state that, even though national judicial system organisation is within the competence of the Member States, it must be planned to guarantee respect for the rule of law and its protection in conjunction with Arts. 2 and 19 TEU. This ensures the independence of the judges who are asked to make decisions regarding the application or interpretation of Union law,[40] thereby ensuring effective judicial protection for individuals.[41] Therefore, the perception at the national (and societal) level does not seem to match a successful adjustment to EU values beyond the formal one.

---

[37] In this sense, see Bobek (2023), p. 373.

[38] This was on the basis of Art. 1 of Commission Decision (EU) 2023/1785, *supra* note 36.

[39] General Court, *Asociația Inițiativa pentru Justiție v. Commission*, T-1126/23 (action brought on 28 November 2023).

[40] See Adam and Van Elsuwege (2018), as well as Adam (2019), who defines judicial independence as both a functional requirement to ensure the effectiveness of Union law and a constitutional requirement thereof, falling within the constitutional characteristics of the Union's legal system.

[41] See Court of Justice, *Asociatia 'forumul judecătorilor din România' and Others*, C-83/19, C-127/19, C 195/19, C-291/19, C-355/19 and C-397/19 (18 May 2021), para. 211, concerning the compatibility with Union law of certain reforms put in place by the Romanian legislature from 2017 to 2019, regarding the organization of the Judicial Inspectorate (C-83/19), the establishment, within the Public Prosecutor's Office, of the Public Prosecutor's Section for the Investigation of Crimes Committed within the Judiciary, SIRG (C-127/19, C-195/19, C-291/19 and C-355/19) as well as the personal liability regime of magistrates. On the judgment see, among others, Dumbrava (2021), Kadlec and Kosar (2022).

5 Conclusion: Alignment to Values as a 'Constant' of the European Integration Process

The ultimate goal of this study was to summarise the major concerns with adjustment to Union principles that appear to be a burden not just for acceding States, but also for Member States themselves. This kind of adjustment is, or at least ought to be, a 'constant' in the European integration process. The difficulty in imposing compliance with the standards requested of the candidate countries on the Member States diminishes the Union's credibility and endangers the validity of its decisions, the efficiency of its policies, and its fundamental foundations. In particular, the rule of law itself, which is a prerequisite for applying for membership, should not be negotiable and should not lead to differentiation that jeopardises the Union's democratic stability and the trust of the candidate nations, who ultimately feel discouraged to 'transform' their legal system and constitutional identity. The tools envisioned (Art. 7 TEU) or later introduced,[42] as well as the Court of Justice's case law on the rule of law as a Union identity value that results in a breach of treaty obligations, are to be regarded as remedies for specific cases and not as general solutions.[43] Despite the systemic violations of the rule of law and the failure of Art. 7 TEU, the Court was able to specify its constituent elements and intervene on the issue of democratic backsliding after accession to the Union thanks to the extensive use of the preliminary reference[44] and infringement procedure.[45] The Court specifically recalls in *Repubblika v. Il-Prim Ministru*[46] how Art. 49 TEU allows any European State to apply for membership in the Union by uniting states that have freely and voluntarily embraced common values, respect those values, and are dedicated to advancing them, as stipulated in Art. 2 TEU. According to the Court, the mutual trust between Member States regarding respect for values implies that, under the combined provisions of Arts. 2 and 49 TEU, a Member State cannot amend its laws in a way that would result in a regression of the protection of the values mentioned in Art. 2 TEU (namely the rule of law),[47] since respect for those values is a prerequisite for the enjoyment of all the rights resulting from the application of the Treaties to that Member State. Furthermore, the Court has confirmed in its decisions

[42] These are, among others, the Commission rule of law framework, the Council's rule of law dialogues, the well-known Regulation (EU, Euratom) 2020/2092, *supra* note 1, as well as the Rule of law in the European Semester and the CERV programme.

[43] In the same direction, the Court has also rejected, albeit under very tight conditions, the implementation of the EAW with a Member State that disregards its values, especially the rule of law. For instance, Court of Justice, *LM,* C 216/18 PPU (25 July 2018), paras. 35–36; Court of Justice, *Criminal proceedings against Lluís Puig Gordi and Others,* C-158/21 (31 January 2023).

[44] On this point, see Daniele (2024).

[45] See Schmidt and Bogdanowicz (2018), Hilpert (2019).

[46] Court of Justice, *Repubblika v. Il-Prim Ministru*, C-896/19 (20 April 2021), paras. 61–62, on the compliance with Union law of the provisions of the Maltese Constitution on the procedure for the appointment of judges.

[47] See, for all, Leloup et al. (2021).

on the Conditionality Regulation that Art. 2 TEU contains values that are embodied in principles that impose legally binding obligations on Member States and serve as the fundamental premise upon which the entire Union order is based, rather than being merely a declaration of political guidelines or intentions. These values thus have a dual meaning: on the one hand, they represent the foundation upon which the European integration process has grown. On the other hand, they define the Union's membership in terms of both membership and the permanence of the States that established mutual trust in that commonality of values.[48] Thus, as has been noted, the values in Art. 2 TEU do not require the creation of new processes or tools for their implementation; rather, they should be strictly adhered to and applied, with particular attention to the rulings of the Court of Justice of the European Union and the European Court of Human Rights, free from daily political scheming and blackmail, guaranteeing a resurgence of constant commitment and consistent execution.[49]

References

Adam S (2019) Judicial Independence as a functional and constitutional instrument for upholding the rule of law in the European Union. In: Craig P, Adam S, Diaz Abad N, Salazar L (eds) Rule of law in Europe perspectives from practitioners and academics. EJTN, Brussels, pp 15–42

Adam S, Van Elsuwege P (2018) L'exigence d'indépendance du juge, paradigme de l'Union européenne comme union de droit. J Droit Eur 9:334–343

Ágh A (2010) Post-accession crisis in the new member states: progressing or backsliding in the EU? Stud Transition States Soc 2(1):74–95

Balfour R, Stratulat C (2015) EU member states and enlargement towards the Balkans. Eur Pol Centre Paper 79(Special Issue):1–250

Bard P, Kochenov P, Pech L, Wouters J (2024) Treaty changes for a better protection of EU values in the member states. Eur Law J (Special Issue):1–16

Bartoloni ME (2022) La natura *sui generis* della Politica Europea di Vicinato: un contenitore di competenze. EUWEB Legal Essays Global Int Perspect 2:8–23

Blanke HJ, Mangiameli S (2013) Article 2 [The homogeneity clause]. In: Blanke HJ, Mangiameli S (eds) The treaty on European Union (TEU). A commentary. Springer, Berlin-Heidelberg, pp 109–155

Blockmans S (2007) Tough love: the European Union's relations with the Western Balkans. Asser, The Hague

Blockmans S, Łazowski A (2006) The European Union and its Neighbours: questioning identity and relations. In: Blockmans S, Łazowski A (eds) The European Union and its Neighbours. A legal appraisal of the EU'S policies of stabilisation, partnership and integration. Asser, The Hague, p 3ff

Blockmans S, Łazowski A (2014) Between dream and reality: challenges to the legal rapprochement of the Western Balkans. In: Petrov R, Van Elsuwege P (eds) Legislative approximation and application of EU law in the eastern Neighbourhood of the European Union. Routledge, London-New York, pp 108–133

48 On the matter, see Russo (2024), p. 56.

49 In this sense, see Bard et al. (2024).

Bobek M (2023) What role for courts in transforming a society? A central European cautionary tale. In: Bobek M, Bodnar A, Von Bogdandy A, Sonnevend P (eds) Transition 2.0. Re-establishing constitutional democracy in EU member states. Nomos, Baden-Baden, pp 361–381
Bosse G (2022) Values, rights, and changing interests: the EU'S response to the war against Ukraine and the responsibility to protect Europeans. Contemp Secur Pol 43(3):531–546
Costea S (2011) EU-Ukraine and eastern partnership: challenges, Progress and potential. Eur Foreign Aff Rev 16(2):259–276
Cremona M (2004) Values in the EU constitution: the external dimension. CDDRL Work Pap 26:1–26
Dabrowski M, Mychenkova Y (2018) The Western Balkans on the road to the European Union. Pol Contrib 4:1–23
Daniele L (2024) I valori dell'Unione nei giudizi nazionali: Stato di diritto e rinvio pregiudiziale. Quad AISDUE 1:1–29
Deana F (2022) L'allargamento dell'Unione europea nei Balcani occidentali: una strada oscura che conduce al nulla? Eurojus 2:171–190
Dumbrava H (2021) The rule of law and the EU'S response mechanisms in case of violation: a Romanian case study. ERA Forum 22(1):437–452
Emerson M, Blockmans S (2022) Next steps for EU enlargement– forwards or backwards? SCEEUS 2:1–13
Fois S (1965) Art. 237. In: Quadri R, Monaco R, Trabucchi A (dirs) Trattato istitutivo delle Comunità economica europea. Commentario. Giuffré, Milan,.p 1717ff
Ghazaryan N (2015) A new generation of human rights clauses? The case of association agreements in the eastern Neighbourhood. Eur Law Rev 40(3):391–410
Gordon C (2010) The stabilization and association process in the Western Balkans: an effective instrument of post-conflict management? In: Hughel J (ed) EU conflict management. Routledge, Abingdon, pp 49–64
Grabbe H (1999) A Partnership for Accession? The implications of EU conditionality for the central and east European applicants. EUI Work Pap 12:1–43
Hanf D, Dengler P (2005) Les accords d'association. In: Louis JV, Dony M (eds) Commentaire Mégret: Relations Extérieures. EUB, Brussels, p 36ff
Hillion C (2010) The creeping nationalisation of the EU enlargement policy. SIEPS 6:7–60
Hillion C (2011a) EU Enlargement. In: Craig P, De Búrca G (eds) The evolution of EU law. OUP, Oxford, pp 188–215
Hillion C (2011b) Evolution of EU Enlargement Policy
Hilpert F (2019) An old procedure with new solutions for the rule of law crisis law. Nordic J Eur Law 2(2):1–22
Hitaj E (2018) L'allargamento dell'Unione Europea verso i Balcani occidentali. Stabilità politica della regione oltre i criteri di Copenaghen? Riv della Cooperaz Giuridica Int 57(1):49–65
Kadlec O, Kosar D (2022) Romanian version of the rule of law crisis comes to the ECJ: the AFJR case is not just about the cooperation and verification mechanism. Common Market Law Rev 59(6):1823–1852
Leloup M, Kochenov D, Dimitrovs A (2021) Non-regression: opening the door to solving the 'Copenhagen dilemma'? All eyes on case C-896/19 Repubblika v Il-Prim Ministru. Eur Law Rev 46:692–703
Mangiameli S (2012) The Union's homogeneity and its common values in the treaty on European Union. In: Blanke HJ, Mangiameli S (eds) The European Union after Lisbon. Constitutional basis, economic order and external action. Springer, Heidelberg, pp 21–46
Maresceau M (1993) Les accords européens: analyse générale. Rev Marché Commun 369:507–515
Maresceau M (2003) Pre-accession. In: Cremona M (ed) The enlargement of the European Union. OUP, Oxford, pp 9–42
Maresceau M (2013) Les accords d'intégration dans les relations de proximité de l'Union européenne. In: Blumann C (ed) Les frontières de l'Union européenne. Bruylant, Brussels, pp 151–192

Mendelski M (2015) The EU'S pathological power: the failure of external rule of law promotion in South Eastern Europe. Southeastern Eur 39(3):318–346

Müller JW (2015) Should the EU protect democracy and the rule of law inside member states. Eur Law J 21(2):141–160

Nicolaides P (2003) Preparing for accession to the European Union: how to establish capacity for effective and credible application of EU rules. In: Cremona M (ed) The enlargement of the European Union. OUP, Oxford, pp 43–78

Nielsen KL, Vilson M (2014) The eastern partnership: soft power strategy or policy failure? Eur Foreign Aff Rev 19(2):243–262

O'Brennan J (2016) The EU and the Western Balkans: stabilization and Europeanization through enlargement. Routledge, London

Petrov R, Van Elsuwege P, Van der Loo G (2015) The EU-Ukraine association agreement: a new legal instrument of integration without membership? Kyiv-Mohyla Law Polit J 1(1):1–19

Pippan C (2004) The rocky road to Europe: the EU'S stabilisation and association process for the Western Balkans and the principle of conditionality. Eur Foreign Aff Rev 9(2):219–245

Rehn O (2005) Speech 'Values define Europe, not borders'. Belgrade, SPEECH/05/32 https://ec.europa.eu/commission/presscorner/api/files/document/print/en/speech_05_32/SPEECH_05_32_EN.pdf

Rizzo A (2011) L'Unione europea e i Paesi dei Balcani occidentali nella prospettiva dell'allargamento. Il Diritto dell'Unione Europea 16(2):445–476

Russo T (2024) Allargamento e membership dell'Unione europea. Editoriale Sci, Naples

Schimmelfennig F (2023) The advent of geopolitical enlargement and its credibility dilemma. In: Dzankic J, Kacarska S, Keil S (eds) A year later: war in Ukraine and Western Balkan (geo) politics. EUI, Florence, pp 185–193

Schmidt M, Bogdanowicz P (2018) The infringement procedure in the rule of law crisis: how to make effective use of article 258 TFEU. Common Market Law Rev 55(4):1061–1100

Sedelmeier U (2005) Constructing the path to eastern enlargement: the uneven policy impact of EU identity. MUP, Manchester

Selulić T (2020) The European Union and the paradox of enlargement: the complex accession of the Western Balkans. Springer, Cham

Szente EZ (2017) Challenging the basic values: problems with the rule of law in Hungary and the failure of the EU to tackle them. In: Jakab A, Kochenov D (eds) The enforcement of EU law and values: ensuring member states' compliance. OUP, Oxford, pp 456–475

Takács T, Jančić D (2016) Fundamental rights and rule of law promotion in EU enlargement policy in the Western Balkans. In: Paulussen C, Takács T, Lazić V, Van Rompuy B (eds) Fundamental rights in international and European law: public and private law perspectives. Asser, The Hague, pp 123–141

Toneva-Metodieva L (2014) Beyond the carrots and sticks paradigme: rethinking the cooperation and verification mechanism experience of Bulgaria and Romania. Perspect Eur Polit Soc 15(4):534–551

Van der Loo G (2016) The EU-Ukraine deep association agreement and deep and comprehensive free trade area. A new legal instrument for EU integration without membership. Brill, Leiden

Van Elsuwege P, Chamon M (2019) The meaning of 'Association under EU Law'. A study on the law and practice of EU association agreements

The manufacturer's authorised representative in the EU is Springer Nature Customer Service Centre GmbH, Europaplatz 3, 69115 Heidelberg, Germany. If you have any concerns regarding our products, please contact ProductSafety@springernature.com

Printed and bound by CPI Group (UK) Ltd, Croydon, CR0 4YY
07/10/2026
02229349-0010